RECURSIVE ORIGINS

RECURSIVE ORIGINS

Writing at the Transition to Modernity

WILLIAM KUSKIN

University of Notre Dame Press

Notre Dame, Indiana

Notre Dame, Indiana 46556
undpress.nd.edu

Manufactured in the United States of America

Library of Congress Cataloging-in-Publication Data

Kuskin, William.
Recursive origins : writing at the transition to modernity / William Kuskin.
pages cm
Includes bibliographical references and index.
ISBN 978-0-268-03325-5 (pbk. : alk. paper) — ISBN 0-268-03325-0 (pbk. : alk. paper)
1. English literature—Middle English, 1100–1500—History and criticism—Theory, etc. 2. Literature, Medieval—History and criticism—Theory, etc. 3. Historical criticism (Literature)—England. 4. Literature and history—England. I. Title.
PR255.K87 2013
820.9'001—dc23

2012050649

∞ *The paper in this book meets the guidelines for permanence and durability of the Committee on Production Guidelines for Book Longevity of the Council on Library Resources.*

For

May

Let us wage a war on totality.

—Jean-François Lyotard, *The Postmodern Condition*

Robert Johnson was like an orchestra all by himself. Some of his best stuff is almost Bach-like in construction. Unfortunately, he screwed up with the chicks and had a short life. But a brilliant burst of inspiration. He gave you a platform to work on, no doubt as he did to Muddy and the others guys we were listening to. What I found about the blues and music, tracing things back, was that nothing came from itself. As great as it is, this is not one stroke of genius. This cat was listening to somebody and it's his variation on the theme. And so you suddenly realize that everybody's connected here. This is not just that he's fantastic and the rest are crap; they're all interconnected.

And the further you went back into music and time, and with the blues you go back to the '20s, because you're basically going through recorded music, you think thank God for recording. It's the best thing that's happened to us since writing.

—Keith Richards, *Life*

CONTENTS

ACKNOWLEDGMENTS

I want to thank Brian Michael Bendis for inspiring *Recursive Origins*, Barbara Hanrahan for encouraging me to write it, and the University of Notre Dame Press for seeing it through to print. Much of the argument was researched during a year-long grant from the National Endowment for the Humanities, and I thank NEH for its support. At the University of Colorado Boulder, the Center for the Humanities and Arts, under the direction of Michael Zimmerman and the oversight of Dean John Stevenson, provided me with funding for travel to various research libraries, and Associate Vice Chancellor Jeffrey Cox of the Office of Faculty Affairs generously gave me a summer research grant to finish the project, as well as some sage advice that I took to heart. I also received a Kayden Research grant from the University of Colorado. Without such support *Recursive Origins* would have been impossible to complete.

Much of my thinking for this book was worked out in the classroom and conference room. I thank my undergraduate students at the University of Southern Mississippi and my graduate students at the University of Colorado. Clayton Lewis led a master class on recursion for my graduate seminar on recursive origins, as did Rob Barnes and Brad O'Sullivan on letterpress printing, and I thank them both. In the middle of the project, Larry Scanlon made a galvanizing observation about my easy use of the phrase "the fifteenth century," one that forced me to revise my thinking and that moved the entire project along. Throughout, the members of the Medieval Writers Workshop, particularly Lisa Cooper, Andrea Denny-Brown, Seeta Chaganti, and

Robert Meyer-Lee encouraged me to pursue recursion as a model. All of these people helped me think through the project in large and small ways, and it is a pleasure to acknowledge their contributions here.

A number of my colleagues commented on specific chapters. Lotte Hellinga and John Goldfinch set the project in motion by inviting me to give a paper on early printing at the British Library. Ruth Evans and Wayne Storey helped me revise chapter 2 for *Textual Cultures* 2.2 (2007). David Glimp, Patrick Cheney, John Watkins, and Curtis Perry read and reread chapter 3, a version of which was eventually published in *Shakespeare in the Middle Ages* (Oxford University Press, 2009). Sarah Kelen painstakingly edited chapter 4 for *Renaissance Retrospections*. I have revised these papers and essays and reorganized their parts into a new whole, and I owe these scholars my deep gratitude. As the text reached completion, I was fortunate to have a number of excellent readers look it over. James Ascher read the introduction and chapter 1. Danny Long and Randall Fullington worked many hours on various drafts, polishing them to a finished state. Professors Kent Cartwright and Martha Rust reviewed the manuscript for the press and provided me with amazingly detailed criticism, capturing the spirit and correcting the flaws of the book far more adroitly than I could have ever hoped. All of these readers' comments were crucial to the final draft, and I offer them my profound thanks.

I have also been lucky to work with the University of Notre Dame Press. Stephen Little shepherded the project to publication with great expertise. Rebecca DeBoer, Wendy McMillen, and Emily McKnight at the Press and Beth Wright of Trio Bookworks turned my manuscript into the book that you now hold in your hands. If the process of transforming ideas into a three-dimensional object is a kind of magic, Rebecca, Wendy, Emily, and Beth are the magicians.

As with my last book, my greatest acknowledgments go to Richelle Munkhoff and Helen Kuskin. Both Richelle and Helen understood how important it was for me to finish *Recursive Origins* and gave me the time to write. Richelle's belief in the initial idea made me believe in it in turn, so it is to her that I owe my greatest thanks.

ILLUSTRATIONS

Introduction

This is a time of transition. The characteristic has been famously ascribed to the Late Middle Ages, specifically to the years just before the advent of the so-called early modern period, when the technology of printing first began to develop. Perhaps it is true now as well, that we endure some great process of change, its outcome just beyond our horizon, linked inextricably to the development of some new form of the book and to some new process of reading we can now only just imagine. Or perhaps every generation inhabits the feeling that it has come to the end of one way of thinking but cannot quite see through to the next, that the forms of the past suddenly offer no clear guidance for the future. In any case, the moment seems one of particular change for the humanities, which is increasingly beleaguered by budget cuts, demands for justification, calls to produce according to measures defined by other disciplines, and shifts in employment patterns. Regardless, two truths seems incontestable: first, that for literary studies this transition appears as a point of indecisiveness in which its cultural capital is depleted and its methodologies are in debate; second, that people need narrative and lyric in their lives, seek out objects representative of these forms, and strive to create their own, notwithstanding the cost in time or finances. The broadest thesis of this book is that we must see these two truths, transition and literature, as intertwined and we must recognize that our recourse lies in our very charge: literary history.

One problem concerns the story we tell of the past. Although literary scholars themselves are often bored by a linear narrative in the texts they study, literary history remains quite progressive, structured by a distinctly modernist understanding of originality that cedes much of the involuted complexity of the literary arts to a straightforward account punctuated by categorical distinctions that beggar their own relevance to the current situation. That literary history moves according to the tick of the clock and the turn of the calendar's page, that it is largely subordinate to political, economic, and ecclesiastical history, that literary greatness remains a test of time distinct from the entertainment industry—these narrative topoi distance the literature of the past from the networks of engagement that define current social practice. Thus, I understand the period of transition we now suffer in literary studies to be due, at least in part, to a kind of intellectual conservatism in one of our major charges, literary history, that has distracted us from elaborating the imaginative processes implicit in artistic reference. Literature is fundamentally of the imagination; in recognizing this, we should also recognize that the telling of its history needn't be shackled to a linear narrative. Chronological progress punctuated by periodic break is not the only way to account for literary time.

Let us follow Keith Richards. We could do worse. This book's second epigraph is a reminder intended to level the theoretical argument of the book overall. Richards can clearly lay some claim to originality in the story of late-twentieth-century popular music. He is also, apparently, quite a reader; whatever the final balance of roles with his coauthor James Fox, in his autobiography he is a reader who writes with a voice distinctive enough that he was honored with the 2011 Norman Mailer Prize for Distinguished Autobiography, an award presented to him by no less a luminary than former president Bill Clinton. Narrating the Rolling Stones' formation early on in *Life*, Richards portrays himself with Brian Jones, huddled in a damp basement flat in Powis Square, as students of the blues. And so the passage sketches a blues canon (represented by Robert Johnson and Muddy Waters), which Richards authorizes as brilliant through a comparison to Bach. He tells, too, of discovering a narrative of the past ("the further you went back") and of the relationship between the individual artist and collective tradition ("this cat was listening to somebody and it's his variation on the theme"), and so comes to a powerful conclusion about music history: "this is not just that he's fantastic and the rest are crap; they're all interconnected." The passage then turns to the process of listening itself, to praising the power of recording and of writing. Listening, reading, consciously tracing things back: these things startle us out of a kind of thinking in which greatness appears as defined by brilliance alone; indeed, they undermine the absolute nature of artistic measure that Richards initially sets out in the passage by emphasizing the importance of interconnectedness over absolute greatness.

In a sense, the passage can serve as an allegory for literary studies over the past twenty years. It narrates a movement from the argument for a pop canon, through the encounter with history and simultaneous deconstruction of the very individual greatness that underwrites canonicity itself, and finally, arrives at the powers of media. As with any provocative deconstruction, the reader is invited to turn the process back on the author himself. Reflecting on his ten-year stint as number 1 on *New Musical Express*'s watch list of Rock Stars Most Likely to Die, Richards hits this head-on:

> I can't untie the threads of how much I played up to the part that was written for me. I mean the skull ring and the broken tooth and the kohl. Is it half and half? I think in a way your persona,

> your image, as it used to be known, is like a ball and chain. People think I'm still a goddamn junkie. It's thirty years since I gave up the dope! Image is like a long shadow. Even when the sun goes down, you can see it. I think some of it is that there is so much pressure to be that person that you become it, maybe, to a certain point that you can bear. It's impossible not to end up being a parody of what you thought you were.[1]

Life follows out the insight "that nothing came from itself" by realizing that Richards, too, is caught in the weaving of interconnection, both because he is a bluesman connected to all other bluesmen and because he is, somehow, woven from a distillation of rock and roll tropes imagined as a structure for the self by a force of desire greater than himself: "They imagined me," he tells us a little further on; "they made me, the folks out there created this folk hero."[2] The same is true for Robert Johnson. "Robert Johnson was like an orchestra all by himself," the earlier passage begins, and in that single line it condenses the entire discussion of the self and artistic history into a simile. Atomized across time, created by pressures so vast as to be only vaguely namable, potentially lost but for the technologies of record, the individual self appears bold and resplendent and full—like an orchestra—in art. In the passage itself, the orchestra harkens forward to that definitive measure of authority, to Bach, but it also locates all the threads of interconnectedness, all the many different voices of the collective, of the "folk," as within Robert Johnson himself.

We know by following Richards's narrative as it unfolds that Johnson cannot be unto himself. His scrappy discography and his experiences growing up in early-twentieth-century America leave us a fragmentary biography, but beyond it, in the moment of simile, we also know the exact opposite: Robert Johnson is fantastic. Of course, the simile is there for us at the start of the passage, but understanding it involves us in a process of tracing things back and forth, of moving from the narrative, through the meditation on art, and back to the lyric realization at its beginning. Such is *Life*. "A strange mystification," Gilles Deleuze and Félix Guattari remark in *A Thousand Plateaus* (1987), "a book all the more total for being fragmented."[3]

Both Richards and his book are groupings of fragments—a ring, a missing tooth, some eyeliner, memories, gossip, pages, tropes, narrative vignettes—that become unified as they loop back on themselves and project the greater totality of a life. The physical book is involved in this process of assembly as well. It is a substitute for the self that becomes unified as we reflect on it, even as it tells us this unity is only imagined—is it half and half?—and announces its joint authorship from the start.

At its core *Recursive Origins* is, as Douglas Hofstadter claims of his great book on recursion theory, an attempt to understand how the self comes to be from inanimate matter, from black ink and pages trapped in time.[4] The reminder Keith Richards gives at the start is that "nothing came from itself. . . . They're all interconnected." The point is obvious, but only by stepping out of the narrative and looping back on it do we realize how completely the single trope "like an orchestra" stages the tensions between individual brilliance and collective participation, between vocal singularity and multiplicity, between temporal atomization and connectedness. Neither pole in the tension is final, so the more we recognize the totality, hear the orchestra, the more we realize the fragmentation of isolation, the lonely brilliance of being "all by himself." So, too, for literary history. In *Recursive Origins* I argue that the dominant narratives of literary studies assert totalizing divisions that insist that things come from themselves. In contrast, I propose that we can best step outside of this narrative, that we can make war on totality, by recognizing that nothing comes from itself unless through a complex process of interconnectedness, of return on precedent, which is no origin at all. Within Richards's reminder, then, lies my specific claim for the book: any committed reader possesses a sense of moving around a text, of return and reflection; indeed, the ability to trace back and forth within a text is what constitutes not only the subject of the reading but also the reader him or herself. By liberating our own reading practices from the categories of period and the grand illusions of origins, not only can we discover connections between books that generations of critics before us have overlooked but, ironically, we can also make new the imaginative process of reading within literary time. In short, by returning to the exigency of literature, we discover both that we are always in transition, always in the tension between fragment and totality, and that our period, as singular as it may be, belongs to the greater whole of literary history.

Observing that one significant failing of literary history lies in its stark inability to negotiate the very birth of modernity at the beginning of the sixteenth century, I frame my thesis in this book through the so-called transition from the Middle Ages to the early modern period. For it is a commonplace assumption in literary criticism that the fifteenth century has little direct influence on the formation of the modern vernacular canon and that the transition from one century to the next is defined by a rupture that both occludes and sustains modernity: *occludes* because as long as criticism argues for a break, writing at the transition to modernity appears truly fantastic, one stroke of genius after the next; *sustains* because as long as we hold these two periods—the medieval and the modern—apart, we can continue business as usual, arguing for the unrivaled originality of the sixteenth century and for its consolidation of vernacular authorship and authority within the totality of the modern.[5] Yet the literary book is a phenomenon so old as to be timeless, and, more locally, fifteenth-century writers thought deeply enough about what constitutes vernacular literary production to create and deploy the very hallmark of modernity, the printing press. Further, they theorized and historicized their labors within an ongoing textual culture spanning manuscript and print formats. Sixteenth-century writers encountered this thinking in the manuscripts and printed books proclaiming Geoffrey Chaucer's, Thomas Hoccleve's, John Lydgate's, William Caxton's, and John Skelton's legacies. Indeed, the canonical figures of the sixteenth century are intense readers of the fifteenth and consciously look back through the editions available to them to its history and poetics as they shape their own. Rather than a literary history defined by a break, then, I suggest that fifteenth-century literary culture reproduces a number of intellectual structures for vernacular literary culture that themselves evolve out of chronologically earlier literature, and in doing so refines them; sixteenth-century writers knew these structures as an inheritance from the past and recur upon them in their own writing. By returning to the very point of transition that instigates modernity, and by recognizing it not as a break but as an intertwined process of reading and rewriting, I hope to provide an alternative model for conceiving of literary history overall.

I make this return largely through William Shakespeare because, like Richards's Bach, he stands as the measure by which all other historical writers are judged as fantastic or crap.[6] Shakespeare is the icon of modernity. Shakespeare, and other major sixteenth-century writers such as Philip Sidney and Edmund Spenser, have long been recognized as making a grand return to the writing of the classical past. Because the sweep of this return is imagined as so vast, it has overshadowed more local and immediate returns upon English writing, suggesting a fundamental break in the chain of reading, so that the sixteenth century appears original even in its return to earlier writing. Shakespeare studies has always been intensely focused on the material record, on what he read and how his writings were produced. Recent work in the field has driven this interest to new insights on his authorship and reception. As Lukas Erne points out in his afterword to the recent collection *Shakespeare's Book* (2008), "the current reconsideration of Shakespeare's authorial standing demonstrates the interrelated areas in Shakespeare studies which are all too often kept safely apart: criticism, textual studies, bibliography, theatre history, reception history, as well as biography."[7] One pragmatic goal of *Recursive Origins* is to add "literary history" to this list and thus to demonstrate how reliant Shakespeare and his editors were upon what are now considered the least canonical of texts: the writings of Hoccleve, Lydgate, Caxton, and the anonymous chroniclers of the mid-1400s. For it is a demonstrable fact that Shakespeare read Caxton, recognized his voice, and drew from his work.

Given that Shakespeare is free to move around time through books, indeed that he looped back on the texts of the more recent past in order to constitute that very past as within a temporal narrative, I suggest that other readers are as well. Each chapter therefore offers up examples of more local recursions in which the readers of the sixteenth and seventeenth centuries produce themselves, their authority, and their period through the fifteenth. As much as these readers—Edmund Spenser, Philip Sidney, "E. K.," John Stow, Thomas Pavier, John Heminge, and Henry Condell—are taken to define the revolutionary energies of the early modern period, yet are so clearly indebted to the writings of the generations before them, I suggest that modernity is far from a distinct historical category but is, in fact, profoundly contingent on the Middle Ages. Liberated from categories derived elsewhere—from political, religious, art, or media history—and from the fantasy of an ultimate escape from the past, literary history affords us a powerful way of constructing ourselves at various points in the flow of time. Thus, I hope to show in what follows that in a technical way by tracing things back we can see that nothing comes from itself, that everybody's connected here, and that this connection occurs most demonstrably, as Richards points out, because of the technologies of memory—writing and recording. My thesis is that literary reading is a way of traveling successfully in time that is in no way diminished by changes in technology and that need not subordinate itself to historical categories. The past is rewritten by the present, which itself is built on the past, creating a recursive loop in how we read the past. Again, our recourse lies in our charge: literature and literary history are deeply interwoven, and in recognizing this, we also recognize our relevance as readers able to move across time.

If modernity and the Middle Ages are totalities created as temporal periods through the manipulation of the literary imagination, it makes sense to look for a governing principle within the technology of reading and writing, an algorithm expressive of the relationship between books and readers. I find this organizing structure in the concept of recursion. I take up recursion in some detail in chapter 1, but it is perhaps worth sketching my understanding of the concept here at the outset. "Recursion" is a term used across domains of knowledge—from computer science and artificial intelligence to theoretical and evolutionary linguistics to the humanities and the fine arts. In the arts, recursion is commonly taken to mean the return of a governing theme or an embedded repetition of the entire art object within itself, such as a picture of the whole picture within the same picture. Recursion is often difficult to separate from self-reference.

Most basically, the difference between the two is that self-reference is an instance of referral, while recursion is a dynamic process.

For example, M. C. Escher's famous *Drawing Hands* (1948; Figure I.1) is both self-referential and recursive: self-referential because it literally illustrates hands drawing themselves; recursive because it uses this self-reference to produce a representation about the nature of representation itself. The recursion, therefore, is produced not so much by the instance of self-reference within the picture as by the interplay between the art object and the viewer, which can only be described as the process of engagement—viewing or reading. In the same way, a line of computer code is not a dynamic process in and of itself so much as a significant part of a program that depends on a user's (or another computer program's) engagement to initiate it toward an output. In the case of *Drawing Hands*, the viewer is invited to pursue the tangled loop of the two hands to a larger statement about representation, one that teasingly implies that the artist is a component part of the production process he also governs. In this way, *Drawing Hands* forces a reflection on the involute relationship between part and whole, execution and intention, object and meaning.[8] For a computer program, the output appears more literal, some on-screen representation or electronic signal triggering additional programs. In *Drawing Hands* the output is more ephemeral—the understanding that the artist, M. C. Escher, is somehow within and without the art object, dominating it and produced by it. Thus, for this book, I define recursion as a trope of return that produces representation through embedded self-reference.

My definition suggests at least three implications. Primarily, it defines recursion as a trope, an identifiable and formal turn (Greek: *tropos*, "a turn"). In chapter 1 I draw a connection between recursion and metonymy, in that both are tropes that associate part and whole, but more broadly, my definition of recursion as a trope is meant to underscore its formal quality across a variety of disciplines and its productive nature, its ability to turn a given linguistic construction into another figuration. Tropes produce representation, whether in computer algorithms, linguistic constructions, or art objects. In computer programming this representation is the result of the successful

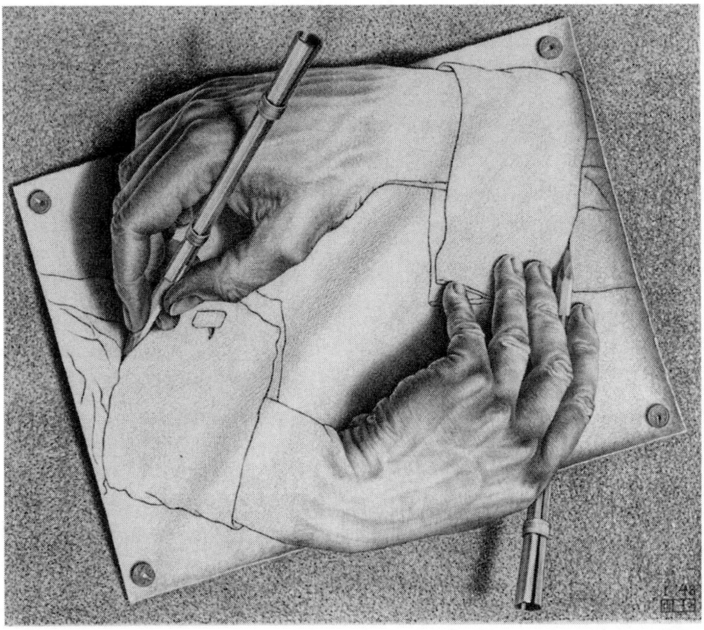

Figure I.1. Recursion in the visual arts. M. C. Escher, *Drawing Hands* (Lithograph, 1948), www.mcescher.com.

execution of a set of procedural steps. In artificial intelligence and linguistics, it is the emergence of complexity, either as a seemingly autonomous intelligence or as linguistic statements, from a definable set of elements. In the arts, the distinction between the trope and the effect produced by the trope is much finer. This is an important point: few end users of a computer program appreciate the coded turns that create the final representation. In the arts, the turn on language is often part of the aesthetic goal, so that the final representation produced is often intentionally paradoxical.

Again, Escher's *Drawing Hands* provides a useful example. For on the one hand, the recursive effect of *Drawing Hands* is its successful representation of the hands of the artist; on the other hand, it is the statement *about* the successful representation of these hands. The lithograph insists that these two hands—embodiment and commentary—are inseparable and self-generative, yet on some profound level we recognize them as quite separate: one a clever representation of ink and paper, the other an idea about artistic creation delivered as a fleeting truth beyond the literal, generated not so much by the artist's hands as by his imagination. Yet we also know that Escher is dead, and that the fact is that the ink and paper ultimately do generate whatever representation we perceive. This duality is only magnified when one takes into account the reprints of *Drawing Hands* in books and in the posters hanging in dorm rooms and engineers' offices, each reprinting Escher's original lithographic representation, itself a representation of the very process of representation. And even at all these layers of remove, *Drawing Hands* produces the sense that somehow the imagination of the man represented by the name M. C. Escher exists in each of these reproductions. *Drawing Hands* thus achieves representation as both a literal document and a figural statement, producing what I would call the fruitful paradox of recursion in the arts: that the literal and figural forms of art are simultaneously and separately part of the troping process that produces representation. That *Drawing Hands* is paradoxical might give us pause—after all, formal paradox is anathema for computing—but it should also remind us that from the perspective of producing a sense of figural meaning through self-reference, *Drawing Hands* is not paradoxical at all: it is efficient.

The manifold nature of *Drawing Hands*' representative capability thus suggests the second implication of my definition: recursion calls attention to the media of transmission. For if *Drawing Hands* shows us anything, it shows us that material and figural forms operate together. This is clear in such a visual object, and it reminds us that script, type, and code are also visual signs and their physical display as numbers, letters, and punctuation actively shapes how they produce a representation. In chapters 3 and 4 I term the double—material and rhetorical—structure of literature "textual formalism" and suggest some of the tropes early printers use—typeface, the margin and header, the title page, dates, printer's marks—to evoke meaning from the page. In this, I am in absolute agreement with Marshall McLuhan's primary dictate, "the medium is the message," or more elaborately, "the 'content' of any medium is always another medium," insofar as he recognizes that media has a representative force and that objects of representation always loop back on themselves, containing the past within them.[9] Ultimately, however, McLuhan is deeply invested in the modern narrative; he insists that by making it new, by inventing some new display of words in prose, in verse, in machine language, we can throw off the past and so move from hot to cool, to infinity and no doubt beyond. The very term "recursion" suggests otherwise. (Re)cursion contains within it a return to writing, no matter the format. As much as "cursive" leads us back to the Latin *curere*, "to run," its linguistic root points to an essential commonality for screen-based digital books and codex-based manuscript and print books alike: all are machines for compilation, for executing textual commands, for "running" the codes of language to a larger sense of meaning. There is no reason to be myopic. The book is a broad term that subsumes a variety of physical manifestations—tablet, roll, codex, digital display. Each kind of book provides a particular physical structure for the reader somewhat different from the next, but just so: no form is static; each is a vehicle for running the words of authors, scribes, printers, and programmers; and each contains a procedure for its use. Given this, my second point is that print does not simply remediate manuscript production in a teleological process by which one medium interpolates another, but that all forms of the book return on the human imagination's primary ability to use language. Indeed, Noam Chomsky famously postulates that recursion is a linguistic principle that plumbs deeper than writing, deeper even than grammar, to organize human language at a root level. In treating the material and figural nature of representation, then, our emphasis should fall less on the notion of revolution between one particular form and the next across history than on the process of embedding—on *recursion*—in all textual systems, whether materialized on clay tablets, papyrus scrolls, manuscript or printed codices, computer screens, or the human imagination.

My third point returns us to Keith Richards's essential insight: outside of the confines of a linear narrative of time, everything is interconnected. Recursion is a trope that allows us to understand these connections in a nonlinear pattern of association. As Richards says, nothing comes from itself, and the sooner we recognize this fact, the sooner we can also recognize that our ability to imagine the future and the past allows us to move within time unbounded by the narrative delivered upon us. It is in this unbounded movement that we are capable of finding who we once were and who we might still be. Books are especially powerful instruments for such self-discovery, because they allow us to move according to contiguity of pages, and in this they give us opportunity and ability to leap across time, to inhabit any number of pasts and incorporate them into our present. This is the particular allure of books—that they engage the reader in time travel and so move him or her outside of his or her self by moving more deeply inwards—for no matter the mode of delivery, we are driven to read and to recur upon ourselves imaginatively in the texts we deem literary. What we discover in the recursive functionality of literary books is that we are part of the algorithm of time and we exist, as constitutive parts, within its whole.

In its emphasis on rethinking the relationship between literature, period, and time, my project shares much with that of Kathleen Davis's *Periodization and Sovereignty: How Ideas of Feudalism and Secularization Govern the Politics of Time* (2008) and with that of Jonathan Gil Harris's *Untimely Matter in the Time of Shakespeare* (2009). The sense of opening outward to new temporalities is common to all three projects. "The topic of multiple temporalities," writes Davis, "cannot be usefully broached, I suggest, until the process and the effects of periodization have been taken into account. Periodization as I address it, then, does not refer to a mere back-description that divides history into segments, but to a fundamental political technique—a way to moderate, divide, and regulate—always rendering its services *now*."[10] Harris, too, describes the multiple temporalities possible within literature:

> Temporality, then, is not just a singularity reified in an object. It is, more accurately, a polychromic network that collates various actors—human and inhuman, animate and inanimate, subject and object—from past and present. On occasion, some of these

> "actors" might *seem* not to act at all. But even in such instances they are crucial to the polychromic network and the temporality it produces. The temporality of supersession needs the supposedly inactive past matter it negates; likewise the temporality of explosion needs the present matter that it shatters. It is only the temporality of conjunction that foregrounds what is suppressed by both supersession and explosion: how past and present work together, and how they are reworked by the imagination of the theorist, to produce the temporalities of matter.[11]

At times in this book, I will pause to underscore moments I find similar to what Davis calls "political technique" and temporalities similar to what Harris calls "supersession," "explosion," and "conjunction." Overall, though, what I understand to bind Davis's and Harris's projects to my own is not merely an interest in laying aside period to explore time but a sense of push and pull in the constitution of period, a knowing embrace and alienation on the part of certain writers that simultaneously makes and rejects the past in the service of the now. Harris's sense of literary explosion, with its sudden realization of the insufficiency of category and corresponding awakening to the power of the imagination, particularly as it occurs through metonymy, is common to my own reading, and I hope to further his effort.[12] With Davis, I conclude that, "in an important sense, we cannot periodize the past."[13] No longer constrained by period, we can move across literary time more fluidly.

Recursive Origins consists of five chapters, each pointed at redefining a significant moment of modern origins—book, poet, dramatic quarto, form, edition—as recurring on the literature of the English Middle Ages. The chapters move through five textual objects that illustrate recursive origins: Martial's epigram on the codex format, Spenser's claim to be the "new Poete" in *The Shepheardes Calender*, Shakespeare's first dramatic quarto in print, Caxton's first printed book in English, and the First Folio.[14] Each of these is certainly an originary moment in literary history, but each is also contingent, dependent on its material form, on readers, and on the very past it contrasts its novelty against. In my readings, I attempt to describe these contingencies as processes of recursion, to freeze them and demonstrate how they work, but it needs be stated up front that recursion is an algorithm—its essential nature is to run. Thus my illustrations must be taken as a kind of stop-action process that captures the powerful and dynamic process of production and consumption occurring in that amazing verb "to read."

Chapter 1 reads the first literary poem of books, Martial's epigram on authorship, to define three aspects of recursion significant to the project as a whole: period, trope, and temporality. Chapter 2 turns to poetic persona through a reading of Edmund Spenser's *Shepheardes Calendar*, a powerful moment of origins that begins by citing John Lydgate: "Vncovthe Vnkiste, Sayde the olde famous Poete Chaucer: whom for his excellencie and wonderfull skil in making, his scholler Lidgate, a worthy scholler of so excellent a maister, calleth the Loadestarre of our Language." This citation was carefully noted by Spenser's readers, such as Thomas Speght, who comments on it in his 1598 edition of Chaucer's *Workes*. Thus, I argue that at the very moment at which the early modern poet is taken to break from what Speght terms those "most unlearned times," Spenser in fact recurs upon those times, drawing out a structure of literary history crafted by Lydgate and dependent on the nature of writing itself. Chapter 3 pursues a similar strategy within a second moment of origins, Shakespeare's first appearance in print in the 1594 quarto version of *2 Henry VI*. Titled *The First Part of the Contention Betwixt the Two Famous Houses of Yorke and Lancaster*, this booklet imagines the medieval past as deeply textual and shows Shakespeare, as well as his collaborators and editors, as reading history, particularly *Holinshed's Chronicles*, to produce the past as past. Drawn directly from the anonymous London chronicles of the mid-1400s, *Holinshed's Chronicles* is derivative of the very past Shakespeare uses it to historicize. Shakespeare's print origins thus lead us into a hall of mirrors, in which temporal distance is created neither through origins nor through progress so much as through a reflective effect, in which text after text reduplicates an event. Thus, chapter 1 lays out my application of recursion, and the subsequent two chapters argue that the significant moments of origins for the early modern period—the birth of the modern poet and appearance of Shakespeare's dramatic literature in print—are recursively intertwined with the literature of the previous century, demonstrably contingent upon and subordinating the literary culture of John Lydgate and William Caxton.

Broadly, I follow Patrick Cheney's argument in *Shakespeare's Literary Authorship* (2008) "that Shakespeare is an alert reader of Spenser's laureate self-fashioning," and so in my discussion of the canon, I follow Spenser with Shakespeare.[15] I differ with Cheney's argument, breathtaking as it is, in that I do not insist on Shakespeare's primacy, so much as on his and his printers' ability to construct authority from preexisting models. Shakespeare is dazzling, but we should acknowledge that a complex system of laureate poetics in print preexisted the Elizabethan age and very much defined the terms of its literary culture.[16] Chapters 4 and 5 use two of Shakespeare's plays to read this engagement. Chapter 4 combines the themes of authorship, print publication, history, and recursion in a reading of Shakespeare's *Troilus and Cressida*, a text usually studied in comparison to Chaucer's *Troilus and Criseyde*. I discuss it in terms of the first book printed in English, William Caxton's *Recuyell of the Historyes of Troye*. My argument here is both technological—that the origins of Shakespeare's play are mediated not by authorship but by form—and aesthetic, that the aesthetics at work in Caxton, and before him in Lydgate's *Troy Book*, are manifest in Shakespeare's play. Chapter 5 makes a similar claim for Shakespeare's canon overall. Here I turn to the 1619 collection of Shakespeare plays known as the Pavier Quartos. These are ten plays in quarto format, the first three of which have running signatures. Predating the First Folio, Pavier's collection offers a threefold return to history: it organizes select plays around the theme of the English past, it partially embodies this organization in a material form authorized by Shakespeare's identity, and it emphasizes the way this past is historically engaged in literary production. In contrast, the Folio asserts Shakespeare's identity as an author not by history but by genre. Its assertion of authorship is a silent appropriation of the past that quite literally papers over Shakespeare's recursive origins, making him appear sui generis. My point in these two chapters, as with *Recursive Origins* overall, is that if we lay aside the governing assumption that the sixteenth century enacts a break with the Middle Ages from which Shakespeare emerges, we can find clear and firm bridges between the two periods. And if modernity and the Middle Ages are functions of one another, if even that great icon of modernity, Shakespeare, is produced from medieval texts, perhaps our own great transition, thrilling as it may be, can be understood less as a revolution than as a recursion to where we have already been.

Literary studies reiterates modernity's revolutionary break with the past as a foundation on which to build ever-increasing levels of theoretical complexity. If we turn to the so-called origins of English modernity in the mid to late sixteenth century and, more specifically, to the major authors Spenser and Shakespeare, we in fact discover no such break; indeed, we discover the writings of Lydgate, Caxton, and the anonymous London Chroniclers, as well as the aesthetic of the early printed book, an aesthetic based heavily on the medieval manuscript *mise-en-page*. Noting that the so-called moment of origins is less a comprehensive return to the classical past than a cycling through of local recursions on immediate precedents, we are challenged to think of other ways that literary history might be imagined—to develop a theory of the book as productive of period and transcendent of temporality itself—and in doing so to claim our authority as readers. For we are readers of literature, and in this identity we might discover not only totalities of temporal organization but ourselves as ever-changing constructions. Our recourse lies in our charge. Literature drives us to read, and reading sustains literature, allowing us to live continuously throughout time.

ONE

Machine Language

Three Implications of Recursion for Literary History

Literary history is the story of influence. Its central tenet is that no one writes alone, that all writers derive originality by precedence, creativity through imitation, and distinction from established structures for literary production. Literary studies has told this story across the tables of contents of anthologies and publishers' catalogues, each section of which—"The Middle Ages," "The Early Modern Period," "The Eighteenth Century," "Modern Literature," "The Postmodern"—is arrayed like the chapters of a novel or the acts of a play, discrete units that combine to tell a grand narrative. Such an organization contains more than one contradiction: literary history as a continuous trajectory *and* a sequence of periods, each a moment of origins unto itself; literature as an autonomous discipline *and* subordinate to historical groupings, themselves defined by political, economic, and ecclesiastical events; authorship as filtered through temporal and generic contexts *and* as immortal, an expression of individual genius beyond time itself. Given the general acceptance of these contradictions, they seem essentially paradoxes, apparently contradictory ideas that are nevertheless true, necessitated by the vast scope and complexity of such a story. Rather than accepting paradox, I suggest these contractions are just that, logical incompatibilities, and should alert us to the dangers of too absolute a subscription to a chronological narrative of period. When the categories of chronology and period are loosened, we can see these contradictions less as paradoxes sustained in their truth by the extraordinary dictates of modern historicity than as simply error messages created when the spiraling relationship of reading and writing is reified against the grid of chronological time. By laying aside the dictates of chronology and period, we can understand literary history as neither progressive nor revolutionary but as a story of influence in which the past is never completely superseded by the present but is instead embedded within every literary page, each a point of origin in its own right, and accessible through the technologies of reproduction that enable the literary imagination. Atomized across a linear narrative of temporality, we are always alone; distilled into each moment, each point in the enduring circuit of production and consumption, the past exists with us as a facet of some greater totality that we only partially fulfill.

One way out of the paradoxes of literary history is through the object of the book. The printed book is traditionally taken as the definitive marker of modern literary culture. Much work on the history of the book falls into the same kind of categorical distinctions as literary history itself, distinctions that attempt to pair the various technologies of literary production with chronologically grounded historical periods. The scholarship on the codex, for example, often separates out scribal production as the signature of the premodern and print as the hallmark of the modern. Yet print is essentially extruded from the logic of manuscript reproduction. We see this in the manufacture and design of type that re-creates handwriting in metal, in the construction of a machine from the bits and pieces of existing craft forms—the wine press, metallurgy, book manufacture—and, finally, in the very imagination of a production system bent not on the creation of something new but on maximizing the volume of original copies. I suggest, then, that one way of meaningfully incorporating the premodern into our postmodern condition is by recognizing print as an extension of manuscript practice. Books know no historical boundary. Indeed, "book" itself is an umbrella term covering many different textual formats: clay tablets, scrolls, pamphlets, codices, and electronic readers, each with its own particular technological structure and economy of meaning. The particular element that defines the codex is the binding together of separate parts—leaves of wood, slate, papyrus, paper, folded quires—into a coherent whole. This sense inflects all things carried by the book: literature, history, and the self. Thus, I argue that books, those most material of objects, have an immateriality about them—a poetry—and that this poetry is defined by one overriding trope: metonymy.

In this chapter, I establish the book as a poetic trope by reading two moments of book history, Martial's second of his revised epigrams and William Caxton's first print of Boethius's *Consolation of Philosophy*. Both writers present the codex as an associative technology—hence my emphasis on metonymy, the trope of association. For both, too, the codex creates the delicate connection between part and whole that we also see in metonymy: it holds everything together even as it reveals that everything is discrete. Metonymy accomplishes this effect through the figural connections implied by troping; codices accomplish it through the binding that defines their format. Further, both writers push this observation toward larger claims about the individual self as sustained within time, not a revolutionary force breaking from it. Thus, I argue that in emphasizing the role of novelty in literary production, we have told a story of modernity. This story ultimately results in a series of contradictions that appear as paradoxes as long as we hold to the narrative of chronology and period. By laying aside these structures, we can begin to imagine a literary history that does not depend on a modern narrative but is free to move through time. Given this, I propose a literary history not of the novelty of print culture and the modern period but of a book culture that relies on the tangible presence of the past within the very technologies of representation that are commonly taken to define modernity.

One place to begin a discussion of the tension between chronology and period, then, is at the very moment of print in the passage between the Middle Ages and the early modern period. The major literary histories of this transition published by Oxford and Cambridge well illustrate the contradictions at this moment. For example, the scholars collected within David Wallace's *Cambridge History of Medieval English Literature* (1999) report the birth of a formal vernacular poetics in the thirteenth century and a vibrant fourteenth-century period, followed in the fifteenth century by, as Wallace tells it, "various forms of retreat" at the end of the Middle Ages.[1] Such a retreat allows for a moment of origins in the sixteenth century, as argued in David Lowenstein and Janel Mueller's *The Cambridge History of Early Modern English Literature* (2002), which proclaims itself a "new history of early modern English literature" and announces "the triumph of the book" and "the emergence of the author" as early modern events.[2] James Simpson's *1350–1557: Reform and Cultural Revolution*, volume 2 of *The Oxford English Literary History* (2002), proposes the exact opposite. Here modernity signals less a moment of revolutionary triumph than one of shutting down, and so Simpson presents a heroic Late Middle Ages, replaced "in the first half of the sixteenth century, [by a] culture that simplified and centralized."[3] The tension between progress and rupture is more stark and tragic in Simpson's telling than in Wallace's or Lowenstein and Mueller's; nevertheless, in each case the influence of the past is paradoxically acknowledged as foundational to English poetics, authorship, and the vernacular book and as sealed off by a break that transforms the Middle Ages into the modern. By accepting such contradictions as unavoidable and sustainable, these scholars implicitly write them as paradoxes and, always claiming the clarity of temporal description, produce the fifteenth century as a period of transition that separates the more coherent periods and therefore sustains the paradoxes. Ironically, as critics have moved from characterizing this transition as the Renaissance to the early modern period, this explanation has become more totalizing, more in the service of modernity overall, even as it has become more theoretical.

These studies evoke an obvious question regarding this space of transition: What would it mean to consider the fifteenth century as a new period unto itself? Such a project began in the 1980s with Paul Strohm's "Chaucer's Fifteenth-Century Audience and the Narrowing of the 'Chaucer Tradition'" (1982) and David Lawton's "Dullness and the Fifteenth Century" (1987), which still define the essentially contradictory understanding of its place in literary history.[4] Here Strohm argues that the period immediately after Chaucer's death is characterized by an aesthetic disengagement with ambiguity in English writing and with politics as well; Lawton, on the other hand, argues that it creates a public sphere in which poetry played a vibrant and political role. A. C. Spearing's *Medieval to Renaissance in English Poetry* (1985) articulates the argument for a backward movement in the English fifteenth century, writing that "measured by the doctrine of artistic progress which the Renaissance invented, [Chaucer's followers] move back rather than forwards."[5]

Two books in the 1990s, Seth Lerer's *Chaucer and His Readers: Imagining the Author in Late-Medieval England* (1993) and Larry Scanlon's *Narrative, Authority, and Power: The Medieval Exemplum and the Chaucerian Tradition* (1994), propose other ways of thinking about the period. Lerer suggests a system of textual production in which the act of reading shaped future acts of writing. Scanlon describes a history of the exemplum that traversed period. Jennifer Summit's *Lost Property: The Woman Writer and English Literary History, 1380–1589* (2000) presses such an exploration of textual and generic production to questions of gender and canon. Still, Spearing essentially lays out the model of the major literary histories from Oxford and Cambridge, one in which English poetry can be told as a progressive narrative from the fourteenth century into the fifteenth that reverts even in its progress so as to create an intellectual gap between Chaucer and Wyatt that allows for the emergence of the early modern period as a Renaissance. The argument is contradictory because it asserts that chronology is an essential gauge for narrative progress—the grid of historical causality—and fundamentally irrelevant to the grand narrative of literary culture, which moves forwards and backwards in time, defined by revolution as its organizing feature.

The past ten years have seen a burst in edited collections and single-author monographs studying the relationship between the Middle Ages and the early modern period. These take roughly three approaches—period, chronology, and biography—and for each, the fifteenth century remains a liminal space bracketed by some governing condition that contains it within the larger narrative of modernity. We see this first in studies that leapfrog over the period entirely. Gordon McMullan and David Matthews's *Reading the Medieval in Early Modern England* (2007), for example, investigates transition through the large-scale categories of "medieval" and "modern"; others, such as Theresa Krier's edited collection *Refiguring Chaucer in the Renaissance* (1998), explore a particular author in the Middle Ages and in the Renaissance. These studies effectively rationalize the paradox contained within the notion of transition by passing over the years between 1400 and 1550 so that the object of the medieval past—romance, Chaucer, Langland—remains a long way from its appearance in the modern present. Here, progress occurs in centuries so that rupture is folded into the absent middle years.

Second, studies such as Daniel Wakelin's *Humanism, Reading, & English Literature 1430–1530* (2007) or Alexandra Gillespie's *Print Culture and the Medieval Author: Chaucer, Lydgate, and Their Books, 1473–1557* (2006) identify what Helen Cooper and Sally Mapstone call "the long fifteenth century," a chronological duration perhaps not associated directly with a century so much as with a theme of transition—the initial development of humanism or of print authorship, for instance.[6] These studies, too, ultimately encase larger questions that might destabilize the development of one period after another—what does it mean for humanism to be a premodern event?, for example—within the confines of period.

Third, studies such as Maura Nolan's *John Lydgate and the Making of Public Culture* (2005) and my own *Symbolic Caxton: Literary Culture and Print Capitalism* (2008) negotiate the break between the past and the present through the coherence of biography. Whether or not Caxton's work troubles the notion of capitalism, as I argue in that book, can certainly be debated, but regardless of the outcome, the issues remain bracketed by his biography. Each book premises its argument on the coherence of larger narrative totalities and thus predefines the object of study as somewhere between the modern and the medieval. Hence, the fifteenth century rationalizes two competing explanations for historical change—*progress* and *period*—to ensure that time marches on but that this march does not confuse the larger totalities involved. In such a narrative, the fifteenth century is written out as the space of paradox. The Greek for paradox, *paradoxos*, means "strange," and this hints at the fifteenth century's role in the modern narrative: it is a strange space in which the narrative structure of chronology can effectively be reserved to facilitate the development of a new period without destabilizing the narrative overall. The fifteenth century as paradox permits contradiction.

To a large extent, this paradox is a function of narrative. Stories have beginnings, middles, and endings, and so the Middle Ages must come to a close before modernity can start. That this narrative should work through the notion of a radical break with the past is what Fredric Jameson terms "the sign of modernity." This sign, he explains in *A Singular Modernity: Essay on the Ontology of the Present* (2002), writes the paradox of chronological progression and historical break as a narrative trope. The essay begins with Jameson's critique of Jean-François Lyotard's definition of the postmodern, as future (*post*) anterior (*modo*), which he dismisses as "one of the oldest models of temporality on the books, namely the cyclical one, which alone could authorize the suitably outrageous position that postmodernism does not follow, but rather precedes, true modernism as such, whose return it prepares." Jameson concludes that Lyotard's "embarrassment suggests two useful conclusions," the necessity of narrative and of novelty:

> "Modernity" is then to be considered a unique kind of rhetorical effect, or, if you prefer, a trope, but one utterly different in structure from the traditional figures as those have been catalogued since antiquity. Indeed, the trope of modernity may in that sense

> be considered as self-referential, if not performative, since its appearance signals the emergence of a new kind of figure, a decisive break with previous forms of figurality, and is to that extent a sign of its own existence, a signifier that indicates itself, and whose form is its very content. "Modernity" then, as a trope, is itself a sign of modernity as such.[7]

Jameson rewrites Lyotard's circular logic as a process of narrative signification, in which the grand narrative of modernity is self-constituting, creating itself through its own sign for self-reference. In doing so, Jameson modifies his great mandate, "always historicize," to the first of his laws or maxims: "we cannot not periodize."[8] In his particular telling, Lyotard's future anterior becomes a two-stage theory of modernity, a narrative of the first or classical modernists and then of late modernists, a Cold War ideology of modernism that he associates with Wallace Stevens and the New Critics. Jameson suggests that his project belongs to the aesthetic sphere, but only after roundly stating, "I believe that the only satisfactory semantic meaning of modernity lies in its association with capitalism"[9]—and who can object? For the category of capitalism rationalizes all literary contradictions from without, setting an undisputable trajectory for literary history itself: from capitalism forward.

Whatever confusions over this narrative that have been created by the fifteenth century can be relegated to its overall strangeness; whatever incoherent medievalisms in economic practice that appeared in the sixteenth, seventeenth, eighteenth, nineteenth, twentieth, or twenty-first century can be designated overdetermined structures in dominance within a narrative condition defined outside of literature. Capitalism defines the terms, which are linked to the sixteenth century by definition so that the sign of modernity is both historically validated and self-referential. The literary histories I have mentioned above operate accordingly. That is, they write the story of modernity by identifying the moment of originality, the decisive break, as the signifier that indicates itself: modernity's arrival is defined by originality; originality is definitive because it defines the arrival of a new period. The question of period can only produce Spearing's conclusion that the period of transition marks a move backward rather than forward, for exactly the reason Spearing states: we measure according to a doctrine of artistic progress that we define a priori as modern and as capitalist.

There seems to be no escape. For example, in *Poets and Power from Chaucer to Wyatt* (2007), Robert J. Meyer-Lee argues persuasively for moving the origin of the self-citing, autobiographical author in English from Chaucer in the fourteenth century and Spenser in the sixteenth to John Lydgate in the first half of the fifteenth.[10] The thesis is shocking, but only in its specifics, not in its general subscription to the terms of chronology and rupture, for it affirms that there really is no avoiding what Jameson calls the rewriting function of the modern narrative—that such a narrative will always assert originality at a new moment—and so we may as well prepare ourselves for no end of outrageous revelations about the birth of the modern as the marker of historical break slides forward and backward on the horizon line of chronology.[11] Thus, even as the recent studies search out alternate patterns of organization—Wakelin discovers a recursive pattern in the poem *Knyghthode and Bataile* and Meyer-Lee argues for "a revisionary point of origin"—they remain contained within an overall subscription to period that leaves the notion of revolution in place.[12] They cannot not periodize. Therefore the question "What would it mean to consider fifteenth-century literary culture as a new period?" forecloses on the project of revision before it is even begun. As a result, though we now know more about English writing up to 1557, we still know precious little about the ways Chaucerian manuscript literary culture is organically connected to sixteenth-century poetics and even less about the reasons major sixteenth-century writers such as Sir Philip Sidney, Edmund Spenser, and William Shakespeare looked to fifteenth-century literary culture for the plots, linguistic tone, and physical shape of their own works. The main obstacle to our understanding is the narrative format of historical period, which dictates the questions we ask of literary history. Ironically, then, rather than troubling the preexisting narrative of medieval and modern, the emergence of this new period confirms what we already know. The contradictions of literary history are underwritten by the sign of modernity, a sign that sustains contradiction as a paradox of narrative. A literary history of modernity that seeks to think through the trope of modernity remains to be told.

The central argument of *Recursive Origins* is that period is a poor measure of literary history. Its guiding question asks not about period so much as what it would mean to think about the relationship between texts without the unifying categories—medieval, early modern, the fifteenth century, print culture, capitalism—of modernity. Its thesis is that a better measure of literary history lies in a material sense of literary form. In her introduction to the *PMLA*'s special issue on the history of the book, Leah Marcus points out that "when critics speak of 'formalism,' they usually mean verbal form; in contrast, book historians keep redrawing the boundary separating the words themselves from extrinsic features such as spelling, spacing, and typeface. Far from replacing hermeneutics by pedantry, book history insists that every aspect of a literary work bears interpretation—even, or especially, those that look most contingent."[13] Medievalists, so long intimate with the history of the book through manuscript and early print studies, have been surprisingly slow to assert a role in the larger book history Marcus writes of here. As Jessica Brantley discusses in a more recent issue of *PMLA*, "medieval studies can benefit enormously from helping to write this more capacious history of the material text."[14] With some sympathy to notions of New Formalism, then, I propose a return to formalism and note that rhetorical formalism is *material*. Rhetorical form appears before the reader as a text, and this means that it is embedded within a physical object and embodied within the page.[15] Moreover, this embodiment is mediated by scribes, printers, and editors who count out meter, regularize genre, and organize it according to a particular aesthetic. Historically, this creates persistent and often irresolvable problems of authorial intention and canonicity—witness the problems of attribution in both the Chaucerian manuscripts and the Shakespearean quartos—but it also insists that a work transcends temporal period as books continue to communicate their contents well past the date they were produced.

The double investment of form, that it is material as well as verbal, suggests a way around abstract categorical boundary lines. In place of period, then, I offer the process of recursion as a formal principle of textual production. I borrow the term "recursion" first from computer science, where it describes an algorithm based, like Jameson's sign of modernity, in self-reference. Recursion is the process by which a system—a computer, the human mind—performs a complex operation through self-reference: a recursive function calls upon itself. How does a robot count one hundred boxes if its program only states how to count one box? It keeps revisiting the problem, temporarily bracketing ("pushing") the total number of problems so as to reduce each encounter by one (n – 1), time and time again ("stacking"), until it can execute the task of counting one box. Once it has done this—essentially ordered the problem into a sequence of nested or embedded subproblems—it can apply its primary and defining rule again and again, working its way back up the stack of problems ("popping") until all the boxes have been counted. The actual counting only occurs as the robot works its way back through the stack. Done correctly, the robot effectively performs an operation it isn't programmed to accomplish—it can count any number of boxes—by referencing itself in a series of subroutines tailored to the parameters of the problem, upon which it "bottoms out" and stops calling upon its one defining rule, and works its way back up the tree of nested self-referential calls. If the subroutines are not nested properly, the recursive program will fall into an infinite loop, repeating the process of self-reference endlessly, or it will simply grind to a halt. If the subroutines are nested correctly, the problem is solved not through iteration but through return.

The important point is this: the robot uses self-reference, but this only becomes recursive in the dynamic process of embedding and self-citation. Thus, it may look like the robot is programmed to count to one hundred, but it is in fact equipped with a more simple and more elegant tool: recursive self-citation. The distinction may appear very fine in such a basic example, but it is important because it illustrates a process that is scalable without limit and capable of containing within itself no end of internal recursive functions.

The elegance of recursion is that it seems to hint at some elusive truth of self-reference in numbers, words, and images. "What is recursion?" asks Douglas Hofstadter in the Pulitzer Prize-winning masterwork on the subject, *Gödel, Escher, Bach: An Eternal Golden Braid* (1979).[16] He concludes,

> Sometimes recursion seems to brush paradox very closely. For example, there are *recursive definitions*. Such a definition may give the casual viewer the impression that something is being defined in terms of *itself*. That would be circular and lead to infinite regress, if not to paradox proper. Actually, a recursive definition (when properly formulated) never leads to infinite regress or paradox. This is because a recursive definition never defines something in terms of itself, but always in terms of *simpler versions* of itself.[17]

Recursion's flirtation with paradox is suggested most famously by the woodcuts of M. C. Escher in which hands draw themselves (see the Introduction, Figure I.1), monks walk onwards toward their starting point, and water cascades from below. Surely these images suggest a paradox, but their magic exists in their sense of suspension, the sense that their structure could unfold indefinitely, as an ongoing spiral of self-reference. "Like Oroboros, the mythical snake which, biting its own tail, represents the endless round of existence," writes W. Tecumseh Fitch in "Three Meanings of 'Recursion'" (2010), "recursive functions take their own past output as their next input, and potentially allow (in absence of processing limitations) indefinitely complex output from even the simplest of functions."[18] Recursion suggests a cycle of production. Case in point: the mathematician, Leonardo Pisano Bigolio (circa 1170–circa 1250), known as Fibonacci (son of Bonaccio), observes in his 1202 *Liber Abaci* ("The Book of Calculation") a hypothetical scenario for calculating the reproduction of rabbits. His formula, which follows, produces a sequence of numbers: 1, 1, 2, 3, 5, 8, 13, 21, 34, 55, 89, 144, 233, 377, 610, 987, 1597, and so forth, in which each new value is the sum of two previous values.[19]

Fib (1) = 1
Fib (2) = 1

For all numbers $n>1$:
$$Fib(n) = Fib(n-1) + Fib(n-2)$$

The Fibonacci Sequence is known as a "renewal equation," one that uses the present and past to predict the future.[20] The reverse is also true: each number within the Fibonacci string contains within it its own code for generation so that the statement *of* the numbers is self-referentially a statement *about* the numbers. Thus, a recursive system has no preordained structure beyond self-reference and embedding, only a rule for writing out a sequence of nested steps and then reading those steps in the process of execution. This functionality, this sense of writing out the sequence of self-references and then rereading back up the chain, is encapsulated in the very term "(re)cursion," which produces new writing by returning upon existing writing. A recursive program writes itself out and then reads itself back, elaborating and interpreting itself in a temporal gesture that exists in time not as progress but as a looping return. Given this, perhaps the Ouroboros, suggesting as it does a continuous circle, is the wrong image for recursion, which when done correctly overcomes an endless cycle of repetition to become productive, moving to produce a new output or suggesting some larger intelligence at work. The magic of Escher's *Drawing Hands*, after all, is not simply the circularity of their representation, their self-reference, but that they spiral outwards to refer elusively to the intelligence that conceived them. When graphed, the Fibonacci Sequence produces a spiral, the center point of which is known as "the eye of God," and this seems a better representative image for the process of recursion overall.[21]

A recursive program appears, therefore, self-authored and thus self-determining; it appears to come from self-reference alone, from its sense of itself. Because of this, recursion has been especially useful to modeling language and artificial intelligence. It is an essential feature of linguistic theory since Noam Chomsky's *Syntactic Structures* (1957). Chomsky furthered his notion of recursion in *The Minimalist Program* (1995), arguing that a single mechanism, "Merge," is the sole recursive interface between the senses and cognition.[22] More recently, Marc D. Hauser, Chomsky, and Fitch in their path-breaking essay in

Science, "The Faculty of Language: What Is It, Who Has It, and How Did It Evolve?" (2002), extend this thesis to evolutionary linguistics to argue that language building, in the narrow sense of internal language, "only includes recursion and is the only uniquely human component of the faculty of language."[23] Recursion is a structure for language capable of building complex sentences through embedding in much the way the robot builds a principle for counting from a single principle. N. Katherine Hayles explains this process as the emergence of intelligence from a recursive procedure: "Emergence implies that properties or programs appear on their own, often developing in ways not anticipated by the person who created the simulation. Structures that lead to emergence typically involve complex feedback loops in which the outputs of a system are repeatedly fed back in as input. As the recursive looping continues, small deviations can quickly become magnified, leading to the complex interactions and unpredictable evolutions associated with emergence."[24]

Recursion's importance lies in its formal way of imagining much larger systems of representation. In this, it is a literal arrangement of language—the computer code work in a recursion program, the nesting of phrases within language assembly—that also figures the process of representation itself: from Escher's hands, his intelligence. Used in computer code, artificial intelligence, linguistic theory, evolutionary linguistics, and the arts, it is a deeply interdisciplinary term, a trope applicable to a variety of modes of knowledge production. In each of these disciplines, the term is inflected somewhat differently, but in all cases it refers to a process of return that produces representation through embedded self-reference.[25]

Literary production is involved in a similar process of self-reference. We can examine how self-reference works by revisiting the first literary meditation on the codex format: the second epigram by Marcus Valerius Martialis (Martial, circa 40–104 CE) of his revised *Epigrams* (circa 103). Here Martial launches a theory of the book close to its historical origins:

> Qui tecum cupis esse meos ubicumque libellos
> et comites longae quaeris habere viae,
> hos eme, quos artat brevibus membrana tabellis:

scrinia da magnis, me manus una capit.
  ne tamen ignores ubi sim venalis et erres
urbe vagus tota, me duce certus eris;
  libertum docti Lucensis quaere Secundum
    limina post Pacis Palladiaeque forum. (I.2)

> You who want to have my books with you wherever you go, and who are looking to have them as companions on a long journey, buy these, which the parchment confines within small covers: give cylinders to the great, one hand can hold me. That you should not be ignorant of where I am on sale and wander aimlessly over the whole city, with me as your guide you will be certain: look for Secundus, the freedman of learned Lucensis, beyond the threshold of the Temple of Peace and the Forum of Minerva.[26]

Martial's is an epigram of self-reference. Most broadly, it is concerned with referencing its particular format, explicitly contrasting the rolls that hold the writing of the great against its small covers and handheld size. Rolls were far and away the accepted format for written literature in Roman culture.[27] Martial's epigrams were specifically bound in codices. The format was two boards inlaid with red or black wax in their centers and stitched together so they folded in on themselves, protecting their contents. Codices developed so that additional wooden, parchment, or papyrus leaves could be nested within the boards, but their association with writing on wax made them a transient form for the classical and Roman worlds, one used for drafts, lessons, reckonings, and messages rather than to preserve literary, historical, or philosophical texts. Thus, as much as Martial seems to suggest permanence for his work—it is a guide to the city to be taken wherever the reader goes—the material format is generally associated with ephemeral writing. Martial refers to his codex as a *libellus*, which William Fitzgerald points out is a pun, meaning both an individual petition and a complete booklet of petitions.[28] In a sense, the term encapsulates the problem of durability latent in Martial's epigram: as individual petitions, epigrams are momentary poems of wit; bound together as a booklet, they are a literary statement. The *libellus* is a double self-reference, a way of talking about the genre of epigram as occasional poetry and an individual author's *oeuvre*, and about the notion of poetry as individual writing as well as a definitive physical collection. It asks, "What is a book of epigrams?"—ephemeral writing or literature—and in doing so suggests the tension of metonymy, specifically of synecdoche, the relationship of part and whole, as spanning material and generic classification—the individual pages that constitute the unified book, the epigrams that constitute the poetic collection. From self-reference to self-reference, the second epigram moves from a discussion of itself as a material artifact to one of itself as a literary artifact.

Self-reference occurs yet again in the epigram's sketch of the economy through which it floats—the buying and selling, reading and using of books. In this expanded field, Martial's discussion relies overtly on metonymy proper—change of name—in that it substitutes an object, the book, for the author, Martial himself. The trope works through substitution, so that the book is both literally and figuratively a first-person guide to Rome. Further, Martial describes this figuration as moving within the city, which is, more broadly still, a renaming of reading as travel. Thus, the epigram traffics in a number of tropes of substitution—metonymy and synecdoche—to suggest the master-trope of substitution itself: metalepsis. Metalepsis is an ambitious trope indeed, one Harold Bloom famously discusses as "a word . . . substituted metonymically for a word in a previous trope, so that a metalepsis can be called, maddeningly but accurately, a metonymy of a metonymy," and Gérard Genette interprets as a layering of narrative functions.[29] All of this occurs within Martial's epigram: the synecdoche for the individual epigram as a book of epigrams written on the individual page standing for the book of pages; the metonymy of the book as author within the metonymy of reading as travel; the metalepsis of the reader-as-traveler with Martial within his poetic evocation of Rome. And so the epigram nests its self-references so that it moves from its confines within two covers, then constructs writer and reader and, finally, arrives at a larger world of people and places. Martial's variations on metonymy supply the epigram with an internal organization, a series of self-referential layers involving form, genre, and literary history, which as the reader moves through, unfolding into meaning, become a recursive process for constructing the author from the book.

Recursion and metalepsis share a particular organization of embedded substitution, that nesting quality, which they elide in the magic of language well used. Brian Cummings describes metalepsis as working through stages of substitution in which some are left out, creating a compression that makes the reader forget the stages themselves and wonder at the effect overall: "if a metalepsis comes off, part of the sheer thrill of success is precisely this sense of a sharing of something recondite or mysterious, the way language pulls things together which seem in principle to be far apart."[30] This quality—that the linguistic process that produces the final effect is elided in the successful execution of the effect itself—is much the thrill of recursion, which accomplishes an end result—all those boxes counted!—from a basic principle that seems far from the task at hand. It is also the magic of Escher's prints, which manage to depict a kind of elision of logic right in front of the viewer's eyes, connecting water so it flows up and down at the same time, showing us hands that cannot actually draw themselves but nevertheless do, and implying an artist who is ultimately an autonomous human being as somehow created from his drawings. It is also the risk: recursion brushes paradox in much the way metalepsis brushes catachresis, so that either the magic occurs or fails completely; either the computer program writes out and reads back all its self-references effectively and produces an effect, or it crashes and suddenly becomes frustratingly visible as lines of code or an error message; either the visual illusion of water flowing upwards is created, or the effort seems entirely amateurish; either a metonymy produces a figural effect, or it becomes awkwardly visible as literal language. The same is true for books more generally, which, in all their forms, layer discrete page after page to create an entity that is ultimately only a conduit, a mediating substrate, but that thrillingly substitutes for the artistic abstraction—the ideal work of the artistic imagination. Metalepsis, recursion, and books are, in this way, tropes of mediation. That is, they work through a careful sequence of self-references—the intermediate steps of the computer program's "stack," the layered metonyms within an overall conceit, the individual pages linked together—that are all elided in the magic of language well used in order to create an emergent effect, which in this case is the voice of the author.

Martial's epigram makes its claims specific to the codex. Unlike a broad definition of the book spanning a number of different material forms, the codex is fundamentally defined by its bound nature that combines parts into a whole—pages into a book—while sustaining these parts still as separate units. Martial's point appears to be that the trope of metonymy, particularly the operation of synecdoche as represented by the word *libellus*, evokes a tension within the codex form between atomized part—page or epigram—and unified whole—identity or book—that operates materially and rhetorically beyond the historical moment in which it was produced. In this sense, Martial's epigram speaks in the first person, both in Martial's voice and in the voice of the book that the reader carries about Rome. So the book is coded to produce from itself a return to an earlier moment of writing, which, when read, it enacts in the present through the function of reading as imaginative writing. It creates Martial in the present from his writing in the past. This earlier writing is, of course, itself also a prior moment of scribal, editorial, and authorial reading and revision, a layering of efforts that pull together through the production process. In this, codices perpetually teeter on paradox: threatening to engulf the reader in a regressive cycle of reading and to fade into antiquity themselves, they inhabit multiple temporalities—the imagined past of writing, the present of reading, other moments of reading recollected—that their readers inhabit simultaneously. From this spiraling energy of production emerges an intelligence, a voice, that transcends time itself. In Martial's epigram, this is a cynical sensibility not of Juvenalean outrage or of Ovidian exile, but of playful self-promotion that is beyond Martial and the reader both, a feeling of the postmodern within the antique. As soon as we recognize this voice as speaking to us, we too have entered into the process of mediation, moving the poem beyond bare self-reference and participating in the magic of nesting that defines metalepsis and recursion.

Historically, Martial's use of the book, as original as it may be, did not sway Roman literary culture from the roll, which remained the primary literary mode. For Roman literature, Martial gives us a recursive origin for the codex, a moment of origins that sets out, with some sophistication, the complexity of issues surrounding the book, authorship, and literary fame, repeating it and repeating it but drawing no greater revolutionary force. In fact, shortly after Martial's observation, the early Christian communities at Antioch and Jerusalem developed the codex from a secondary writing aid to a major textual form. By the fourth century, the codex rivaled the roll, so much so that the term *biblios* became commonly used for school texts or Christian books in Antioch; by the fifth century 89 percent of all remaining Greek books are in the form of the codex. In a quantifiable way, the representative potential inherent in the codex found an audience in Christian readers and writers, and this energized its technological development. The early Christians' predilection for the codex has no clear explanation beyond the jointly physical and discursive capacities suggested by Martial: codices imply a unified canon even if the actual texts they contain are only fragmentary. In each case—material surface and linguistic depth (juxtaposition), change of name (object for author) and part for whole (a selection of texts representing a total collection)—the codex operates through a singular tropological principle: metonymy.

Medieval bookmakers developed both an apparatus for internal organization and an articulate understanding of the roles of the individuals who create the book from the scribe, through the compiler and commentator, to the author.[31] As a balance to Martial's epigram, I offer a book at the end of the medieval spectrum: William Caxton's first edition of Geoffrey Chaucer's translation of Boethius's *Consolation of Philosophy*, known as the *Boece*. In the *Consolation*, Boethius is visited in prison by the allegorical representation of philosophy in the form of a robed woman, who attempts as best she can to explain to him the physical and ethical organization of the universe as his historically true execution looms before him. Jean de Meun suggested the importance of translating the text in the *Roman de la Rose*, and Chaucer translated it early in his literary career, beginning a tradition that includes translations by John Walton (1410), George Colville (1556), Queen Elizabeth (1593), and Michael Walpole (1609).

Caxton printed Chaucer's *Boece* as *Boecius* amidst his first series of Chaucerian poetry, which included a number of smaller half-sheet quartos of poems by John Lydgate and Chaucer as well as a folio edition of the *Canterbury Tales*. A reproduction of Chaucer's translation, Caxton's *Boecius* is ostensibly a historical point of departure in which the tradition transitions into print. As a printed edition with no clear source, however, it has the authority of a manuscript witness to the past. It is an original copy.[32] Thus, Caxton's *Boecius* is very much a recursive text. Rhetorically, it uses self-reference to create different levels of truth, embedding the event of Boethius's imprisonment into a fictional environment to generate a philosophical truth. Materially, its trajectory through time enacts a series of secondary embeddings, one translation after another. On this level, the printed *Boecius* recurs on the handwritten *Boece* without superseding it; both remediate an earlier manuscript, which itself remediates not actual speech so much as Boethius's self-referential, imaginative dialogue with Philosophy. This sequence of self-references produces a series of remediations that leads not, as Marshall McLuhan might predict, to a fundamental moment of break from orality into a one new textual reality followed by the next, so much as a base case in which, like the Fibonacci numbers, the initial sequence is not zero—the utter absence of writing as orality—but the repeated copying of manuscript and manuscript that leads into print. That is, *Boecius* makes obvious the progressivism that underwrites the Gutenberg galaxy—orality, handwriting, print, digitization—and offers a compelling reminder that forms of textuality recur on one another outside of a linear sequence of technological progress.

Boecius is nevertheless a text of voices. In places, Caxton's text reads almost as a prompt book, indicating "B." and "Phîa." to distinguish the speakers from the thick, black printed page. In the final book, Philosophy describes a world of successive representations in which each lived moment is an image of the dwelling of God carried through time (see Figure 1.1). "This litel momente," she tells Boethius, "the whiche p*re*sence of this litel & swift momente for that it bereth amaner ymage or liknes of the ay dwelling of god." Her description is almost cinematic. Flattening out experiential perception to an image, she describes reality within the temporal condition as a flow of images before the individual, who perceives them as an ongoing sequence. Philosophy continues: "It grau*n*teth to suche maner thinges as it betideth to / that it semeth hem as these thinges han*n* ben / & ben." Succession—time proceeding as things have been and been; language ordered in speech and on the page—defines the temporal condition. "Therfore," Philosophy concludes, "it rauisshed & toke the infinite wey of tyme + that is to seye by succession / & by this maner it is done / for that it shuld contynue the lyf in goyng + of the whiche life hit ne mighte not + enbrace the plente of dwelling." This is the unfathomable difference between earthly representation and godly dwelling: the images of God's dwelling are ravished—hastened on and perhaps violated by this haste—as they enter into the infinite way of time, life ongoing. In Philosophy's simile these images appear flattened out, the visual perception of the individual who experiences them as fleeting within time, but we must always remember that they are not images so much as the dimensional space that the individual occupies. "Late vs seye thenne sothly that god is eterne + and that the world is perpetuell," Philosophy tells Boethius, and this is effectively as far as she can go: the temporal condition presents in perpetual motion what God conceives as spatially eternal.

The result is that Philosophy is able to articulate free will and foreknowledge. Living by succession in perpetual motion, perceiving only representative images of things that have been and been, mortals perceive action as autonomous choices leading into a future that they perceive as unfolding in a linear pattern. God does not perceive images in motion:

> And the scyence of him that ouerpassith alle temporall momente dwellith in simplicite of his presence / And enbraceth and considereth all the infinite spaces of tymes preterites and of tymes futures + And loketh in his simple knowyng all thinges of preterite / right as they were done presently right nowe / If thou wolt thenne thinken and auysen the prescience + by whiche hit knoweth alle thynges + thou ne shalt not demen hit / as prescience

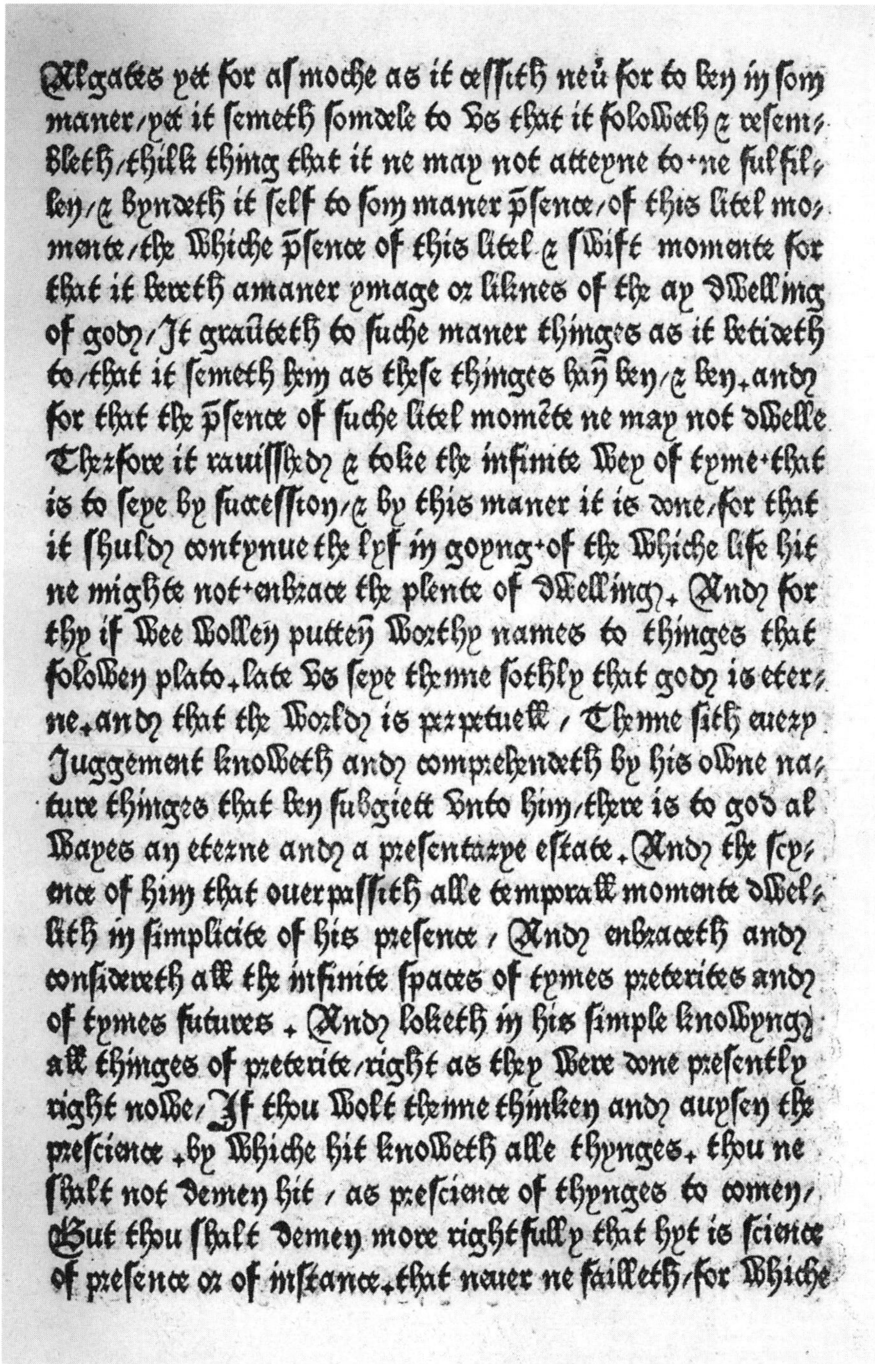
Algates yet for as moche as it cessith neū for to ben in som
maner/yet it semeth somdele to vs that it foloweth & resem-
bleth/thilk thing that it ne may not atteyne to·ne fulfil-
len/& byndeth it self to som maner p̄sence/of this litel mo-
mente/the whiche p̄sence of this litel & swift momente for
that it bereth amaner ymage or liknes of the ay dwellyng
of god/It grauūteth to suche maner thinges as it betideth
to/that it semeth hem as these thinges han ben/& ben·and
for that the p̄sence of suche litel momēte ne may not dwelle
Therfore it rauisshed & toke the infinite wey of tyme·that
is to seye by successiō/& by this maner it is done/for that
it shuld contynue the lyf in goyng·of the whiche life hit
ne mighte not·enbrace the plente of dwellyng·And for
thy if wee wollen putten worthy names to thinges that
folowen plato·late vs seye thenne sothly that god is eter-
ne·and that the world is perpetuell/Thenne sith euery
Juggement knoweth and comprehendeth by his owne nature thinges that ben subgiett vnto him/there is to god al
wayes an eterne and a presentarye estate·And the scyence of him that ouerpassith alle temporall momente dwel-
lith in simplicite of his presence/And enbraceth and
considereth all the infinite spaces of tymes preterites and
of tymes futures·And loketh in his simple knowyng
all thinges of preterite/right as they were done presently
right nowe/If thou wolt thenne thinken and auysen the
prescience·by whiche hit knoweth alle thynges·thou ne
shalt not demen hit/as prescience of thynges to comen/
But thou shalt demen more rightfully that hyt is science
of presence or of instance·that neuer ne failleth/for whiche

Figure 1.1. Levels of recursion and Caxton's Type 2. *Boecius de consolacione philosophie* (Westminster: William Caxton, 1478), unnumbered pages, *STC* 3199, © The British Library Board. All rights reserved.

> of thynges to comen / But thou shalt demen more rightfully that hyt is science of presence or of instance

God sees time as a density of space. He quite literally dwells in the moment of the infinite—all presents and futures as a point. Fibonacci begins his *De Practica Geometrie* with the words "the point is that which lacks dimension; that is it cannot be divided," and this is how God perceives reality: each moment in divine reckoning in eternity contains within it the successive actions that mortals perceive as perpetual motion. This motion is the circularity that dominates the *Consolation of Philosophy*, the spinning of Fortune's wheel, the nested spheres of the universe, the progression of chapter after chapter, meter after prose, within the text. From God's vantage, all this motion is essentially local, nested within an indivisible unity.

Hofstadter writes of the recursive nature of electrons that "every real particle's existence therefore involves the existence of infinitely many other particles, contained in a virtual 'cloud' which surrounds it as it propagates. Each of the virtual particles in the cloud, of course, also drags along its own virtual cloud, and so on ad infinitum."[33] This is an account of reality as a density of particles recursively operational within clouds of successive stacks of activity, perceived by us as a solid structure moving through time. In effect, Philosophy's God sees that time as just such a density. In Hofstadter's and Philosophy's accounts, reality appears as a totality when viewed from a higher perspective, a simultaneous writing and reading of each recursive stack that occurs so quickly as to appear fixed. On the local level, the level of Boethius's imprisonment and of the subatomic particle, this totality appears as a series of internal recursions, cycles and sequences played out over and over. Even more locally, these cycles themselves are invisible, and reality appears simply arbitrary, one event after another. Thus, Boethius can only perceive himself as existing in the succession of instances, forever unfolding within time, a string of self-references that can only be held together by calls but is never available to itself as a totality.

In the last sentence of the *Boecius*, Philosophy tells Boethius that it is of vast importance to recall that every act must be fulfilled as if it is part of an overall system, a functional part of the cloud of particles that constitute reality: "Areyse thy couraige to rightfull hopes Yelde thou humble prayers and highe + grete necessite of prowesse and of vertue is encharged and commaunded to you if ye nyl not dissimulen / sith that ye worchen and done + that is to seyne youre dedes & your werkes / beforn*e* the eyen of the Iugge that seeth and also that demeth alle thynges / Deo gracias." The great eye of the judge sees all things. Its sweep accounts for all time, all actions, and all decisions in an instance, as a unity, a solid. To dissimulate would be to conceal the many self-references, the individual calls and cycles, implicit in all things. As Philosophy's charge extends through the second person, the reader, too, is challenged to imagine God's perspective, to remember that what he or she perceives as the forward moment of time is a solid object in the eye of the judge where the record is never expunged, the film never burned, the pages never shredded. Thus, Philosophy reminds us that there is no escape from the past, no simple process of forgetting past actions and relegating them to a fleeting history.

In his epilogue to *Boecius*, Caxton seems to find the density that Philosophy describes for reality in the object of the book itself. Here, he presents the book as a palimpsest of agents. "Boecius was an excellente auctour of dyuerce bookes craftely and curiously maad in prose and metre," he tells us, continuing, "Maister Geffrey Chaucer hath translated this sayd werke oute of latyn in to oure vsual and moder tonge + Folowyng the latyn as neygh as is possible to be vnderstande," and finally concluding, "I William Caxton haue done my debuoir & payne tenprynte it in fourme as is here afore made." On one level, the epilogue suggests a sequence of individuals responsible for the text: Boethius is the author, Chaucer the translator, and Caxton the printer. On this level, Caxton's discussion of these roles becomes, if not less profound, at least less elaborate with every stage—authorship, translation, printing. On another level, however, author, translator, and printer are all unified by the tangible nature of the book. Boethius makes books craftily and curiously in prose and meter, and Chaucer works language as if in metal, making it ornate and fair, so it lasts through time, perpetually. Caxton is least descriptive about his own work, which is of course the most material of all, finding it his duty to print the book in the form the reader now encounters it. The larger point is that we create ourselves in literature in many ways, and one way is through the materiality of the book we contrive to represent physically the individual as a simple point within each page's time, one after the other in succession and bound together as a whole.

Caxton seems to mean that books grant their readers the perspective of God. In the epilogue he explicitly tells the reader, "For in the sayd boke they may see what this transitorie & mutable worlde is And wherto euery man*n* liuyng in hit / ought to entende." The book represents this mutable and transitory world. Reading through its pages, we both perceive its fictional representations, its many voices in motion, as within the time of reading and as a totality. The book allows us to move through it, like a lived reality, and to stop the forward moving succession and to dwell on one point, one word, one letter. The page that presents these very passages is dense with such letters (see Figure 1.1). Crucial here is the care with which Caxton's type founder, Johannes Veldener, takes to re-create the particular qualities of an individual hand. This typeface is known as Caxton's Type 2, which he introduced in 1475 as a specific alteration of his aesthetic plan. Lotte Hellinga has pinpointed the introduction of Type 2 as part of Caxton's move from Ghent to Bruges.[34] Caxton's Type 1, she argues, is specifically modeled on the Flemish script of the scribe David Aubert. Type 2 is a more upright, rounded, bolder face. Traditionally, Type 2 is thought to indicate Caxton's turn to economy because it is smaller than Type 1, but Hellinga points out that it is in fact undergirded by a larger body and thus takes up the same amount of space in the form. Its chief effect is aesthetic, a re-creation of a particular scribal hand, that of Colard Mansion of Bruges. In the narrowing succession of makers of the text, each of whom is more physically intimate with the text but receives less mention, Colard Mansion becomes the unnamed but most palpably manifest presence in *Boecius*. His hand makes the *Consolation of Philosophy* readable, part of temporal representation by succession, so that letter follows after letter, creating the voices of Boethius and Philosophy. Each one of these letters is a cloud of historical action—of authorial intention, of translation, of scribal copying, of printing, of typecasting, of Colard Mansion—so the printed page recurs on manuscript technology, as an embedded representation within it, not as a progressive replacement before the reader's eyes, making him or her the great judge situated at the stable center point in the recursive spiral, the so-called eye of God. As the reader's eyes sweep the page from this locus, they take in the recursive structure as a totality that projects in the succession of letters, the layering of ink and paper, a tangible representation of time as a solid object. Caxton's point, put more explicitly, is that *Boecius* is a formal system of layered self-reference and that, in this, it presents a self-consciousness, a hand, a voice, an authorial intention, but it is also a totality, a density, that allows the reader to step back from the transitory and mutable temporal world and read from the vantage point of God's intention.

To take up Philosophy's challenge is to read without dissimulating, simultaneously attentive to temporal sequence and immediate presence. A literary history that cannot not periodize must turn away from this project and find totality elsewhere: in modernity, in period, in capitalism, in the unity of the visionary self who can stand apart from the sequences of time and be unto himself. Paul de Man famously argues that "modernity exists in the form of a desire to wipe out whatever came earlier in the hope of reaching at last a point that could be called a true present, a point of origin that marks a new departure."[35] Such is the power of novelty to deny the past entirely in a bid for everlasting presence, from which the paradoxical sequence of attempts to name a true point of origins, a true beginning of the historical present. Literary historians have followed this protocol, writing it into the story of the past they tell as a fundamental trope. One way out of this paradox is through recognizing the recursive function within literary production; for the physicality of the book suggests that its patterning lies not merely in progressive chronology, but in a return to the past through the physical text.

Because the physical axis is so important to literature, conceiving of literary history has less to do with a linear movement backward and forward along a sliding scale of artistic progress and technological development than with understanding how the material intrusion of chronologically older items into later points in time constitutes a powerful form of knowledge. A literary history of the book would register this duality, this simultaneous process, in its story of influence, not so much chronological linearity punctuated by a break into a new period than the continued unfolding of the presence of the past within the literary object itself. Books are steeped in time but also stand apart from it, their contents at once produced at a discrete moment and reproduced into the present through the sheer fact of physical endurance and the act of reading. Put more plainly, books complicate period through the banal observation that they remain to be reread long after they are written and printed.

If we lay aside our commitments to the totality of modernity, and instead recognize a literary culture of contingency mediated by the physicality of books, we can chase back across the firewall of 1500 to develop a more supple understanding of the local recursions within English writing and discover, in fact, that the major English vernacular writers who lived during the 1400s are not hemmed in by period but instead influence the writers of the late 1500s in tangible ways. Not only do books endure, but they are also reprinted: all of Lydgate's major texts—the *Troy Book*, the *Siege of Thebes*, and the *Fall of Princes*—were printed in the 1500s, and much of William Caxton's print portfolio—the *Recuyell of the Histories of Troy*, the *Canterbury Tales*, the *Confessio amantis*, *Le Morte Darthur*, and Aesop's fables, to name only his major literary texts—were reissued after his death. Clearly, Spenser and Shakespeare were readers of John Gower, Lydgate, Caxton, and Sir Thomas Malory, and consciously looked to their writing. For example, though Spenser boldly asserts the title of "the new Poete" in print, he relies not just on Malory's *Le Morte Darthur* for the *Faerie Queene*, but on Lydgate's *Fall of Princes* for the epistle to *The Shepheardes Calender*, and on Skelton's persona, Colin Clout.[36] Shakespeare drew directly on Caxton's *Recuyell* for his *Troilus and Cressida*.

The challenge of literary inheritance lies in the threat of infinite regression, anonymity in the trajectory of time. To escape the regressive pull of anonymity and time, sixteenth-century writers frame literary history through a recursive definition in which the fifteenth century is an elided step in the thrilling magic of literary origins. Thus writers such as Spenser create Lydgate as a fifteenth-century scholar, barely an author, even as they perceive his voice in their present, in order to shape their own work into coherence. Recognizing the past, sixteenth-century writers appropriate its forms from persona to typography, but encapsulate them within a period, denying the very influences they read in order to accomplish the thrill of poetic creation, of recursion, the effect of which is the appearance of origins from a system of reference. In this model, modernity is produced through existing texts, which writers themselves return to but render invisible through the idea of historical break. My point is that as literary historians we cannot simply be dazzled by the magic of language well used but instead must record the spiraling references within the codes of literary production.

In a sense, the process I describe is not dissimilar from Harold Bloom's notion of misprision in that it suggests the pointed misreading of the past on the part of the strong readers who define modernity. My claims are both narrower and broader than Bloom's. His is fundamentally a story of modernity, one premised on the idea that "Shakespeare belongs to the giant age before the flood, before the anxiety of influence became central to poetic consciousness."[37] Here is revolution in all its glory: a theory for all poetry that depends on a decisive break from a utopian past that can never be fully accounted for by the terms presented but in fact supplies those same terms. Bloom is precise about his claim that Shakespeare creates a rupture in literary history that separates us from the generous dispensation of premodern history. "To say that Shakespeare and poetic influence are nearly identical," he writes, "is not very different from observing that Shakespeare is the western literary canon."[38] To this point, my claims are narrower: the textual evidence demonstrates that Shakespeare read Caxton and drew from his translations, embedding their plots and aesthetic within his own work, illustrating a local recursion upon English writing. Given that Caxton's main work reproduces preexisting texts and thus recurs on the literary traditions of the Middle Ages, my claims are also broader than Bloom's. For Bloom cannot significantly account for Shakespeare beyond this great claim for origins and so does not propose a coherent English literary history so much as a manifesto for the ideology of modernism itself: that modern culture defines literary greatness as a break with a past, which it performs over and over in a recursive loop producing nothing but its own error message that, like Boethius trapped in time himself, we read as our state of being.

I suggest that recursion, that the material trope of the book, provides a more powerful rationale, one that moves beyond modernism to suggest a relationship between technology and rhetoric within literary production. That is, I suggest we recognize that literary history provides us with a complex story of subordination and mediation that spans periodic division. My evidence for the importance of this argument lies simply in that I see no other account for accommodating Lydgate, Caxton, and their contemporaries within the sixteenth-century giants of modernity, Spenser and Shakespeare. That is, either we accept that the contradictions in our current narrative are true, and in doing so simply accept modernity as our paradoxical state of being, or we actually read the evidence before us in the text of the past.

Thus I argue that medieval literary thinking is central to modern literary history, not as a simple precursor or antecedent but as a productive element interior to it. In this, *Recursive Origins* charts a process of influence more similar to what Bruce Holsinger describes in *The Premodern Condition* (2005) or Jennifer Summit in *Memory's Library* (2008) than to Bloom's anxiety of influence.[39] This is not as simple as Bruno Latour's slogan, "We have never been modern," which juxtaposes to modernity only the empty category of the premodern.[40] Rather it is, as Lyotard suggests, to make war on the totality of modernity by demonstrating how the past and the present exist in a nonlinear narrative relationship, the one always inflecting and revising the other. In this, I am perhaps true to Bloom's ultimate goal when he writes, "I mean something more drastic and (presumably) absurd, which is the triumph of having so stationed the precursor, in one's own work, that particular passages in his work seem to be not presages of one's own advent, but rather to be indebted to one's own achievement, and even (necessarily) to be lessened by one's greater splendor."[41] This is, as I read it at least, to approach Lyotard's definition of the postmodern in which future comes first, creating the past before either can exist in a temporal relationship.

Recursion therefore allows us to return to Lyotard's embarrassment. "A work can become modern only if it is first postmodern," writes Lyotard, concluding that "postmodernism thus understood is not modernism at its end but in the nascent state, and this state is constant."[42] Jameson reads Lyotard as proposing a circular history, one ultimately doomed to repeat the master narrative of modernity. By folding Lyotard into a circular history, Jameson writes him as the Ouroboros eating its own tail in an endlessly circular loop of modernity, which produces break after break, ceaselessly making it new. This is a less than generous reading of Lyotard, who argues that language is coherent not within a master narrative but within smaller narrative sequences. Lyotard's understanding ultimately seems more true to Boethius's assessment of the perpetual temporal cycles within a single point in space and to Hofstadter's recursive atomic clouds, both of which propose spirals of self-referential production clustered within what appears to be a unidirectional trajectory of time. Thus, I read Lyotard's postmodernism as not circular at all but recursive, nesting its conclusions within larger spirals of meaning that are productive, rather than returning on themselves in closure. Given this, the functional self-reference within the narrative of literary history is not the trope of modernity; that way of analysis only leads to paradox, to a relentless insistence that we cannot not periodize even when periodization is clearly incoherent. The grand statement of originality, of being, is in fact cobbled together piecemeal from the fragments of the past that remain compelling even as they are constructed as antique.

If we acknowledge that there are no absolute moments of origin, and that novelty ultimately finds its origins as a self-referential part of some larger sequence, then literary modernity cannot be premised on a historical break so much as on local textual encounters in which the past is reasserted and remade in the present. One powerful expression of and apparatus for this system of return is the book, and by viewing it as a means of reading temporal connection, *Recursive Origins* reframes three main theses concerning period, trope, and temporality for literary history:

1. *Period:* The Renaissance may have invented the doctrine of artistic progress, but such a concept is not an objective measure of scholarship so much as a narrative structure. Charged with telling a narrative that spans medieval to modern, current literary critics hew to this structure, refurbishing it through ongoing claims for the novelty of the sixteenth century: a New Historicism that champions sixteenth-century authorship as an original event, a book history that triumphs early modern printing as a revolutionary culture, and a literary history that locates its own origins in the Renaissance. In each case this argument imagines literary traditions as both passing from the Middle Ages to modernity and essentially revolutionized in that passage. I term this the "organizing principle of paradox" and argue that these are not paradoxes at all, but merely contradictions. I note there is significant evidence that rather than breaking from the past into a new literary culture, sixteenth-century writers and printers repeat its terms by subordinating them to historical narrative so as to construct their own efforts as foundational. Thus, I suggest that periodicity has too long dominated the narrative of literary history and argue that any serious consideration of the continuities inherent in literary texts must recognize that the history of vernacular literature lies less in a moment of origins than in the continual reworking of literary authority.
2. *Trope:* Recursion is a way of reorienting our thinking about literary history. Premised on nested self-reference within a functional system, recursion shares qualities with that trope of association, metonymy. One imaginative expression of both of these tropes, recursion and metonymy, is the codex. Codices are metonymic machines in that they gesture toward a unified meaning through the juxtaposition of pages, mediate between parts and unified wholes, stand in for their authors through a change of name, and allow their readers to imaginatively jump from one narrative moment to the next; they are also recursive in that their textual forms embed earlier textual forms within them to achieve their functionality. Further, they suggest the enduring nature of technical and tropic forms so that the so-called medieval is inscribed within the very technology that defines modernity: the printed book.

The vessel of narrative knowledge, the codex, offers an escape from narrative, and as we leave its dominion, we can reflect on the vastness of its shaping force.

3. *Literary Time:* The process of literary history often appears a species of naturalism, the settling of literary accounts according to a yearly plan. We have conceived of this as a move between periods and centuries and organized our discipline accordingly. Nevertheless, literary reading is both linear and recursive, sequentially moving through words and pages while simultaneously returning upon itself in reflection. This process stands in some contrast to the way time is often perceived as unidirectional, forever evolving. By discovering the recursive process within the apparently sequential nature of language itself, I suggest we can move away from the paradox of modernity and begin to appreciate better what we have always known: that the power of literature is that it allows us to embark on a temporal exploration uninhibited by the categorical limitations of our bodies and our selves. Literature affords a unique perception of time that we often take for granted, yet it nevertheless constitutes the many selves of history not as linearly distant from the temporal moment but as perceivable, palpable in the imagination.

TWO

The Poet

Edmund Spenser's *Shepheardes Calender* and the Construction of Modernity

The major poets of English literature who are copied over in manuscript during the 1400s—Geoffrey Chaucer, John Gower, William Langland, Thomas Hoccleve, and John Lydgate—are reprinted in the sixteenth century. If we see these reprints as merely static containers, and thus insignificant because they are not original, we can maintain a firm distinction between precedence and innovation, and so separate the late Middle Ages from the early modern period. If we instead take seriously the enduring power of books as part of literature's imaginative purchase, part of its ability to be renewed with each reading, we must also allow that the transition to modernity is contingent upon their enduring presence.

Contingency carries a heavy weight. The writers immediately following Chaucer negotiate it by simultaneously consolidating his writing as canonical and authorizing their own, and their method for doing so is of a piece with the logic of scribal reproduction, a practice that endorses authority by copying it over, producing Chaucer as a poet by reproducing his lines as encased within both manuscripts and tradition alike. The printing press, an apparatus for textual reproduction produced from the bits and pieces of other forms of craft knowledge (the wine press, metallurgy, book manufacture), is born from this same logic. Yet such a strategy is fraught with the risk of infinite regression, and by participating so completely in the Chaucerian mode, Hoccleve, Lydgate, James Stewart, William Caxton, and the various anonymous poets who appear in miscellanies of Chaucer's works are easily absorbed into his shadow as derivative. Observing this, sixteenth-century writers appropriate past literary forms, from persona to typography, but encapsulate them into period, which they brand "darcke"—distinct rather than contingent. In this formulation, fifteenth-century literary culture emerges as a totality that actively inflects how early modernity is written, and the modern, in turn, casts it as anterior to itself, contained within historical narrative.

What is learned in the sixteenth century, then, is subordination. "Why England, (the Mother of excellent mindes,) should bee growne so hard a step-mother to Poets?" asks Philip Sidney in *An Apologie for Poetrie.*[1] The question proposes a powerful analogy between vernacular letters and a lost childhood, one in which the recent literary past is figured as the harsh middle years that the mature adult escapes. But who suffered this adolescence, and what did they write? Sidney's memory apparently fails, though the books that contain the names are obviously within his reach: the *Apologie* itself is intimately connected to *The Shepheardes Calender*, which freely alludes to John Lydgate and John Skelton and is clearly familiar with their texts, fluent in their poetics. Still, Sidney imagines English literary history as a romance of lost origins, and so his argument makes a long return to classical models as the rightful paternity of English poetry. The current scholarship essentially accepts this view to assert a moment of break in literary history when the terms of literature change.[2] Rather than suggesting modernity occurs because the English writers of the late Middle Ages stop being read, I argue that modernity occurs *because* they are read so deeply that they must be subordinated. Thus, in order to make his own work cohere, Edmund Spenser constructs Lydgate as a tertiary writer in *The Shepheardes Calender*, even as he reads his work, perceives his voice, and cites him as a poetic precursor for the present. Reading and writing occur in a dynamic circuit of literary reproduction that transcends any simple notion of historical break.

I organize my case through two sixteenth-century prefaces. First, I offer a reading of the opening sentence of E. K.'s "Epistle to Harvey," which fronts Spenser's 1579 *Shepheardes Calender*. Lynn Staley Johnson remarks that E. K. operates as a "literary memory" for *The Shepheardes Calender*, a persona who contextualizes it in literary tradition.[3] I argue that this memory has been largely forgotten; indeed, as Paul de Man suggests, such forgetting is a necessary part of the story modernity tells of itself. The Epistle serves an important function within the poem, mediating its wealth of literary allusions in much the same way that its physical format as a book unifies its diverse parts into a whole.[4] E. K. cites Lydgate's *Fall of Princes* in the opening of the Epistle, and I trace this citation through that text, looping it from *The Shepheardes Calender* to Sidney's *An Apologie for Poetrie*. The same passage is then cited in the preface to Thomas Speght's 1598 *Workes of Chaucer*.[5] Speght's edition presents Chaucer's poetry as a part of literary history, and accordingly it not only collects a number of fifteenth-century poets with Chaucer but also includes an extended apparatus for remembering: Speght's own preface and letter to his readers, Francis Beaumont's preface "to his very louing friend, T. S.," William Thynne's letter to Henry VIII from his 1532 edition of Chaucer, a literary biography, and a glossary.[6] This collection of material illustrates the way literary precedence is simultaneously embraced and distanced in the service of modern literary history. In place of a literary history defined by break, then, I offer one of involution and subordination: Chaucer, Lydgate, Caxton, and even Hoccleve actively inflect how modernity is written; E. K., Spenser, and Speght recognize these influences but also alienate them into history so as to write themselves modern while simultaneously reading deeply into the past's rhetoric. As a result, the fifteenth and sixteenth centuries appear discrete even as one is woven from the other in a literary history of materiality and allusion, projected into abstraction as the rupture in time itself that defines historical period. In this spiral of citation and subordination, identification and alienation, selection and authorization, Lydgate is the mark of recursion that allows us to read the code work of modernity for the persona of "the new Poete."

E. K.'s "Epistle to Harvey" is a letter about the crafting of literary letters. This can be seen superficially in the contrasting layout of the first facing pages of *The Shepheardes Calender* (see Figure 2.1). Here, the opening poem, "To His Booke," by the mysterious Immeritô, evokes a Chaucerian tradition of tentativeness about authorial control through a revision of Chaucer's famous invocation of classical authority at the end of *Troilus and Criseyde*:[7] "Goe little booke: thy selfe present / As child whose parent is vnkent" (π¶.i^{v}), writes Immeritô, using the "Go little book" trope both to recall Chaucer and to introduce his own possession of the text. Witness the passage as it appears in the 1561 Stow edition, printed by John Kingston for Wight:

> Go litel boke, go my litell tregedie
> There God thy maker yet er that I die
> So sende me might to make some comedie
> But litell boke, make thou none enuie
> But subiect ben unto al poesie
> And kisse the steppes, wher as thou seest pace
> Of Vergil, Ouide, Homer, Lucan, & Stace.[8]

The passage is reminiscent of Martial's epigram on the book in that it sets out a substitution of the book for the author, which it then inserts into an internal literary world where authors appear as icons of literary history. Within this formulaic setting, Immeritô transforms

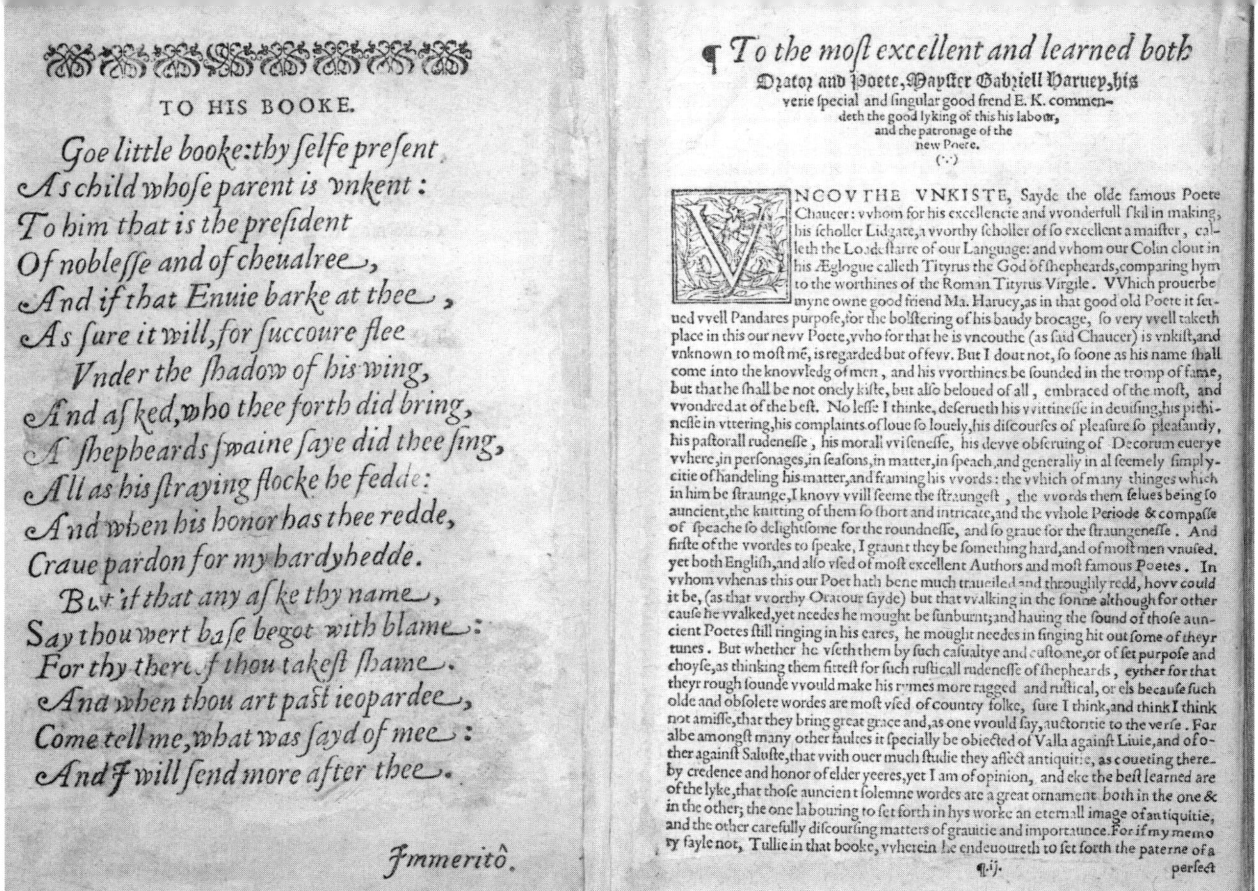

TO HIS BOOKE.

Goe little booke: thy ſelfe preſent,
As child whoſe parent is vnkent:
To him that is the preſident
Of nobleſſe and of cheualree,
And if that Enuie barke at thee,
As ſure it will, for ſuccoure flee
Vnder the ſhadow of his wing,
And aſked, who thee forth did bring,
A ſhepheards ſwaine ſaye did thee ſing,
All as his ſtraying flocke he fedde:
And when his honor has thee redde,
Craue pardon for my hardyhedde.
But if that any aſke thy name,
Say thou wert baſe begot with blame:
For thy thereof thou takeſt ſhame.
And when thou art paſt ieopardee,
Come tell me, what was ſayd of mee:
And I will ſend more after thee.

Immeritô.

¶ To the moſt excellent and learned both
Orator and Poete, Mayſter Gabriell Haruey, his
verie ſpecial and ſingular good frend E. K. commendeth the good lyking of this his labour, and the patronage of the new Poete.

(∵)

VNCOVTHE VNKISTE, Sayde the olde famous Poete Chaucer: vvhom for his excellencie and vvonderfull ſkil in making, his ſcholler Lidgate, a vvorthy ſcholler of ſo excellent a maiſter, calleth the Loadeſtarre of our Language: and vvhom our Colin clout in his Æglogue calleth Tityrus the God of ſhepheards, comparing hym to the worthines of the Roman Tityrus Virgile. VVhich prouerbe myne owne good friend Ma. Haruey, as in that good old Poete it ſerued vvell Pandares purpoſe, for the bolſtering of his baudy brocage, ſo very vvell taketh place in this our nevv Poete, vvho for that he is vncouthe (as ſaid Chaucer) is vnkiſt, and vnknown to moſt mē, is regarded but of fevv. But I dout not, ſo ſoone as his name ſhall come into the knovvledg of men, and his vvorthines be ſounded in the tromp of fame, but that he ſhall be not onely kiſte, but alſo beloued of all, embraced of the moſt, and vvondred at of the beſt. No leſſe I thinke, deſerueth his vvittineſſe in deuiſing, his pithineſſe in vttering, his complaints of loue ſo louely, his diſcourſes of pleaſure ſo pleaſantly, his paſtorall rudeneſſe, his morall vviſeneſſe, his devve obſeruing of Decorum euerye vvhere, in perſonages, in ſeaſons, in matter, in ſpeach, and generally in al ſeemely ſimplycitie of handeling his matter, and framing his vvords: the vvhich of many thinges which in him be ſtraunge, I knovv vvill ſeeme the ſtraungeſt, the vvords them ſelues being ſo auncient, the knitting of them ſo ſhort and intricate, and the vvhole Periode & compaſſe of ſpeache ſo delightſome for the roundneſſe, and ſo graue for the ſtraungeneſſe. And firſte of the vvordes to ſpeake, I graunt they be ſomething hard, and of moſt men vnuſed, yet both Engliſh, and alſo vſed of moſt excellent Authors and moſt famous Poetes. In vvhom vvhenas this our Poet hath bene much traueiled and throughly redd, hovv could it be, (as that vvorthy Oratour ſayde) but that vvalking in the ſonne although for other cauſe he vvalked, yet needes he mought be ſunburnt; and hauing the ſound of thoſe auncient Poetes ſtill ringing in his eares, he mought needes in ſinging hit out ſome of theyr tunes. But whether he vſeth them by ſuch caſualtye and cuſtome, or of ſet purpoſe and choyſe, as thinking them fitteſt for ſuch ruſticall rudeneſſe of ſhepheards, eyther for that theyr rough ſounde vvould make his rymes more ragged and ruſtical, or els becauſe ſuch olde and obſolete wordes are moſt vſed of country folke, ſure I think, and think I think not amiſſe, that they bring great grace and, as one vvould ſay, auctoritie to the verſe. For albe amongſt many other faultes it ſpecially be obiected of Valla againſt Liuie, and of other againſt Saluſte, that vvith ouer much ſtudie they affect antiquitie, as coueting thereby credence and honor of elder yeeres, yet I am of opinion, and eke the beſt learned are of the lyke, that thoſe auncient ſolemne wordes are a great ornament both in the one & in the other; the one labouring to ſet forth in hys worke an eternall image of antiquitie, and the other carefully diſcourſing matters of grauitie and importaunce. For if my memory fayle not, Tullie in that booke, vvherein he endeuoureth to ſet forth the paterne of a

¶.ij. perfect

Figure 2.1. Two introductions of the New Poet. *The Shepheardes Calender* (Hugh Singleton: London, 1579), ¶.i^v^-¶.ii, *STC* 23089 RB69548, reproduced by permission of the Huntington Library, San Marino, California.

Chaucer's relationship of author and book into one of parent and child, which he folds into a generalized pastoral world so that "make thou none enuie" in *Troilus* becomes an allegorical scene ("And if that Enuie barke at thee" and later: "A shepheards swaine saye did thee sing"). The action of writing is figured through a range of existing historical tropes for authorship and thus constructs literary history through allusion. Immeritô readily concedes that such a literary history is impure—"But if that any aske thy name, / Say thou wert base begot with blame," he tells his progeny—but the terms of his concession are nevertheless aestheticized so as to remain an idealized inheritance from the self-effacing English author and piping Virgilian swain alike. "Come tell me, what was sayd of mee: / And I will send more after thee": in such a literary history the ready concession of blame is merely an additional occasion to write because it leads Immeritô further into this pastoral world. In the opening poem, Immeritô constructs an idealized literary history in which the admission of failure is in fact a consolidation, a chance to circulate one's name and produce more poetry.

Facing Immeritô's opening poem is the dedicatory headnote to, and the beginning of, E. K.'s "Epistle to Harvey." Harvey was a reader of Chaucer as well, and the marginal notes in his copy of the 1598 edition of Chaucer's works comment on Spenser's and Shakespeare's literary status. In contrast to the aestheticized literary history of authorship in "To His Booke," this page focuses on literary making in the here and now. The headnote presents the Epistle as a letter between friends interested in good poetry:

> ¶ *To the most excellent and learned both*
> Orator and Poete, Mayster Gabriell Haruey, his
> verie special and singular good frend E. K. commen-
> deth the good lyking of this his labour,
> and the patronage of the
> new Poete.[9]

Here, Harvey is styled as an orator and poet, and the initials "E. K." suggest a range of possible personae for the Epistle's author. Perhaps

Spenser's Cambridge contemporary Edmund Kirke, perhaps a familiar but otherwise anonymous editor, or perhaps a loose persona for Spenser himself, the abbreviated identity sets up what is to follow not simply as an announcement of the New Poet but as a personal recommendation that becomes a proclamation only as it is made public.[10] In fact, the headnote's layout and language, even the curious little decorative marks that set it apart from the text of the Epistle, echo the 1579 edition's title page, which puts the entire book in the context of patronage by offering it "TO THE NOBLE AND VERTV- / *ous Gentleman most worthy of all titles* / both of learning and cheualrie M. / Philip Sidney" (π¶.i). Thus, if Immeritô's poem on the facing page entreats Spenser's little book to go forth into a figural setting of allusion, the title page and the headnote to the Epistle announce the audience that is to receive it. In this transition from literal text to figural world and back again to literary letters—this expanding and flattening out of poetry into commentary that occurs on the two facing pages—the headnote is no less figural than the poem, just differently so, for it creates an imaginative space for the reader to situate him or herself as a voyeur, reading, as it were, over the shoulder of these gentleman literary aficionados. The distinction between the two tellings of literary history, Immeritô's and E. K.'s, is captured superficially on the page itself: one figures the passage of authority through the almost fluid italic column of verse, capped by a floral decoration; the other literalizes its declaration through a solid column of black ink topped by a tight wedge. The Epistle is a letter about literary letters: it is as concerned with the *litera* (the literal), and its pages are dominated by an almost solid sheet of letters themselves, yet because it imagines itself and the following poem as circulated among an ideal audience, which it too places in dialogue with literary history, it is also about the ideals of reading and writing.

Within the Epistle, E. K. offers a literary history concerned with just such a process of constructing a public statement as private. Where Immeritô's poem idealizes its history—writing the scene of Chaucerian rhetoric as inhabited by a Virgilian swain—the Epistle's first sentence teaches a more pragmatic lesson in how to write. E. K. begins: "VNCOVTHE VNKISTE, Sayde the olde famous Poete

Chaucer: whom for his excellencie and wonderfull skil in making, his scholler Lidgate, a worthy scholler of so excellent a maister, calleth the Loadestarre of our Language: and whom our Colin clout in his Æglogue calleth Tityrus the God of shepheards, comparing hym to the worthines of the Roman Tityrus Virgile" (¶.ii.). E. K. opens by returning the reader to Chaucer's *Troilus and Criseyde*, specifically to Pandarus's advice to Troilus that "Unknow unkist, and lost that is unsought."[11] Chaucer's Pandarus is a master rhetorician, one who teaches Troilus not only to write love letters but also to write them naturally, as a performance: "Ne scriueinishe or craftely thou it write / Beblotte it with thy teares eke alite," he tells Troilus, cautioning, "And if thou write a goodly worde all soft / Though it be good, rehearce it now to oft."[12] What Pandarus teaches is an artifice that denies itself, an artifice that appears unmediated but is by definition all the more artificial for doing so.[13] E. K. goes on to explicate the passage in terms of literary fame, telling Harvey, "for that he is vncouthe (as said Chaucer) is vnkist, and vnknown to most me*n*, is regarded but of few." E. K.'s lesson is to risk publicity; it is also to write what you want others to read: here Pandarus's "unknow" is cited (insistently so) as "vncouthe," a word similar in meaning but emphasizing strangeness and leaning—almost—toward "indecorous," a use the *Oxford English Dictionary* first records in 1589. E. K. ascribes just this quality—a strangeness that remains, barely, on this side of decorum—to the New Poet's verse: "the words them selues being so auncient, the knitting of them so short and intricate, and the whole Periode & compasse of speache so delightsome for the roundnesse, and so graue for the straungenesse" (¶.ii.). Indeed, he tells Harvey that it is just such a quality of decorous strangeness that marks the New Poet's achievement over other authors and allows him to "restore, as to theyr rightfull heritage such good and naturall English words. . . . For what in most English wryters vseth to be loose, and as it were vngyrt, in this Authour is well grounded, finely framed, and strongly trussed up together" (¶.ii.^{v}). The Epistle's addressee and authorship imagine the kind of readership necessary to appreciate Spenser's work, and its contents construct authority by citing literary precedent and, simultaneously, silently revising that precedent to fit a particular telling of literary history.

As constructed as it is, the Epistle nevertheless offers a specifically fifteenth-century articulation of Pandarus's advice. This is clear in the way his first sentence casts Chaucer as an author mediated by his major reader: John Lydgate.[14] Lydgate writes of Chaucer that "off oure language he was lodesterre" in his English version of Laurence de Premierfait's second, amplified French translation of Giovanni Boccaccio's *De Casibus Virorum Illustrium*, which Lydgate produced for Humphrey, Duke of Gloucester, between 1431 and 1439.[15] James Simpson points out that the *Mirror for Magistrates* was a "main channel for the survival of Lydgate's reputation as a secular poet," but Lydgate's major works were available in print throughout the century.[16] Richard Pynson printed the *Fall of Princes* in 1494 and again in 1527; John Wayland printed the text in 1554, as did Richard Tottel.[17] Pynson published Lydgate's massive *Troy Book* in 1513, Thomas Marshe published it in 1555, and Thomas Purfoot published a version in 1614.[18] Further, Wynkyn de Worde printed *The Siege of Thebes* in 1497, a text featured in the title of the 1561 *The Woorkes of Geffrey Chaucer, Newly Printed, with Diuers Addicions, Whiche Were Neuer in Printe Before, with the Siege and Destruccion of the Worthy Citee of Thebes, Compiled by Ihon Lidgate, Monke of Berie*, and collected with Chaucer's works in the 1598 and 1602 editions.[19] In this inclusion, Lydgate's authority is both lessened—he is made a mere appendage to Chaucer, a compiler—and powerfully transformed into an essential part of the Chaucerian canon. Up to and including the seventeenth century, then, Lydgate was a named writer, one continuously read from the time of his writing, and therefore a model for contemporary writers. E. K.'s opening sentence may trace a history beginning with Chaucer and ending with Virgil, and his glosses within *The Shepheardes Calender* may offer a direct comparison between these two poets, but first he constructs Chaucer through Lydgate's telling of authority.

Understanding Lydgate's influence is no straightforward task. If Pandarus's lesson is about the performance of writing—the necessity that it appear impromptu and unrehearsed most especially when it isn't—Lydgate's is about the consolidation of literary authority. Seth Lerer has identified this as the twofold process of authorizing and selecting at the heart of fifteenth-century writing, and we can read it clearly in the prologue to the very work E. K. cites, *The Fall of Princes*.[20] Here Lydgate is initially concerned with authorizing his work as belonging to a specifically vernacular tradition, and so he underscores its origination with Boccaccio and its passage through French to himself. In the same vein, he accounts for Chaucer's works by listing them off, placing Chaucer in the context of Petrarch, Boccaccio, Seneca, and Cicero. This is of a piece with Chaucer's own agenda: Chaucer catalogs his writings in a number of instances and clearly associates himself with such classical predecessors at the end of *Troilus and Criseyde* in the lines Immeritô alludes to in the *Calender*'s opening poem. Thus Lydgate's first consolidation authorizes his work through a broad, and broadly humanist, claim that vernacular writing offers an authority comparable to classical precedent.

Lydgate then selects a Chaucerian style to inhabit as his own. So, just as Troilus's inability to write occasions Pandarus's instruction in an aesthetic contrived as natural and defenseless when it is most thrusting, Lydgate learns from Chaucer an aesthetic of refinement that belittles its claim to authority ("go little booke") at the same moment it seizes that authority. David Lawton argues that "dullness is the mark of a fifteenth-century poet; but, conversely, a true mark of a fifteenth-century poet is to deny being a poet—to abrogate, that is, any specialized status (beyond financial reward) that poetry might bring."[21] Dullness, the poetics of self-reference as self-denial, is what Spenser learns from Lydgate, and it is exactly what makes *The Shepheardes Calender* so difficult. For the poem's many voices—Immeritô's, E. K.'s, Colin's, the shepherds'—stage a series of assertions of, feints at, and deferrals to authority that seem simultaneously to deny the possibility of a unified poetic voice and also to speak as one, as Spenser.

Immeritô, for instance, initially appears as an autonomous poet able to confirm the project overall, but the more we understand him, the more we see him not as a poet but as an allegory for self-denial (his name means "the undeserving one"), a proxy for Spenser, and thus evidence of the poem's complexity and the poet's cunning. Rather than a legitimate voice, Immeritô is yet another self-reference, a sign that whatever one may understand of what is to come, Spenser is well ahead, seeding in allusions and self-effacing protestations that the reader may never plumb. In Immeritô we should see that self-denial is always an instance of self-reference, a complex undercutting of authority premised on the prior admission of that authority. This twofold process is ostentatiously self-conscious and deeply contrived. As Pandarus tells Troilus, blot the tears into the page a little; it lends credibility.

The twofold structure of authorizing and selecting authority is fundamental to the Chaucerian tradition and acknowledged in Spenser's (and E. K.'s) various appropriations. It is, at heart, the recursive procedure of producing a representation through an embedded self-reference because it produces literary authority by citing it first. Allowing the subordination of one poet to the next, denial facilitates a sequencing of self-references that conspire to the final statement: poetic authority. Thus, Lydgate represents himself as a poet by embedding the representation of Chaucer as a poet within his poetry, and, in turn, Spenser does the same for Lydgate. The trope appears throughout fifteenth-century poetry, and Lydgate is not the only model E. K. makes use of in *The Shepheardes Calender*. In the Epistle, E. K. obfuscates the source of the *Calender*'s governing poetic persona, making it familiar ("our Colin clout") while holding off any mention of its origin until his first gloss to "Januarie," where he explains "COLIN Cloute) is a name not greatly vsed, and yet haue I sene a Poesie of M. Skeltons vnder that title. But indeede the word Colin is Frenche, and vsed of the French Poete Marot" (A.ii.^{v}).

Critics have tended to read heavily here, claiming Skelton as lost to literary history. For example, A. F. Marotti argues for Skelton's ultimate irrelevance to the poet laureates of the sixteenth century: "The editions of his works that survive present him as 'Skelton Laureate,' 'Skelton Poet Laureat' or 'Skelton Poeta,' titles that emphasize his academic credentials and allude to his occasional courtly verse but do not seriously assert cultural authority within the print medium—something that might be claimed for the sixteenth-century editions of Chaucer's collected works, for example, Thynne's published in 1532."[22] Marotti suggests that the books bearing Skelton's title—the multiple editions proclaiming "Master Skelton, Poet Laureat," on their title pages—do not assert cultural authority in print;[23] indeed, he argues that the books of Chaucer's poetry before Thynne's 1532 *Workes of Geffray Chaucer* are symbolically different from those printed after the first third of the sixteenth century. The tacit assumption is that fifteenth-century writing, bound to manuscript or incunabular format as it is, does not "seriously assert cultural authority within the print medium." Yet neither the cultural authority of the vernacular poet laureate nor the collected-works format is unique to sixteenth-century print production; both, in fact, rely on the twofold recursive mechanism of authorizing and selecting outlined by Lerer and so clearly utilized by Lydgate in the *Fall of Princes*.

We can see this in an early manuscript bearing Skelton's poetry, B. L. MS Royal 18.D.ii. Originally owned by William Herbert, Earl of Pembroke, this manuscript compiles Lydgate's *Troy Book* and *The Siege of Thebes* with Skelton's early poem, "Elegy on the Earl of Northumberland," and its illuminated letters boldly proclaim Skelton's laureate status. The manuscript is organized according to the double Chaucerian rhetoric: it *authorizes* certain styles of writing—vernacular, Chaucerian, courtly, ornate—in order to *select* an authorial role for cultural authority—the poet laureate. Skelton is quite aware of this process, writing Chaucer, Gower, and Lydgate into his *Garlande of Laurell* as acknowledging his arrival at Fame's court. Jane Griffiths writes that "Skelton momentarily seems to base his own claim to authority upon his position within that tradition, and not upon his individual voice," which brings him into what she terms a "chain of transmission":

> The inscription of Chaucer, Lydgate, and Gower as Skelton's readers places them not only as the origin but as the end of the chain of transmission, and by implication positions Skelton not as the inheritor of their authority but as an original with authority of his own. Thus, in Skelton's treatment of the idea of writing as part of a chain of transmission, the chain does not run from the original source to the reader through the mediation of the writer, but from the writer to the reader, mediated through the text.

> Whereas the former view tends to gloss over inevitable changes of meaning, the latter gives them full acknowledgement, and the writer becomes the origin rather than the inheritor of meaning. . . . Contrary to first impressions, then, Skelton may be viewed, like the later laureates Spenser and Jonson, as "the thing of great constancy" at the centre of his work.[24]

Griffiths describes a recursive algorithm for literary authority that produces the persona of the poet as the originator, not the inheritor, of literary authority. Skelton banked upon this role in print: Caxton's own assertion of Skelton's title in the preface to his *Eneydos* presents him as a cultural authority over vernacular writing from the 1490s, and Griffiths argues that Skelton's "deployment of titles is consistent and controlled and that the obsession with the author's status may be construed as the poet's own."[25] Though Griffiths doubts that these titles reproduced Skelton's authority clearly after his death, David Lee Miller points out that they nevertheless endured, so that "Spenser would have seen himself foreshadowed in such passages."[26] The terms "foreshadowed" and "obsession" undercut the impressively strategic nature of such authorial construction as a poet. Skelton's claim to authority is never simply anxious or academic: it is a rhetorical deployment of material and intellectual forms toward the symbolic construction of cultural authority that works by recognizing certain roles in the past, acknowledging them as models, and then using the text to mediate one's self-presentation as original in the present.

The same is true for the so-called single editions of Chaucer's poetry before William Thynne's 1532 *Workes*. Thynne's edition is often cited as historically important for demonstrating the growing sense of the English canon in the early sixteenth century.[27] A similar case has been made for Richard Pynson's 1526 edition because its separate units seem designed to be joined together, looking ahead to the concept of the collected works.[28] Yet the technique of compiling separate texts into a greater whole is a fundamental part of the English tradition of vernacular manuscript production and can be seen in the manuscripts of the Oxford Group from the first half of the fifteenth century.[29] It is also a functional part of early printing: Caxton printed two discrete runs of Chaucerian material, one produced in the mid to late 1470s and covering quarto and folio editions of works by Lydgate and Chaucer and a second printed almost entirely in 1483, featuring new works by Gower and Chaucer and a reprint of the *Canterbury Tales*.[30] Caxton's buyers purchased these editions and assembled them into personal collections: witness the Bishop Moore quarto binding together, among other pieces, Lydgate's *Stans puer ad mensam*, *The Churl and the Bird*, *The Horse, the Sheep and the Goose*, and *Temple of Glass*, with Chaucer's *Temple of Brass* and *Queen Anelida and the False Arcite*; witness the folio-sized volume of Roger Thorney that assembles Caxton's 1483 *Canterbury Tales* and *Troilus and Criseyde* with a paper manuscript copy of Lydgate's *Siege of Thebes*.[31] As with Thynne, Stow, and later Speght, these books collate not simply texts by Chaucer but his cultural authority as well. What Thynne's edition makes *explicit*—the nature of the collected works—is in fact *implicit* in the design of Caxton's texts, in the recursive process by which certain texts are authorized as canonical and then selected as a unit: the collected works.

Caxton's prose works much the same way. Caxton embeds allusions to Chaucer's poetry, as well as to works he does not print, such as Lydgate's *Troy Book* and *Siege of Thebes*, into his prose prefaces.[32] Unmarked, these references imply a certain familiarity with the Chaucerian tradition in manuscript and circulate this familiarity in the print medium. For example, Caxton's first extended piece on Chaucer, his epilogue to the 1478 *Boecius*, draws on his own edition of the *Book of Courtesy*. Similarly, his prologue to the second edition of the *Canterbury Tales* draws on a number of allusions to Lydgate's *Troy Book* and *Siege of Thebes*, and to Chaucer's own *Clerk's Tale*. Caxton's writing is often dismissed as "secondhand" or "advertising talk"—some sort of rudimentary marketing, which, as Robert Costomiris puts it, "compromises [its] worth"[33]—but he essentially follows the same rhetorical strategy as Lydgate: he authorizes certain writings and then selects from them a language for his own statement. In effect, Caxton's assembly practices and editorial commentary work the same way: both suggest to the reader certain fundamental units for composition, in the form of either individual texts or discrete poetic allusions, which they offer as parts of the larger, imaginary, unity of English literature. In the Skelton manuscript and the Caxton print, cultural authority is not bifurcated across book technologies or medieval and modern periods but derived from the ongoing manipulation of material and intellectual aspects of literary production according to the practices of an overall textual culture.

The complexity inherent in this rhetorical mechanism for the production of literary authority is captured in Lydgate's term "loadestarre." Etymologically derived from Old Norse, the "lodestar" is ostensibly a guiding star, and on the most obvious level, this is what the word signifies in E. K.'s Epistle: Lydgate simply praises Chaucer for guiding English poetry.[34] E. K. also announces at the beginning of his Epistle that the method of "our poet" is to knit together and truss up ancient words, and I would suggest this is especially true for the word "lodestar," for it weaves together its greater significance through allusion to prior writing, allusion we can begin to read by following the word deeper into Lydgate. In book 2, chapter 13 of the *Fall of Princes*, Lydgate applies the term to Dido, calling her, as is recorded in Tottel's 1554 edition, the "lode sterre of all good gouernance" (fol. liii). Dido is frequently associated with the origins of writing, and in this section Lydgate connects Dido's literary legacy to a history of writing stemming from the Phoenicians.[35] Tottel's 1554 edition presents this as (fol. li^v):

> Cadmus found first letters for to wryte,
> Gaue them to Grekes as made is mencion,
> whose brother Fenix as Clerkes eke endite
> found fyrst the colour of vermilion:
> and of Cartage the famous mighty towne.
> This sayd Ddio [*sic*] her story doth expresse,
> How she was both quene and founderesse.

Here is a history for the origins of writing that intertwines public and literary authority. This suggests a second level of meaning for the word "lodestar," one evoking the way writing embodies various kinds of cultural authority: applied to Chaucer, the lodestar signifies that eloquence produces a particularly literary authority; applied to Dido, it signifies the way writing materially communicates authority in the historical record. The passage is not only interested in literary production as linguistic, however; it also asserts that writing is a material endeavor involving the fabrication of letters, the use of inks, and the historical communication of a technology from one culture to the next. Dido's fame as "both quene and founderesse" of Carthage perseveres because of her connection to the founding of writing; indeed, in Lydgate's telling it almost seems that Cadmus first invented letters to spread her fame ("This sayd Ddio her story doth expresse"). Jonathan Goldberg relates Cadmus's story in connection to Erasmus and to the development of sixteenth-century writing manuals.[36] Yet the link between Dido, Cadmus, and the Phoenician origination of writing is in no way unique to Lydgate's or Erasmus's interests: besides featuring here in his *Fall of Princes*, it is a significant part of Caxton's *Eneydos* and figures, too, in Skelton's translation of the *Bibliotheca historica*. Thus on a third level, the lodestar suggests a particular interest in the way material and intellectual forms of literary production conspire to produce authority.

We can follow the lodestar further into literary history by tracing it back to Chaucer. Chaucer uses the word in *The Knight's Tale* to describe the painting of Callisto turned to Ursa Major in the Temple of Diane ("And afterward was she made the lode sterre").[37] In *Troilus and Criseyde*, Troilus, in bed, laments to himself about Criseyde ("Who seeth you now, my right lode sterre"),[38] and in the "Litera Troili," the final letter Pandarus instructs Troilus to write, he tells her,

> And if so be my gilt hath death deserued
> Or if you list no more upon me se
> In guerdon yet of that I haue you serued
> Beseche I you, mine owne ladie fre
> That hereupon ye woulden write me
> For loue of God, my right lode sterre
> That death maie make an ende of al my wer.[39]

In each case—Callisto's metamorphosis into the stars, Troilus's two mournful evocations of Criseyde—the lodestar signifies a woman of both artifice and loss. So it is, too, with Chaucer's depictions of Dido in the *House of Fame* and *Legend of Good Women*. Jennifer Summit argues that in these texts Dido embodies "the textual instability that underlies an idealized model of tradition but that is also hidden from view."[40] Exposure: Dido embodies a literary past of failure but also of revelation. Her story reveals that the claim to origins offers no guarantee of stability in literary history. In telling Dido's story, Lydgate knows that regardless of her political authority, her example is famously negative, and that to be like Dido is to be all too visible in literary history as a failure, a counterweight to literary fame.

Here, then, the lodestar knits together a web of at least four strands of meaning: in the first, it suggests the fullness of Chaucer's singular precedence in literary history as the guiding light of English letters. In the second, Lydgate's linkage of Chaucer's authority as a founding poet and Dido's as a political founder suggests an overlap between literary and political authority. In this connection is the third strand of meaning: the lodestar recalls a material history of writing in which the actual production of letters leads directly to the symbolic production of authority. Yet Chaucer's own use of the term both reminds us that artifice offers no guarantee of fame and recalls a sense of textual instability, of the greater loss to history, which Chaucer feminizes. Thus, through a fourth strand the lodestar evokes E. K.'s initial reading of Pandarus's advice: "vnkown to most me*n*, is regarded but of few," nothing risked leads to nothing gained, but above all, nothing is promised; everything must be constructed to protect against the destructiveness of history. All four strands, but especially the fourth, are graphically encapsulated in Tottel's compositor's transposed setting of Dido as "Ddio," a mistake that records her name for posterity but does so incorrectly, denuded of her royal authority and almost parodic of her special purchase on the permanence of writing.

Dido also returns us to *The Shepheardes Calender*, specifically to "Nouember," which presents Spenser's only rendition of her history. Ostensibly, Lydgate's Dido and Spenser's Dido are far apart. Lydgate tells the story of Dido as queen of Carthage and explicates the loss of her "grene youth flouring with al pleasance" with "¶ Le enuoye direct to widowes, of the translatour," in which he encourages widows to be chaste with the refrain "to folow Dido ye was quene of

Chartage" (Tottel, fol. liii). His is an allegory of loss, which he explains straightforwardly enough. Colin Clout's song, immersed in pastoral motifs as it is, bears no explicit allegorical meaning beyond E. K.'s announcement that "the personage is secrete, and to me altogether vnknowne," no clearer conclusion than his argument that it is "farre passing his reache, and in myne opinion all other the Eglogues of this booke" (fol. 44), no explication more profound than its overriding tone of mourning. "Nouember" is also an eclogue of apprenticeship, one E. K. positions as an "imitation of Marot his song" (Marot who was previously associated with Skelton through the persona of Colin Clout) and one in which Thenot directly asks Colin to teach him. As Thenot says (fol. 44^{v}),

> Nay, better learne of hem, that learned bee,
> And han be watered at the Muses well:
> The kindlye dewedrops from the higher tree,
> And wets the little plants that lowly dwell.

As much as November is a song of loss, it is also a song evoking the power of songs, a song calling to the muses for education. Again, the lesson of the Chaucerian tradition is one of self-reflection and self-construction, and this is how E. K. has positioned Lydgate all along—as a model for self-construction and a warning at the beginning of the project. What Spenser learns from Lydgate is that literary authority is premised on the public consolidation of an authorial role, and so he constitutes Lydgate as a "scholler" specifically to appropriate that role for E. K., whom he contrives as his own Lydgate capable of explicitly authorizing and selecting rhetorical elements that the other personae who dominate the book—Immeritô, Colin, Thenot, Piers—leave for the reader to work out. In *The Specter of Dido*, John Watkins writes that Spenser "recalls Chaucer both as a mentor and as a potential threat to his Virgilian identity," and this is unquestionably true.[41] Just as true, however, is that Lydgate is a mentor and threat to Spenser. The lodestar shows not only the specter of Dido but also the specter of Lydgate, for on one level, Lydgate is an author involved in exactly the kind of vernacular humanism that interests Spenser and thus operates as a model and a guide to the construction of literary authority; on another, he is a "Ddio," part of the intervening past that must be bracketed off in order to idealize the New Poet. What Spenser takes from Lydgate is a self-conscious ambivalence about literary history and the knowledge that for his poetic persona to appear successfully, he must accomplish the poetics of denial almost invisibly. For as presented in the Cadmus legend, the production of letters creates a lodestar, a public marker for history that can tell either of genius or of infamy, either of the magic of literary production that results in a fame capable of surmounting literary history or the failure of language itself in which all those lines of poetry appear for naught and produce only a garbled message, "Ddio."

More to the point, Lydgate is threatening to our own account of literary history. For if we acknowledge that books transmit cultural authority across historical and technological boundary lines, that this transmission process is defined neither by linear progress nor by sudden break, and that writers as often dismissed as John Lydgate constitute important parts of it, we need to reassess some basic assumptions about the perspicuity of so-called late medieval thinking, the originality of so-called early modern print culture, and the nature of literary history overall. Indeed, these assumptions are deeply held in literary criticism. For example, recent discussions of New Formalism and of Historical Formalism continually return to Sidney's *Apologie for Poetrie*, and through him to Aristotle and Horace. The *Apologie* is broadly taken to be a rebuttal to texts that would excoriate poetic making, such as Stephen Gosson's 1579 *Schoole of Abuse*.[42] Gosson's text was of course dedicated to Sidney, whose essay takes the occasion of defense to stage a larger theory of poetics. Like Spenser, Sidney cites Chaucer's *Troilus and Criseyde* as a literary precedent, writing "*Chaucer*, vndoubtedly did excellently in hys *Troylus* and *Cresseid*; of whom, truly I know not, whether to meruaile more, either that he in that mistie time, could see so clearely, or that wee in this cleare age, walke so stumblingly after him. Yet had he great wants, fitte to be forgiuen, inso reuernt antiquity" (I4). Here Chaucer appears out of the mists of time, a prescient antique. What is more marvelous, asks Sidney, that Chaucer could produce poetry or that the contemporary reader, able to see so much more clearly, cannot match him? Just so, few medieval authors are presented by New Formalists; the implicit statement is a proscription: in our own time of cultural degradation we would do well to return to formalism so as to renew our commitment to the ever-incomplete project of modernity, identified with Sidney's essay. And in so searching out our link in the modern past, we would be surprised to find that the medieval, enveloped in the darkening mists of time as it is, has any relevance at all.

Sidney searches the present for poetic making. "I account the *Mirrour of Magistrates*, meetely furnished of beautiful parts," he remarks, and he lauds "the Earle of Surries *Liricks*, many things tasting of a noble birth, and worthy of a noble minde. The *Sheapheards Kalender*," too, "hath much Poetrie in his Eglogues" (I4r-v). He pauses over "*Gorboduck*." But when Sidney looks back on literary history, he sees a fairly empty landscape in which the only English authors that intrude into his line of sight to the classics are Chaucer and Gower:

> Let learned Greece in any of her manifold Sciences, be able to shew me one booke, before *Musæus*, *Homer*, & *Hesiodus*, all three nothing els but Poets. Nay, let any historie be brought, that can say any Writers were there before the*m*, if they were not men of the same skil, as *Orpheus*, *Linus*, and some other are named: who hauing beene the first of that Country, that made pens deliuerers of their knowledge to their posterity, may iustly chalenge to bee called their Fathers in learning: for not only in time they had this priority (although in it self antiquity be venerable,) but went before them, as causes to drawe with their charming sweetnes, the wild vntamed wits to an admiration of knowledge. So as *Amphion* was sayde to moue stones with his Poetrie, to build Thebes. And *Orpheus* to be listened to by beastes, indeed, stony and beastly people. So among the Romans were *Liuius*, *Andronicus*, and *Ennius*. So in the Italian language, the first that made it aspire to be a Treasure-house of Science, were the Poets *Dante*, *Boccace*, and *Petrarch*. So in our English were *Gower* and *Chawcer*. (B2r-v)

"Shew me one booke," Sidney calls out, and so finds the origins of writing in a history of poetry—Musaeus, Homer, Hesiod, Orpheus,

Linaus, Amphion, Livy, Andronicus, and Ennius—that charts a material legacy of books and writers that "made pens deliuerers of their knowledge to their posterity." These men are the fathers of poetry, suggestively necessary for England (that mother of excellent minds). Still, what appears a linear history of poetics, moving from the Greeks through the Romans to Italy and England, is in fact a rhetorical arrangement that can only be answered in the negative: Amphion "was sayde" and Orpheus was "listened to." Amphion and Orpheus—the putative fathers before Musaeus, Homer, and Hesiod—are singers, not writers at all; they can never "shew me one booke" because their work is ephemeral. The call for evidence is a rhetorical confirmation of the power of both poetics and Sidney's particular rendition of English literary history. Between Sidney's final citation of the major fourteenth-century poets—Dante, Petrarch, Boccaccio, Chaucer, and Gower—and his own efforts lies a chasm of poetic making demanding a long return through the ages to song.

"Shew me one booke," Sidney challenges, and in a sense *The Shepheardes Calender*'s citation of Lydgate is an answer to the challenge before it is offered. For if we can trace Sidney's allusion to Amphion back to Horace's *Ars poetica*, which announces both Amphion and Orpheus, we can also follow it back through Spenser's citation of Lydgate, back to *The Fall of Princes* and *The Siege of Thebes*, both of which mythologize Amphion's poetic song. This later text is particularly relevant because it too narrates the origins of writing in order to comment on current English poetics. Begun in the spring of 1421 and finished shortly before Henry V's death in August 1422, *The Siege of Thebes* was widely circulated in manuscript and became increasingly associated with *The Canterbury Tales* in print across the fifteenth and sixteenth centuries, embedded in the encomia and books that constitute Chaucer's authority. Though he did not print it, William Caxton drew on it for his praise of Chaucer in his prologue to his 1483 edition of *The Canterbury Tales*; it was compiled with Chaucer's work in the Thorney and the Fisher *Sammelbände*, and, again, it was printed by de Worde in 1497 and conflated into the Chaucer canon, included in *The Canterbury Tales* from the Stow edition.[43]

The inclusion is fitting, for in the prologue to *The Siege of Thebes*, Lydgate writes himself into *The Canterbury Tales*: he describes how he meets the pilgrims in Canterbury and is commanded by the Host to tell his own tale on the journey back to London. Lydgate chooses to tell the precursor to Chaucer's *Knight's Tale*: the tale of Oedipus and the fall of Thebes. In bringing Chaucer's pilgrims out of Canterbury, Lydgate affirms the narrative order of *The Canterbury Tales*; in telling the precursor to its first tale, he undermines its structural order, looping back from his chronological place at the end to a narrative position at the beginning. Authorizing and selecting, Lydgate sets up the double rhetoric recursion: he embeds Chaucer's authority within the poem as preexisting his own, autonomous within literary history; indeed, he writes that Chaucer is a specifically national poet, the "Floure of Poetes, throughout all Bretaine" who "neuer shall, appallen in my minde."[44] At the same time, he appropriates Chaucer's authority wholesale, using it to represent himself as a poet. Hence the double rhetoric: Lydgate authorizes *The Canterbury Tales* as a genre—he actually names it the "Canterburie tales" in his prologue—precisely so he can select this genre for himself and, casting Chaucer so ruthlessly into history that he is not even present as a pilgrim, exploit it to his own ends.

In referencing Lydgate's commentary on Chaucer, Spenser does more than show Sidney one book; he leads him to an elaborate theory of literary reproduction. Germaine Warkentin writes: "I think it would be possible to argue that the purpose of the *Defence* is less to exalt poetry than to provide a kind of 'creation myth' for history."[45] This is Lydgate's purpose as well. Lydgate drew much of the *Siege* from a French redaction of Statius's *Thebaid*, entitled the *Roman de Edipus*. In this telling, after Oedipus dies, his sons Eteocles and Polynices fall to war over the throne of Thebes. In the opening of the poem Lydgate sets out Amphion, the founder of Thebes, as a governing exemplum for poetic eloquence in the service of political authority. Directing us back to his sources, the anonymous *Roman de Edipus* and Giovanni Boccaccio's *Genealogiae deorum gentilium*, he tells, as Stow records it,

> Rede her bookes, and ye shall finde it so
> How this kyng, this prudent Amphion

With his swetenesse, and melodious soun
The citee built, that whilom was so strong
And Armonie, of his swete song
By vertue onely, of the weribles sharpe
That he made, in Mercuries Harpe
Of whiche the stre*n*ges, wer not touched softe
Whereby the walles, reised weren a lofte
Without crafte, of any mannes hande
Full yore ago, midde of Grekes lande.[46]

Amphion illustrates a seamless union of literary and political rhetoric. As much as he is a poet, he is king; as much as his words are utilitarian, they are also harmonious. He is like Chaucer: where Amphion's "swete song" raises the walls of Thebes, Lydgate announces in his opening prologue that Chaucer's "sawes swete" construct English literature.[47] Just as Lydgate describes Amphion as the "Chief cause" of the foundation of Thebes, he fashions Chaucer as the "Chief Registrer" of *The Canterbury Tales*.[48] But Amphion is also like Dido, for Thebes is the most negative of exempla, and Lydgate pointedly elides the generations of Theban rulers separating Amphion from Laius so that Amphion reads as the only significant precursor to the Oedipal tragedy: "Fro kyng to kyng, by succession / Conueiyng doune, by the stocke of Amphion / Ceriously by line, all the discent."[49] Stow's edition presents the passage as carefully bracketed out with printed rubrics so as to highlight that the "Example good of kyng Amphion" is directly followed by "how the line of Amphion by discente, was conueighed to kyng Laius."[50] The implication is clear: "But of cursed stocke, cometh unkinde blood," but only by implication, never by definition.[51] *The Siege of Thebes* is not just a tragic romance; it is literary history as well. Including as it does Lydgate's recursion on Chaucer, it specifically participates in the English Chaucerian tradition, but it also goes on to write a larger literary history for vernacular letters. Like Spenser, Lydgate insists on the efficacy of vernacular eloquence for diplomacy but notes that such eloquence always bears the risk of failure, and so he uses the twofold rhetoric of authorizing and selecting to attempt to secure Chaucer's authority for himself.

If we look at the sixteenth-century editions of Chaucer contemporary to *The Shepheardes Calender*, we can see that Spenser's appreciation of Lydgate's precedence was, in fact, carefully noted by his readers, such as Francis Beaumont, who comments on it in Speght's 1598 edition of Chaucer's *Workes*. These writings can help us understand the construction of sixteenth-century literary history as distinct from the past. The very title of Beaumont's preface, "F. B. to his very louing friend, T. S.," suggests the same technique for crafting an ideal public audience through the performance of intimacy that we see in "E. K.'s Epistle to Harvey." Citing Horace, F. B. likens the decline of vernacular language to the ripening of fruit and notes that even the Latin language aged, concluding: "But yet so pure were *Chaucers* wordes in his owne daies, as *Lidgate* that learned man calleth him *The Loadstarre of the English language:* and so good they are in our daies, as Maister *Spencer*, following the counsaile of *Tullie in de Oratore*, for reuiuing of antient wordes, hath adorned his owne stile with that beauty and grauitie, which *Tully* speakes of" ($\pi 3^v$). The passage applies E. K.'s Epistle to the broader service of explaining the historical development of literary history. E. K.'s "Loadestarre of our Language" becomes "*The Loadstarre of the English language*," a phrase slightly less private and intimate and slightly more focused on the notion of a specifically English canon. Still, both E. K. and F. B. construct Lydgate as capable of acknowledging Chaucer's genius, naming him the lodestar and thus ratifying Spenser's own selection of a poetic "stile." In turn, they also argue that the immediate literary past, the literary culture from which Lydgate comes, separates the present from a more fruitful language. The fifteenth century is precisely what constitutes the intervening past that denigrates Chaucer's pure words so that they are barely recognizable as eloquent in the present.[52] This same sentiment is available in E. K.'s Epistle as well, where he writes that "Our Poet" has "laboured to restore, as to theyr rightfull heritage such good and naturall English words, as haue ben long time out of vse & almost cleare disherited" (¶.ii.^{v}). Lydgate is both necessary to the articulation of poetic authority and part of the past that clouds the present's view. In effect, he is created as paradox, as the mediating gateway both for figuring the past and for the process of literary reading in the present.

If the early modern return to the past seeks to recuperate Chaucer from what Speght terms those "most unlearned times" (π3), this return occurs through the simultaneous deployment and denial of fifteenth-century writing; it occurs through the paradox of modernity that stages the fifteenth century as a strange transition period that separates the past from the present.

What stands out in the sixteenth-century editions of Chaucer's works, therefore, is not the concept of cultural authority or of literary history, nor the process of recursion itself, but the need to make this history explicit, to encapsulate it outside the literature itself. This is in distinct contrast to Chaucerians, such as Hoccleve, Lydgate, and Caxton, who fold their praise of Chaucer into their poetry, writing it in the case of Lydgate as the prologue to his own telling of Thebes, in the case of Hoccleve as the motivating occasion for his major poem *The Regement of Princes*, and in the case of Caxton as the rhetorical bedrock of literary praise. In turn, Speght's edition writes literary history from explicit examples of Hoccleve's *Regement of Princes*, Lydgate's *Troy Book*, and Caxton's *Book of Courtesy*. For example, in the section of his *Life of Chaucer* entitled "His bookes," he recounts Chaucer's canon, ending

> The Letter of Cupid is none of Chaucers doing, but was compiled by Thomas Occleue of the office of the priuie Seale, sometime Chaucers scholler. The which Occleue for the loue he bare to his Master, caused his picture to be truly drawen in his booke *De Regimine Principis*, dedicated to Henry the fift: the which I haue seene, and according to the which this in the beginning of this booke was done by John Spede, who hath annexed thereto all such cotes of Armes, as any way concerne the Chaucers, as he found them (trauailing for that purpose) at Ewhelme and at Wickham. (c.i.)

The passage asserts Speght's encounter with manuscript culture, and in it he identifies Hoccleve in the same terms as Spenser identifies Lydgate: as a scholar rather than a poet. In fact, the text identifies Speght's own portrait of Chaucer as a copy from Hoccleve's *Regement* (see chapter 5, Figure 5.7). Turning the page, Speght not only acknowledges Hoccleve but also uses the next section, titled "His Death," to assemble the fifteenth-century praise of Chaucer (see Figure 2.2). And so the reader is presented with a two-page spread depicting Hoccleve's stanza on Chaucer's portrait, the epitaph to Chaucer by Stephanus Surgionus contained in Caxton's *Boecius*, two more passages from the *Regement*, Lydgate's "Loadstar" passage from *The Fall of Princes*, and finally an obscure passage from Caxton's *Book of Courtesy*. The very arrangement separates poetry from literary history by moving between roman and black-letter type to offer the poems as textual artifacts recovered from history and exposed for the reader.

Black letter is unanimously understood as indicating a popular audience. As opposed to the more learned roman, it is the "English letter."[53] The distinction, as Zachary Lesser notes, carries deep social connotations: "Since the beginnings of modern bibliography in the early twentieth century, scholars have asked the black-letter typography of 'cheap print' (broadside ballads, chapbooks, romances) to serve as a 'social discriminant' in differentiating 'high' from 'low' readers" within the conservative nature of middle-class reading in print."[54] The identification of this debased form of literary culture with the "English letter" fits neatly into a literary history of immaturity, in which England comes into literary consciousness slowly, only by outgrowing the fifteenth-century past. As Lesser points out, the editions of named English poets, of the chronicles, of law books, of dictionaries, can hardly be for "low" or beginning readers, and so Lesser reads black letter as a nostalgic impulse, "a powerful combination of Englishness (the 'English letter') and past-ness (the 'antiquated' appearance of black letter by the seventeenth century)."[55]

If black-letter type evokes nostalgia on the page, it is a complicated and threatening nostalgia, one less the province of antiquated recollection than of representation itself. Like Caxton's Ghent and Bruges faces, black letter possesses a deep aesthetic history. It first appears in 1489 as Caxton's last font, Type 8, cut by Ulrich Gering in Paris.[56] This is a gothic, or *textura*, face, usually reserved for liturgical texts. Gering's version is more graceful than the Flemish types Caxton had previously used, and it softens the perpendicular style by

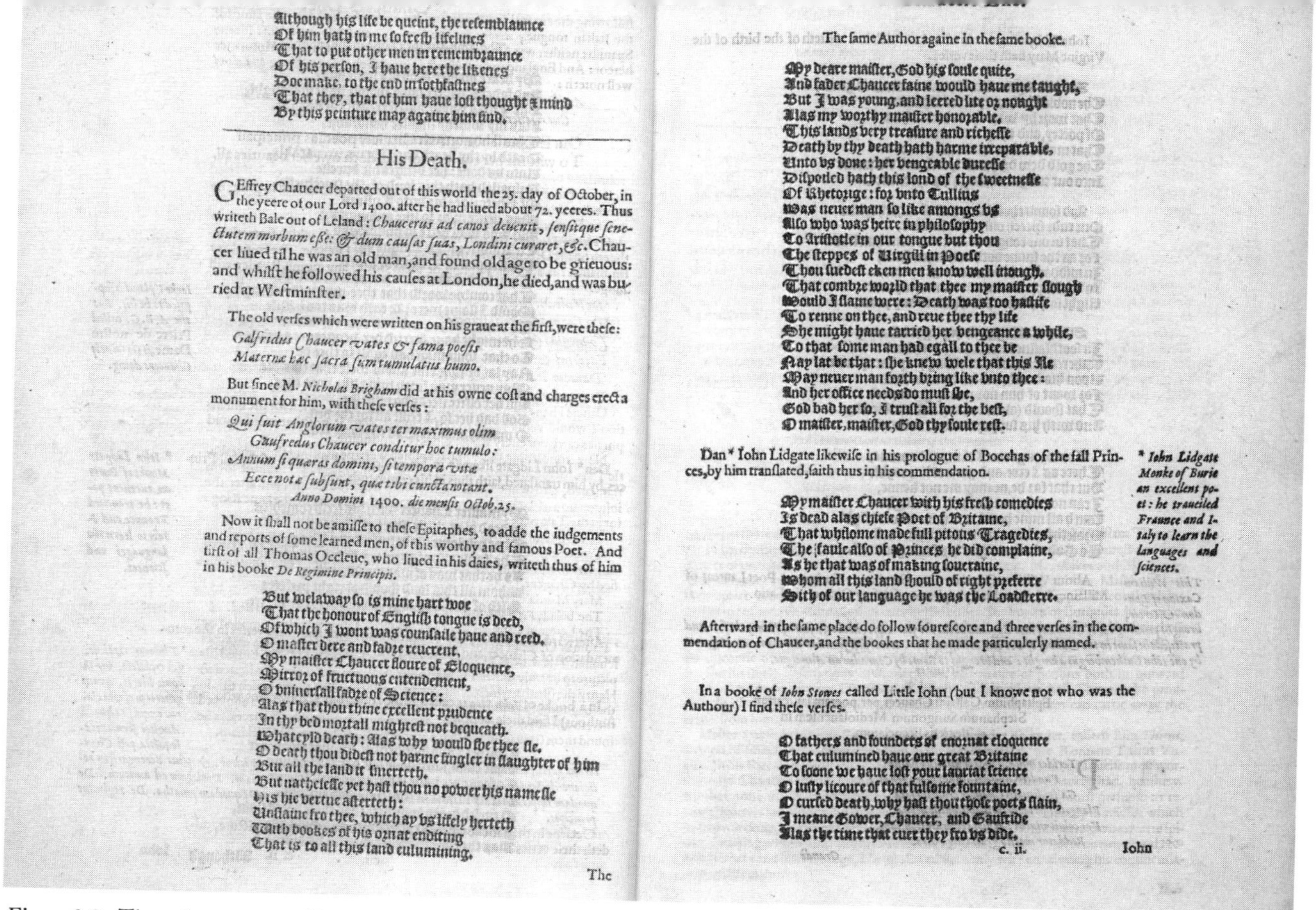

Although his life be queint, the resemblaunce
Of him hath in me so fresh liflines
That to put other men in remembraunce
Of his person, I haue here the likenes
Doe make, to the end in sothfastnes
That they, that of him haue lost thought & mind
By this peinture may againe him find.

His Death.

GEffrey Chaucer departed out of this world the 25. day of October, in the yeere of our Lord 1400. after he had liued about 72. yeeres. Thus writeth Bale out of Leland: *Chaucerus ad canos deuenit, sensitque senectutem morbum esse: & dum causas suas, Londini curaret, &c.* Chaucer liued til he was an old man, and found old age to be grieuous: and whilst he followed his causes at London, he died, and was buried at Westminster.

The old verses which were written on his graue at the first, were these:

Galfridus Chaucer vates & fama poesis
Maternæ hac sacra sum tumulatus humo.

But since M. *Nicholas Brigham* did at his owne cost and charges erect a monument for him, with these verses:

Qui fuit Anglorum vates ter maximus olim
Gaufredus Chaucer conditur hoc tumulo:
Annum si quæras domini, si tempora vitæ
Ecce notæ subsunt, quæ tibi cuncta notant.
Anno Domini 1400. *die mensis Octob.* 25.

Now it shall not be amisse to these Epitaphes, to adde the iudgements and reports of some learned men, of this worthy and famous Poet. And first of all Thomas Occleue, who liued in his daies, writeth thus of him in his booke *De Regimine Principis.*

But welaway so is mine hart woe
That the honour of English tongue is deed,
Of which I wont was counsaile haue and reed,
O master dere and fadre reuerent,
My maister Chaucer floure of Eloquence,
Mirror of fructuous entendement,
O vniuersall fadre of Science:
Alas that thou thine excellent prudence
In thy bed mortall mightest not bequeath.
What eyld death: Alas why would she thee sle.
O death thou didest not harme singler in slaughter of him
But all the land it smerteth.
But nathelesse yet hast thou no power his name sle
His hie vertue asterteth:
Unslaine fro thee, which ay vs lifely herteth
With bookes of his ornat enditing
That is to all this land enlumining.

The

The same Author againe in the same booke.

My deare maister, God his soule quite,
And fader Chaucer faine would haue me taught,
But I was young, and leered lite or nought
Alas my worthy maister honorable,
This lands very treasure and richesse
Death by thy death hath harme irreparable,
Unto vs done: her vengeable duresse
Dispoiled hath this lond of the sweetnesse
Of Rhetorike: for vnto Tullius
Was neuer man so like amongs vs
Also who was heire in philosophy
To Aristotle in our tongue but thou
The steppes of Uirgill in Poese
Thou suedest eken men know well inough.
That combre world that thee my maister slough
Would I slaine were: Death was too hastife
To renne on thee, and reue thee thy life
She might haue tarried her vengeance a while,
To that some man had egall to thee be
Nay lat be that: she knew wele that this Ile
May neuer man forth bring like vnto thee:
And her office needs do must she,
God bad her so, I trust all for the best,
O maister, maister, God thy soule rest.

Dan * Iohn Lidgate likewise in his prologue of Bocchas of the fall Princes, by him translated, saith thus in his commendation.

* *Iohn Lidgate Monke of Burie an excellent poet: he traueiled Fraunce and Italy to learn the languages and sciences.*

My maister Chaucer with his fresh comedies
Is dead alas chiefe Poet of Britaine,
That whilome made full pitous Tragedies,
The faule also of Princes he did complaine,
As he that was of making soueraine,
Whom all this land should of right preferre
Sith of our language he was the Loadsterre.

Afterward in the same place do follow fourescore and three verses in the commendation of Chaucer, and the bookes that he made particulerly named.

In a booke of *Iohn Stowes* called Little Iohn (but I knowe not who was the Authour) I find these verses.

O fathers and founders of enornat eloquence
That enlumined haue our great Britaine
To soone we haue lost your laureat science
O lusty licoure of that fulsome fountaine,
O cursed death, why hast thou those poets slain,
I meane Gower, Chaucer, and Gaufride
Alas the time that euer they fro vs dide.

c. ii. Iohn

Figure 2.2. The *mise-en-page* of literary history. *The Workes of Our Antient and Lerned English Poet, Geffrey Chaucer* (London: Adam Islip, 1598), c.iv–c.ii, *STC* 5077 RB84666, reproduced by permission of the Huntington Library, San Marino, California.

including *bastarda* capitals with *textura* lower cases for capital C, E, P, S, T, and V. In contrast, roman type is famously thought to be inspired by the stone-cut inscriptions of ancient Rome, revived in fifteenth-century Italy. The very name "roman" derives from French booksellers who referred to it specifically as type from Rome, and today it is epitomized by the work of Venetian printers and type founders such as Nicolas Jensen, Francesco da Bologna, and Aldus Manutius in the last decade of the fifteenth century. It is, of course, also an adaptation of scribal handwriting, in this case Carolingian book hand.

Stanley Morison attributes the formal elements of early humanistic script to Niccolò de Niccoli, who he argues established it in place of the Bolognese and Florentine book hands between 1395 and 1400 exclusively for capturing the historical authority of classical Latin texts. Morison argues that Niccoli's "intention was, in the first place, to collect ancient manuscripts of classical authors, to study their texts; and, secondly, by refashioning the 'forma di lettere' to produce transcriptions in 'period' style, or, in Niccoli's own words, 'all' antiqua.'"[57] Conrad Sweynheym and Arnold Pannartz produced a text of Cicero's *De Oratore* in 1465 at their monastic press at the Benedictine house Santa Scolastica, Subiaco, and it features the first roman type. The first English roman was introduced by Richard Pynson in his 1509 *Sermo Fratris Hieronymi de Ferraria* and the *Oratio* by Petrus Gryphus.[58] Thus, the "forma di lettere" of black letter is nostalgic but also complex: it tells the history of English literature as it emerges into its own mode from a hybrid of native, French, and Burgundian traditions; overlaps between vernacular and liturgical works; and takes on its own representative force in print. What is implicit in Caxton's type therefore becomes an explicit representation in Speght's contrast with roman.

Similarly, the movement from Caxton's fifteenth-century quartos and folios to Speght's 1598 edition of Chaucer does not mark the origination of cultural authority so much as a transformation from implicit structures for readership to an explicit apparatus. And this too is contained within the word "lodestar": what Chaucer and the writers through Caxton leave *implied* about the cultural authority of literary production, in the forms and history of textual culture, and in the story of Dido and its counterstory of loss, becomes *explicit* in the sixteenth-century story of vernacular letters as it returns to fifteenth-century writing, coughing up its literal misrepresentation of the past as the history of "Ddio."

In this process of moving from implicit to explicit forms, Lydgate is subordinated, folded into history not as an author but as an explicit part of the canonizing procedure, a scholar. The transformation is actually prefigured by Lydgate, implicitly in his subordination of Chaucer in *The Siege of Thebes* and somewhat more explicitly in his discussion of literary precedent and translation in *The Fall of Princes. The Fall of Princes* contains an extensive discussion of rhetoric, especially at the end of book 6, where Lydgate describes Bocas—ostensibly Boccaccio, but very much a character within the story who frets about the language he should use to tell his stories and reacts to their contents—as "astonyed" and "abashed.dull of his courage," and lacking cunning and language to praise Cicero (Tottel, fol. i^{v}). As in *The Siege of Thebes*, Lydgate creates an interplay of exchanges between his language for recognizing past greatness and greatness itself, so Bocas's language for Cicero is also the language that Lydgate himself uses when he describes the task of writing on Chaucer in *The Siege of Thebes*. The process folds in on Lydgate, both in his own staging of himself as a Canterbury pilgrim, a kind of Chaucer, and as he is represented in later printings of his works. For example, Lydgate is labeled the translator of *The Fall of Princes* on the title page of Pynson's second edition, and the title is adopted by both John Wayland and Richard Tottel in their 1554 editions. In his preface, Wayland also claims to have augmented the text, telling in his preface, "I haue added a continuacion of that Argument, concernynge the chefe Prynces of thys Iland, penned by the best clearkes in such kinde of matters that be thys day lyuing, not unworthy to be matched with maister Lydgate."[59] In casting Lydgate as a translator or a clerk, Pynson, Wayland, and Tottel position him one step further from the seat of rhetorical authority, Cicero, whom he refers to as "of eloquence the lanterne and the light" (Tottel, fol. clxi^{v}), one step further too from what he calls that "inward corage" that every writer must have that enables "the cause searched why he stant desolate" (Tottel, fol. clxiii[v]). So we can imagine an elided middle, a space in which Bocas pales in comparison to Cicero and Lydgate is merely a translator of Bocas, ultimately a worthy scholar for Chaucer and not unworthy to be matched by one of Wayland's clerks. Yet in *The Fall of Princes*, Lydgate writes that Cicero himself is foremost a translator of "Grekish bokes of olde antiquitie, / Made of Rethorike, & in theyr vulgar song / He translated into Latin tong" (Tottel, fol. clxi). In positioning Lydgate as a translator, ostensibly a subservient role comparable to the clerks of the day, these printers write him more explicitly into the history of writing as comparable to Cicero. Lydgate is made a translator, then, but this makes him, too, in his own language, more like Cicero, surpassing even his model, Boccaccio, and thus more closely achieving a closer affinity with Chaucer. In effect, the recursion occurs as Harold Bloom suggests: in a chronological future that recurs so powerfully on the chronological past that it is able to rewrite it. Sidney is able to forget Lydgate in *An Apologie for Poetrie* precisely because Spenser already showed him the book, but even so this does not so much deny Lydgate as subordinate him according to the terms available.

The process by which Lydgate becomes a translator should remind us that the setting out of "the new Poete" in print is not so much a break from the past into a new concept of writing as it is a continuation and competitive return to it, an appropriation that, as Lydgate suggests in the prologue to *The Fall of Princes*, all authors do. Again, I turn to Tottel's edition (fol. A.1):

> Thing y[e] was made of auctors the*n* beforne,
> they may of newe find and fantasye,
> out of olde chaffe, trye out wel clene corne,
> make it more fresh and lustie to the eye:
> Their subtil wit, and their labour applye,
> with their colours agreable of hewe,
> make olde thinges for to seme newe.

Lydgate's lines recall Chaucer's *Parliament of Fowls*, where he writes "for out of the olde feldes, as men saieth, / Cometh all this newe corne, fro yere to yere / And out of old bookes, in good faieth / Cometh all this newe science, that men lere."[60] This same passage heads one of the variant title pages to Speght's 1598 Chaucer's *Workes*. Nestled in a sculptural surround, is the passage translated in roman type:

CHAVCER
Out of the old fields, as men sayth,
Commeth all this new corn, fro yere to yere:
And out of old books, in good fayth,
Co*m*meth al this new science that men lere.

Here is a conscious declaration of the power of old books. Speght's edition also reproduces, among its prefatory matter, William Thynne's early preface to his 1532 edition as "The Epistle of William Thinne to King Henry the eight." This piece contains a history of writing tracing back to the origins of writing with the Phoenicians. Here I cite from Speght's edition: "But in processe of time, by diligence or pollicy of people, after diuers fourmes, figures, and impressions in mettall, barkes of trees, and other matter vsed for memory and knowledge of things, then present or passed, sundry letters or carects were first amonges the Phenices deuised and found, with suche knittinges and ioinings of one to another, by a merueilous subtilty and craft" (¶i.). According to Thynne, "impressions in mettall" appear among the alternative technologies explored by the Phoenicians at the origins of writing. What Thynne describes—"impressions in mettall"—is precisely what fifteenth-century printers such as Gutenberg and Jensen perfected: the mixing of alloys so that impressions of characters could be punched into metal. This history of writing becomes, in Thynne's telling, a history of eloquence as well. Literary production is therefore threefold: physical, rhetorical, and ultimately historical. And this is essentially what is learned from the fifteenth-century discussion of the history of writing. Again, this appears in Speght (¶i.^{v}):

> For though it had been in Demosthenes or Homerus times, when all learning and excellency of sciences, flourished amongs the

> Greekes, or in the season that Cicero Prince of eloquence, amonges Latins liued, yet had it beene a thing right rare and straunge, and worthy perpetuall laud, that any clerke by learning or witte, could that haue framed a tongue before so rude and imperfite, to such a sweete ornature and composition, likely if he had liued in these daies, being good letters so restored & reuiued as they be

The passage recalls E. K.'s own assertions of classical precedent in arguing for the importance of an English poetic eloquence embodied in Chaucer. And like Immeritô's opening poem, it is saturated with embedded allusions, here to Caxton's 1483 edition of *The Canterbury Tales*, which opens by praising clerks: "Grete thankes lawde and honour / ought to be gyuen vnto the clerkes / poetes and historiograhs" of the past that have produced "monumentis wreton."[61] Speght begins his own epistle "To the Readers" with a trope from Caxton as well: "Some few yeers past, I was requested by certaine Gentlemen my neere friends, who loued *Chaucer*, as he well deserueth; to take a little pains in reuiuing the memorie of so rare a man, as also in doing some reparations on his works, which they iudged to be much decaied by iniurie of time, ignorance of writers, and negligence of Printers" (π2^{v}). Every reader of Caxton knows the diverse gentlemen, friends, and acquaintances that seem to crowd his shop with requests for English literature. For Speght, though, these readers demand not an original impression of an English text but a reviving of memory. In this, they are like E. K., fictions or half-fictions that present a "literary memory." Yet they are also representative of a kind of memory that simultaneously asserts an active forgetting: in Caxton's preface to his 1483 *Canterbury Tales*, the anonymous gentleman convinces Caxton "I erryd in hurtyng and dyffamyng [Chaucer's] book in dyuerce places" (aii^{v}). Caxton's story is self-incriminating; Speght's incriminates the past. What is original to Thynne and reproduced in Speght, then, is not so much the genealogy of writing, which comes to them directly through the editions they read, but the way originality is imagined as an explicit return to the past that subordinates that past even as it relies on it.

For the Chaucer canon, the moment of origins is always a return. This is *literally* true in that the 1483 *Canterbury Tales* returns to a new manuscript source to revise the first edition. It is *rhetorically* true in that the story told within these editions of Chaucer always features a bibliographical return: Caxton tells a story of correction, one that arcs back in time "for to satysfye thauctour," even as his narrative acknowledges the utter impossibility of returning to the past and retracting the earlier edition. Thynne, too, must search out the early editions, and Speght, in turn, is driven back to read Hoccleve in order to derive Chaucer's legacy. And it is *historically* true for the afterlife of *The Canterbury Tales* in that the strangely looping origin stories are reprinted over and over again: Pynson's and de Worde's editions through to 1526 reprint Caxton's initial story, and Speght's edition reprints Thynne's in 1598. For Caxton, as for the printers following him, the material text is neither a moment of origins nor a linear replacement; rather, it is both derivative and atemporal: derivative because it is reliant on *The Canterbury Tales* of the past, hence always invested in a return to precedence, to a previous manuscript, to Caxton's print; atemporal because it stands outside narrative to offer some sort of direct contact with the author and to communicate *The Canterbury Tales* to its reader in whatever present the book finds itself.

This return becomes more palpable the deeper we look. David Carlson points out that all of the illustrations in the printed *Canterbury Tales* through to John Stow's 1561 edition follow the patterns set by Caxton's second edition, patterns that, Carlson argues, "derive from a programme of miniatures in a manuscript of which only a few leaves now survive, the 'Oxford fragment.'"[62] Indeed, Thynne's printer, Thomas Godfray, and the printer of the 1542 edition of Thynne's *Workes*, Richard Grafton, actually used Caxton's woodcut blocks to illustrate the text. The 1561 Stow edition is similar, reusing the blocks from Pynson's 1492 version, themselves copies of Caxton's. The various printed *Canterbury Tales* return to the past in different ways: they change the *Tales*' order and add new ones; they introduce various readings from manuscripts; they compile the *Tales* with other works. Nevertheless, they never demonstrate an absolute break: their publishers return to existing prologues, reprinting Caxton's and Thynne's voices through multiple editions; their editors concentrate on printed copy texts; and their compositors handle the very same blocks of wood. Touching these objects, using them to craft Chaucer's poetry just as the generation before them had done, these people could not help but recognize the continuity of their project. The afterlife of *The Canterbury Tales* is recursive: that is, though the editions can be cataloged according to a narrative of progress and rupture, the texts loop back on themselves to weave the past into the present.

The lasting presence of books complicates any reckoning of time. A major problem for historicizing Chaucer within literary history is realizing this quality intellectually, and so critics have tended to think very literally here, finding the readers of these editions to be antiquarians, grappling with the language of the past. While the printed books of 1483 may appear old in 1598, neither they nor the print shop they were created by is technologically foreign. Given this, the printing of books holds a peculiar relationship to time in a number of ways. On the local level, when printers turn their press from the daily income of jobbing work to an edition, they are making a long-term investment that will tie up their capital and production cycle for an extended period of time, often years.[63] Printers and publishers could not turn from the basic economy of printing, which is based in broadside ephemera, to this large-scale endeavor if they did not see that there was an ongoing market for a new edition and if they were not reckoning time in the long term. That printed books were necessarily available for purchase for many years after they were printed implies the publisher's ability to forecast the relationship between the production, consumption, distribution, and reproduction of books at the outset. By definition, then, the printing and selling of an edition thus occurs in a slower register of economic time than a broadside.

Further, regardless of the destruction of books during the Reformation, from Caxton on, all the print shops that engaged in printing Chaucer based their work directly on earlier volumes. Thus, when Thynne or Stow or Speght—or any of their editors or letter writers—speak of temporal distance between their volumes, they are figuring time while holding their predecessors' works in their hands and are therefore reminded, in a tangible fashion, that the work before them, and their work too, is durable. They know this neither as antiquarians nor as archivists but as participants: their eyes see it, their hands hold it, and their compositors' fingers literally manipulate the same blocks of wood as their predecessors. As these compositors set to work, they adjust these blocks of wood, feel the letters, and copy out the line breaks from their exemplar; as they disassemble their work for the day, they clean the ink off the wooden blocks, repair them of any damages, and sort all the type away. Speght's team did this exactly as de Worde's team did before them. For book culture, then, Chaucer could never really be locked away, either in the books or in the practice of bookmaking. When Speght writes about the past, he does so knowingly, in what Jonathan Gil Harris terms "supersessionary time, with its simultaneous recognition and distancing" of the past.[64] Within this process of recognition and distancing temporality occurs at different paces, each of which layers the past and the present unevenly, so that at times it seems far away, and at times it seems within the moment. The vehicles of textual mediation, books at times transmit the past with no mediation at all and so make the past immediate.

The development of literary history is both material and intellectual. It is easy to chart this development as linear, a progressive movement away from the unique Chaucerian manuscripts of the early fifteenth century, through William Caxton's, Wynkyn de Worde's, and Richard Pynson's early editions of Chaucer's *Canterbury Tales*, superseded by the 1532 *Workes of Geffray Chaucer Newly Printed*, an edition that parallels the intellectual unfolding of the modern vernacular author.[65] This reading misses the way books encounter time. As Caxton writes, books are monuments: recopied, reprinted, and reread, they are material objects that speak the past directly to the present. Ultimately, this does assert a paradoxical sense for literary history. On the one hand, it suggests a chronological progression of ideas bound by time in which one literary movement follows the next. On the other, it recalls that books are transcendent of local history and insistent on their terms through their survival in the hands of readers. We can ignore this particular paradoxical arrangement if we so choose by substituting one of chronology and period that imagines a linear and progressive history of authorship, in which each author improves on the next in much the same way that each new edition corrects its predecessor's errors, so that the past is sealed away, without major writers, without an editorial sensibility, without the tools of modernity. In this vein it is tempting to read *The Shepheardes Calender's* proclamation of "the new Poete" as a progressive step toward the 1611–12 collected works, the title page of which announces Spenser as "Englands Arch-Poët," to see Spenser's formation of himself as an author as reflecting a larger development of English literary culture—in short, to read literary biography as paralleling literary history itself.[66] Indeed, a significant body of New Historicist writing makes this claim strongly, connecting a particular generation of sixteenth-century writers with the emergence of literary authority. Such a story parses the complex circulation of ideas and books into discrete manuscript and print cultures. As a result, fifteenth-century literary production—both its material and its symbolic forms—remains poorly recognized.

Alternatively, and more wisely in my view, we can acknowledge literary history as involute. Texts do not evolve in a linear pattern; they are crosscut by separate traditions, corruptions, and interpretations. This complexity is true for authorship and authority as well. Thus literary history evolves as a web of connections, a weaving that recalls the root meaning of the word "text." Within such a process of change, authors do exactly as F. B. suggests: they knit or truss together influences, or as Thynne puts it, "with suche knittinges and ioinings of one to another, by a merueilous subtilty and craft." And so E. K. is a memory for *The Shepheardes Calender* just as he claims for the New Poet: a knitting up of language's history. Sidney himself underscores this notion, writing "thus much is vndoubtedly true, that if reading bee foolish, without remembring, memorie being the onely treasurer of knowlede, those words which are fittest for memory, are likewise most conuenient for knowledge. Now, that Verse farre exceedeth Prose in the knitting vp of the memory" (G3). Acknowledging the power of this memory suggests that the period from the late 1400s to the late 1500s is less a retreat from the public assertion of a poetic authority, less a clear simplification of a heterodox literary culture in the sixteenth century, less a sudden coalescence of a newfound print culture than a process of continued mediation in which certain writing is actively cast as part of the past even as it is reworked in the present.

Such a conception of literary history suggests that Spenser took part not so much in a specific print culture as in a larger textual culture intimate with manuscript practice. Spenser surely made changes to this culture, but not through an outright break with it so much as through a return to some of the essential features of that past that paradoxically initiate originality. Though generations of readers may change, the books that disseminate English authorship and authority continue to offer models well into the sixteenth and seventeenth centuries.[67] Such is literary history as an acknowledgment of the symbolic presence of the past in the books that constitute English writing: a recursive origin.

THREE

The Dramatic Quarto

Recursion in William Shakespeare's *2 Henry VI*

Edmund Spenser, Philip Sidney, and William Shakespeare secure their literary authority in print across the 1590s. The decade is marked by Spenser's and Sidney's publications, each of which names their authority on its title page. Not only are two editions of *An Apologie for Poetrie* printed posthumously under Sidney's name in 1595, but the *Arcadia* is printed as "*written by Sir Philippe Sidnei*" twice in 1590, and again in 1593, 1598, and 1599. *Astrophel and Stella* is published twice in 1591 and two more times in 1597, always as by "Sir P. S."[1] Spenser, too, emerges as a named author in print across the 1590s. The 1579 *Shepheardes Calender* bears only Sidney's name on its title page: "*Entitled to the noble and vertvous gentleman most worthy of all titles both of learning and cheualrie M. Philip Sidney*," and though this text is reprinted throughout Spenser's lifetime, in 1581, 1586, and 1597, it never carries his name on the title page, perhaps because of the play with identity within the text itself. Spenser's second publication, the 1580 *Three Proper, and Wittie, Familiar Letters* is simply "betwene two Vniuersitie men," and his third, the 1582 *De rebus gestis Britanniae*, is elusively attributed to "E. S." In 1590 the *Faerie Queene* is printed in three variants, one of which identifies Spenser on the inside of the title page. After 1590, the issue of authorship seems settled: all of Spenser's work beside the *Calender*—the 1591 *Complaints, Daphnaïda, Prosopopoia*; the 1592 *Axiochus*; the 1595 *Amoretti and Epithalamion* and *Colin Clouts Come Home Againe*; and the 1596 *Faerie Queen, The Second Part of The Faerie Queene, Fowre Hymnes,* and the *Prothalamion*—name him up front.[2] The 1590s are no less important for Shakespeare's authorship, and Shakespeare studies over the past decade has recognized that the quartos published in these years stage his authority as both a poet and a playwright.[3]

Like Sidney and Spenser, then, Shakespeare becomes a named author in the 1590s. Like them, too, he comes to this authority by situating himself in relationship to the English past. Where Sidney and Spenser draw on and occlude the fifteenth century in literary history, Shakespeare dramatizes its political history. Yet the history Shakespeare draws on is itself difficult, less an object framed by temporal distance, a break into modern scholarship, than the past's own report of itself reproduced in the sixteenth-century present. Such a history cannot help but be self-referential, not to a modern present but to the earlier source material that is itself based on the manuscript tradition of the *Brut* that it reproduces. Hence the insistence by sixteenth-century writers on their modernity: they must constrain self-reference, subordinate it by any means necessary—typography, antiquarianism, claims to scholarship—or else become the Ouroboros and fall into an endless cycle of repetition in which self-reference operates like a hall of mirrors, leading forever backwards to some prior moment of record, always re-creating some receding present and never producing the output: *that was the past; this is the present.* Thus, just as Lydgate intrudes on the Spenserian rhetoric of authorship, the anonymous chroniclers of the mid-1400s intrude on sixteenth-century historians; and just as Spenser subordinates Lydgate, interpolating him into his own poetic in order to stage the arrival of the New Poet in print, these historians bracket themselves as separate from the past they read, marking it as the past. In contrast, Shakespearean drama embeds history into the overall genre—the literary dramatic quarto—as a formal principle, a trope. By so embedding self-reference as a representative strategy, the dramatic quarto becomes an object separate from the larger genre of history and casts history into the past and authorship into the present. So conceived, history is the self-referential trope, the recursive circuit, within the literary dramatic quarto.

Still, Shakespeare's emergence as an author in the 1590s presents a significant problem for the status of print evidence. His first publication seems to resolve the problem straight away: the 1593 *Venus and Adonis*, published and printed by Richard Fields and sold by John Harrison, is a high-priced quarto with a dedication to Henry Wriothesley, Earl of Southampton and Baron of Titchfield, and signed "William Shakespeare."[4] This book of poetry comes at the beginning of what Peter Blayney has identified as a surge in play registration and publication from December 1593 through May 1595, perhaps as publicity for the reopening of the theaters after the plague. The Shakespearean texts printed during this period suggest the generic possibilities of the moment: in 1594 Thomas Millington published an anonymous quarto edition of *2 Henry VI*; Harrison published an edition of *Lucrece* and, now in control of the rights, a second edition of *Venus and Adonis*, both signed by Shakespeare in the dedication; and Millington and Edward White produced an anonymous edition of *Titus Andronicus*. In 1595 Millington published an anonymous version of *3 Henry VI*, and Harrison followed with a third edition of *Venus and Adonis*.[5] Blayney records the best-selling dramatic quartos through to the seventeenth century as tragedies—the anonymous *Mucedorus* as the most reprinted title, followed by Christopher

Marlowe's *Tragicall History of the Horrible Life and Death of Doctor Faustus*, and then by Thomas Kyd's *The Spanish Tragedie*. The fourth, fifth, and sixth most reprinted titles on Blayney's list are Shakespeare's *1 Henry IV*, *Richard III*, and *Richard II*. Still, as Blayney points out, *Venus and Adonis* "out-sold [Shakespeare's] best selling play by four editions."[6] Book history would seem to offer the clear distinctions of Shakespeare's career in print from the start, a conclusion Peter Stallybrass and Roger Chartier have recently summed up as "the authorial Shakespeare was above all Shakespeare the poet, not Shakespeare the dramatist."[7]

This conclusion appears neatly underwritten by a broad generic division. Accordingly, Harrison publishes Shakespeare the Courtly Poet, and Millington markets an anonymous writer of spectacular dramatic history. Within five years of that first *Venus and Adonis*, however, the separation becomes less than clear: in 1598 Shakespeare is named on the title pages of *Love's Labour's Lost* and two editions of *Richard II*, in 1599 he is similarly named on the title page of *1 Henry VI*, and by the very beginning of the seventeenth century he is named as the author of the 1602 editions of *Merry Wives of Windsor*, *Richard III*, and *Hamlet*.[8] Pointing out this marked shift in attribution, Lukas Erne writes in *Shakespeare as Literary Dramatist* that "no playwright's name appears as suddenly and as often as Shakespeare's does between 1598 and 1600," concluding, "it is no exaggeration to say that in one sense, 'Shakespeare,' author of dramatic texts, was born in the space of two or three years at the end of the sixteenth century."[9] Erne attributes this change to a group of anthologies and literary histories, chiefly Francis Meres's 1598 *Palladis Tamia*, which places Shakespeare in the company of Geoffrey Chaucer, John Gower, John Lydgate, Philip Sidney, Edmund Spenser, Samuel Daniel, Michael Drayton, and William Warner, and in so doing "turned 'Shakespeare' into a name with which publishers expected to make money."[10]

Stallybrass and Chartier take up a similar view, citing Shakespeare's inclusion in printed commonplace books: "Shakespeare thus emerges as a canonical English poet in a bound volume neither through poems nor through his plays but rather through individual 'sentences' (of 10 or 20 syllables) extracted from his works."[11] The argument writes a circle: Shakespeare is defined as literary because his writing is recognized as belonging to the genre of literature. Yet this is to return the problem (how to account for the appearance of Shakespeare in print) as its own solution (by the appearance of Shakespeare in print). Although print history would seem to offer clear-cut evidence—the named *Venus and Adonis*, the anonymous dramatic quartos—the texts themselves offer no clear guidance as to why Shakespeare's name is extended from poetry to drama during the 1590s, no apparatus beyond those ambiguous title pages, no E. K. or Immeritô to explain their status. The closer we look at the generic distinctions, the more they seem superimposed over the print record.[12] For example, Erne writes that "even though modern scholarship has often opposed the poet to the playwright, 'playwright' is in fact a term that came into use after Shakespeare's writing career, and the term Elizabethans used to designate a writer of plays is precisely that of 'poet.'"[13] Observing this fact, Erne, Stallybrass, and Chartier look elsewhere for a gloss. More fundamentally, however, the problem with Shakespeare's authorship is internal to the plays themselves and intrinsic to their appearance in history: as with Spenser, the assertion of literary presence from history is a fraught endeavor, one that questions the derivation of literary identity from historical process.

If the early quartos suggest anything, it is that Shakespeare's emergence in print is connected with the construction of history as a dramatic genre. On the one hand, this genre, "history," has tremendous explanatory force. "A large, hungry, and committed continent-wide market for historical narrative was in place by the accession of Elizabeth in 1558," writes M. Rick Smith. "Indeed," Smith continues, "drama about the past—whether the legendary or the historical past—was the genre that launched the Elizabethan theater in the 1580s as a paying proposition."[14] On the other hand, it replicates the larger problem, for the parameters of this genre, "drama about the past," are shifty in the 1590s.[15] For example, the 1594 version of *2 Henry IV* advertises itself on its title page with successive triangular paragraphs of historical detail but ultimately brands the characters' fates as tragedy (see Figure 3.1). Similarly the 1595 octavo of *3 Henry VI* is titled *The True Tragedy of Richard Duke of Yorke.* The titles obfuscate:

unnamed, clearly different from prompt books, and shifting between history and tragedy, they make their contents difficult to classify without a priori distinctions of literature, history, and drama. Hence the problem for Shakespeare's emergence in print: so clear in hindsight—Shakespeare the named poet, Shakespeare the anonymous dramatist—it is premised on a slippery distinction between literature and history, to which the texts themselves continually lead back around, and in which Shakespeare's emergence as an author is strangely imbricated in the construction of the past to no clear generic ends. "The evidence really suggests," David Scott Kastan writes, "that, as it gets published, the printed drama becomes a category of its own, competing in the marketplace with other recognizable categories of reading material like literature, religion, and history."[16] The problem of sorting English history from English dramatic literature is part of the work of the 1590s, part of what Sidney, Spenser, Speght, Meres, and Shakespeare all attempt to resolve. How this sorting occurs in the early quartos, how the specific genre of authorial, printed, dramatic texts about history emerges from the swirl of textual experimentation, and why it involves the fifteenth century remain unexplained.

Following David Lawton, then, I argue that "we shall not understand . . . Shakespeare's history plays without an understanding of the interweaving of genre in fifteenth-century public poetry."[17] And so I turn back to Lydgate. In Tottel's 1554 edition of *The Fall of Princes*, Lydgate comments on the overlap between literature and history in his envoy to the Tragedy of Ariadne:

> This tragedye maketh a memorie
> of Dukes tweine, and of their high renouns
> And of their loue write a great historie,
> and how they conquered diuers regions,
> gouerned cities, countries and eke tounes
> till fortune their prowesse dyd appalle,
> To shewe their sugre was meynt w*ith* bieter gall.[18]

"This tragedye maketh a memorie," Lydgate remarks. Sidney and Spenser also acknowledge the importance of memory in literary

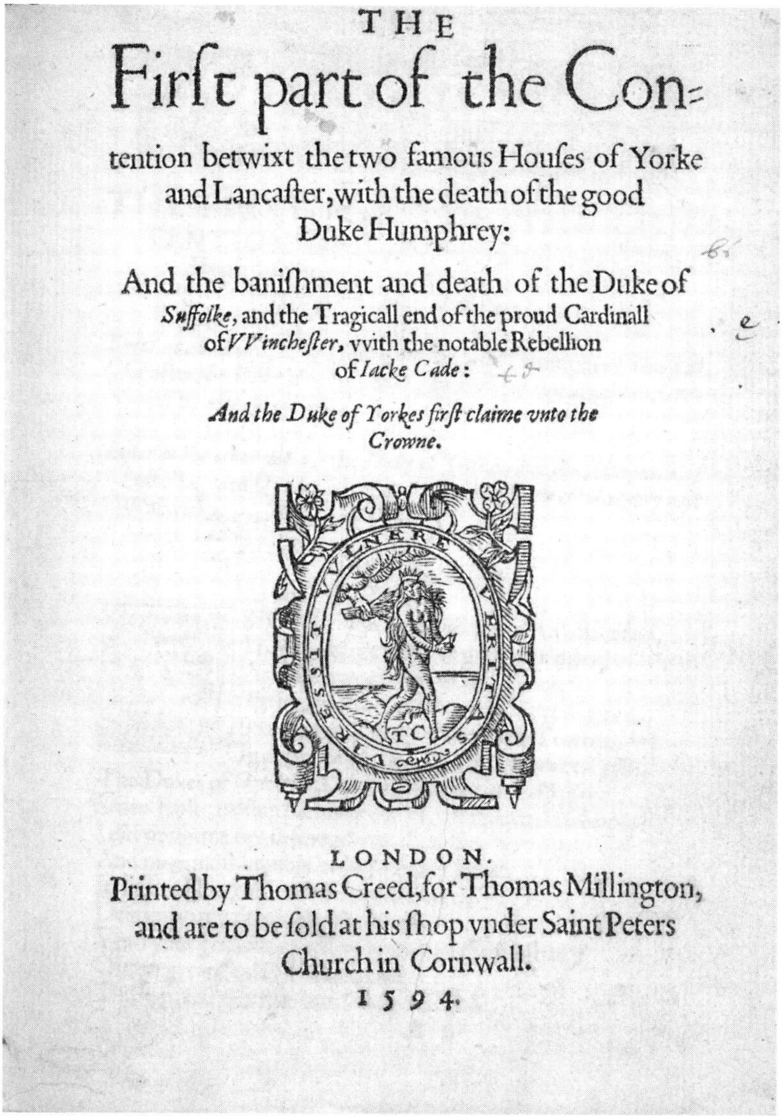

THE
Firſt part of the Con-
tention betwixt the two famous Houſes of Yorke
and Lancaſter, with the death of the good
Duke Humphrey:
And the baniſhment and death of the Duke of
Suffolke, and the Tragicall end of the proud Cardinall
of *VVincheſter*, vvith the notable Rebellion
of *Iacke Cade*:
*And the Duke of Yorkes firſt claime vnto the
Crowne.*

LONDON.
Printed by Thomas Creed, for Thomas Millington,
and are to be ſold at his ſhop vnder Saint Peters
Church in Cornwall.
1594.

Figure 3.1. The tragedy of history: Shakespeare's entry into the market for dramatic literature. *The First Part of The Contention* (London: Thomas Creede for Thomas Millington, 1594), title page, *STC* 26099, reproduced by permission of the Folger Shakespeare Library.

construction but reverse the equation so that the knitting up of memory makes literature, and thus they devise ways of shaping memory so that history remains separate from contemporary literary making. In contrast, Lydgate writes that tragedy asserts a generic force over memory itself, embedding any knowledge of the past in the literary form of the exemplum. The *de casibus* tradition, of which Lydgate's *Fall of Princes* is a major part and from which develops the *Mirror for Magistrates*, is based on this overlap—that the histories of kings illustrates the great truth of tragedy that "fortune their prowess dyd appalle."

Chaucer, of course, writes such tragedies in the *Monk's Tale* and in the *Legend of Good Women*, which contains within it the legend of Ariadne as well as that of Lucrece, and like *Venus and Adonis* draws heavily from Ovid. In that poem, Venus is overcome with desire, pining for her diffident lover, and so removes herself from the world and "meanes to immure her selfe, and not be seen."[19] She is thus withdrawn but also fully seen as a literary figure: Is not Venus a loadstar, a negative historical example of literary fame like Dido? And is not *Venus and Adonis*—the marker of Shakespeare's emergence as an author, reprinted some sixteen times before 1640, imitated frequently, yet ultimately marginal to his modern canon—just the text that Dido would produce for literary history, one paradoxically essential to and lost from the narrative of literary greatness overall, one printed (and so exposed) but also immured so as not to be seen? Embodied in Dido, Venus, and eventually Lydgate, this counterhistory of loss, of literary anonymity, underwrites literary history, so that Chaucer, Lydgate, Sidney, Spenser, and Shakespeare are, as Meres writes them, linked, but in no easy alliance of absolute authority. Rather, they each struggle to emerge from the overwhelming generic authority of the past.

I suggest that one way into this problem is by returning to a moment of textual origins freighted with epoch-making significance: the first appearance of a Shakespeare play in print.[20] Printed by Thomas Creede for Thomas Millington as an anonymous quarto in 1594, this is *The First Part of the Contention Betwixt the Two Famous Houses of Yorke and Lancaster*, and it reports, in a somewhat short version, the play now known as *2 Henry VI*. *The Contention* was followed in 1595 by an octavo printed by Peter Short, also for Millington and also unattributed, entitled *The True Tragedie of Richard Duke of York and the Death of Good King Henrie the Sixt* and now known as *3 Henry VI.* In 1600 Millington had Valentine Simmes reprint *The Contention* and William White reprint *The True Tragedie.* These two plays were produced in continuous register in 1619 by William Jaggard for Thomas Pavier as *The Whole Contention*, "newly corrected and enlarged" and "Written by William Shake-speare, Gent." This last version presents the plays with *The Late, and Much Admired Play, Called, Pericles, Prince of Tyre*, and together the three seem to begin a much larger collection, which I will take up in chapter 5.[21] It is not until the 1623 Folio, however, that the *Henry VI* plays are rationalized into the second and third parts of a continuous narrative, fronted by *The First Part of King Henry the Sixt.*

Scholarly discussion of *The Contention* tends to focus on its textual authority, and the play has served as the centerpiece for the argument that the early quartos are memorial reconstructions, the detritus of print history that obscures the authorial canon.[22] My interest in this quarto—be it pirated copy, collaborative precursor, or Shakespearean abridgement—is that it is a concrete moment of origins that troubles the notion of origins overall. For regardless of our assessment of its authority, *The Contention* both records Shakespeare's early interest in the fifteenth century and reveals his emergence in print not as a clean break but as a convoluted process of repeated return, a first appearance in print that is, essentially, the second part of an ongoing story that blurs the distinctions of genre. *The Contention* offers us a recursive origin: literally the text launches Shakespeare's career as a literary dramatist; it shows us not a clean break with the past so much as a return to it in the middle of things.

The Contention is thus a metonym for my argument as a whole. For not only does it represent the complex process of textual development eclipsed by the reassuring movement of chronology and the drama of originality, but the fact that it is a significant moment of origins long denied authority as a "bad quarto" underscores my point overall: that the narrative of modernity insists on forgetting the complexity of the literary record and instead looks to places external to the text itself to write literary history. In an attempt to recapture some of that record, my investigation moves through four main texts to show how the earliest dramatic quarto distinguishes itself and so manages the past as a platform for literary making.

First, I note that the two main printed versions of *2 Henry VI*—*The Contention* and the First Folio's *Second Part of Henry the Sixt*—use the book as a trope within their plots. This suggests that the return to the past featured in these plays is imbricated in the very form of that return: the book. I trace the plays' interest in the history of the book back to its sources to point out a supremely self-reflective moment: the entry on the invention of printing in the Holinshed Syndicate's 1587 *Chronicles of England* and from there to a similar passage in William Caxton's 1480 *Chronicles of England*.[23] But even at this level of analysis there exists no point of origins, for Caxton's own telling of the invention and spread of print—surely a self-reflective moment if ever there was one—is in fact a generic reproduction of earlier manuscript chronicles. This brings me to what I see as a significant point: the historical form of the book asserts a structural force within the writing on the history of the book. This structural force—I call it "textual formalism"—is literally impressed into the pages that tell English history by pen and press, creating a kind of loop in which the books of history embody the history of books through an ongoing reproductive cycle of self-reference. Thus, *The Contention*'s figuration of the book allows us to see a formal continuity between manuscript and print into the sixteenth century that short-circuits historical distance by pointing out that a history built only on reproducing self-reference has no purchase on its own terms. So sixteenth-century editors of history—Edward Hall, John Foxe, and John Stow, the Holinshed Syndicate—struggle to bracket the past in various ways but in fact reproduce it and reveal the scaffolding of modernity in exceptional clarity, demonstrating the material and intellectual continuities between manuscript and print.

Shakespeare, his printers, and his collaborators take a different tack. *2 Henry VI*—particularly the Folio version—actively subordinates the past, embedding the self-references that constitute history within a larger narrative of reading and writing. Neglecting its own authority, *The Contention* does this somewhat haltingly but successfully enough to stand as a literary object separate from history. I suggest as my final point that an alternative to the ambivalent literary history of chronological progress and revolutionary break lies in the movement from self-reference to embedded subordination, from reproduction to recursion, a process that legitimizes print drama as a unique genre.

The book—or more generally, textuality—is a central conceit in both versions of *2 Henry VI*.[24] Much of *The Contention* is organized around physical scraps of texts. The play's motivating occasion, the announcement of marriage between Henry and Margaret, is affirmed by "the Articles confirmde of peace" (Q1, A2^{v}), and the peers' dismay with the deal contained therein is explicitly textual. "Duke *Humphrey* lets it fall," the Quarto's stage directions announce (Q1, A2^{v}), and York frames his objection through his reading of history: "As I haue read, our Kinges of England were woont to haue large dowries" (Q1, A4). Later, Suffolk and the Queen's conspiracy grows while reading the Petitioners' "writings," which are, like the early articles, remarked on in *The Contention*'s stage directions as physically present ("He teares the papers," Q1, B2^{v}). Later still, Lady Eleanor uses a "scrole of paper" to conjure spirits (Q1, B4^{v}), and this scroll is poured over on stage no less than three times: once by Sir John in the conjuring ("*Elnor*. Here sir *Iohn*, take this scrole of paper here," Q1, B4^{v}); once by Buckingham in the discovery ("*Buc.* See here my Lord what the diuell hath writ," Q1, C1); and once again by Buckingham in the accusation ("*Reads*. The Duke yet liues, that Henry shal depose . . ." Q1, C3^{v}). Subsequently, Eleanor is marked with "verses written on her backe and pind on" (Q1, D2). As the action becomes more intense, texts remain in the forefront: Henry learns of Stafford's death and Jack Cade's rebellion by letter (Q1, F4^{v}), and, of course, Jack Cade rants and raves against textuality. As *The Contention*'s version is almost a third shorter than the Folio's, and contains more detailed stage directions, its rendition of the fifteenth-century English court contains a palpable density of textual emphasis.

If *The Contention* depicts the English past as fundamentally textual, it also insists that we take these texts as meaningful in a variety of ways: they are physical objects within the world that are read, dropped, passed around, shredded, and pinned on a person's back; they are symbolic objects as well, conduits for information, signs of authority, and markers of identity. As such, they often perform a double service within the play. So just as William de la Pole uses the articles to promote himself to the Duke of Suffolk, these articles also lie behind his eventual impeachment. Similarly, Lady Eleanor employs the scroll to conjure spirits, and this same scroll is thus proof that she consorts with them. York's first major speech captures this duality well, summing up the problem with Henry's kingship in a single line: "Whose bookish rule hath puld faire England downe" (Q1, A4ᵛ). Taken literally, York's assessment objects to Henry's religiosity, to his willingness to defer all matters to The Book. So, too, in the Quarto Margaret complains that Henry's "eyes are alwaies poring on his booke" (Q1, B2ᵛ). The book is also a cogent symbol for Henry's authority, a reminder of his God-given role as king, a tangible expression of his values, a marker of his honest piety. The critique of "bookishness" ultimately cuts both ways, alternately revealing Henry as too otherworldly to rule and the English court as too worldly to be ruled. Many years ago Margaret Deanesly characterized fifteenth-century England by its "extreme booklessness," and the description stuck.[25] *The Contention* imagines the exact opposite: a fifteenth century so entirely written out that texts figure both the constitution and the critique of its polity.

Emerging as the driving rhetorical force in the play after Humphrey and Suffolk have been eliminated, Jack Cade brings its critique of bookishness to a head. In the Quarto, Cade's charges begin with the trial of the Clarke of Chattam (who is to be hanged, "with his penny-inckhorne about his necke," for the crimes of being able to write his name, possessing a book with red letters, and "setting of boyes coppies," Q1, F3ᵛ), proceed to a tirade against the very materials of writing ("Why ist not a miserable thing, that of the skin of an innocent lamb should parchment be made, & then with a litle blotting ouer with inke, a man should vndo himselfe," Q1, G2), and culminate in the trial of Lord Saye, whom Cade condemns (Q1, G2):

> thou hast most traitorously erected a grammer schoole, to infect the youth of the realme, and against the Kings Crowne and dignitie, thou hast built vp a paper-mill, nay it wil be said to thy face, that thou kepst men in thy house that daily reades of bookes with red letters, and talkes of a Nowne and a Verbe, and such abhominable words as no Christian eare is able to endure it. And besides all that, thou hast appointed certaine Iustises of peace in euery shire to hang honest men that steale for their liuing, and because they could not reade, thou hast hung them vp: Onely for which cause they were most worthy to liue.

Initially, Cade's ravings seem haphazard, a broadside attack on writing by the semiliterate, but his insistence on the doubling, physical, and symbolic nature of texts continues the play's drift. For according to Cade the materials of books—parchment, ink, and paper mill—are inseparable from the authority they disseminate. So he points out that one can no more strike out the nouns and verbs of social injustice than the books and schools that construct them as authoritative. His observation—that textual authority works against the illiterate ("and because they could not reade, thou hast hung them vp")—has an undeniable rightness to it, and his logic is to eliminate the symbolic axis of textual representation entirely, to reduce all representation to a kind of empiricism, the reiteration of the obvious. So he knights his fellows: "Kneele downe Iohn Mortemer, / Rise vp sir Iohn Mortemer . . . kneele downe Dicke Butcher, / Rise vp sir Dicke Butcher" (Q1, F4). "O monstrous simplicitie," laments Stafford in response (Q1, F4^{v}), and this is precisely how Cade replaces the play's earlier rhetoricians, Suffolk and Humphrey: he simplifies Suffolk's carefully nuanced appropriation of royal authority at the beginning of the play to parodic self-invention ("I learnt it my selfe," he announces of his lineage in the Quarto, F4; in the Folio he is even more freewheeling: "I inuented it my selfe," F1, 139), and he reduces Humphrey's lament on the destruction of historical monuments ("Ah Lords, fatall is this marriage canselling our states, / Reuersing Monuments of conquered *France*, / Vndoing all, as none had nere bene done," Q1, A3) to a celebration of the destruction of the written record. Cade is like York: both object to a "bookish rule" and in doing so underscore that books present a powerful trope for the construction and dismantling of authority.

All four characters, Suffolk, Humphrey, York, and Cade, are self-aware—the one so deeply scheming, the other so earnest, the third so self-righteous, the last so absurd—because they each have a profound sense that the texts that constitute them can be manipulated. This defines the *2 Henry VI* plays' depiction of the fifteenth century as well as the plays' relationship to their sources. For example, Cade's first speech is derived from details culled from Holinshed's record of the 1381 Peasants' Revolt as well as from the actual 1450 Cade Rebellion. *The Contention* introduces Cade with this conflation (Q1, F3^{v}):

> *Cade.* Therefore be braue, for your Captain is braue, and vowes reformation: you shall haue seuen half-penny loaues for a penny, and the three hoopt pot, shall haue ten hoopes, and it shall be felony to drinke small beere, and if I be king, as king I will be.
> *All.* God saue your maiestie.
> *Cade.* I thanke you good people, you shall all eate and drinke of my score, and go all in my liuerie, and weele haue no writing, but the score & the Tally, and there shalbe no lawes but such as comes from my mouth.

Holinshed's *Chronicles of England* tells that John Tiler changed his name to Jack Straw, led the rebels out of Essex to Kent, and "therefore willed them to make them readie to ioine with them for their obteining of libertie, and reforming of the euill customs of the realme."[26] Later, in London, it records that Wat Tyler "should saie with great pride the day before these things chanced, putting his hands to his lips, that within foure daies all the lawes of England should come foorth of his mouth."[27] Vowing Straw's reformation and claiming Tyler's kingship, Cade is a synthesis of these two figures.[28] In the play, Cade's is an explicitly textual reformation, and this too finds its echo in *The Chronicles of England*'s report of the 1381 uprising: the rebels "purposed to burne and destroie all records, euidences, court-rolles, and other minuments, that the remembrance of ancient matters being remooued out of mind, their landlords might not haue whereby to chalenge anie right at their hands."[29] Cade's motives are not so pragmatic and instead contribute to rebellion as a twofold break: within the play, Cade overthrows—reforms, he says—the normal value of things so that names no longer equate to a tangible value (seven halfpenny loaves are now worth a penny and a three-hoop pot shall have ten hoops). More broadly, Cade also overthrows the plot's governing structure. For according to Robert Adger Law's collation of the plays against Hall's and Holinshed's chronicles, Cade's are the only scenes in the entire trilogy that distort the chronicles' chronology by more than a decade.[30] In short, by conflating the historical rebellion in 1450 with that of John Ball, Jack Straw, and Wat Tyler in 1381, Shakespeare inserts a recursive relationship to the past into the midst of a trilogy that is overwhelmingly chronological and progressive.

Cade's rebellion is therefore thematically bookish and structurally recursive. It is recursive because it enacts a trope of return that produces the representation of Cade through embedded self-reference. The feeling of recursion is particularly intense because the two qualities—theme and structure—are interwoven around textuality, so that as Cade focuses the plot on books and reading, the play enacts a return upon its source texts that is out of step with its generally progressive reading of history. Given this representational strategy, we should be surprised not to find these elements intimate on the formal level as well, woven into *2 Henry VI*'s treatment of textuality overall. We can pursue the issue further through the Folio version of Cade's itemization of Saye's crimes, which includes printing: "Thou hast most traiterously corrupted the youth of the Realme, in erecting a Grammar Schoole"; blusters Cade, continuing, "and whereas before, our Fore-fathers had no other Bookes but the Score and the Tally, thou hast caused printing to be vs'd, and contrary to the King, his Crowne, and Dignity, thou hast built a Paper-Mill" (F1; 141). Holinshed's *Chronicles of England* is specific about the history of printing, including it in the entry for 1459 (see Figure 3.2):

> ¶The noble science of Printing was about this time found in Germanie at Magunce by one Iohn Cuthembergus a knight: one

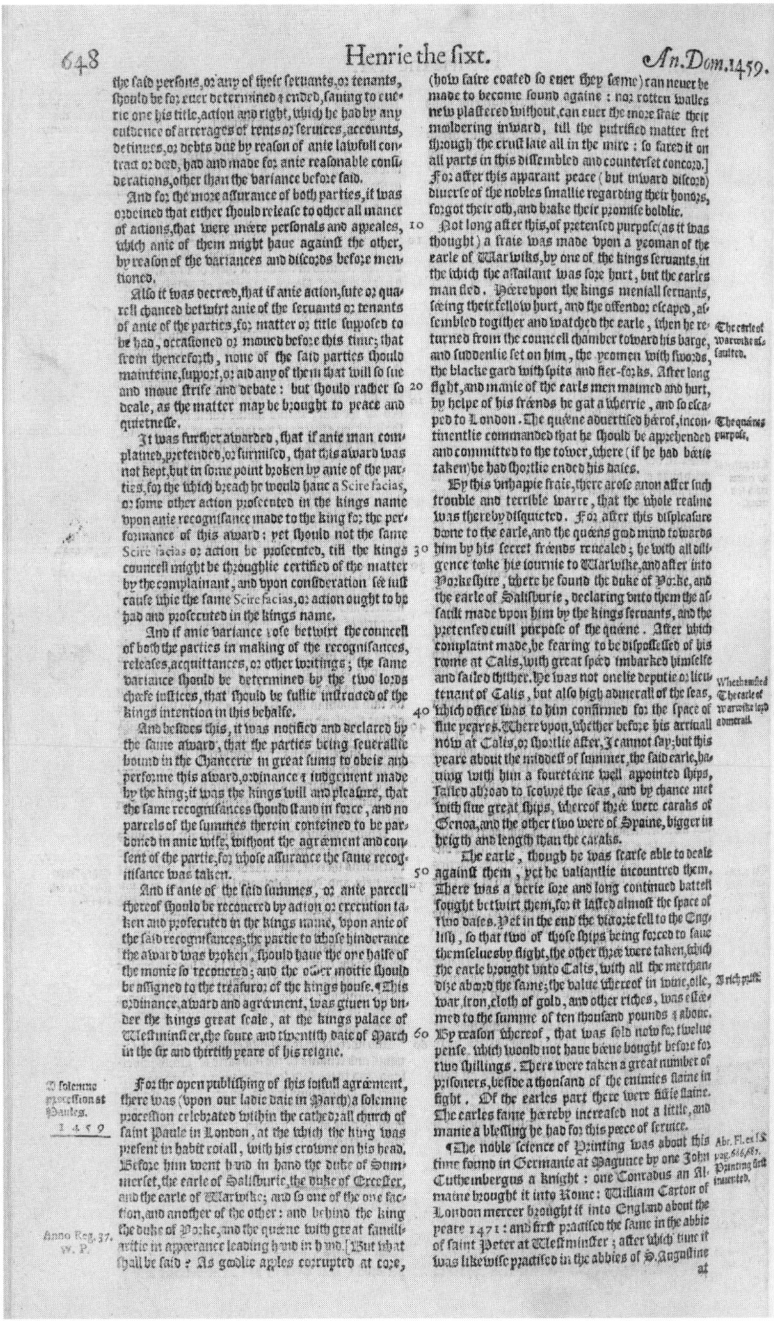

the said persons, or any of their seruants, or tenants, should be for euer determined & ended, sauing to euerie one his title, action and right, which he had by any euidence of arrerages of rents or seruices, accounts, detinues, or debts due by reason of anie lawfull contract or deed, had and made for anie reasonable considerations, other than the variance before said.

And for the more assurance of both parties, it was ordeined that either should release to other all maner of actions, that were méere personals and appeales, which anie of them might haue against the other, by reason of the variances and discords before mentioned.

Also it was decreed, that if anie action, sute or quarell chanced betwixt anie of the seruants or tenants of anie of the parties, for matter or title supposed to be had, occasioned or moued before this time; that from thenceforth, none of the said parties should mainteine, support, or aid any of them that will so sue and moue strife and debate: but should rather so deale, as the matter may be brought to peace and quietnesse.

It was further awarded, that if anie man complained, pretended, or surmised, that this award was not kept, but in some point broken by anie of the parties, for the which breach he would haue a Scire facias, or some other action prosecuted in the kings name vpon anie recognisance made to the king for the performance of this award: yet should not the same Scire facias or action be prosecuted, till the kings councell might be throughlie certified of the matter by the complainant, and vpon consideration sée iust cause whie the same Scire facias, or action ought to be had and prosecuted in the kings name.

And if anie variance rose betwixt the councell of both the parties in making of the recognisances, releases, acquittances, or other writings; the same variance should be determined by the two lords cheefe iustices, that should be fullie instructed of the kings intention in this behalfe.

And besides this, it was notified and declared by the same award, that the parties being seuerallie bound in the Chancerie in great sums to obeie and performe this award, ordinance & iudgement made by the king; it was the kings will and pleasure, that the same recognisances should stand in force, and no parcels of the summes therein conteined to be pardoned in anie wise, without the agréement and consent of the partie, for whose assurance the same recognisance was taken.

And if anie of the said summes, or anie parcell thereof should be recouered by action or execution taken and prosecuted in the kings name, vpon anie of the said recognisances; the partie to whose hinderance the award was broken, should haue the one halfe of the monie so recouered; and the other moitie should be assigned to the treasuror of the kings house. ¶This ordinance, award and agréement, was giuen vp vnder the kings great seale, at the kings palace of Westminster, the foure and twentith daie of March in the six and thirtith yeare of his reigne.

A solemne procession at Paules. 1459

For the open publishing of this ioifull agréement, there was (vpon our ladie daie in March) a solemne procession celebrated within the cathedrall church of saint Paule in London, at the which the king was present in habit roiall, with his crowne on his head. Before him went hand in hand the duke of Summerset, the earle of Salisburie, the duke of Excester, and the earle of Warwike; and so one of the one faction, and another of the other: and behind the king the duke of Yorke, and the quéene with great familiaritie in appearance leading hand in hand. [But what shall be said? As goodlie apples corrupted at core, *Anno Reg. 37. W. P.* (how faire coated so euer they séeme) can neuer be made to become sound againe: nor rotten walles new plastered without, can euer the more staie their moldering inward, till the putrified matter fret through the crust late all in the mire: so fared it on all parts in this dissembled and counterfet concord.] For after this apparant peace (but inward discord) diuerse of the nobles smallie regarding their honors, forgot their oth, and brake their promise boldlie.

Not long after this, of pretensed purpose (as it was thought) a fraie was made vpon a yeoman of the earle of Warwiks, by one of the kings seruants, in the which the assailant was sore hurt, but the earles man fled. Héerevpon the kings meniall seruants, séeing their fellow hurt, and the offendor escaped, assembled togither and watched the earle, when he returned from the councell chamber toward his barge, and suddenlie set on him, the yeomen with swords, the blacke gard with spits and fier-forks. *The earle of Warwike assaulted.* After long fight, and manie of the earls men maimed and hurt, by helpe of his fréends he gat a wherrie, and so escaped to London. The quéene aduertised héerof, incontinentlie commanded that he should be apprehended and committed to the tower, where (if he had béene taken) he had shortlie ended his daies. *The quéenes purpose.*

By this vnhappie fraie, there arose anon after such trouble and terrible warre, that the whole realme was thereby disquieted. For after this displeasure doone to the earle, and the quéens good mind towards him by his secret fréends reuealed; he with all diligence tooke his iournie to Warwike, and after into Yorkeshire, where he found the duke of Yorke, and the earle of Salisburie, declaring vnto them the assault made vpon him by the kings seruants, and the pretensed euill purpose of the quéene. After which complaint made, he fearing to be dispossessed of his roome at Calis, with great spéed imbarked himselfe and sailed thither. He was not onelie deputie or lieutenant of Calis, but also high admerall of the seas, which office was to him confirmed for the space of fiue yeares. *Whethem. The earle of warwike lord admerall.* Therevpon, whether before his arriuall now at Calis, or shortlie after, I cannot say; but this yeare about the middest of summer, the said earle, hauing with him a fouretéene well appointed ships, sailed abroad to scowre the seas, and by chance met with fiue great ships, whereof thrée were caraks of Genoa, and the other two were of Spaine, bigger in heigth and length than the caraks.

The earle, though he was scarse able to deale against them, yet he valiantlie incountred them. There was a verie sore and long continued battell fought betwixt them, for it lasted almost the space of two daies. Yet in the end the victorie fell to the English, so that two of those ships being forced to saue themselues by flight, the other thrée were taken, which the earle brought vnto Calis, with all the merchandize aboord the same; the value whereof in wine, oile, wax, iron, cloth of gold, and other riches, was estéemed to the summe of ten thousand pounds & aboue. *A rich prise.* By reason whereof, that was sold now for twelue pense, which would not haue béene bought before for two shillings. There were taken a great number of prisoners, beside a thousand of the enimies slaine in fight. Of the earles part there were fiftie slaine. The earles fame héereby increased not a little, and manie a blessing he had for this peece of seruice.

¶The noble science of Printing was about this time found in Germanie at Magunce by one Iohn Cuthembergus a knight: one Conradus an Almaine brought it into Rome: William Caxton of London mercer brought it into England about the yeare 1471: and first practised the same in the abbie of saint Peter at Westminster; after which time it was likewise practised in the abbies of S. Augustine *Abr. Fl. ex I. S. pag. 686, 687. Printing first inuented.*

at

Figure 3.2. The printed history of printing. *The Firste Volume of the Chronicles of En - gland, Scotlande, and Irelande* (London: Henry Denham for John Harrison, George Bishop, Rafe Newberie, Henry Denham, and Thomas Woodcock, 1577), page 648, *STC* 13569.2pt 1, reproduced by permission of the Folger Shakespeare Library.

> Conradus an Almaine brought it into Rome: William Caxton of London mercer brought it into England about the yeare 1471: and first practised the same in the abbie of saint Peter at Westminster; after which time it was likewise practised in the abbies of S. Augustine at Canturburie, saint Albons, and other monasteries of England.[31]

The passage tells a clear history of the book: printing is invented in 1459 (or "about this time") and comes to England in 1471, "after which time" it is further disseminated across a number of monasteries. The dates are fairly close to our own understanding, which posits the invention of print somewhat earlier—after 1450—and records Caxton importing this technology into England somewhat later, in 1476, as a secular and urban experience. By any reckoning, printing, even more fantastically than the paper mill (which seems to have only come to England in 1495), occurs after the events of *2 Henry VI*. Moreover, that any discussion of printing at all should be *inserted* into Cade's speech in the Folio is at odds with our sense of that text's authority. Madeline Doran and Peter Alexander both conclude that the Quarto is a memorial reconstruction of a more authoritative text, in part because of its carelessness with historical detail. This argument presents the Folio as a general straightening out of the plays, one that asserts authorial control in proportion to historical accuracy. The Cade passage above reasserts anachronism in Cade's speech in the midst of such a process, making the play's book history less historically cogent even as the Folio reorganizes the Henry trilogy in sequential continuity. Breaching the plot's temporal frame, the discrepancy brings Cade's critique of textual authority to a larger reflection on the constitution of historical authority itself. That is, the play presents a world defined by its textuality, which it illustrates by constructing and destroying its characters through texts. In the main, it restrains this process from the backbone of chronological history it uses for the plot, preferring to tell the past as a progressive story. But throughout the Cade section, when authority is most under assault, it abandons chronology and seeks out a more thematic organization for the historical past, one that doubles back on chronology to link Cade with

Tyler and Straw. The Folio's particular revision around printing takes this reorganizing sensibility one step further by calling into question the authority of documentary history even as it consolidates the plays in a progressive sequence overall.

Wrapped up in the history of printing, the emergence of Shakespeare's work in print, the relationship between texts and authority, and the constitution of the past, Cade's telling of the history of printing offers a supremely self-reflective moment, a moment in which theme and structure come together to create a character who not only speaks of the problems of textuality but is also generated out of the manipulation of historical texts and who, when revised, becomes even more indicative of the ways historical details can be inserted within a new narrative that is at odds with the narrative from which the details were taken. Cade may not be psychologically self-reflective, but he is self-reflective in that his complaints about the manipulations of printing within the plot reflect the way his self—his character, his identity—is constructed from manipulations of the historical record. I suggest that such inward turning is implicit in book history and especially so in the history of the book.[32]

Caxton discusses the development of printing in his 1480 *Chronicles of England*. This text is based on the *Brut*, which tells the history of England from its legendary founding to 1333, variously extended in manuscript.[33] Caxton added a 1419–61 continuation, which he also used for his "liber ultimas" of his 1482 *Polychronicon*.[34] The entry on printing thus presents a uniquely self-reflective moment: a historical account of printing written by the first English printer and presented in the first printed history of England. If we turn to the actual page of Caxton's *Chronicles of England* on which it appears, Folio page Y1^{v}, we can better appreciate both the self-conscious nature of fifteenth-century literary culture and its methods of reproduction (see Figure 3.3). At first glance, the page seems entirely unselfconscious about history. Beginning with a chapter heading that focuses on a particular moment in the Wars of the Roses, it quickly splinters into the chronicle form: here four great fish are landed between "Eerethe" and London (notably, a "mors marine"—a seahorse or walrus—a swordfish, and two whales); there Lord Egremont is imprisoned and Warwick

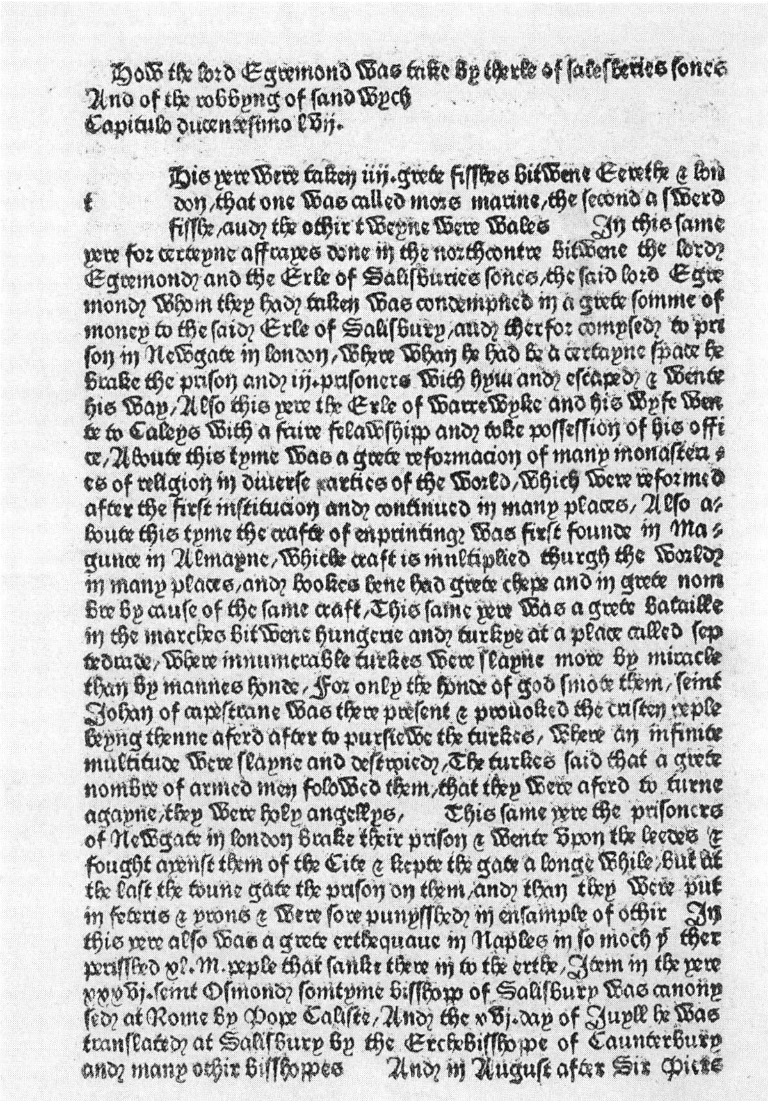

How the lord Egremond was take by therle of salesberies sones
And of the robbyng of sandwych
Capitulo ducentesimo lvij.

This yere were taken iiij. grete fisshes bitwene Erethe & lon
t don, that one was called mors marine, the second a swerd
fisshe, and the othir twayne were wales In this same
yere for certeyne affrayes done in the northcontre bitwene the lord
Egremond and the Erle of Salisburies sones, the said lord Egre
mond whom they had taken was condempned in a grete somme of
money to the said Erle of Salisbury, and therfor commysed to pri
son in Newgate in london, where whan he had be a certayne space he
brake the prison and iij. prisoners with hym and escaped & wente
his way, Also this yere the Erle of Warrewyke and his wyfe wen
te to Caleys with a faire felawship and toke possession of his offi
ce, Aboute this tyme was a grete reformacion of many monaster
es of religion in diverse parties of the world, which were reformed
after the first institucion and continued in many places, Also a
boute this tyme the crafte of enprinting was first founde in Ma
gunce in Almayne, which craft is multiplied thurgh the world
in many places, and bookes bene had grete chepe and in grete nom
bre by cause of the same craft, This same yere was a grete bataille
in the marches bitwene hungerie and turkye at a place called sep
tedrade, where innumerable turkes were slayne more by miracle
than by mannes honde, For only the honde of god smote them, seint
Johan of capestrane was there present & prouoked the cristen peple
beyng thenne aferd after to pursiewe the turkes, where an infinite
multitude were slayne and destroyed, The turkes said that a grete
nombre of armed men folowed them, that they were aferd to turne
agayne, they were holy angellys, This same yere the prisoners
of Newgate in london brake their prison & wente upon the ledes &
fought ayenst them of the Cite & kepte the gate a longe while, but at
the last the toune gate the prison on them, and than they were put
in feteris & yrons & were sore punysshed in ensample of othir In
this yere also was a grete erthequaue in Naples in so moch þ ther
perisshed xl. M. peple that sanke there in to the erthe, Item in the yere
xxxvj. seint Osmond somtyme bisshop of Salisbury was canony
sed at Rome by Pope Caliste, And the xvj. day of Juyll he was
translated at Salisbury by the Erchebisshope of Caunterbury
and many othir bisshoppes And in August after Sir Pierse

Figure 3.3. Documenting the origins of print in print. *Chronicles of England* (Westminster: William Caxton, 1480), Y1v, *STC* 9991, reproduced by permission of the Folger Shakespeare Library.

and his wife take possession of Calais; elsewhere there is a miraculous intervention on the part of some angels in the war against the Turks; now a prison break occurs in Newgate, now an earthquake in Naples; and then the Wars of the Roses continue on the next page with Warwick, York, and Salisbury's alliance.[35] Between Warwick's trip to Calais and the war with the Turks, apparently, both monastic reform and printing occur:

> Aboute this tyme was a grete reformacion of many monasteries of religion in diuerse parties of the world / which were reformed after the first institucion and continued in many places / Also aboute this tyme the crafte of enprinting was first founde in Magunce in Almayne / whiche craft is mnltiplied [*sic*] thurgh the world in many places / and bookes bene had grete chepe and in grete nombre by cause of the same craft /

Taken with the rest of the page, the commentary presents two more atomized events in the overall list, associated with the rest not by analysis but by proximity and accretion. Indeed, the page as a whole seems at odds with itself, the overwhelming solidity of its black rectangle of ink opposed to the fragmentary connections it develops between events. Yet, given the compression of the chronicle format, the passage is surprisingly insistent on the profound nature of this "reformacion" and "the crafte of enprinting." These are both "grete" changes to existing social practices, "the first institucion" and the existing book economy; both, too, are explicitly of global proportions and in this differ from the discrete catching of fish or even the Wars of the Roses itself, which is presented as of more local consequence. The explicit grouping of these two events, concerned as they are with discourses of belief and communication, suggests in some oblique way a potent if unarticulated relationship between them. In this, Caxton's account appears simultaneously knowing and arbitrary, paradoxically aware of the historical changes it records and opaque to any causal connection. Like Tottel's "Ddio," this awkward combination of insight and naïveté is captured on Caxton's page in the misplaced "n" in his statement that print is "mnltiplied thurgh the world," which defines one of print's very first moments of self-reflection as a typo.

This paradox should not distract us from the governing condition at work in the passage—reproduction—which it illustrates on at least three levels. First, Caxton's *Chronicles of England* is a reproduction of manuscript sources, an extension of scribal practices. Caxton derives his continuation from two sources: the *Fasciculus temporum*, written by Werner Rolewinck and printed by Caxton's longtime associate Johannes Veldener in Cologne in 1474 and then again in Louvain in 1475, and the *London Chronicles*, a variegated group of urban and secular fifteenth-century chronicles organized by mayoral year. He adapts both of these to the *Brut* format. Mary-Rose McLaren counts forty-four extant manuscripts of the *London Chronicles* but speculates "that in the mid fifteenth century there were almost certainly hundreds of *London Chronicles* in circulation."[36] Two surviving *London Chronicles*, B.L. MS Cotton Vitellius A.xvi and the *Great Chronicle of London* (CLC/270/MS03313, formerly MS Guildhall 3313), also record the invention of printing.[37] Both manuscripts report printing in terms very similar to Caxton's.

Cotton Vitellius tells of the Wars of the Roses, of the "greate ffysshes . wherof one was callid mors maryne and the second a swerdfysshe and the other .ij. were whalis," and of Egremont's imprisonment. It passes over the great Reformation but mentions the mayor of London's intervention into a dispute between the Duke of Somerset and John Nevile, and then some Frenchmen in Sandwhich, before returning to Warwick and his wife in Calais, and then finally coming to print: "Also this yere began the Crafte of Enp*ri*ntyng of Books which was ffoundyn In a towne callid magounce in Almayne" (see Figure 3.4). *The Great London Chronicle* includes the same incidents, "Also this yer*e* began the crafte of Enprentyng of bookis which was ffoundyn In A toune callid magounce in Almayngne" (see Figure 3.5).[38] The two manuscripts are visually similar as well: the *Great London Chronicle* breaks the events into separate lines, but both head the page with the regnal year and organize the individual entries by mayoral year. By comparison, Caxton's text is much more dense. Still, revolution and originality seem the wrong measure of print technology and of Caxton's writing, which are profoundly conservative of both form and content.

Caxton emphasizes this tangible durability of writing in a number of his prologues, particularly in his preface to the *Polychronicon*, in which he discusses history as a genre separate from "the terryble feyned Fables of Poetes." Caxton drew this prologue from a French version of Poggio Bracciolini's Latin translation of Diodorus Siculus's *Bibliotheca historica.*[39] "Historye," writes Caxton, "is a perpetuel conseruatryce of thoos thynges / that haue be doone before this presente tyme / and also a cotydyan wytnesse of bienfayttes of malefaytes / grete Actes / and tryumphal vyctoryes of all maner peple."[40] In contrast, Caxton defines the exemplary value of poetry as based in eloquence:

> By Eloquence the grekes ben preferryd in contynuel honour to fore the rude barbares / Oratours and lerned clerkes in like wise excelle vnlerned and brutyssh peple / Syth this eloquence is suche that causeth men emonge them self somme texcelle other / after the qualyte of the vertue and eloquence be seyn to be of valew / For somme we Iuge to be good men digne of laude / whiche shewe to vs the waye of virtue / and other haue taken another waye for tenflamm more the courages of men by fables of poesye / than to prouffyte And by the lawes and Institutes more to punysshe than to teche Soo that of thyse thynges the vtylyte is myxt with harme / For somme sothly techyth to lye / But historye representynge the thynges lyke vnto the wordes / enbraceth al vtylyte & prouffite.[41]

Caxton is clear about genre: both history and poetry are of value. History figures "thinges lyke vnto the words"; it is still tropological, and Caxton's definition emphasizes simile, but its representative force is based on verisimilitude. "Fables of poesye" mix utility with harm, so that exemplarity is interwoven with the ability to enflame passion. This difference sets poetry apart from history and, according to Caxton at least, separates the Greeks from the "rude barbares."

Caxton's conception of history is that it conserves the past, reproducing it as witness, and so his historical writing, let alone his

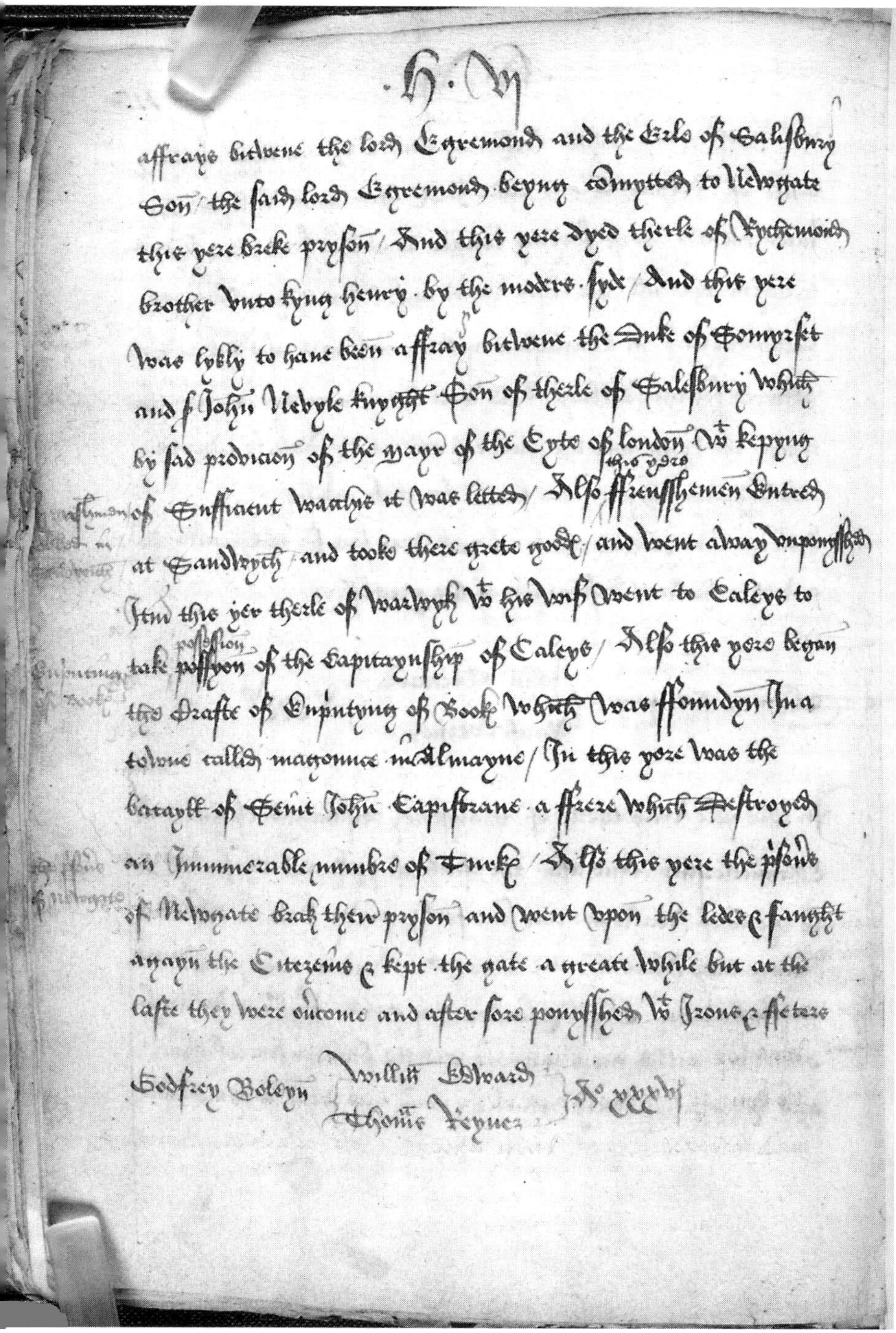

·h·vj

affrays bitwene the lord Egremond and the Erle of Salisbury
Son the said lord Egremond beyng comytted to Newgate
this yere brake pryson And this yere dyed therle of Rychemond
brother unto kyng henry by the modres syde And this yere
was lykly to haue been affray bitwene the duke of Somyrset
and s John Nevyle knyght Son of therle of Salesbury which
by sad prouision of the mayre of the Cyte of london wt keping (this yere)
of sufficient wacche it was letted Also ffrensshemen entred
at Sandwych and toke there grete good and went away unponysshed
Item this yer therle of Warwyk wt his wif went to Caleys to
take possession of the Capitaynship of Caleys Also this yere began
the Crafte of Enpryntyng of Book which was ffoundyn In a
towne called magounce in Almayne In this yere was the
bataylle of Seint John Capistrane a ffrere which destroyed
an Innumerable numbre of Turkes Also this yere the prisoners
of Newgate brake there pryson and went upon the ledes & faught
agayn the Citezeins & kept the gate a greate while but at the
laste they were ouercome and after sore ponysshed wt Irons & ffeteres

Godfrey Boleyn   William Edward   Thomas Reyner   No xxxvj CCC

Figure 3.4. The handwritten origins of print. *The London Chronicle*, Cotton Vitellius A. X. VI., 113v,

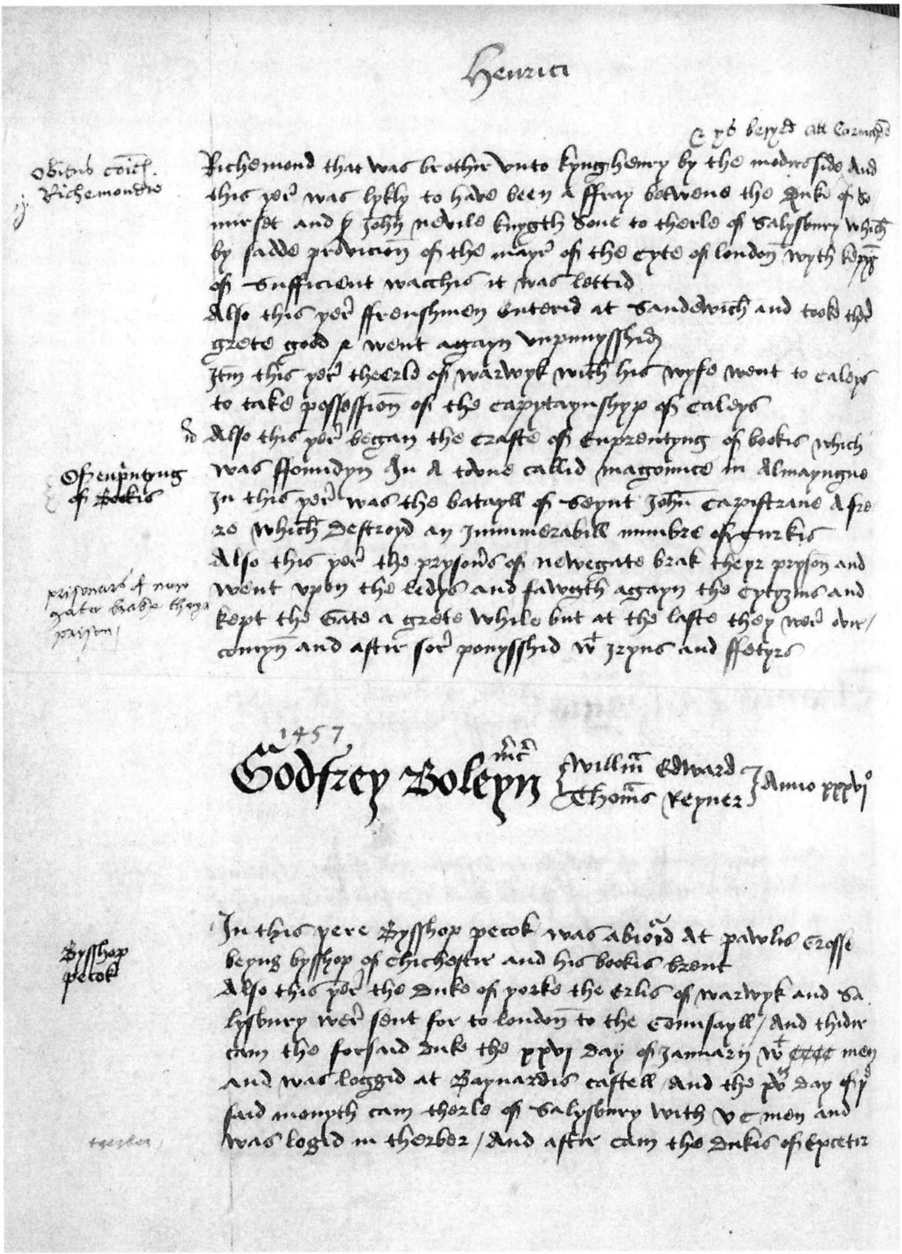

Henrici

Richemond that was brother vnto kyng hemry by the moders side And
this yer was lykly to have been a ffray betwene the Duke of So
mersett and Sir John nevill knyght sone to therle of Salysbury which
by sadde provision of the mayr of the cyte of london wyth kepyng
of sufficient wacche it was letted
Also this yer frenshmen entered at Sandewich and took the
grete good & went agayn vnpunysshed
Item this yer therle of warwyk with his wyfe went to calys
to take possession of the capytaynshyp of calys
Also this yer began the crafte of enpryntyng of bookis which
was ffounden in A towne called magounce in Almayngne
In this yer was the batayll of Seynt John capystrane after
which destroyed an innumerable nombre of turkis
Also this yer the prysoners of newgate brak theyr pryson and
went vpon the ledys and faught agayn the cytyzins and
kept the gate a grete while but at the laste they were ov/
comyn and aftir sore ponysshed wt yrons and ffetyrs

1457

Godfrey Bolleyn mr — Willm Edward, Thomas Reyner — Anno xxxvj

In this yere Bysshop pecok was abiurd at powlis crosse
beyng bysshop of chichestir and his bookis brent
Also this yer the Duke of yorke the erlis of warwyk and Sa
lysbury were sent for to london to the counsayll / And thider
cam the forsaid Duk the xxvj day of Januarij wt CCCC men
and was logged at Baynardis castell / And the xv day of the
said moneth cam therle of Salysbury with v c men and
was logid in therber / And aftir cam the Dukis of Excetir

Figure 3.5. The handwritten origins of print, redux. *The Great Chronicle of London*, CLC/270/MS03313, CLXI[v], reproduced courtesy of the City of London, London Metropolitan Archives.

material reproduction of the manuscript page, cannot be intellectually exclusive to print production. Indeed, the prologue announcing this conclusion also performs it, by conserving Poggio's original even as it reproduces it in English. The issue here is not simply the remediation of an earlier form but sustaining a sense of return, conserving it, through a variety of iterations, from Latin, to French, to English. The same logic dominates the text's material iterations, so that though Caxton produces manuscript in print, a number of manuscripts were copied out from his text as well.[42] If there is any difference between manuscript and print beyond the particular mechanics of composition and impression, it lies in print's ability to energize this reproductive system.

Thus, my second point about print reproduction: it is exponential. That is, though the *Chronicles of England* follows manuscript practice, the influx of volume provided by print technology insists that it develops according to a radical curve: print keeps on reproducing, not just books but its own terms for greater reproduction, which in turn allow for the reproduction of even more books at even more locations. This is borne out by the *Chronicles of England* bibliography. *The Chronicles'* importance lies not simply in its popularity—it remained in 181 English manuscripts, 49 Anglo-Norman manuscripts, and about 20 Latin manuscripts, and its popularity in the late Middle Ages, as Lister Matheson points out, was exceeded only by the Wyclifitte Bible—so much as in its structural position within an exponentially expanding reproductive sequence.[43]

Caxton's *Chronicles of England* was reproduced on a massive scale. Not only did his continuation serve as the base text for his addition to the *Polychronicon*, from which Caxton also spun off his short *Discripcion of Britayne* in 1480, but he reprinted the *Chronicles* in 1482.[44] In 1483, the Saint Albans Schoolmaster printer revised this text for his own edition, *Cronicles of Englonde with the Frute of Timis*, and following him, William de Machlinia produced a copy of Caxton's version from his shop in London in or around 1485. In 1493 Gerard de Leew, working in Antwerp, reprinted the *Chronicles* as the *Cronycles of the Londe of Englond* for importation into England, and shortly after taking control of Caxton's Westminster shop, Wynkyn de Worde reprinted the Schoolmaster Printer's version in 1497, pairing it with the *Discripcion of Britayne.*[45] If we assume, as is fairly accepted, a print run of five hundred copies per edition, the *Chronicles of England* circulated in approximately three thousand copies by 1500. Even if we discount this number, de Leew's willingness to invest in the text for importation into England suggests an ongoing demand for books, which the six editions answer with a large number of individual copies. The books continued: de Worde reprinted the Schoolmaster's version in 1520 and the matched set in 1502, 1515, and 1528, as did Julian Notary in 1504 and 1515, and Richard Pynson in 1510.[46] Yet the *Chronicles of England* was not even the most reprinted title of the fifteenth century, which is John Mirk's *Festial.*

These statistics pose a fundamental question about the relationship between print and social change: Where did the demand for English history come from? The question is not rhetorical. Manuscript production could, apparently, already meet a demand for hundreds of copies of the *Brut* and *London Chronicles.* Obviously, our own fondness for an English fifteenth century of booklessness is not prepared to theorize such change. Print energized the volume of reproduction, but knowing that fact offers no clear explanation for the notion that supply itself could drive demand, for the tightness of the circuit between production and consumption such that the one could in fact create the other, or for the drastic changes in literacy, distribution, storage, wholesaling, and even the conversation habits of individuals over dinner that such a large number of books implies.[47] One answer lies in Caxton's commentary on print, which—in contrast to the *Great Chronicle of London*—emphasizes that print multiplies books as well as knowledge.

My third point, then, is that Caxton's comments on printing are about the power of reproduction, about the way objects and knowledge can expand at a nonlinear rate that is neither progressive nor periodic; rather, their expansion spirals outward according to its own, as-yet-unknown algorithm. Print is revolutionary, perhaps, but not as a break from the past so much as a revolving multiplication of both production and consumption. As manuscript continuation, as exponential system, and as self-referential history, fifteenth-century literary culture may well be intertwined in a number of paradoxes, but this does not mean that it does not have some sense of the process that defines it, and that process is reproduction.[48]

It is worth pausing to examine a version of Caxton's text, the 1483 *Cronicles of Englonde with the Frute of Timis* produced at Saint Albans by the so-called Schoolmaster Printer, to better understand the subtlety capable within this literary economy.[49] This name, the Schoolmaster Printer, is supplied in Wynkyn de Worde's colophon to his 1497 edition of the text, in which he announces that the text was "enprynted by one somtyme scolemayster of saynt Albons."[50] The press at Saint Albans produced a total of eight texts: six neatly printed Latin texts between 1480 and 1481, followed after a brief hiatus in 1482 by two more roughly produced but thematically and technically adventurous vernacular works, the *Cronicles* and the *Boke of St Albans*. Overall, the press remains little understood and may represent separate printers working at Saint Albans with the "Schoolmaster" acting as an editor, translator, and writer for the press's two last productions. Regardless, both the Latin and the English print runs began with titles lifted from Caxton's portfolio, the 1480/81 *Nova rhetorica* and the 1483 *Cronicles*. In fact, the tendency to reproduce Caxton's work dominates not only the Saint Albans press's choice of texts but its aesthetic texture right down to the paper substrate: five of Saint Albans's twelve different paper stocks are also found in Caxton's books, and the Saint Albans's typefaces echo Caxton's own.[51]

In any case, the voice that emerges from the prologue to the *Cronicles* announces the text's novelty: "¶In thys neew translacion ar contened many notabull and meruelles thyngys."[52] From our perspective, any novelty to be associated with the *Cronicles* appears within the umbra of Caxton's influence. Still, the *Cronicles* is indeed "neew" on a number of counts: beginning with an original table and prologue to the reader, it is adorned with original woodcuts, uses color printing for its initials and lombards, and closes with the very first English trademark.[53] And if the Saint Albans printer's typeface reproduces Caxton's style, it does so as an original copy: Nicolas Barker has argued that the Saint Albans type was not imported, as Caxton's was, but created by a punchcutter working in England. Barker terms Saint

Albans Type 1 an English "court hand."[54] In the Saint Albans *Cronicles*, as in fifteenth-century literary production overall, derivativeness paradoxically constitutes originality.[55]

The Saint Albans printer's selection of titles, as well as his type and paper, suggest that he thought broadly about printing overall, noting carefully what Caxton was accomplishing in Westminster but also developing his own sense of the production process, his own craft. This quality is also apparent in the Schoolmaster's modifications to Caxton's text and his own original writing. Most obviously, the Schoolmaster moves Caxton's entry on printing from its place beneath the four great fish to a specific note on the second-to-last leaf of the book (k viii):

> Nota. Printerys of bokis wer this tyme mightely multeplied in maguncie & thurgh out the world .and thei began frist and ther held the craftis. And this time mony men began for to be more sotell in craftis and suyfter then euer they wer a fore.

The note is reminiscent of Caxton's entry, but separated out from the block of text and sequestered at the end of the book as it is, it creates printing as an autonomous event. The Schoolmaster also revises Caxton's commentary to underscore printers' "sotell" refinement of the craft (such as Saint Albans's own introduction of color printing) and the advancement in speed. Further, the note appears amidst a progressive history of popes appended to Caxton's update that continues through to "Sixtus the iiij. a Ianuens and a frere minore wos Pope after Paule. and is yit at the makyng of this boke," bringing the *Cronicles* up to date (k viii^{v}). Further still, as the popes the Schoolmaster chronicles—Eugenius, Calixtus, Paulus, and Pius—were all involved with exactly the kind of monastic reform Caxton mentioned in his earlier comment, the Schoolmaster's continuation dovetails with Caxton's other major difference from *The London Chronicles* in manuscript. The Schoolmaster in fact leaves the initial mention of reform untouched and then reintroduces the topic at the top of k viii, the page in which he discusses printing. Indeed, immediately after the note on printing, the Schoolmaster inserts a discussion of Pope Pius II's career as poet laureate under the name of Aeneas Sylvius. This passage is also lifted from Caxton, where it appears on Y2^{v}, and the Schoolmaster leaves it in that original position while reiterating it in this final passage.

The result is that the Schoolmaster highlights printing by separating it out in an autonomous note that reflects on his own efforts, and then he reattaches the issue to ecclesiastical reform, not simply as a coterminous event but as a part of literary production—eloquence—that is imagined as a province of the pope himself. Specifically, the revision implies that printing is not divorced from eloquence and authority in both its form and its content. More broadly, it demonstrates how the reproduction—the reprinting, the rearrangement, and the alteration of a preexisting text—can generate an original statement. This is the process of textual formalism: the physical manipulation of textual form within an existing generic structure that permits a revised intellectual statement.

The Schoolmaster's prologue to the *Cronicles* instructs his readers in just this textual formalism. The prologue promises to elaborate "the ordyr off thys boke and the thyngis that be spokyn of" (aii^{v}) and ends by concluding that "this ordyr is kepyt in all the boke of euery thyng in his place as it is sayd a foor" (aiii^{v}). In part, the Schoolmaster's concern with order is intellectual, and so he lists his sources (aii), itemizes the "vii partes" of history (aii^{v}), and underscores the six things necessary to understand the chronicle itself (aii^{v}–aiii^{v}). It is also physical: the Schoolmaster opens the book by instructing the reader how to use signatures to navigate through the text: "And ye must vnderstond y*at* eueri leef is markid vnder with A. on . ij . iij. & iiij . & so forth to viij . all the letters . an what sum eu*er* ye fynd shortli writin in this table . ye shall find oppenli in the same letter" (a).[56] Over the course of the prologue, he explains how to use the marginal header to move through the seven parts of history: "¶And so in eu*ery* part of thes . vij . partes is shewed the most and necessary actys of all the kyngis of Englond & ther namys wrettyn abooe in the margent that euery man may fynd them soon" (aii^{v}). From this prologue it is possible to come to some understanding of fifteenth-century English printing's poetics of reproduction. On the one hand are the rhetorical tropes of the printed page—the prologue to the reader, the type, the leaf, the signature marks—and the schemes of arrangement—the "margent," the header—which the printer can manipulate for an effect ranging from an aesthetic evocation of English writing, through an organizational structure for the book that mirrors an intellectual structure for history, to a specific point about the importance of a particular event. On the other hand, these are interwoven with, but also somewhat separate from, the book's content ("what sum eu*er* ye fynd shortli writin" and "necessary actys of all the kyngis of Englond"), which the Schoolmaster also manipulates through the more rhetorical tropes of reiteration and amplification. Neither a simple reproduction of Caxton's *Chronicles* nor a completely new edition, the Schoolmaster's *Cronicles* reflects on these formal elements of the book through a complex sequence of self-references that constitute its content, structure, and voice. That his voice is so carefully integrated with defining itself in terms of the book but has nevertheless been lost to literary history is both ironic and also understandable: another demonstration of the counterhistory of loss that underwrites literary fame.

Overtly, the sixteenth-century chronicles seem conceptually removed from such a literary culture of reproduction. Witness Edward Hall's epistle to his 1548 edition of *The Union of the Two Noble and Illustre Famelies of Lancastre & Yorke*:

> Sithe the ende of Frossarte whiche endeth at the begynnyng of kyng Henry the fourthe, no man in the Englishe toungue, hath either set furth their honors accordyng to their desertes, nor yet declared many notable actes worthy of memorie dooen in the tyme of seuen kynges, whiche after kyng Richarde succeded: Excepte Robert Fabian and one with out name, whiche wrote the common English Chronicle, men worthy to be praysed for their diligence, but farre shotyng wide from the butte of an historie.[57]

Hall records two chronicles since Froissart's: an anonymous chronicle and Robert Fabian's. Accordingly, the hundreds upon hundreds—if not thousands upon thousands—of editions featuring Caxton's and the Schoolmaster's prose, the hundreds of *London Chronicles* in manuscript, are all simply as "one with out name, whiche wrote the common

English Chronicle." This general anonymity authorizes Hall's own chronicle, which begins with Henry IV. Yet reproduction underwrites these editions' presentation of the history of print even as they argue for such clear difference.

The page from Holinshed's *The Chronicles of England* offers a convenient example (see Figure 3.2). In place of whales and earthquakes, the Holinshed Syndicate presents an orderly narrative of the Wars of the Roses carefully calibrated to reflect chronological progression. The entry on printing is particularly saturated with this overall interest in ascribing events to a certain moment in time: the year 1459 is cleanly separated from the previous year by a marginal notation, the passage on printing is set off yet again by a paragraph mark and another marginal comment, and the founding of print is itself separated from its specific arrival in England in 1471. Indeed, the page layout—with its two narrow columns, its orderly paragraphs all carefully indented, its delicate marginalia—contributes to this chronological clarity with striking contrast to Caxton's block of text. Yet the closer we look at the sixteenth-century chronicles, the more they appear indebted to fifteenth-century manuscripts: *The Chronicles of England* in fact sandwiches the story of print between Warwick's journey to Calais and his union with York and Salisbury. Similarly, Richard Pynson's 1516 *Newe Cronycles of Englande and of Fraunce*, reprinted by William Rastell in 1533 as *Fabyans Cronycle*, actually reproduces the entry on printing quite clearly, down to the four fish (now "wo*n*derfull fyshys"), and cites the *Polychronicon* as a source, which as we have seen reprints the *Chronicles of England*.[58] Edward Hall follows fifteenth-century historiography as well: under his entry around the year 1458, he lists the conflict between Egremont and Salisbury, Salisbury's escape from imprisonment, and the invention of print: "In which season, the craft of Printyng was first inuented in the citie of Mens in Germanie, to the great furtheraunce of all persons, desiryng knowledge or thyrstyng for literature," which is followed by the pact between York, Salisbury, and Warwick.[59] To the best of my knowledge there is nothing about the year 1459, about Egremont's escape, or about the Yorkist coalition that insists on the inclusion of printing at this point. The year 1459 is an arbitrary date; rather, it is not arbitrary at all: it reveals that early modern printing relies on the manuscript and incunable for its internal organization, indeed, for its sense of itself.

In truth, it cannot be otherwise: the *Great Chronicle of London* was owned by John Foxe and John Stow, a significant member of the Holinshed Syndicate responsible for preparing the 1587 revision. Both Stow and Foxe thought they were working with the manuscript version of Fabyan's *Newe Cronycles*; Stow in particular referred to it as "Fabian's MS" and marked it, as well as MS Vitellius A.xvi (the other manuscript to include mention of printing), and the other *London Chronicles* he used for his various printed histories.[60] These manuscript origins structure the pages of *The Chronicles of England*: they are intellectually present in the choice of events on the page, they are aesthetically evoked through the black-letter type that emulates the typeface Caxton introduced in 1489, and they formulate the terms by which early modern history reflects on its own history of printing. Even the marginalia in *Holinshed's Chronicles* is forecast, not by the print form in Caxton, but by Stow's handwritten notes in the manuscripts (see Figures 3.4 and 3.5).

These examples are an important reminder, for it is still a commonplace that print introduces conceptual and technological fixity to an otherwise fluid medium: witness D. R. Woolf's assertion in *Reading History in Early Modern England* that "print made possible the establishment and reproduction of accurate texts, but it also prohibited further substantive intervention in those texts."[61] Caxton is quite articulate about the conservative nature of history, and he carries out his theoretical understanding of genre by physically reproducing the manuscript sources faithfully. These manuscripts are as organized and as accurate as the printed histories derived from them. Indeed, their structural uniformity and similarity in content is impressive. Ultimately, print has no special relationship to fixity other than in its typecasting techniques, in its paper-drying process, and in certain mechanical adjustments made to the form. It is but one technological element in an overall mode of production that incorporates manuscript practices, such as collation, rubrication, book binding, and the elaborate *ordinatio* of the book refined over centuries. The anonymous scribes of the *London Chronicles* and the *Brut* manuscripts, Caxton, Fabyan, Grafton, Hall, and the Holinshed Syndicate all participate in this common system of textual reproduction. The pages they produce speak of the continued structural presence of manuscript practices in early modern texts, not simply in their aesthetic arrangement but in their report of the way their makers think about textual production, which appears deeply contingent on the past. Hall, Rastell, and the Holinshed Syndicate subordinate this past through their epistles and the shape of their pages, but they do not break from it. Given this continuity, it strikes me as premature, to say the least, to speak of a "print culture" in the sixteenth century.

In sum: the terms of chronicle history change between 1480 and 1587. The stories told by Caxton and the Holinshed Syndicate are vastly different, the one governed by the paradoxes of reproduction, the other by the exigencies of a chronological narrative of political events. One look at the page makes it impossible not to recognize and acknowledge this difference. It is tangible. Still, the so-called early modern histories are nevertheless structured on multiple and profound levels by manuscript production protocols, which they recur upon by embedding their form and content within themselves. In the particular instance of the history of print, this asserts a *durable formal structure* within the chronicles' account of print history. This affinity is obscured by the sixteenth-century chroniclers and antiquarians, such as Hall and Stow, who assert their chronological distance from the fifteenth-century past as a conceptual distance, and by sixteenth-century poets, such as Sidney, who fashion analogies of historical rupture that elide the fifteenth-century into a painful adolescence, one by implication best left forgotten. Shakespeare's Jack Cade shows us this obscurantist rhetoric: he decries printing, though according to the historical accounts that contrive his identity he should not know what it is. The moment we acknowledge his protest and step out of the progressive sequence of historical narrative to recognize him as a recursive construction, we also become aware that print history is not linear, that in fact the most self-reflective moment in the history of printing is ironically the most derivative of manuscript culture. The Folio's *Second Part of Henry the Sixt* can tease out these problems of the history of the book to a greater extent than *The Contention* precisely because the Folio's structure—its use of a generic framework, its insistence on chronological sequence—subordinates the past to a greater extent overall, making most explicit the jarring discrepancy of Cade's complaint. Still, in both cases the plays insist that textual authority is relentlessly double: the terms that allow it to construct authority as self-aware also undermine that authority, and so at its most absurd it launches its most sweeping critique.

Amidst an ongoing world of bookish self-reference, Cade is thus the sign of recursion that moves the play from historical record to literary critique. For more than simply a character, Cade is a recursive function, an instance of self-reference contrived by embedding a return upon its very constitution, and thus he drives the play forward to be productive of something other than history: literary drama. Cade is not the only character that does this, though he does it most flamboyantly. Rather all the main characters recognize to some degree that, walled in by texts as they are, any chance they have at self-reflection appears, like the various chronicle commentaries on printing, to be prefigured by some other text, to be caught in allegory. At the end of *2 Henry VI*, Young Clifford formulates this very problem through an allusion to the *Aeneid*. Coming across his father's body on the battlefield of Saint Albans, he uses this allusion to frame himself as the loyal son. In the *Contention* this reads (Q1, H3):

> Immortall hate vnto the house of Yorke,
> Nor neuer shall I sleepe secure one night,
> Till I haue furiously reuengde thy death,
> And left not one of them to breath on earth.
>
> He takes him vp on his backe.
> And thus as old Ankyses sonne did beare
> His aged father on his manly backe,
> And fought with him against the bloodie Greeks,
> Euen so will I.

The stage directions set up a parallel that Young Clifford's lines elaborate: visually, but also rhetorically, the action of taking up his father modifies his "immortall hate," explaining it not simply as hate but as a moment of carrying paternity onwards, a statement of cultural heritage and identity. The passage is more elaborate in the Folio, with a section frequently attributed to a mature Shakespeare (F1; page 145, O3^{r-v}):

> Henceforth, I will not haue to do with pitty.
> Meet I an infant of the house of Yorke,
> Into as many gobbits will I cut it
> As wilde *Medea* yong *Absirtis* did.
> In cruelty, will I seeke out my Fame.
> Come thou new ruine of olde Cliffords house:
> As did *Æneas* old *Anchyses* beare,
> So beare I thee vpon my manly shoulders:
> But then, *Æneas* bare a liuing load;
> Nothing so heauy as these woes of mine

In both texts, Young Clifford realizes that literary precedent underwrites his current state. In the Quarto the stage directions ask the reader to imagine him lifting his father and thus make the connection to Aeneas as he does. Less is left open in the Folio, where the lines make the link explicit. Further, in the Quarto the allusion suggests that Young Clifford must seek revenge; in the Folio it circumscribes his position before he comments on his father: his "immortall hate" is now "cruelty," and the literary reference gives him license to and a model for any form of violence. Subsequently, Young Clifford's assessment of this Virgilian parallel leads him to realize not just that he is like Aeneas, but that his situation is far more desperate: "*Æneas* bare a liuing load, / Nothing so heauy as these woes of mine." In both Folio and Quarto, Young Clifford finds himself within a preexisting narrative, hemmed in by a prior tragic exempla; indeed, the weight of it presses him down.

"Tragedye maketh a memorie," remarks Lydgate in *The Fall of Princes*, and such is exactly the case with Young Clifford, who defines his experience according to the tragedy. Lydgate's line encapsulates the connection between historical and literary exemplarity—that both demonstrate the turn of Fortune's wheel—and suggests the problem of literary inheritance: memory involves precedence, and no sooner than it is acknowledged than one becomes like Dido, encased in a narrative external to oneself, subsumed in tragedy. Recall Humphrey's lament on Suffolk's treaty with France: "Ah Lords, fatall is this marriage canselling our states, / Reuersing Monuments of conquered *France*, / Vndoing all, as none had nere bene done" (Q1, A3). In the Folio, Humphrey's speech is expanded into a statement on the power of books (F; M3, 121; I.i.93–100):

> Fatall this Marriage, cancelling your Fame,
> Blotting your names from Bookes of memory,
> Racing the Charracters of your Renowne,
> Defacing Monuments of Conquer'd France,
> Vndoing all as all had neuer bin.

Humphrey's speech echoes the terms of Caxton's prologue to the 1482 *Polychronicon*, where he praises "wryters of hystoryes," by comparing historical writings to cities and laws because, he writes, "truly many of hye and couragyous men of grete empryse / desyryng theyr fame to be perpetuelly conseruyd by lyberal monumentis / whiche ben the permanente recordes of euery vyrtuouse and noble Acte."[62]

For Caxton and the historians that follow him, the monumental nature of the book includes within it a mandate for reproduction, and so he allows for no erasing of character, no blotting of names, and no cancellation of fame in historical writing. Humphrey understands the book by the same terms, but like Cade he speaks not of the reproduction of that past so much as its subordination to some other force—righteous justice, tragic realization, political manipulation—that thrusts him into Fortune's turning wheel, to be ground up like the rest in the *de casibus* tradition. My point is neither that *2 Henry VI* imagines the fifteenth century as unable to manipulate texts nor that Humphrey is some sort of modernist finally able to realize appropriately historical distance. Quite the opposite: the play stages a series of readers of social and literary history precisely to identify that the struggle with historical narrative is the struggle with textuality, and thus writes the literary condition into the performance of the lived reality of the past. Young Clifford and Humphrey appear stunned at their situation—devastated, really—and this is part of the play's realization. Jonathan Gil Harris notes "the play's recognition that the Catholic past is less divided from the Protestant moment than all too present within it—and with potentially explosive consequences."[63] I read such an explosion as what Sarah Beckwith terms "the *radical* nature of Shakespeare's medievalism," because if the past is contained within *The Contention*, it is barely so, always impinging on the construction of history to break into the narrative of the present and rupture the delicate levels of subordination that separate moments in time, writing it out in a narrative.[64]

Shakespeare constructs himself as an author by constructing the fifteenth century. In so doing he, and his printers, engage both with the literary marketplace and with generic form, shaping fifteenth-century cultural history in much the way Spenser, Sidney, and Speght shape its literary history, as well as the quarto format, into a literary product. Thus, he dramatizes the fifteenth-century past as a coherent period to be understood as a narrative on the installment plan, and in doing so he represents it but also constructs it as distinct from the present as drama is from history. That is to say, tentatively: barely escaping the horrible realization that time threatens to collapse in on us, that the past is never really at bay, that our consciousness is truly a thin strip, and that we remember much more than we can ever organize in a linear narrative. This realization—that memory is like history and threatens to dissolve a progressive narrative of the self—erupts at moments in Shakespeare's plays and in Shakespearean scholarship, which currently grapples with his identity as an author. With this, Shakespeare presses closely to the ruthless circularity of Dido, of Lydgate, of a Venus who would remove herself and not be seen, to emerge, perhaps awkwardly, into the literary marketplace through the genre of the print quarto. From such a sequence of embedded self-references, by which the past is put forth through the very representations it contrives of itself, Shakespeare emerges as a gentleman author in print.

FOUR

Form

William Caxton's *Recuyell* and William Shakespeare's *Troilus and Cressida*

The recent writing on Shakespeare and the Middle Ages tends to imagine his engagement with the past as enacting a long reach back across the chasm of the Reformation and Tudor history to Chaucer, who appeared to him in William Thynne's and Thomas Speght's canonical editions, and to the mystery plays he assumedly watched.[1] The argument conceives of literary history as bracketed off by period and mediated by authorship. Yet to imagine it as such is ultimately to abandon our disciplinary charge in favor of the grand narratives of monarchical and ecclesiastical fortunes from which literary critics exhume, like the ruins of some lost civilization, powerful moments of authorship.[2] Certainly literature is politically inflected, but it is also formally structured, and it is to the history of these forms that writers of all ages turn.

In place of period, then, I suggest a twofold formal structure: (1) rhetorical in the received tropes and schemes of literary expression and (2) material in the documentary modes that physically articulate and archive literature. Because the physical axis is so important to literature, conceiving of this dual formalism in terms of temporality has less to do with a transition from one period to the next and with authorship as an abstraction capable of withstanding the hazards of time than with understanding how the material intrusion of chronologically older items into later points in time constitutes a powerful aesthetic and intellectual effect. The result of releasing literary history from these predetermined categories is, somewhat ironically, to perform a corrective recursion and recognize the intervening time obscured by periodization. It is, in short, to discover the impact of what William Caxton terms "the terryble feyned Fables of Poetes" of the elided transitionary period as part of Shakespeare's works. As a result, Shakespeare's emergence as an author occurs not only through the construction of the fifteenth century in dramatic narrative but also through the reproduction of its textual forms.

Fifteenth-century writers and printers were well aware of the way textual formalism constitutes the literary subject. One powerful example exists in book 3, chapter 18, of William Caxton's *Recuyell of the Histories of Troye* (1473/74), the section in which Caxton translates Guido delle Colonne's ekphrasis of Hector's tomb (see Figure 4.1). Ornately crafted, the tomb features four golden pillars supporting a golden tabernacle encrusted with precious stones and images of angels. Above this is set "a grete ymage of gold that was maad after the semblance of hector" brandishing a naked sword at the Grecian encampment. "In the myddes of the tabernacle [in] a place voyde," Caxton continues, "the maysters setted and putte the body of hector in flesshe and in bones y cladde in his beste garementes and robes. And stood right vp on his feet . . . veryly in lyke wyse as he had ben on lyue." The tomb thus presents a double image: here is the semblance of Hector; here is Hector. Which is the more daunting, it asks, the golden statute or the standing body? Yet Hector's body is not presented as simply the natural original set out for comparison, innocent of human contrivance; rather, it is itself preserved so that it "myght endure so a longe tyme in that wyse with oute corupco*u*n by certayn scyence," not embalming but simply a vessel placed on "the sommet or toppe of the hede of hector" that drips fluid "doun in to alle the membres of the bodye." Plasticity in representation is ekphrasis's governing theme, and so this passage gives us artifice layered upon artifice, for here there is no natural world to contrast human construction, only repeated forms of representation: the saturated body, the golden effigy, and the literary trope.

In his epilogue to book 3 of the *Recuyell*, Caxton makes a similar distinction between assumed naturalness and fabrication for the printed page, remarking that he has "practysed ⁊ lerned at my grete charge and dispense to ordeyne this said book in prynte after the maner ⁊ forme as ye may here see / and is not wreton with penne and ynke as other bokes ben." The *Recuyell* is printed in Caxton's Type 1, the face cut for him by the master type-designer of the Low Countries, Johannes Veldener, to echo David Aubert's scribal hand. By commenting on this echo, Caxton draws it to the reader's attention, underscoring that the page is not a transparent vehicle for literary meaning but a contrivance, a figuration evoking a prior form, a representation no more natural than Hector's tomb. If the ekphrasis of Hector's tomb sets the reader on notice regarding any presumption of naturalism in the story's evocation of the Trojan heroes, Caxton's epilogue turns this on the page itself, casting its typographical metallurgy as an ekphrasis of literary writing. Bruce Holsinger writes, "ekphrasitic poetics elaborate a kind of literary hall of mirrors: a recursive self-reflexivity that is also a self-reflectivity, a mode in and by which literary language gazes at the visual as a lens upon the beauty of its own performance."[3] Representation is everywhere—in the doubling figures, the evocation of the Trojan past, the page's letters—and nowhere is it to be taken for granted: troping in the *Recuyell* cuts

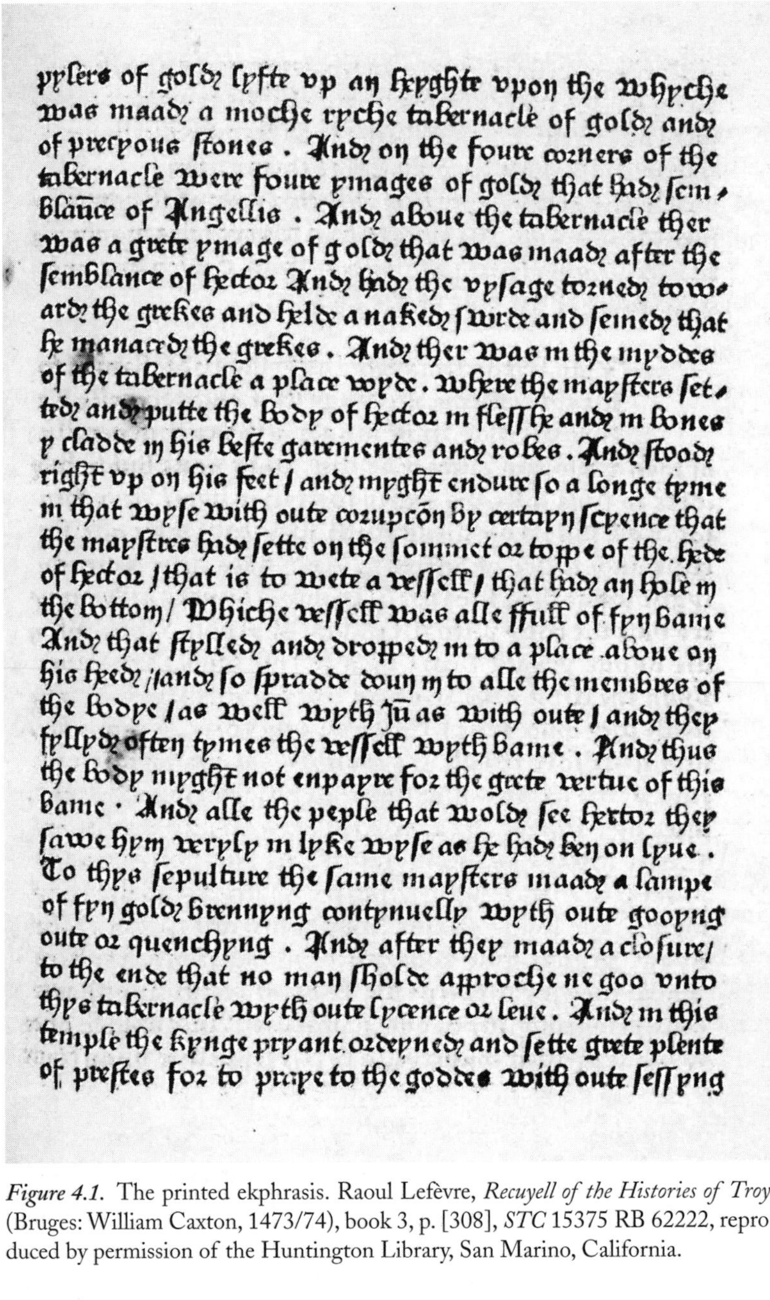
pylers of gold lyfte vp an heyghte vpon the whyche
was maad a moche ryche tabernacle of gold and
of precyous stones . And on the foure corners of the
tabernacle were foure ymages of gold that had sem-
blaūce of Angellis . And aboue the tabernacle ther
was a grete ymage of gold that was maad after the
semblance of hector And had the vysage torned toward the grekes and helde a naked swerde and semed that
he manaced the grekes . And ther was in the myddes
of the tabernacle a place wyde . where the maysters setted and putte the body of hector in flesshe and in bones
y cladde in his beste garementes and robes . And stood
right vp on his feet / and myght endure so a longe tyme
in that wyse with oute corupcōn by certayn scyence that
the maystres had sette on the sommet or toppe of the hede
of hector / that is to wete a vessell / that had an hole in
the bottom / Whiche vessell was alle ffull of fyn bame
And that stylled and dropped in to a place aboue on
his hede //and so spradde doun in to alle the membres of
the bodye / as well wyth īn as with oute / and they
fyllyd often tymes the vessell wyth bame . And thus
the body myght not enpayre for the grete vertue of this
bame . And alle the peple that wold see hector they
sawe hym verely in lyke wyse as he had ben on lyue .
To thys sepulture the same maysters maad a lampe
of fyn gold brennyng contynuelly wyth oute gooyng
oute or quenchyng . And after they maad a closure /
to the ende that no man sholde approche ne goo vnto
thys tabernacle wyth oute lycence or leue . And in this
temple the kynge pryant ordeyned and sette grete plente
of prestes for to praye to the goddes with oute sessyng

Figure 4.1. The printed ekphrasis. Raoul Lefèvre, *Recuyell of the Histories of Troye* (Bruges: William Caxton, 1473/74), book 3, p. [308], *STC* 15375 RB 62222, reproduced by permission of the Huntington Library, San Marino, California.

across any easy division between literary contents and printed form. Caxton's version of Hector's tomb achieves mimesis through a reproduction process that is jointly material and rhetorical, that insists on the verisimilitude of its re-creation of preexisting forms while underscoring its own artificiality.

My guiding question in this chapter, then, is what does it mean to stand at Hector's tomb? On one level, such a question asks after local literary history: What does it mean to build the Troy story on the same ground as past writers? On another level, it asks after the story we tell of literary influence. That is, as we come across the ruins of Hector's tomb in the manuscripts and printed books that constitute our gateway into the past, what do we see? The traditional report has been of a chasm at the exact point of the fifteenth century, a rupture in the panorama of authority and inheritance that invites us to look backward to Chaucer's Middle Ages and forward to Shakespeare's Renaissance. Thus, when Shakespeare returns to the literary past in *Troilus and Cressida*, he is understood as engaging in a long look back across largely unobstructed terrain, his gaze falling not on the fifteenth century, which he thought and wrote so much about, but on Chaucer.[4] This is of a piece with our understanding of Shakespeare's age, one sealed off from fifteenth-century tellings of Troy by milestones such as John Bale's 1548 literary history, Gavin Douglas's 1553 *Eneados*, and Chapman's 1598 translations.[5] In such a model, Chaucer may come before Shakespeare chronologically, but we in fact read him after Shakespeare because his importance is predefined by a narrative structure that is essentially modern, that finds literary greatness in novelty, and that writes literary history as a paradoxical combination of linearity and break. Still, there can be no doubt: Shakespeare's main source for *Troilus and Cressida* is chapters 12 through 17 of book 3 of William Caxton's *The Recuyell of the Histories of Troye*.[6]

The Recuyell is another overtly recursive text. As Caxton's first independent production, it initiates English printing. Reprinted no less than sixteen times, it appears to have had continuous readership through the eighteenth century.[7] In his prologue, Caxton announces that his text comes from three books by the Burgundian court writer Raoul Lefèvre chronicling the three falls of Troy. Lefèvre developed the first two of these from Giovanni Boccaccio's *Genealogia deorum gentilium* and based the third on Guido delle Colonne's 1287 *Historia destructionis troiae*, itself a silent revision of Benoit de Sainte-Maure's twelfth-century *Roman de Troie*. Caxton offers his version of this final destruction of Troy, *The Recuyell's* third book, as a prose alternative to John Lydgate's *Troy Book*, and the association is carried into the sixteenth century, even as Caxton's persona as the first English printer is subordinated to his role as a translator, his language adjusted to fit contemporary standards. Read as merely a source for Shakespeare, *The Recuyell* is no more than a mumble from the caesura separating medieval and modern, a bit of debris for collectors and aficionados reporting nothing significant. Read as part of an ongoing exploration of English form that reproduces a network of texts dating from the thirteenth through the fifteenth century, however, it is a significant moment of origins for English printing that travels through time in a spiral of reproduction and so significantly complicates the clear boundaries of period to argue for a notion of literary history as a process of inheritance, revision, reproduction, and recursion rather than a timeline marked by breaks.

The center of my argument in this chapter is that the issue of representation so alive in the ekphrasis of Hector's tomb is a fundamental theme of Shakespeare's *Troilus and Cressida*—not by accident but by design. For Shakespeare followed *The Recuyell* in the course of his play, and the trace of this engagement remains to us not merely in the quartos and folios labeled with this name but in the sixteenth-century witnesses to Caxton's and Lydgate's works, such as William Copland's 1553 *Recuile of the Histories of Troie . . . Translated out of Frenche in to Englishe by Wyllyam Caxton* and Thomas Marshe's 1555 version of the *Troy Book*.[8] Speaking through the technology of the book, these texts all share a thematic interest in textual formalism; that is, they imagine literature as achieving its representative force by intertwining rhetorical and bookish forms. Because Shakespeare's *Troilus and Cressida* relies first and foremost on Caxton's *Recuyell of the Histories of Troy*, we should be cautious about broad and commonplace distinctions between medieval and modern literature and instead be willing to imagine how textual formalism sustains literature long after its inception. When folded over onto temporality, textual formalism suggests an alterative mode of reading literary history, one that describes not medieval otherness and early modern origins, but the structural problems of representation implicit in vernacular literary production and the power of the literary imagination to overcome those problems.

For *Troilus and Cressida* is a problem, and its problems are inseparable from its material embodiment.[9] These coalesce in the prefatory pieces that front the quarto and folio versions of the play. Both are qualifications of sorts, second thoughts to first attempts inserted after the printing process had begun. The first occupies two leafs asserted onto the initial version of the 1609 quarto, printed by George Eld for Richard Bonian and Henry Walley, and comprises a new title page and an epistle to the reader. This new title page reproduces the earlier title page's format—its engraved design and printer's identification are identical with the first version, which was apparently left standing in the form—but renames the play from *The Historie of Troylus and Cresseida* to *The Famous Historie of Troylus and Cresseid* (see Figure 4.2).[10] It also replaces the original title's performance history ("*As it was acted by the Kings Maiesties* / seruants at the Globe") with plot synopsis ("*Excellently expressing the beginning* / of their loues, with the conceited wooing / of *Pandarus* Prince of *Licia*"). This is followed by the epistle (¶2$^{r–v}$), which Leslie A. Fiedler terms "the earliest extended response to Shakespeare as a writer of comedy."[11] Titled "A neuer writer, to an euer reader. Newes," the epistle contradicts the permission granted on February 7, 1603, to James Roberts in the Stationers' Register, which reports "The booke of Troilus and Cresseda as yt is acted by my lo*rd* Chamb*er*lens Men," as well as the original title page's production history by announcing "Eternall reader, you haue heere a new play, neuer stal'd with the Stage, neuer clapper-clawd with the palmes of the vulger, and yet passing full of the palme comicall."[12] Hence the problems with *Troylus*: the play is "famous" yet its own epistle claims that it has never been acted; it is a history full of the "palme comicall"; its original state occurs not once, but twice.[13] The epistle attempts to consolidate these problems by connecting the play's literary kind (history or comedy) to its material state (theatrical record or freestanding commodity) and offering up a single generic entity—the published, but not played, quarto comedy—but the connection is difficult at best, undercut by the print history surrounding it and the labored explanation within it.

These problems are obviated in the First Folio, which rigorously defines the plays according to author and genre in the authoritative folio-book format. The fit is not quite so seamless in quarto: cheap, dispensable, and unbound, the quartos grasp at formal descriptions to articulate what they are, and so their title pages gesticulate broadly with literary terms before resorting to plot summary while alternately claiming, ignoring, or feinting at authorial identity. We can parse these problems into discrete instances and understand them as the specific confusions of individual printers, but collectively they speak of the difficulty of matching rhetorical and material literary categories. So the quartos exist in a transformational state somewhere between ephemera—the playwright's imagination, the company's improvisation, the live performance, the foul papers, the cheap pamphlet—and the definitive single-author book. As a result they possess the indeterminate literary authority of "bad," memorial, or draft texts. Thus the *Troylus and Cresseid* epistle takes up a problem central to the quartos overall: literary form, or how to classify—materially as a book and rhetorically as an artwork—the play's representational status.

If genre is the epistle's theme, transformation is its mode. "And were but the vaine names of commedies changde for the titles of Commodities, or of Playes for Pleas," it imagines, "you should see all those grand censors, that now stile them such vanities, flock to them for the maine grace of their grauities: especially this authors Commedies, that are so fram'd to the life, that they serue for the most common Commentaries, of all the actions of our liues" (¶2). Changing the title from comedy to commodity or fixing it in legal terms as a plea, the Never Writer tells us, makes the play's benefits so obvious that even the vain censor would see them.[14] This is just what the printer George Eld's revision has done to the title page: it has transformed the play into a commodity through the techniques at his disposal. So the new title page revises the play's name and erases its performance history to make it an autonomous textual object; so the epistle helps this

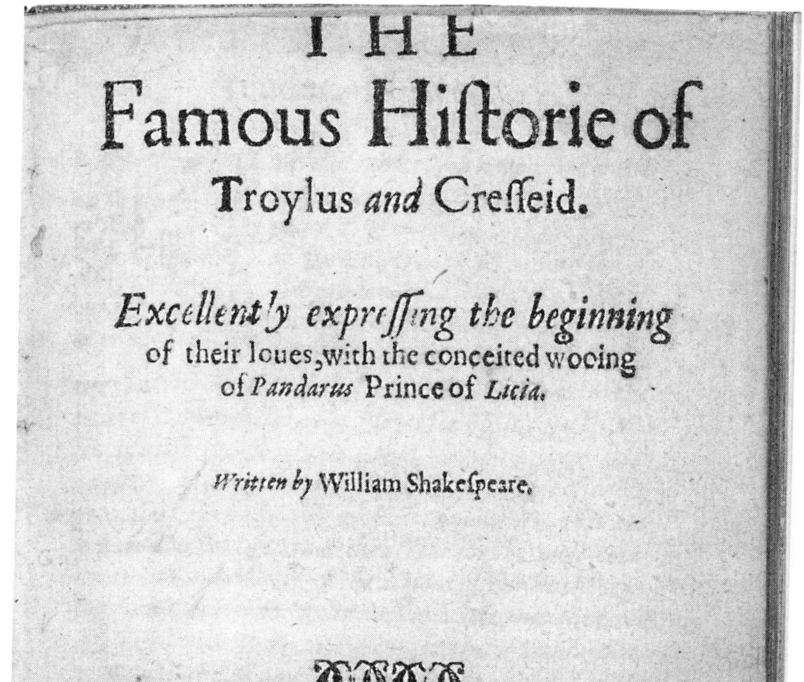

THE

Famous Hiſtorie of

Troylus *and* Creſſeid.

Excellently expreſſing the beginning of their loues, with the conceited wooing of *Pandarus* Prince of *Licia.*

Written by William Shakeſpeare.

LONDON

Imprinted by *G.Eld* for *R. Bonian* and *H. Walley*, and are to be ſold at the ſpred Eagle in Paules Church-yeard, ouer againſt the great North doore.

1609.

Figure 4.2. Second thoughts on *Troilus. The Famous Historie of Troylus and Cresseid* (London: George Eld for Richard Bonian and Henry Walley, 1609), title page, *STC* 22332, reproduced by permission of the Folger Shakespeare Library.

transformation along by moving the contents from history to comedy and then to commodity. The point is that the epistle is not naïve to the complexities of form; however hyperbolically, it presents a transformation of rhetorical and material genres to articulate whatever coherency it can for the quarto as a unified object.

The possibility of transformation is within the epistle in other ways as well. For example, the epistle stakes out a number of finite subject positions—it is written by the "neuer writer," who later assumes the first person, I; we are the "euer" or "Eternall" reader, later "you"; there is also the theatre-going audience, the Censors, and the author. The Never Writer initially casts distinctions between these groups—writers write and readers read, the audience is vulgar, the censors are obtuse—which he soon clouds through the very notion of commodity circulation. So, if the Censors flock to the author's comedies when they are renamed, "when hee is gone," the Never Writer hypothesizes, "and his Commedies out of sale, you will scramble for them, and set up a new English Inquisition" (¶2^{v}). Both Censor and reader not only jostle for texts but do so in a strangely clerical mode: the Censors apparently suppress them, and the reader would set up an English Inquisition. As much as this inquisition is specifically English, the readers are vulgar clerics at that, and so reader, Censor, and audience member are all ultimately connected through their mutual consumption and regulation of English texts. In its slippery way, then, the epistle suggests that textual transformation organizes individuals—reader, writer, author, censor, audience—into a collectivity. Indeed, all these subject positions come together in the play, which comments on "our liues." Thus, in delivering the work from "the smoaky breath of the multitude" (¶2^{v}), the epistle effectively recreates the disparate collective of a theatre-going audience as a textual audience, looking ahead to the constellations of identification between insular community and anonymous commerce, between private and public, that Pandarus makes overt in his closing address to the "Brethren and sisters of the hold-ore trade."[15] The epistle argues that the latent power of comedy to unify—one capable of moving from audience to reader in the transformational process of its own construction—is made palpable as the work becomes a textual commodity.

This recognition is essential to the play's authority, for it is the engagement with the author's wit through the text that changes people so that they "haue found that witte there, that they neuer found in them-selues" (¶2). If genre is the epistle's theme and transformation its mode, literary authority is its product.

Transformation is also a theme in the preface to the First Folio's version of *Troilus*, albeit in a different register. Unlisted in the opening catalogue, *The Tragedie of Troylus and Cressida* is a late addition to the Folio, one only announced on the first page of the play itself, which is wedged between *The Life of King Henry the Eight* and *The Tragedy of Coriolanus*. Again, this late addition grapples with issues of genre: on the one hand, it summons up yet a third literary genre to describe the text, "tragedie"; on the other, it reinscribes the play in a supremely literary material genre: the single-author edition. And again, the modification is essentially an afterthought, for there are a number of variations of the play's initial page: the play seems to have first been placed after *Romeo and Juliet* (a version remains with the last page of *Romeo* on its opening recto) and later inserted after *Henry the Eight* with an entirely blank opening recto.[16] The final version includes a prologue on this recto (see Figure 4.3). Like the epistle it replaces, the prologue enacts a formal reading of the play. Ostensibly, this reading is entirely concerned with narrative: "IN Troy there lyes the Scene: From Iles of Greece," the prologue opens, continuing, "The Princes Orgillous, their high blood chaf'd / Haue to the Port of Athens sent their shippes / Fraught with the ministers and instruments / Of cruell Warre." On this level, the prologue orients the reader to the plot, a necessary step because, as it points out, the play itself "Leapes ore the vaunt and firstlings of those broyles, / Beginning in the middle: starting thence away." Plot leads directly to genre, and on a second level the prologue's epic troping and heroic tone position it on the high ground between history and tragedy, paralleling its physical place in the First Folio's collection of plays.

On a third level, the prologue's scene setting is self-consciously theatrical even as it is textual: addressing the readers as "faire Beholders," it announces that "our Play" jumps into the middle of things, so as to cover only "what may be digested in a Play." Just as the epistle

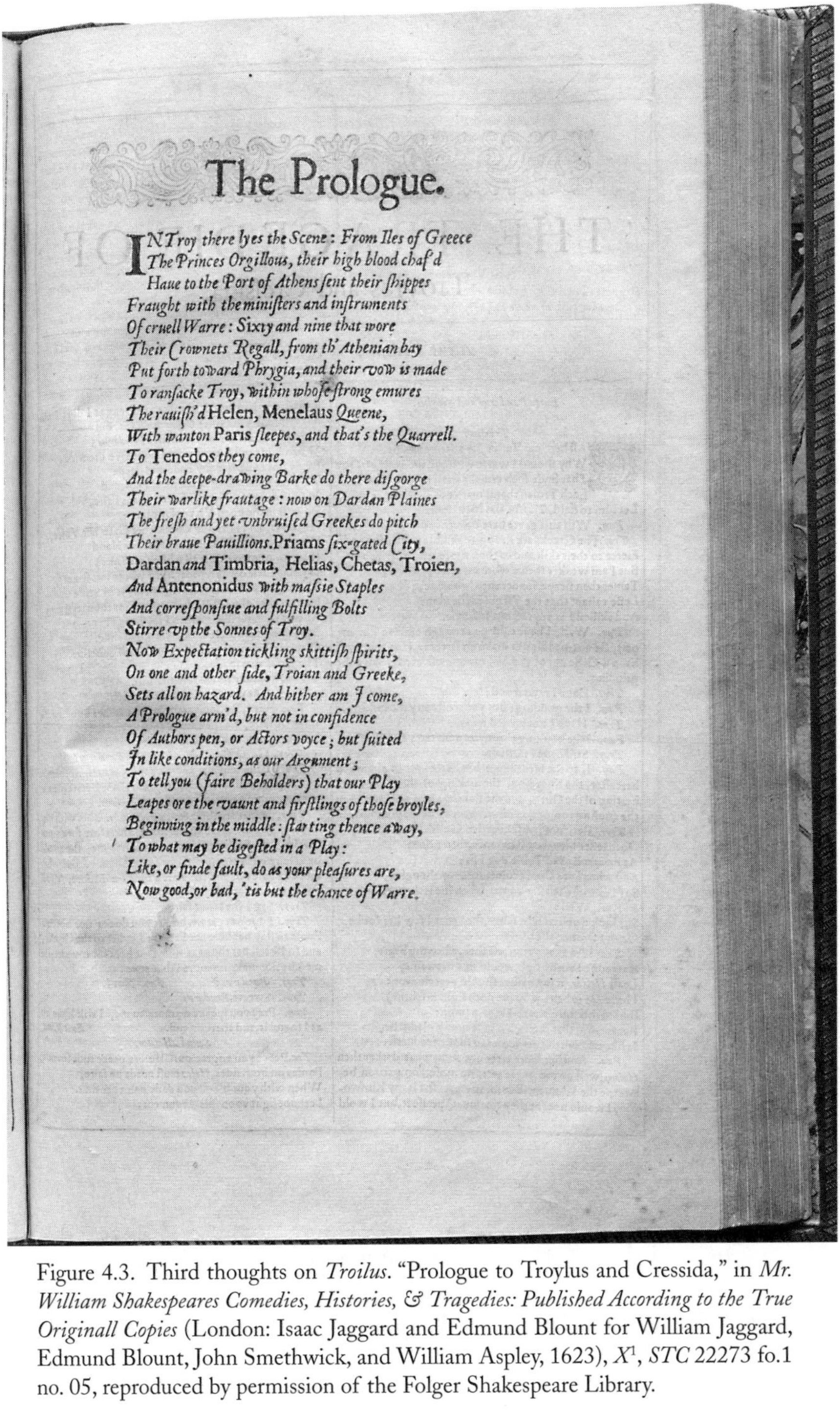

The Prologue.

IN Troy there lyes the Scene: From Iles of Greece
The Princes Orgillous, their high blood chaf'd
Haue to the Port of Athens sent their shippes
Fraught with the ministers and instruments
Of cruell Warre: Sixty and nine that wore
Their Crownets Regall, from th'Athenian bay
Put forth toward Phrygia, and their vow is made
To ransacke Troy, within whose strong emures
The rauish'd Helen, Menelaus Queene,
With wanton Paris sleepes, and that's the Quarrell.
To Tenedos they come,
And the deepe-drawing Barke do there disgorge
Their warlike frautage: now on Dardan Plaines
The fresh and yet vnbruised Greekes do pitch
Their braue Pauillions. Priams six-gated City,
Dardan and Timbria, Helias, Chetas, Troien,
And Antenonidus with massie Staples
And corresponsiue and fulfilling Bolts
Stirre vp the Sonnes of Troy.
Now Expectation tickling skittish spirits,
On one and other side, Troian and Greeke,
Sets all on hazard. And hither am I come,
A Prologue arm'd, but not in confidence
Of Authors pen, or Actors voyce; but suited
In like conditions, as our Argument;
To tell you (faire Beholders) that our Play
Leapes ore the vaunt and firstlings of those broyles,
Beginning in the middle: starting thence away,
To what may be digested in a Play:
Like, or finde fault, do as your pleasures are,
Now good, or bad, 'tis but the chance of Warre.

Figure 4.3. Third thoughts on *Troilus*. "Prologue to Troylus and Cressida," in *Mr. William Shakespeares Comedies, Histories, & Tragedies: Published According to the True Originall Copies* (London: Isaac Jaggard and Edmund Blount for William Jaggard, Edmund Blount, John Smethwick, and William Aspley, 1623), *X*[1], *STC* 22273 fo.1 no. 05, reproduced by permission of the Folger Shakespeare Library.

constructs shifting categories of transformations—from history to comedy to commodity, from individual reader to textual community, from ephemera to literature—the prologue transforms the play once again. Underscoring its gravity and theatricality to produce the play as a textual experience of drama, the prologue retrofits it to the context of the Folio collection of stage plays. Overall, then, both prologue and epistle are formal pieces designed to work in conjunction with the material format of the individual text. Their dynamic interaction is imbricated in specific questions of genre—of the literary genres of history, tragedy, and comedy and the print genres of the quarto play text and the single-author folio edition. It cannot be otherwise. The text is produced through rhetorical and material forms; the two are inseparable for a written document to successfully perform the authority we accord literature.

Like the epistle before it, then, the prologue is caught up in a transformation of genre from an ephemeral action—a play that leaps and vaunts—to a textual thing: "And hither am I come, / A Prologue arm'd, but not in confidence / Of Authors pen, or Actors voyce; but suited / In like conditions, as our Argument." As opposed to the quartos, which teeter on the brink of incoherence as they attempt to produce literary authority in a textual form, the First Folio is so confident in the efficacy of its generic classifications that any loosening of its hold, any reminder that these once were performance pieces, any suggestion that the plays leap and vault of their own imaginative accord appears a mere feint and ultimately underscores its definitive nature as a record of Shakespeare's work. As neither author's pen nor actor's voice, this prologue is fundamentally different from, say, that of *Pericles*, in which Gower enters as an author from the past. For this is a textual voice, an overview of "our Argument," a reading. Specifically, it reads the first eleven chapters of *The Recuyell*, book 3, presenting a montage of essential moments. It sketches *The Recuyell*'s plot, and turning to Copland's 1553 edition, we can read of the "sixty & nine . . . [that] assembled at the porte of Athenes," of their arrival at "the porte of Thenedon," of the encounter on "a greate playne . . . out of the gate named Dardan," and finally of the "sixe principal gates: of Whome that one was named Dardane, ye seco*n*de Timbria, the thirde

Helyas, the fourthe Chetas, the fifte Troyen, and the sixt Antenorides."[17] The prologue picks out lexical details from *The Recuyell* as well, such as Priam's definition of the Greeks as "orguyllous and proude," that they are "chauffyd," that the Grecian "quarel" is specifically that Helen is "rauysshed," and that their tents are "pauyllon[s]."[18]

These details locate the prologue's reading almost exactly. Caxton first printed *The Recuyell* in Bruges in 1473 or 1474; it was revised and reissued in London by his successor Wynkyn de Worde in 1502 as *The Recuyles*, with a variant in 1503. In 1553 William Copland collated these two editions into a third, *The Recuile*, one closer to Caxton's original but following de Worde's double-column format and indexing conveniences while adding roman chapter headings. This text was, in turn, "Newly corrected, and the English much amended, by *William Fiston*" for Thomas Creede and Valentine Simmes's 1596/97 *Destruction of Troy . . . Translated out of French into English, by W. Caxton*. De Worde's edition names the last of the six gates of Troy "ammorydes," not "Antenorides," as in all the other editions.[19] When the prologue cites the six gates, then, it reveals the particularities of its reading, eliminating de Worde's edition as a possible reference. Similarly, Phiston modernized Caxton's language for the 1596/97 version, substituting "pride," "insolent," "high minded," and "hautinesse" for "orgulous" at every turn.[20] The prologue's language also rules out this edition and points specifically to either Copland's 1553 *Recuile* or, more speculatively, to Caxton's original.

The prologue sets the scene, therefore, in both literal and figural terms. Literally, it provides a context for the play's plot, formulating a review of Caxton's Troy story, indeed an explicit reading of Caxton or Copland that hangs on the gates of Troy and the word "orgulous." Figuratively, it defines the text's genre as a play within a definitive collection and, cuing the reader to the upcoming "orgulous" tone as high and somewhat old fashioned, suggests its subgenre as a tragedy, though its physical location in the Folio's organizational framework hedges this definition by placing it in a liminal zone between genres. Appearing neither in Chaucer's *Troilus and Criseyde* nor in Lydgate's *Troy Book*, this term, "orgulous," is not Chaucerian. For Phiston, it is archaic and thoroughly negative, a synonym for excessive pride. Caxton uses it in this manner as well, especially as a doublet with "proud." For instance, in his 1474 *The Game and Play of Chess*, he writes "For hit happeth oftetyme that the ministris by theyr pryde and orgueyll subuerte Iustice and do no ryght," and in the 1477 *Historie of Iason* translates, "Men saye / that the most orguilloust & proudest creature that is / is the deuill."[21] Both of these texts come, like *The Recuyell*, from Caxton's experience of Burgundian literary culture: printed immediately after *The Recuyell* in Bruges, *The Game and Play of Chess* is Caxton's second English text, and though he prints *Iason* in England, it is also by Lefèvre.

"Orgulous" appears in a text authored by an Englishman as well and is throughout *Le Morte Darthur*, which features, among other instances, the "castel Orgulous" in book 9, chapter 3, and the names "Sire Bellangere le orgulous" in book 19, chapter 11, and "Belliau*n*ce le orgulus" in book 8, chapter 41. King Arthur comments on it as an attribute of his character about which he is circumspect: "Thenne arose Arthur / and wente to syr Vwayn and said to sire Tristram we haue as we haue deserued / For thurgh our orgulyte we demaunded bataille of you."[22] One is not always so self-reflective. For example, the first book of *The Recuyell* recounts "orguyllous serpentes," and Bellerophon and Perseus come upon "beastes [that] were cruell and ful of orgueyll"—these creatures are no doubt mighty and proud but inchoately so, not in the sense implied by Arthur's self-criticism.[23] The *Oxford English Dictionary* traces the word's origins to "an unattested West Germanic noun with the sense 'excellence, pride' (compare the corresponding adjective represented by Old High German *urguol* 'famous, renowned')," and this root meaning describes Caxton's use well: Orgulous is a sense of excellence. Perhaps justified, perhaps inarticulate, it is nevertheless so extreme as to be dangerous, as to be satanic.[24]

Book 3 of *The Recuyell* is the most orgulous of all. Where Caxton uses the word four times in books 1 and 2, he uses it five times in book 3 alone, all before the second battle scene and therefore in the portion mapped out by the First Folio's prologue. This is concentrated orgulty. In book 3, chapter 8, Agamemnon addresses the Grecian host at Thenedon "as a good captaine ought," announcing "that it please the gods that it be wythout pryde and felonnye. For it is so that of the sine of pride growe all other vyces, and that ye goddes resist and wythstonde the orgulous and proude people. And therfore we ought to put away pride fro our werkes."[25] Agamemnon names orgulous pride a sin and suggests that the Grecian mission be without it, a dispassionate act of martial justice. He continues: "kynge Pryant dyd dooe requyre vs by hys specyal messangers that we should rendre to him hys Syster Eione: that by our Orguyell and Pryde we woulde not delyuer her agayne, and yf we had delyueryd and sente her home agayne: these euelles had neuer happend."[26] Here Agamemnon voices Priam's accusation from book 3, chapter 1: "for so litle a cause or trespasse as ye know how the grekes by theyr orguyel ben comen in to thys countrey. . . . And for these thynges me semeth that it shoulde be well reason that by the helpe of ye goddes that resist the orguyllous and proude."[27] Yet Agamemnon delivers this observation flatly, not to contest Priam's point so much as to affirm it. He continues, "And there is none of vs that knoweth what shal happen to hym good or euyl." Agamemnon goes on to insist on the rightness of the Grecian claim, to predict the destruction of Troy, and to announce that posterity will favor the Greeks, but ultimately he offers no greater guarantee than this series of observations: the gods resist the orgulous and proud; we could have avoided war; we did not; none of us now knows his fate. Through our orgulty we demanded battle of you, laments Arthur to Sir Tristram, but reflecting on this truth, however profoundly, hardly mitigates its consequences. "Orgulous" defines the third destruction of Troy not simply as of pride, but of a pride that, although self-knowing, plunges headlong into self-destruction.

"Now good, or bad, 'tis but the chance of Warre," closes the prologue to the Folio's *Troylus*, and Caxton's Agamemnon would agree, for both stories write war as the unavoidable and unpredictable consequence of self-proclaimed excellence. The characters in both stories recognize this fact, as Agamemnon does, but are far too orgulous to stop themselves. So in the First Folio version of *Troylus and Cressida*, Ulysses thinks through exactly this problem with Nestor ("I haue a young conception in my braine, / Be you my time to bring it to some shape").[28] "This 'tis," he reflects, "Blunt wedges riue hard knots: the seeded Pride / That hath to this maturity blowne vp / In ranke *Achilles*, must or now be cropt, / Or shedding breede a Nursery of like euil / To ouer-bulke vs all." According to Ulysses, Achilles's pride is a wedge in the Grecian alliance and undoes the knot that binds their union. Such is Ulysses's thinking earlier in the act, when he announces, "This Chaos, when Degree is suffocate, / Followes the choaking," which is to say that such pride will overwhelm the collectivity.[29] Ulysses mulls the metaphor over with Nestor, and by turns Achilles's pride is a wedge loosening a knot of rope and, simultaneously, a chisel splitting a knot in a plank of wood. From woodworking to horticulture: Achilles's "seeded pride" is growing, and growing recklessly, becoming bloated, blocking the sun from the rest of the plants in the nursery—as Ulysses said earlier, so follows the choking. This subtlety with metaphor marks a powerful difference between *Troilus and Cressida* and *The Recuyell*, which is far less delicate with language. Regardless, both versions are concerned with the proper representation of heroic excellence.

Given this overriding theme, Ulysses has less interest in eradicating orgulty than in managing it. He asserts that the Greeks are disorganized, but this assertion provides no brake, no caution against self-inflation. In fact, he implies that perhaps the Greeks are not orgulous enough ("Degree being vizarded"). Thus the conception in Ulysses's brain ages, and the metaphor (pride is a wedge, pride is a chisel) changes to pride is a pruning knife, transforming its destructive force into a tool for Grecian victory, exactly the turn Ulysses takes later in the play when he maneuvers Achilles into meeting Hector in combat. In its insistence on the necessity of orgulty, the entire speech on degree never attains the introspection or regret of Arthur's one-sentence remark to Sir Tristram. Indeed, just the opposite is true: rapacious self-promotion is exactly as necessary in the public sphere as Achilles is to the Grecian cause. For Ulysses, therefore, Achilles's greatest offense is not his orgulty but his willingness to indulge in misrepresentation: "He Pageants vs," Ulysses complains; "He acts thy Greatnessse in."[30] The utility of pageantry is a given in *The Recuyell* and *Troylus* alike, one Ulysses can hardly object to: strutting and posturing are both stories' means of introducing heroes. Rather, Ulysses lays a specific problem of genre at Achilles's tent. According to Ulysses, Achilles makes the Grecian heroes ridiculous: "From his deepe Chest, laughes out a lowd applause, / Cries excellent, 'tis *Agamemnon* iust. / Now play me *Nestor*; hum, and stroke thy Beard. . . . 'Tis *Nestor* right . . . Or, giue me ribs of Steele." Ulysses cannot even summon up Achilles's rendition of him, only comment obliquely that Achilles calls his kind of strategizing "Bed-worke, Mapp'ry, Closset-Warre." Achilles mixes genres, transforming the heroic into farce: "As stuffe for these two, to make paradoxes," he characterizes the Grecian princes not as the stuff of history or tragedy but of a subgenre of theatrical entertainment at the Inns of Court.[31] Ulysses names this kind of pageantry "pale, and bloodlesse Emulation," and this defines his objection overall: the representation is not robust and full blooded. It borders on sickly.

"What is mesmerizing about the idea of emulation," writes Eric Mallin, is that it brings together competition and representation. "For, as a mimetic act, emulation is always to some degree an aesthetic one as well. It is a poetics of success through imitative conduct."[32] This sense of emulation is exactly at issue in Hector's tomb, for following Guido, Caxton describes art as appearing to emulate nature—the golden statue mimicking the real body, the typeface indistinguishable from pen and ink—when in fact it competes with layers of contrivance: the preserved corpse, the rhetorical trope, the technology of writing. And so the threat of sickness: Hector's tomb epitomizes the attempt to represent adequately heroic excellence and the equivalent risk that such an attempt will miss its mark to become bloated and appear merely gaudy—or worse, distended. This is a worry that thoroughly permeates *Troilus*: Ulysses observes that the "enterprize is sicke," Thersites ruminates on the "botchy core" at the heart of things, and the undertow of prostitution, with its hazy connection to disease and plague, taints any possibility for straightforward romantic love in the play.[33] In both Caxton and Shakespeare, representation walks the line between veneration and corruption, a truth for fifteenth- as well as sixteenth-century writing.

The Shakespearean version nuances the existing interest in orgulty by bringing to the story a sophistication in language that frames every passage as a meditation on the limits of trope. With this it intertwines material and rhetorical formalism in the characters' very lines. For example, Hector finds himself read by Achilles and blusters at the book simile, arguing that it specifically fails to account for the depth he would claim for himself: "O like a Booke of sport thou'lt reade me ore: / But there's more in me then thou vnderstand'st."[34] Similarly Troilus, Cressida, and Pandarus are all too aware that posterity will flatten them out, reducing them to words—characters as letters on a page rather than as people. "Let all constant men be *Troylusses*, all false women *Cressids*, and all brokers betweene, Panders," Pandarus proclaims, his bravado cloaking the truth that they are already booked, already read over by generations of readers, already flattened into icons.[35] In this, it strikes me as somewhat disingenuous to read Shakespeare's Cressida in comparison to Chaucer's Criseyde, because to do so is to imagine that the thousands of editions of *The Recuyell* and the *Troy Book* that stand between them had never been published, to pretend that reader and writer come to this character in a vacuum, as if by the sixteenth century she had no intervening figuration in English literature other than Chaucer's.

The obvious truth is that Achilles, Hector, Troilus, Pandarus, Cressida, and the rest are already entombed, already representations of a prior figuration speaking about the process that simultaneously constitutes and limits their evocation. So, though they may not possess the emotional depth of Malory's and Caxton's Arthur, they betray a sophistication about the status of representations that eludes *The Recuyell*'s blocky personages. "Words, words, meere words," moans Troilus, "no matter from the heart," and to say this is to reflect on how Shakespeare's characters are like Hector's corpse: representations with the semblance of life but lacking internal depth.[36] In this, they are indeed self-aware but obliquely so, as Holsinger's self-reflexive and thus self-reflective commentary on literary form rather than as psychologically real.

"Orgulous" is therefore a powerful sign at the head of the *Tragedie of Troylus and Cressida*, though at our first encounter we may not know how to read it. On reflection, it guides the reader in a number of ways. Literally, it marks the prologue's reading matter. On this level the prologue's opening lines, "IN Troy there lyes the Scene: From Iles of Greece," amount to much the same as the first line of Caxton's third book, "For to entre tha*n* into yᵉ mater," in that they invite the reader to lay aside much of the story and concentrate on the war over Helen.[37] So the prologue signals its reading of Caxton's *Recuyell*, or more likely Copland's *Recuile*, and indeed much of *Troilus and Cressida* draws from the eleven chapters it covers: for example, the Trojan women at the city walls; Hector's caution about war and Paris's endorsement of war; and Ulysses's description of Troilus as "a second hope, as fairely built as *Hector*," forecast by Caxton's description that "he resembled moche to Hector, and was the seconde after hym of prowesse."[38] The action of Shakespeare's play occurs from chapter 11's "second battle" through Hector's death in chapter 17, and here too we find much of the play adumbrated by Caxton's prose. Act 4 uses Hector's recognition of Ajax (picking up the specific term "cosyn germayne") and the interview in Achilles's tent ("Achilles behelde hym gladlye for asmuche as he had neuer seen hym unarmed").[39] The rush of act 5 draws out the Trojan attempt to dissuade Hector from combat as he and Troilus arm and also lifts the name of Hector's horse ("Galathe"), Diomedes's capture and delivery of Troilus's horse to Cressida, Hector's penchant for taking armor, his encounter with Achilles in which Achilles is forced to retire, and Achilles's questionable victory.[40] The burning misogyny that underwrites the play overall is a set piece in *The Recuyell*, one its narrative voice often pauses to mitigate or explain away.[41] In fact, the play's somewhat abrupt ending stops just before chapter 18, the chapter describing "the ryche sepulture of Hector." More broadly, the prologue's use of "orgulous" stakes out *Troylus and Cressida*'s overriding genre and theme. Generically, it marks a transformation of narrative material from the generic category of a *recueil* (from the *Oxford English Dictionary*, "a literary compilation or collection") into that of a textual drama leaning from history to tragedy.[42] Thematically, it concentrates this drama on the way self-approbation leads to self-destruction. In the process of transformation overall, the prologue folds the physical problems of genre into the play itself. That is, just as the quarto's title page and epistle focus on the movement from ephemeral production to commodity, denying the one in order to emphasize the other, the First Folio's prologue positions the play as about literary genre and heroic representation. Indeed, it wraps plot, genre, and theme together to suggest a number of thematic and historical relationships between fifteenth-century prose story and seventeenth-century dramatic text.

These relationships demonstrate the power of the book to transcend temporal distance. It is worth pausing over the sixteenth-century publication history of the Troy story to illustrate the point in detail. The version of *The Recuyell* preceding Eld's 1609 quarto of *Troylus* is Creede and Simmes's 1596/97 *Destruction of Troy*, modernized by Phiston. Creede and Simmes were far and away the most ambitious printers of Shakespeare's quartos, printing for publishers such as Thomas Millington, Andrew Wise, Thomas Pavier, and Nathaniel Butter.[43] The closeness between Eld's quarto of *Troylus* and their version of *The Recuyell* suggests that the products connect across various generic boundaries. That is, finding in the quarto format a certain generic looseness, Creede, Simmes, Eld, Bonian, and Walley exploit it, bringing to market products associated in plot and theme. Indeed, Creede and Simmes seem to have divided the production of the *Destruction* so as to separate out the final book, printed by Simmes in 1597. This third book has a unique title page (see Figure 4.4), suggesting its autonomy as a product. Eld's *Troylus* has grillwork identical to Simmes's *Destruction*, and Creede's 1607 edition is quite similar as well. The two texts make a matched set.

The strategy of matching prose and drama is not unheard of in Shakespeare publication: witness interconnections between the 1609 quarto of *Pericles*, printed by William White for Henry Gosson, and George Wilkins's 1608 *The Painfull Aduentures of Pericles Prince of Tyre As It Was Lately Presented by the Worthy and Ancient Poet Iohn Gower*, printed by Thomas Purfoot for Nathaniel Butter.[44] In fact, there are a number of similarities between these two pairs, *Pericles* and *The Painfull Aduentures*, and *Troylus* and *The Recuyell*: both *Pericles* and *Troilus and Cressida* have a strong English literary history, the one stemming from Gower, the other from Caxton, and both, more tangentially, from Chaucer; both, too, have an awkward relationship to the First Folio, the one eliminated entirely, the other a late addition.

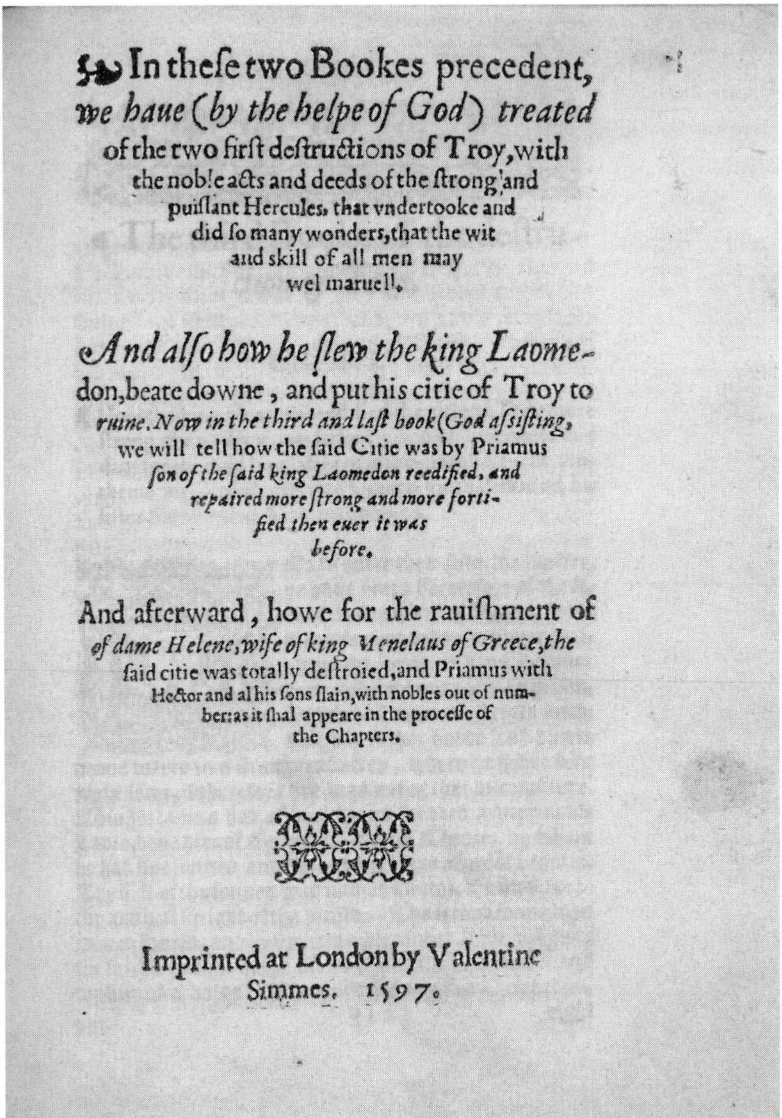

In theſe two Bookes precedent, *we haue (by the helpe of God) treated* of the two firſt deſtructions of Troy, with the noble acts and deeds of the ſtrong and puiſſant Hercules, that vndertooke and did ſo many wonders, that the wit and skill of all men may wel maruell.

And alſo how he ſlew the king Laomedon, beate downe, and put his citie of Troy to *ruine. Now in the third and laſt book (God aſsiſting,* we will tell how the ſaid Citie was by Priamus *ſon of the ſaid king Laomedon reedified, and repaired more ſtrong and more fortified then euer it was before.*

And afterward, howe for the rauiſhment of *of dame Helene, wiſe of king Menelaus of Greece, the* ſaid citie was totally deſtroied, and Priamus with Hector and al his ſons ſlain, with nobles out of number: as it ſhal appeare in the proceſſe of the Chapters.

Imprinted at London by Valentine Simmes. 1597.

Figure 4.4. Repositioning Caxton. *The Auncient Historie, of the Destruction of Troy* (London: Valentine Simmes, 1596/7), title page for book 3, *STC* 15379, reproduced by permission of the Folger Shakespeare Library.

From the vantage point of an established literary history the First Folio is a print masterstroke, yet it is only one material articulation of the possible ways of collating Shakespearean authority, one not necessarily exclusive of other connections. By 1623 Creede and Simmes had printed Phiston's 1596/97 version of the *Destruction of Troy*, and Creede had also gone on to print another edition in 1607, as had Barnard Alsop in 1617. The First Folio was, of course, reprinted in 1632, 1663, and 1664; *The Recuyell*, too, was reprinted across this period, in 1636, and after that in 1663, 1670, 1676, 1680, and 1684.[45] The significant dates here—the 1597 *Destruction of Troy*, the Stationer's report that the play was acted in 1603, Creede's 1607 solo edition of the *Destruction*, Eld's 1609 quartos of *Troylus*, and the seventeenth-century reprinting of Shakespeare's and Caxton's editions—point to a complex intertwining of commercial interests in which prose and play versions appear as complementary products. *Troylus and Cressida* and *The Recuyell* are dynamic partners in print, articulating two literary genres against one another in the symbolic production of literature in a material form.

As much as this pairing implies the immediacy of Caxton's work for Shakespeare's, the editions themselves assert a vast temporal distance. For example, Creede's title page for the entire *Destruction of Troy* develops the material from the prior editions into a modern achievement, both visually and intellectually (see Figure 4.5). The first reprinting of *The Recuyell*, Wynkyn de Worde's 1502/03 edition, had already introduced a number of changes to Caxton's original plan. De Worde created a title page where Caxton had none, added woodcuts, edited and deferred the initial preface, inserted an extended table at the beginning of the text, and merged Caxton's three books into one. In unifying the books around an opening table, de Worde also eliminated Caxton's prologue and two epilogues on the birth of printing, instead finishing the text with a version of Caxton's printer's device and a colophon identifying his shop in London at the sign of the sun (see Figure 4.6). The next significant edition is by William Copland in 1553. Copland's father (or perhaps father-in-law), Robert Copland, worked with de Worde as a translator, editor, and contract printer, eventually opening his own shop. William Copland diverged from de Worde's model by restoring Caxton's paratextual matter, converting the initial preface into a title page, and revising de Worde's table into smaller inserts at the end of books 2 and 3. These decisions reassert the major divisions between the books overall, and so Copland returned Caxton's first-person epilogues as well. The restoration suggests Copland had access to one of Caxton's Bruges editions, now eighty years old.

Creede and Simmes's title page revises the information from Copland's preface into a monumental page, almost an engraving on paper. Here Caxton's manifold roles are divided: he is named a translator—"*Translated out of French into English, by* W. Caxton"—but not an editor or a printer, roles that are divided between the other participants. The text itself is "Newly corrected, and the English much amended. By William Fiston," and Creede is its printer, a role that is divided yet again in book 3, which has a separate title announcing Simmes as its printer. The edition is fronted by an opening epistle, "The Printers to the curteous Reader," which pulls together these various agents into a single voice. The passage concludes as follows:

> And whereas before time, the Translator William Caxton, being (as it seemeth) no Englishman, had left very many words mere French, and sundry sentences so improperly Englished, that it was hard to vnderstand, we haue caused them to bee made plainer English: and if leiure had serued, wee would haue had the same in better refined phrases, and certaine names that bee amisse, conferred with Authours, and made right.[46]

The passage presents Phiston's work as the recovery of the text from obscurity. It is tempting to read Phiston's commentary quite literally, as simply evidence of historical distance, an indication that Caxton's language had become remote by 1596. In this, his comments are reminiscent of William Thynne's assessment in his 1532 edition of Chaucer's *Workes* of Chaucer's English as "rude and imperfite," and of Robert Crowley's discussion of the language of *Piers Plowman* and of the Wycliffite Bible.

In these editions of the *Canterbury Tales*, *Piers Plowman*, and the Wycliffite Bible, the language is of the past but nevertheless

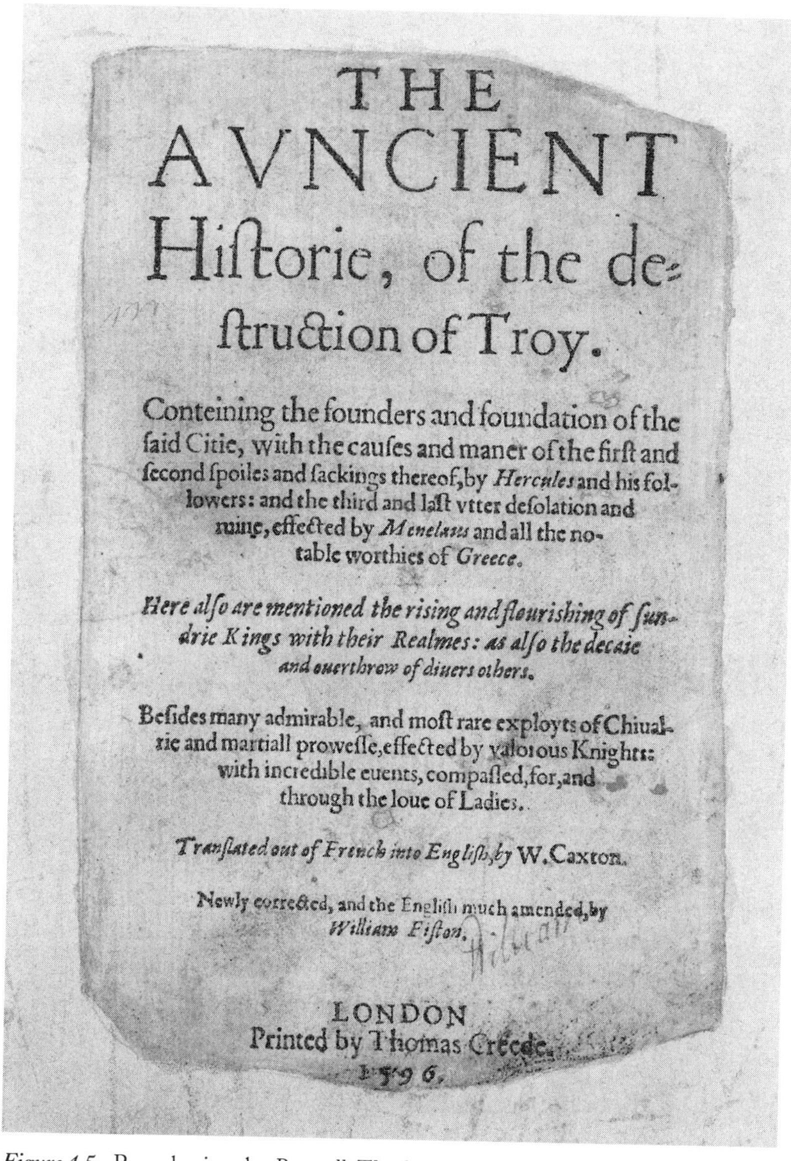

THE
AVNCIENT
Hiſtorie, of the de-
ſtruction of Troy.

Conteining the founders and foundation of the ſaid Citie, with the cauſes and maner of the firſt and ſecond ſpoiles and ſackings thereof, by *Hercules* and his followers: and the third and laſt vtter deſolation and ruine, effected by *Menelaus* and all the notable worthies of *Greece*.

Here alſo are mentioned the rising and flourishing of ſundrie Kings with their Realmes: as alſo the decaie and ouerthrow of diuers others.

Beſides many admirable, and moſt rare exploytes of Chiualrie and martiall proweſſe, effected by valorous Knights: with incredible euents, compaſſed, for, and through the loue of Ladies.

Tranſlated out of French into Engliſh, by W. Caxton.

Newly corrected, and the Engliſh much amended, by *William Fiſton.*

LONDON
Printed by Thomas Creede.
1596.

Figure 4.5. Repackaging the *Recuyell*. *The Auntient Historie of the Destruction of Troy* (London: Thomas Creede, 1596/97), title page, *STC* 15379, reproduced by permission of the Folger Shakespeare Library.

prynce of the chyualrye of the worlde
slewe with his hande by ryall fayete
xviij. kynges by his oonly prowesse w
out eyyll thought. that is to wete the
kynge Archylogus. the kynge Prothe
selaus / the kynge Patroclus / the kyn
ge Menon / the kynge Prothenor / the
kynge Archymenus / the kynge Pole
mon / the kynge Eppystropus / the kyn
ge Cedeus / the kynge Doccius / yͤ kyn
ge Polyxenus / the kynge Phybus / the
kynge Anthyppus / the kynge Cenutus
the kynge Polybetes / the kynge Hume
rus / the kynge Fumus / and the kyng
Exampptus. Parys slewe Palamy-
des the Emperour of the hoost of the
Grekes / the kynge Achylles / the kyn
ge Ayax / Ayax and Parys slewe eche
other. Eneas slewe the kynge Amphy
cus / & the kynge Nereus. Achylles sle
we the kynge Cupemus / yͤ kynge Ypo
neus / the kynge Plebeus / yͤ kynge Au
sterus / the kynge Cymoneus / the kyn
ge Euforbius / the kynge Menon and
yͤ kynge Neptolonyus / & also he slewe
Hector that toke none hede of hym / &
Troylus that his Myrondones had
enclosyd and vnarmed. Pyrrus the so
ne of the same Achylles slewe the que
ne Panthasyle & also he slewe the no
ble kynge Pryant whome he founde
vnarmed and without defence as a
cruell tyraunt / he slewe the fayre may
de Polyxene and the best maner de of
the worlde. Dyomedes slewe the kynge Antyppus / the kynge Escorpyous / yͤ
kynge Prothenor and the kynge Ob-
tyneus. &c.

¶ Thus endeth the boke of the recu-
les or syege of Troye. Enprynted in
London in Flete strete at the sygne of
the sonne by Wynken de Worde. The
yere of our lorde god. M. CCCCC.
and. iij.

Figure 4.6. Recursion as embedding. Wynkyn de Worde's trademark, in *The Recuyles or Gaderinge to Gyder of the Hystoryes of Troye* (London: Wynkyn de Worde, 1503), Kk6v, M.24.22 STC 15376 (variant state), reproduced by permission of the Provost and Scholars of King's College Library, Cambridge.

significantly English, and the editors endeavor to recover meaning from history itself, to leap back to an earlier moment of origins in English writing, and they assert that with a little effort the reader can do so as well. Thynne's Chaucer is a model poet, and Crowley concludes that the language of *Piers Plowman* is "somewhat darcke, but not so harde, but that it may be understande of suche as will not sticke to breake the shell of the nutte for the kernelles sake."[47] Ultimately, Crowley finds the Middle English Bible so luminous that "al darke sentences therin maye be vnderstande."[48] Thynne and Crowley acknowledge that the text is difficult, but they fully expect their readers to follow it. Phiston's discussion of *The Recuyell* is fundamentally different. He argues that the text must be recovered not from history but from Caxton: so he brands Caxton's translation "improper" and "hard to understand," so he asserts that the text is filled with corruptions, and so he concludes that the language suggests Caxton was no Englishman. Phiston's critique is therefore ultimately one of authority, not of history, and accordingly Caxton is irredeemable, a foreigner.

Again, it is tempting to read the assessment of Caxton as simply an effect of historical distance: that by 1596 the autobiographical material so finely placing Caxton as an Englishman, so clearly articulating his combined roles as translator, writer, financier, printer, and publisher, had been lost, filtered out by time. Looking through the text, however, it is clear that Phiston used Copland's edition, not de Worde's. We can see this in the way the book divisions fall so as to break the text into separate units and in the way the tables appear at the end of each book. Phiston had access to all of Caxton's material: to his autobiographical prologue, to his careful explanation of his relationship with Margaret of York, to his narrative of the birth of English printing. Phiston actually includes lightly revised selections of this material, all of which is entirely unavailable in de Worde's version. So in the last pages of the second book, Caxton speaks to the reader through Phiston's hand, telling him or her that

> And as for the third booke which treateth of the generall and last destruction of Troy: It needeth not to translate it into English, forasmuch as that worshipfull and religious man Iohn Lidgate

> moonk of Burie did translate it but late, after whose worke, I feare to take upon me (that am not worthy to beare this penner and inke-horne after him) to meddle at'all in that worke. But yet, forasmuche as I am bound to obey and please my said ladies good grace: and also that his worke is in rime: and as farre as I knowe it is not had in prose in our tongue . . . I haue deliberated in my selfe, for the contemplation of my said redoubted Lady, to take this labour in hand.[49]

In "our tongue"—the narrative announces to its reader that Caxton has to be an Englishman; moreover, it offers Lydgate as a clear literary precedent for Caxton and by extension for Phiston. Phiston works more quickly with the epilogue to the third book, leaving much of the discussion of Lady Margaret intact, but editing Caxton's comments on print down to a single phrase: "I have caused this book to bee Printed: that being published the more plentuously, mens turns may be the more easily served."[50] Here the one actual moment of origins in the history of English printing—the moment Caxton decides to print *The Recuyell*—is no origin at all. Caxton seems no Englishman; the birth of printing is simply publishing. Phiston tells a book history replete with citations of Lydgate and tales of female patronage—and thus detailed and knowing—but also resolute that the past is no authority for the present—if leisure had served he might have revised it further still. Here is a literary history of influence and denial, one in which fifteenth-century literary culture actively inflects how modernity is written, even as it is alienated into history.

This alienation has tended to overwhelm the significance of Caxton's understanding of literary history for recent scholarship. Witness James Simpson's argument in *1350–1547: Reform and Cultural Revolution*: "the works of Leland and Bale . . . are, however, the first attempts to shape a British, or even English, tradition as an identifiable national tradition of letters."[51] Simpson's claim for the originality of sixteenth-century writers denies exactly Caxton's point—Caxton premises his authority on his ability to articulate English literary history, to comprehend Lydgate's biography (in Caxton's *Recuyell*, "dan Iohn lidgate monke of Burye"), to assess the texts' circulation in English ("as ferre as I knowe hit is not had in prose in our tonge"), and to account for their transmission ("he translated after some other Auctor"). He does this repeatedly in his prologues and epilogues when he praises Chaucer by weaving his encomium from lines of Lydgate, when he frames his romances in terms of the array of versions available in vernacular languages, and when he links multiple texts in series.[52] As his epilogue to book 2 of *The Recuyell* continues, it is his implicit control of the categories of authorship and literary history that ground his introduction of a new literary genre—the printed English prose *receuil*—as related to, but different from, the preexisting genre of the English verse manuscript. According to Caxton, the introduction of this new form depends on the different aesthetic appeal inherent in different generic forms; as he says, "dyuerce men ben of dyuerce desyres. Some to rede in Ryme and metre. and some in prose." He makes this connection between genre, readership, and desire throughout his career, most famously in the 1483 *Canterbury Tales*, the 1485 *Le Morte Darthur*, and the 1490 *Eneydos*, each of which names authors, includes references to a range of works, and situates the location of reading in Caxton's study. Rather than some sort of instability in authorship or murkiness about literary history—all to be sorted out in the sixteenth century—by the fifteenth century the material text is understood to embody a process of reproduction of vernacular literary history in its relationship to generic form.

The early modern *Recuyell of the Hystoryes of Troye* therefore comes to embody a narrative in which the past is no model for the present but is nevertheless still quite contemporary, still a frame for current writing. Such an ambivalent relationship to history textures the ensuing editions of *The Recuyell*, all of which rely on the Creede and Simmes's edition and carry some version of its epistle. With Barnard Alsop's 1617 edition, these texts bear a title page announcing them "corrected and much amended" and numbering them in sequence. This numbering suggests a linear narrative of book history, a reckoning of time and books as progressively improving. Within such a chronology lies contradiction, however, for Alsop does not claim his edition is the first, but the fifth. Thus, though it derives from Copland's 1553 edition, it traces its origins back to de Worde's 1502/03 edition. *Knowingness*: to make this count, Alsop had to be aware of all the editions before him. Rather than simply positing a linear trajectory, this supplementary edition—the first—implies that the point of origin does not quite start the sequence. Caxton's edition is the repeated first digit in the sequence, the first Fibonacci numeral that occupies two positions at the very beginning of the process. Indeed, de Worde's printer's mark, embedding rather than replacing Caxton's sign in the system of reproduction, suggests this fundamental plan from the start: the past is encased, not replaced, in the present. Linearity premised on break, continuation as revolution—this is a print history that nests the past within it, that loops backwards even as it spirals forward to find its future in the first years of print.

What is amazing about the technology of the book is that because Caxton's *Recuyell* is encased within each new edition, its intellectual statement is never fixed at a single chronological point in time and so never stops articulating a relationship between genres, never stops seeking out new relationships, and never stops transforming the text. Books endure, and whether we imagine the First Folio's prologue to *Troylus and Cressida* an intrinsic part of the original play or an afterthought added in the final production process—a passage intruded from the lost prompt book, a notation added by Shakespeare in some final authorial revision, a contrivance of the Folio's editors—it announces that Copland's 1553 edition (if not Caxton's original) remained in use even as Phiston was revising Caxton's orgulous language and his work was being reprinted by Creede, Alsop, and others. So the quarto and folio versions of *Troilus* are involved in the very process of generic negotiation articulated in terms of verse and prose by Caxton, *simply because Caxton's text was still being read.* Indeed, for these later readers, the project of initiating print, of imagining the relationship between type and handwriting, of assembling literary history is instigated *not* by Caxton's relationship to Lydgate in the fifteenth century but by his relationship to Lydgate in the sixteenth and seventeenth centuries.

For example, the connection Caxton casts between his 1473/74 printed *Recuyell* and some unidentified manuscript of Lydgate's *Troy Book* is recast for the sixteenth-century reader as between it and, perhaps, Richard Pynson's 1513 edition of the *Troy Book*, or between Copland's 1553 edition of *The Recuile* and Thomas Marshe's 1555 *Troy Book*, or between any combination of the above.[53] In "the pistle to the reader" that begins Marshe's edition, Robert Braham takes up this very issue, discussing "Caxtons recueil" (which he terms "but a longe tedious and brayneles bablyng, tendyng to no end") and championing Lydgate ("And so by these degrees, hath bene at the laste by ye diligence of Iohn Lydgate a moncke of Burye, brought into our englyshe tonge").[54] In this way, Braham effectively re-creates the tension Caxton himself perceived in the fifteenth century but does so by triumphing Lydgate for the sixteenth. For the seventeenth-century reader, this network of associations is expanded even more by the ensuing editions of *The Recuyell* and by Thomas Purfoot's 1614 *The Life and Death of Hector . . . Written by* Iohn Lidgate *Monke of Berry*.[55] These texts did not go unread: John Tatlock sources Robert Greene's 1587 *Euphues His Censure to Philautus*, George Peele's 1589 *Tale of Troy*, Thomas Heywood's 1609 *Troia Britanica*, 1611 *Golden Age*, 1613 *Brazen Age* and *Silver Age*, and 1632 *Iron Age*, as well as the plays listed in the "Admiral Fragment" (BL MS Additional 10449) to Caxton's *Recuyell* and Lydgate's *Troy Book*.[56] The central point—to my mind even more important than the print strategies of marketing Troy in various formats—is this durability: the physical nature of the book ensures that it reproduces its contents as immediate. My point is not merely that literature is produced through textual formalism but that this textual formalism is *persistent*, reproducing chronologically older texts not as dormant fossils of an earlier literary period suitable only to antiquarian interests, but as speaking to the reader and therefore actively shaping contemporary writing.

Moreover, the physical page, and not the edition or the ideal nature of the literary work, is the primary instrument of such literary reproduction. For instance, Copland's rendition of *The Recuyell* expresses temporality not as an abstract chronological progression in time, but as a dimensional movement through space (see Figure 4.7). Here de Worde's double columns of text are juxtaposed with roman chapter headings. The effect is to manage the reader, to carry him or her from medieval black-letter text to modern editorial voice and

forowe, for she was his soueraygne
lady of loue, and in semblable wise
Breseyda loued stronglye Troyllus. and she made also the greatest
sorowe of the worlde for to leaue
her soueraygne lorde in loue. There
was neuer seen so mouche sorowe
made betwene two louers at their
departynge, who that lyste to here
of all theyr loue: let hym rede the
booke of Troyllus that Chaucer
made, wherein he shall fynde ẏ story whole, whyche were to longe to
write here, but finablye Breseyda
was led vnto the Grekes whome
they receyued honourably. Among
them was Diomedes that anon
was enflamed wyth the loue of
Bryseyda, whan he sawe her so
fayre, and in ridinge by her side: he
shewed to her all his corage, and
made to her many promysses and
specyally desired her loue, and thā
whan she knew the corage of Dyomedes: she excused her sayinge that
she woulde not agree to him ne refuse him at ẏ time, for her hert was
not disposed at ẏ tyme to answer
other wyse. Of thys answer Dyomedes had greate ioye, for asmuch
as he was not refused vtterly, and
he accompanyed her vnto the tente
of her Father, and halpe her downe
of her horse, and tooke fro her one
of her glooues that she helde in her
handes, and she suffred hym swe-
tely. Calcas receyued her w great
ioye, and whan they were in priue-
tie betwene hem bothe: Breseyda
sayde to her father these and semblable wordes.

HA, a, my father how is thy
wytte fayled that were wōte
to be so wise and the moste honou-
red and belouyd in the citie of troy,
& gouernedst al ẏ was win, and had
dest so manye richesses and posse-
ssions, and hast ben traytour thou
that oughtest to haue kepte thy richesses and defended thy countrey
vnto the death: but thou louest better to lyue in pouerty and in exyle
amonge the mortal enemies of thy
countrey. O how shall this turne
to thy greate vilonye: certes thou
shalt neuer get so muche honoure:
as thou hast goten vilonye, and ỹ
shalt not onli be blamed in thi life:
but ỹ shalt also after thy death & be
dampned in hel. And me semeth yet
it had ben better to haue dwelled
out of the people vpon some yle of
the Sea, than to dwell here in thys
dishonour and vilony, wenest thou
that the grekes holde the for trewe
and faythful, that art openly false
& vntrewe to thy people: Certes it
was not onli the god Appollo that
thus abused thee: but it was a cōpa
ny of deuils. And as she th⁹ spake
her father: she wepte strongly for yͤ
displeasur that she had. &c.

HA, a, my doughter sayd Calcas, than wenest thou it is a
sure thinge to despyte the answer
of the goddes, and specially in that
thinge that toucheth my health: I
know certaynly by their answers
that this warre shal not dure lōge
that the Citie ne shalbe destroyed,
and the nobles also and the burgei
ses, and therfore it is better for vs
to be here safe, than to be slayne
wyth thē: and than finisshed they
their parlament. The comynge of
Breseyda pleased muche to all the
Grekes, and they cam thether and
feasted her, and demaūded of her ti
dynges of Troy and of the kynge

Priant

destruccion of Troye fol.xx ii.

Pryam,and of them that were with in,& she said vnto hem as much as she knew curtoysly.Thā al ẏ greatest that were ther:promysed her to kepe her and holde her as dere as her doughter,and than eche man wente into hys owne Tente,and there was none of hem but that gaue to her a iewell at the departynge,and than it pleased her wel to abide and dwell wyth the Grekes,and forgat anon the noble citie of Troy,and the loue of the noble Troyllus.O how sone is the purpose of a woman chaunged & turned:certes more sooner than a man can saye or thynke,now late had Breseyda blamed her Father of the vyce of traysō,which she her selfe excersised in forgettynge her countrey and her truce frende troyllus.&c.

How the Grekes and troyans begā the sixt batayle that dured by the space of thirty dayes in whiche were many kinges and prices dead of that one syde and of that other,and how diomedes smote doune Troyllus of his horse & sente it to Breseyda hys loue that receyued it gladly.&c.

After the thre monthes of truce passed: on the morne betymes the Troyans apparayled them to batayle.And whan Hector had ordeyned all hys batayles : he issued out first and tooke with him fyftene thousande fyghtynge men and troyllus folowed him with tē thousāde knyghtes,after hym cam Paris wyth thre thousande fyghtynge men and good archers and well horsed . After came Deyphebus wyth thre thousand fyghters, after hym came Eneas and the other all in ordre so mani that there were this daye of the partye of the Troyans:more than an hondered thousande good fyghtyng men and hardy.Of the party of the Grekes came al there fyrst Menelaus with seuen thousande knightes, and after hym Dyomedes with as many, and than achilles that lad also leuen thousande,the kynge Pampitus with a great multytude of knyghtes , and the other after lyke as they were ordeyned. The Kynge Philes aduaunced him alther first, and Hector came agaynste hym so strongly that he slewe hym wyth hys spere.Thā there arose a great crye of his death amonge the Grekes,and the occysion and slaughter began so greate:that it was an horrible sight to se as well of that one syde as of that other.The king Pampitus slewe manye Troyans for to venge the death of his vncle & assayled Hector,but Hector gaue hym so greate a stroke wyth hys swerde that he slewe him also,and for to auēge his death the Grekes slewe manye of the Troyans . Achilles slewe manye noble men, amonge the whiche he slewe the duke Byraon,and Euforbe that was a moche noble man : Hector was this daye sore hurte in the visage and bledde greate plentye of bloud and wyste not who had doen it, and therefore the Troyans reculed vnto the walles,and whan hector behelde and sawe vpon the walles the quene Hecuba his mother and hys systers:he had greate shame,& by greate yre assayled the king Menon cosyn of Achilles,& gaue him so manye strokes wyth his swerde vpon his helme:that he slewe hym seinge Achilles,that wende for to haue enraged and tooke a stronge spere

Figure 4.7. Mediating history. *Recuile of the Histories of Troie* (London: William Copland, 1553), book three, fol. xxvii^{v}–xxviii^{r} (misnumbered xx.ii), *STC* 15378 RB62194, reproduced by permission of the Huntington Library, San Marino, California.

back. Typographically these are graphic tropes for temporality, and if literary language can be defined by troping, I argue that this is true for the material text as well. Further, within this very page, we can see that Caxton himself was intent on managing the readers' relationship to the past in his initial revision of Lefèvre's text, for six lines down the left-hand column, Caxton folds Chaucer's *Troilus and Criseyde* into Guido's *Historia destructionis troiae*, writing, "There was neuer seen so mouche sorowe made betwene two louers at their departynge, who that lyste to here of all theyr loue: let hym rede the booke of Troyllus that Chaucer made, wherein he shall fynde ye story whole, whyche were to longe to write here."[57]

When William Shakespeare moved through this page, as he most likely did, his perception of the relationship between the past and the present was truly involute: Managed by the typography, the page continually reminds him that he is reading a narrative located in the black-letter past but mediated by the roman present. He is no less managed by Caxton's voice from this past, one that reminds him not to forget literary history, not to pass over Chaucer's place in this history, and not to neglect the two stories being told here—one of an arrogant war and one of a betrayed love—than he is managed by his own voice, one that, like any reader's, hears Diomedes's requests, Criseyde's delay, and her speech to Calcus in the right-hand column that he too shall be reduced to a mere representation ("ye shalt not onli be blamed in thi life: but ye shalt also after thy death").

The physical book operates in the same way as its contents: both attempt to represent the fullness of life in a textual form but depend on the reader's engagement—in this particular case Shakespeare's—to give them life. Mimesis in the face of corruption: the book is an orgulous technology. Its potency lies in its excellence in the representation of literary material, and so it transcends its period of origination to communicate its contents beyond their invention. But this excellence comes with no promise. The book moves through time, simultaneously dated, decrepit, a relic of the past, and urgent and alive in its reader's hands. Energized by the press, the book's orgulty represents literature as paradoxical—contained within time and immediate.

Because of this immediacy in relation to time, what we think of as medieval writing is present and alive in early modern poetics. Take, for example, the *Troy Book*. Lydgate, author of courtly and mercantile mummings, was himself a dramatist and in the *Troy Book* dilates on tragedy and comedy as specifically dramatic genres.[58] Like Guido before him and Caxton after him, Lydgate initially describes Troy as a place of artifice by emphasizing the tremendous craftsmanship that goes into Priam's rebuilding of the city. In contrast to both Guido and Caxton, Lydgate introduces an ekphrasis of a dramatic performance during this preliminary section, opening with an excursus on the dramatic forms of tragedy and comedy. Of course, Chaucer famously defines *de casibus* or "Gothic" tragedy in his translation of Boethius's *Consolation of Philosophy* and in the prologue to *The Monk's Tale*. He also cites both tragedy and comedy in *Troilus and Cresyede*.[59] Though Chaucer never articulates a definition of comedy, most scholarship proceeds as if Lydgate's discussion in the *Troy Book* is entirely derivative of this earlier work.[60] As a result Lydgate's dramatic sensibility is perceived as having nothing to contribute to Shakespearean themes. But this is a tautological proof, dependent entirely on eliding the fifteenth century into a long English Middle Ages that finds its significance in Chaucer's initial formulation of courtly writing. In truth both Chaucer's and Lydgate's understandings of tragedy are derivative.[61] Liberated from this predetermined historical structure and recognized as available in sixteenth-century editions, indeed as embedded in publishing schemes and drawn on as a source for a number of plays, Lydgate's *Troy Book* takes on greater importance for literary history. If we turn to Marshe's 1555 edition of the *Troy Book*, we find that Lydgate is interested in exactly the problems surrounding *Troilus and Cressida*: the relationship between the Troy story and genre, and how one genre can transform into the next.

Lydgate expands on Chaucerian tragedy by defining it in relation to comedy. The two have this "fynall difference" he tells us: "¶ A comedye hath in his gynnynge, / A pryme face a maner complaynynge, / And afterwarde endeth in gladnesse," but tragedy "begynneth in prosperitie, / And endeth lykewyse by aduersytie."[62] This conception of tragedy is deeply Boethian—it is centered on a fall—but it is also complementary to comedy, the subsequent rotation of Fortune's wheel that reverses adversity, bringing it to gladness. For Chaucer, tragedy is entirely unidirectional: it is a singular fall from grace epitomized by Adam's choice and brutally reenacted across human history. As a result, Chaucerian tragedy is relentlessly ahistorical, and so Chaucer applies the definition to pagan, Hebrew, and Christian exempla. By defining tragedy in relation to comedy, Lydgate implies that one form might ever be transformed into the next, that the fall might also be a redemption. Lydgate's tragedy is not universal but dependent on history, not a closed form but open to the contingency of events. This is part of Lydgate's definition in that tragedy alone "doth also of the conquest treate, / Of ryche kynges and of lordes great. / Of mighty men and olde conquerours."[63] In this vein, the entire discussion is merely a prelude for the ekphrasis, which writes a historical account of Trojan performance. Here Lydgate depicts the semicircular Trojan theatre on which an altar and pulpit sit. He visualizes the "auncient poete" who mounts the stage. As this poet sings, Lydgate reports, blood leaves his face ("With deadly face all deuoyde of blode"), and a chorus of masked players emerge from a tented section of the theatre.[64] The song continues, cycling from joy to heaviness, from comedy to tragedy, and with this the blood ebbs and flows from the poet's face. The action is paralleled by a transfiguration of the chorus's masks, "So that there was no maner discordaunce, / Atwen his ditees and their contenaunce." Lydgate's emphasis on blood is one with the economy of representation we see in Caxton and Shakespeare, in which the ability to manipulate the presence and absence of blood is no less than the ability to achieve the illusion of representation.

In the *Troy Book*, this first ekphrasis operates as a balance to that of Hector's tomb, the one introducing Trojan art before the war, the other bringing it to its height at the truce just after Hector's death. Lydgate substantially amplifies upon Guido delle Colonne in this second passage, exaggerating both the techniques of preserving Hector's body and its results. "By subtyll crafte as it were lyuynge," Lydgate begins, granting Hector virtual life, "Of face and cheare and of quicke lokinge, / And of coloure southly and of hewe, / Beynge as freshe as any rose newe."[65] Rather than simply a vase that uses the force of gravity to carry fluid through Hector's body, Lydgate's Hector is permeated by "pipes artyfyciall / Through necke and head into many place, / Penetrable by vaynes of the face." Sweetening the colors and heightening the contrivance, Lydgate immerses the reader in formal technique as well as its results. So we are implicitly invited to imagine the labor of making, of threading these tiny rods through Hector's face, his breast, arms, hands, and feet, and tempted to read this into Lydgate's own tropes, his use of simile and amplification to construct the passage overall. This rhetorical amplification has the material result that Hector is, if not sentient, otherwise alive—"Comparisoned as it were semblable, / To a soule that were vegetable, / The whych without sensybelyte, / Ministreth life in herbe, floure, and tre." Caxton's version presents mimesis through reproduction; fitting a printer, his notion of artistic production relies on techniques of material duplication to represent—indeed, replace—the natural world. For Lydgate, the poet, the passage is similarly about reproduction but focused on the way formal artifice—similes and small pipes—narrows the distance between fabricated representation and original life, making a living art lacking only consciousness. In both cases, Hector's tomb is a metonym for literary formalism that combines rhetorical and material making into a single vernacular statement.

Again, Simpson's reading in *1350–1547: Reform and Cultural Revolution* affords a useful contrast to my argument. There he reads Hector's tomb as it is rendered in John Whalley's *Destruction of Troy*, a fourteenth- or early-fifteenth-century descendant of Guido's *Historia.* Simpson argues that "the poet's description of the tomb places so much emphasis on the very ingeniousness of the craftsmen who constructed it that heroism is displaced by admiration for macabre engineering. There is nothing here of the divine technology of the *Aeneid*. . . . There is, certainly, no stellification of dead heroes."[66] Simpson's reading limits the scene to admiration of the gruesome literal, surely a lesser intellectual interest than the divine figuration he finds in the *Aeneid.* Remaining in only one manuscript and never printed, Whalley's telling is minor for literary history, yet as Simpson parallels it with Lydgate's *Troy Book* and does not explore *The Recuyell*, his conclusion must stand for all: "In the fifteenth century the 'tragic' is the preserve of clerics, who certainly address the interests of secular warriors, but who speak from a distinct and partly oppositional discursive position."[67] Without literary history, uninterested in the deeper issues of heroism, insulated by clerical authors, and defined by totalizing genres, Simpson's fifteenth-century literary culture is contained by period. Yet Caxton is no cleric, and Lydgate writes of a fluid sense of tragedy and comedy. Indeed, these blurred distinctions—the mercantile nature of literature, the slippage between genres—define the English editorial problems of *Troylus* well into the seventeenth century. And is it not exactly the issue of stellification that so interests Lydgate, Caxton, and Shakespeare in the notion of orgulty? Is it not exactly the problem of artistic mimesis—the possibility that human labor might figure life from pale and bloodless technology—that Lydgate broaches with his similes and tiny rods and Shakespeare with all the strutting on the stage? As a metonym for art, Hector's tomb demonstrates how the tomb, the book, the performance, the trope, and the typeface are jointly rhetorical and material. Hence my point in insisting on a textual formalism: literary history is a story of imitative conduct, one in which each author—Lydgate, Caxton, Shakespeare—is first a reader who returns to the past through the text and then a writer who engages, and thereby continues, that past. Readership, literary culture, and transformation: literary history differs from political history in that it has the ability to circumscribe temporality to tell not of linearity but of recursion, not of historical period but of transcendence.

What does it mean, then, to stand at Hector's tomb? We should look to Achilles. For the task facing Lydgate—facing Caxton and Shakespeare as well—is to tell a story that has been told before, to represent in the wake of prior writing. Thus, Lydgate's *Troy Book* is filled with commentary on previous writers: on Guido, Homer, Ovid, but above all Chaucer. Yet Lydgate's most involved engagement with Chaucer—when Achilles stands at Hector's tomb—is unmarked. Here, in book 4, Lydgate writes of Achilles's visit to Hector's tomb in terms strikingly reminiscent of Troilus's encounter with Criseyde in the Palladium in Chaucer's book 1. The scenes are parallel: gazing on Criseyde, Troilus is struck through his eyes by her beauty; so too

Achilles gazes on Polyxena. Now hot, now cold, both heroes retreat to their beds.[68] The scenes are overtly about representation. Chaucer's Troilus makes a mirror of his mind in which to view Criseyde; standing before Hector's tomb, Achilles and Polyxena exist in a world of aesthetic contrivance.[69] If Hector's tomb is a metonym for artistic rendering, Achilles comes to it as a representation given life by a silent appropriation from an earlier text, an emulation of Guido's Achilles filtered through Chaucer's Troilus. And thus, Achilles, that most orgulous of heroes, is humbled: in Lydgate, as in Guido and Caxton, it is this scene, and not his love for Patroclus, that motivates his refusal to fight.

But strangely, Lydgate and Chaucer betray an inverted history here. As Larry Benson points out, Lydgate draws his version of Achilles through Chaucer's own appropriation of an early telling of Achilles: "Boccaccio apparently drew suggestions for his account of Troilus's enamorment from an episode in Benoît (17489ff.) telling of Achilles' love for Polyxena, and from his own Filocolo."[70] Lydgate thus performs a sort of double appropriation of Benoît's *Roman de Troie*, once in his translation of Guido's *Historia destructionis Troiae* and once again in his interpolation of Chaucer's *Troilus and Criseyde*, which returns the figuration of Achilles from Troilus back to Achilles. In this, Achilles's experience at Hector's tomb is a model and a guide for the major English authors: Patrick Cheney argues that through the trope of ekphrasis "Shakespeare presents Achilles as a personal figure for the nature of his self-concealing authorship," and Achilles parallels Lydgate in all his major works by embodying what it means to be constituted by prior writing.[71] At Hector's tomb Achilles sets out the parameters of English formalism as neither a break into originality nor a return to a more classical sense of figuration so much as a ceaseless and ongoing process of literary reproduction in which the literary past is never sealed off by historical period but is instead continually reread and rewritten, reproduced across time through the medium of the book.

FIVE

The Edition

Assembly Programs and the Protocols of Canonization

We read in the shadow of the First Folio.[1] That its canon is incomplete, that its internal organization is inconsistent, that its later iterations insert apocrypha—these points do nothing to undercut its relentless coherence: the First Folio takes the ephemera of Shakespeare's legacy—his biography and his theatrical productions—and formally structures them so they appear as unified and as autonomous as the book itself. For the Folio's assertion of categorical unity is threefold at least: rhetorical, in its appeal to the authority of generic distinction; material, in its identity as a freestanding book; and finally, historical, in its refinement of the logic of book assembly into a seamless product. Thus, Gary Taylor writes in his 2006 McKenzie Lectures that "every generalization about 'Shakespeare' as a distinctive and unified whole—which is to say, all modern criticism—derives that totalizing and homogenizing strategy of reading from the 1623 edition: from the visual uniformity of its typography and page design, from the physical unity produced by its printing, sewing, and binding."[2] In short, the First Folio asserts formalism and biographical historicism—the collation of Shakespeare's works according to genre as a way into his individual self—over the fragmentary and partial process of reading. The First Folio's mode is modern; to read its brilliance, yet alone read beyond it, we need to appreciate how the technology of the literary book produces authority.

To accomplish this, I focus my discussion in this last chapter on a group of playbooks known as the Pavier Quartos.[3] These are ten plays in nine quarto booklets published by Thomas Pavier and printed by William Jaggard, who with his son Isaac, Edmund Blount, John Smethwick, and William Aspley, went on to produce the First Folio. The Quartos remain in a variety of forms: in separate pamphlets, in bound books of only a few plays, and in complete collections. Strikingly, though all of the Quartos were printed in 1619, their title pages bear a variety of printers' names and, even more strangely, three groups of publication dates: 1600, 1608, and 1619 (see table).

In 1908 W. W. Greg made the case for their common publication based on the watermarks of their various paper stocks. He explained their heterogeneity as a subterfuge. Pavier, Greg argued, only owned the rights to five of the ten plays and thus disguised the rest in an attempt to circumvent copyright. With this argument, Greg initiated the New Bibliography and consolidated his claim for a science of close reading of the material book as a historical artifact. More recent Shakespeare scholarship has inverted much of what Greg took for granted, so that rather than the fiercely competitive market for unauthorized reconstructions of theatrical performances that he and A. W. Pollard read in book history, the late sixteenth century is now understood as having produced a small but coherent marketplace for

The Early Modern Composite Volume: The Pavier Quartos[4]

Title/STC	*Ownership*	*Imprint and Date*	*Signatures*
1. *The Whole Contention* (STC 26101)	Pavier	T.P., n.d.	A–Q4
2. *Pericles* (included in *STC* 26101)	"derelict" (Greg)	T. P., 1619	Title, R–Aa4, Bb1
3. *A Yorkshire Tragedie* (STC 22341)	Pavier	T. P., 1619	Title, A–C4, D1–3
4. *Merchant of Venice* (STC 22297)	Thomas Hayes (d., acquired by James Roberts, 1600; claimed by Lawrence Hayes, 1619)	J. Roberts, 1600	A–K4
5. *Merry Wives of Windsor* (STC 22300)	Arthur Johnson	Arthur Johnson, 1619	A–G4
6. *King Lear* (STC 22293)	Nathaniel Butter	Nathaniel Butter, 1608	A–H4
7. *Henry the Fift* (STC 22291)	Pavier	T. P., 1608	A–G4
8. *Sir Iohn Old-castle* (STC 18796)	Pavier	T. P., 1600	A–K4
9. *Midsommer Nights Dreame* (STC 22303)	Thomas Fisher (d.)	T. P., 1600	A–H4

dramatic literature, much of it authorized by the playwright.[5] What remains of Greg's argument is the story of origins. As A. S. W. Rosenbach, having purchased the most significant complete composite volumes of the Pavier Quartos, the Gwynn edition (now at the Folger), noted in pencil on its first page, they are "the first attempt at a collection of the works of William Shakespeare. From the library of Marsden J. Perry, Providence R. I., Purchased July 22, 1919. A. S. W. Rosenbach."

Greg asks at the end of his discussion of the Quartos, "What is the disturbance caused to received opinion with regard to the text?," and concludes, "The answer is: Practically none."[6] So he positions the Pavier Quartos as the tentative exploration of a Shakespearean canon that adumbrates the massive statement of the First Folio and of the New Bibliography both, the incipient gesture that accurately locates the construction of Shakespeare's plays in history but ultimately makes no great difference. More recently, in *Shakespeare and the Rise of the Editor in Print*, Sonia Massai has argued convincingly that Pavier's efforts were not illegitimate but in fact connected to the Folio Syndicate through the Jaggards.[7] Nevertheless, for book history and for Shakespeare studies alike, the Pavier Quartos operate like the fifteenth century itself: they are printed across the bleed of literary history and so color its margins by bracketing the unified periods and compendious folio volumes that tell its story but remain only partially meaningful in and of themselves.

In what follows, I read the Pavier Quartos in four points. First, I suggest that the nine booklets phrase Shakespeare's canon as a dramatization of the past, which to a large extent they localize to the 1400s. *The Whole Contention* launches the series with a double bill—*Henry VI*, parts 2 and 3, in one quarto—and so sets out the collection's theme as an implicit return to Shakespeare's first publication (Figure 5.1). Further, as much as the Quartos' title pages assert history as the overriding genre of Shakespeare's work, they present a similarly consistent claim for his authorship: of the nine titles, only *Henry the Fift* neglects Shakespeare's name. Thus my second point: as I argued for *The Contention* in chapter 3, the Pavier Quartos imagine the early to mid-1400s not just as politically unstable but also as consistently literary, deeply invested in rhetorical creation, and pointedly bookish. Authorship and history are linked overtly on the Pavier Quartos' title pages and within their plots, which model reading and writing as processes of interpretive engagement that not only occur in the present but are also projected back as a defining characteristic of the past.

These two points conspire to a third. Rather than imagining an opposition between the Quartos and the First Folio, I suggest we see them as working to the same ends through different means. The

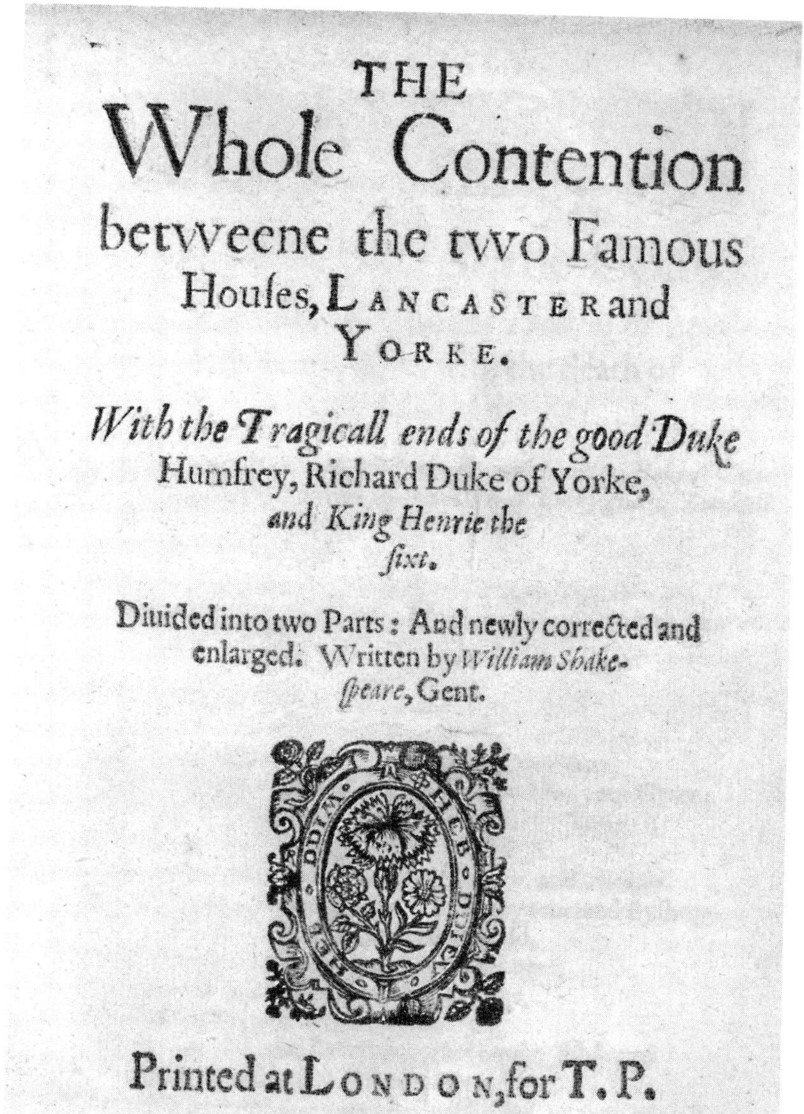
THE
Whole Contention
betvveene the two Famous
Houſes, LANCASTER and
YORKE.

With the Tragicall ends of the good Duke
Humfrey, Richard Duke of Yorke,
and King Henrie the
ſixt.

Diuided into two Parts: And newly corrected and
enlarged. Written by *William Shake-*
ſpeare, Gent.

Printed at LONDON, for T. P.

Figure 5.1. Revisiting Shakespeare's first Quarto. *The Whole Contention* (London: William Jaggard for Thomas Pavier, 1619), *STC* 26101 copy 3, reproduced by permission of the Folger Shakespeare Library.

quarto format demands its reader take an active role in creating the text through booklet assembly. As I underscored in the case of John Lydgate's and William Caxton's production of the Chaucerian canon in chapter 2, quarto compilation was an established manuscript practice, one clearly used by the readers of early printed books. And as I argued for the prose *Recuyell* and dramatic *Troylus* in chapter 4, printers exploited bookish forms for their readers' uses. Made coherent by size and design, the Pavier Quartos offer the purchaser a selection for just such a compilation, and the composite volumes that remain speak of the different collations of booklets readers imagined for the series. Indeed, though the books were entirely printed in 1619, the variety of dates imprinted on their covers provide the reader with the imaginative units for assembling his or her own composite volume as not only thematically about the past but also of a piece with its technology, participating in its textual forms toward both material and figural ends—an overall book that represents the past. In this, the Pavier Quartos are programmed with cultural practices of manuscript assembly that are dependent on the reader's engagement and are capable of exfoliating the history inherent in its pages. Once the reader intellectually engages with the Quartos, he or she is effectively provided with the protocols in the quarto format to assemble the Shakespearean canon through the recognition of history. In this sense, the Pavier Quartos are paradoxical objects: disavowing any claim to "make it new" through their material and intellectual reliance on preprint technologies, they seem resolutely antimodern; alternatively, demanding that each reader conceptualize Shakespeare as reshaping the past, they cast literary authorship and historical period as mutually constituted by each reader. Thus, I argue that the Pavier Quartos complicate the intertwined notions of originality, modernity, and historical break by locating in historical precedent the same material and discursive practices of the literary culture they depend on to reproduce Shakespeare anew.

In contrast, the First Folio routes Shakespeare's canon through the literary structures of genre as presented in its apparatus and *mise-en-page*. In accepting this hardwiring, the Folio's reader cedes productive engagement with the text to its editors. Thus, I read its assertion of authorship as a silent appropriation of preexisting literary technologies that reorganizes the Pavier Quartos' recursive tendencies. In effect, if the Pavier Quartos depend on their readers' participation in assembling the Shakespearean canon, the First Folio is programmed for auto-assembly: its animating scripts run regardless of the reader's engagement so that it produces Shakespeare even when dormant. The Folio contrives literature as autonomous and formal, alienated from history, which—conceived of as existing externally to the book—must actively be brought to bear on the work of art if it is to influence "received opinion." Greg's separation of bibliography and received opinion—indeed, literary studies' continual and ambivalent juxtaposition of formal and historical modes of reading—is latent in the organizing structure of the Folio itself. Laying the Folio's august structure aside, if only for a moment, allows us to recuperate the dynamic relationship between literature and history within modernity and, in turn, see how modernity names that relationship as of the distant past. Thus, my fourth, and overall point: By recognizing that all forms of the book contain programming language, we can develop a literary history for the digital age.

The Pavier Quartos are unified, then, not just by the watermarks that reveal their true dates of publication but as a collection presenting Shakespeare's authorship in relation to history. We can see this in the first three plays—*Henry VI*, parts 2 and 3, and *Pericles*—which were printed with a running signature. Although Shakespeare had acquired a coat of arms as early as 1596 or 1597, *The Whole Contention*'s title page is the first mention of him as a gentleman in print. In effect, the Quarto revisits Shakespeare's first appearance in print in the 1594 *Contention* (see chap. 3, Figure 3.1) by naming him an author. The two plays contained within this quarto are separated by subtitles identifying them as the first and second parts of a continuous narrative, followed by *Pericles*. The planned effect, then, was for the reader to encounter Shakespeare as a gentleman author, to read about the Wars of the Roses, to think through their various struggles, and—after all this—to turn the page and be met by Gower, who emerges from the past as a figure of authority.

These themes of authorship and history are carried through all the Quartos: again, regardless of who we now believe wrote the plays and how we now classify them generically, of the nine separate title pages only one, *Henry the Fift*, neglects Shakespeare's name, and only three claim generic designations far from history: *A Yorkshire Tragedie*, *The Merry Wives of Windsor* (comedy), and *A Midsommer Nights Dreame* (performance). Still, these three plays resonate well with the others, pointing the reader back to Lancastrian history and to Chaucer. The Pavier Quartos are crosscut by this central tension: linked through the overarching themes of authorship and history, they suggest a unity that is fleetingly reinforced by the first three plays' continuous signature; separated by the title pages that announce different dates and printers, neglect or announce Shakespeare's authorship, coalesce and diverge thematically, they remain, still, discrete publications.

This tension is endemic in early seventeenth-century literary collections.[8] Michael Drayton's *Poems*, published by Smethwick in folio the same year as the Pavier Quartos, provides a ready comparison.[9] Drayton is reported in Sir Philip Henslowe's diary as one of the authors of *Sir John Oldcastle*, and *Poems* collects his verse from various quarto editions since the 1590s. The opening title page uses curly brackets to organize its contents, roughly, around the divisions of these preexisting quartos (Figure 5.2). The first section, including "The *Barons* Warres," "*Englands* Heroicall Epsistles," and "Idea," reproduces a selection similar to that published in 1603; the second, Drayton's "*The Legends*," looks back to a collection first published in 1596; and the last includes items from the 1606 edition of *Poems: Lyrick and Pastorall*, which collected his "Odes" and "Eglogs" with "the *Man* in the Moone."[10] In those quartos, the poems follow along with continuous pagination; in the larger folio, each is introduced with an entirely new title page reiterating the date and place of publication as with, for example, THE OWLE (Figure 5.3). This method of introducing continually paginated texts with a separate title page announcing the author, date, and printer holds true for other major collections of the early seventeenth century, such as the 1601 *Works of Samuel Daniel* and the 1616 *Workes of Beniamin Ionson*. The originality of publishing Jonson's works while he was alive has perhaps overshadowed the fact that the premise behind the assembly process is far from unprecedented. As we have seen, the early Chaucerian collections are bound in this way, and *Tottel's Miscellany* is itself a mass-produced commonplace book of poetry. Like the Pavier Quartos, then, these editions present a tension between authorship and canonicity on the one hand and the halting sequence of separate texts on the other.

What distinguishes the Pavier Quartos is that this tension is never resolved; indeed, it appears to have been emphasized as the printing of the texts was carried out. So although the first three plays were produced in sequence, the running signatures were abandoned after the text of *Pericles*, at which point the compositor planned the remaining title pages, beginning with *A Yorkshire Tragedie*, and then left the type laid out so he could create the title pages for *Pericles* through the rest as he composed the form for each first quire (with the exception of the title page for *Midsommer Nights Dreame*, which was set independently).[11] As a result, the Pavier Quartos have no fixed order and remain in a variety of different arrangements, with some books collecting only a few plays, such as the Newberry Library's edition of *The Merry Wives of Windsor*, *Sir Iohn Old-castle*, and *The Whole Contention*, and others (such as Greg's famous example of the Gwynn edition) compiling them all. As with Chaucer, so with Shakespeare: the Pavier Quartos illustrate the twofold process of authorizing and selecting at work in the seventeenth century, for if their title pages authorize certain works as Shakespeare's, their material format provides the reader with a mode of selecting from these works a single volume that represents Shakespeare's canon, challenging the reader to participate by matching and sorting the group into an arrangement of plays that he or she thinks should comprise a literary-dramatic rendition of the past.

As a result, the texts operate as a formal principle for canon construction on at least three levels. First, they embody the recursive structure for canon construction developed by the fifteenth-century Chaucerians. On this level, they operate similarly to the mode of production of the early fifteenth-century Chaucerian manuscripts, which both materially and intellectually build the English canon as an expression of a larger field of texts available. On a second level, the Pavier Quartos add to this process the specific tropes of printing introduced to England in the late fifteenth and early sixteenth centuries:

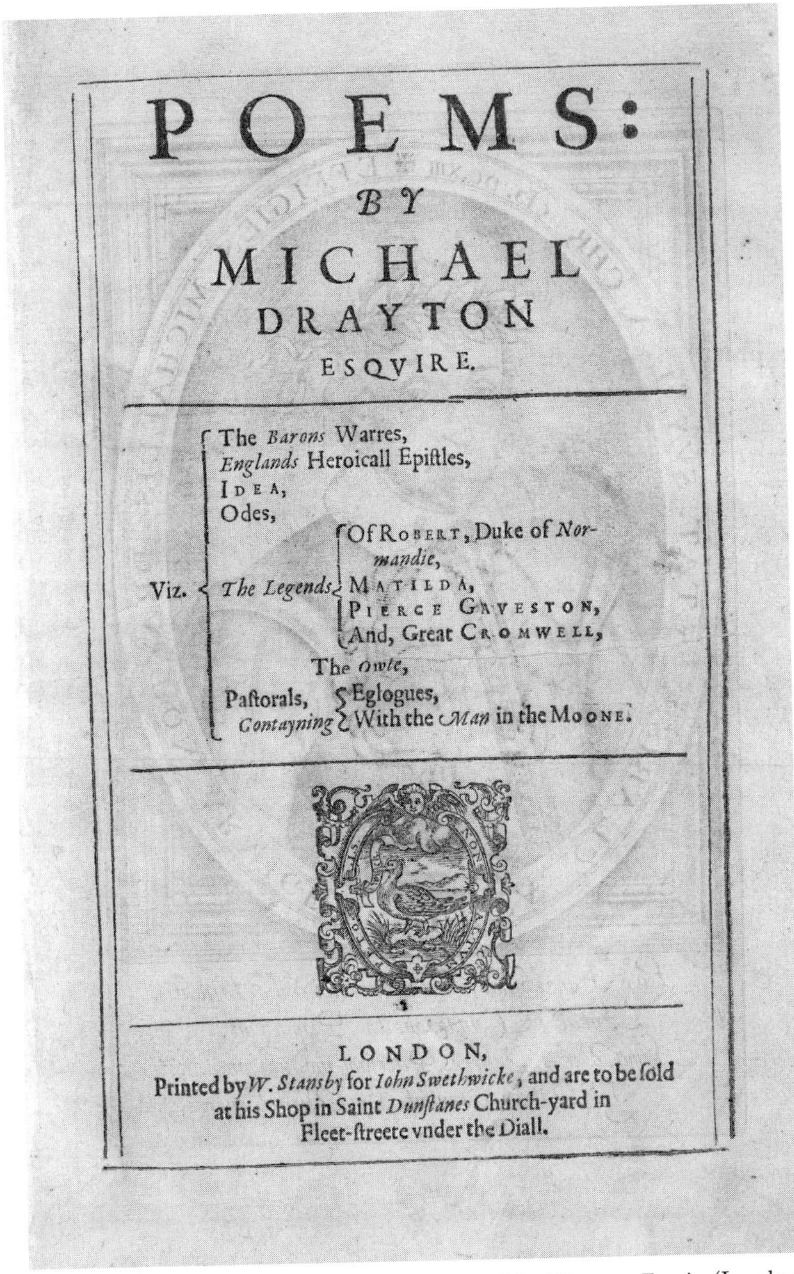
POEMS:

BY

MICHAEL
DRAYTON
ESQVIRE.

Viz.
- The *Barons* Warres,
- *Englands* Heroicall Epiſtles,
- IDEA,
- Odes,
- *The Legends*
  - Of ROBERT, Duke of *Normandie*,
  - MATILDA,
  - PIERCE GAVESTON,
  - And, Great CROMWELL,
- The *Owle*,
- Paſtorals, *Contayning*
  - Eglogues,
  - With the *Man* in the MOONE.

LONDON,
Printed by *W. Stansby* for *Iohn Swethwicke*, and are to be ſold
at his Shop in Saint *Dunſtanes* Church-yard in
Fleet-ſtreete vnder the Diall.

Figure 5.2. A method of compiling. *Poems: by Michael Drayton Esquire* (London: William Stansby for John Smethwick, 1619), title page, *STC* 7222 copy 1, reproduced by permission of the Folger Shakespeare Library.

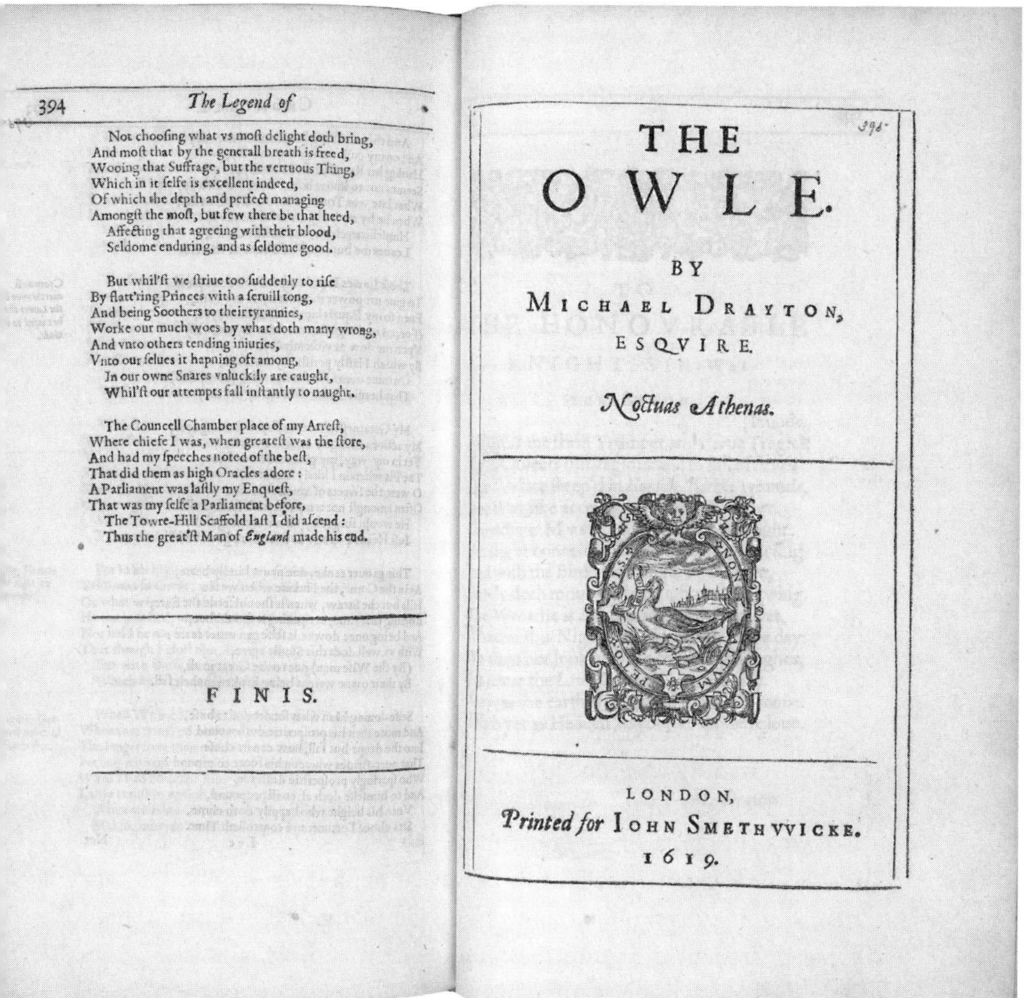

394 *The Legend of*

Not choosing what vs most delight doth bring,
And most that by the generall breath is freed,
Wooing that Suffrage, but the vertuous Thing,
Which in it selfe is excellent indeed,
Of which the depth and perfect managing
Amongst the most, but few there be that heed,
Affecting that agreeing with their blood,
Seldome enduring, and as seldome good.

But whil'st we striue too suddenly to rise
By flatt'ring Princes with a seruill tong,
And being Soothers to their tyrannies,
Worke our much woes by what doth many wrong,
And vnto others tending iniuries,
Vnto our selues it hapning oft among,
In our owne Snares vnluckily are caught,
Whil'st our attempts fall instantly to naught.

The Councell Chamber place of my Arrest,
Where chiefe I was, when greatest was the store,
And had my speeches noted of the best,
That did them as high Oracles adore:
A Parliament was lastly my Enquest,
That was my selfe a Parliament before,
The Towre-Hill Scaffold last I did ascend:
Thus the great'st Man of *England* made his end.

FINIS.

395

THE
OWLE.

BY
MICHAEL DRAYTON,
ESQVIRE.

Noctuas Athenas.

LONDON,
Printed for IOHN SMETHVVICKE.
1619.

Figure 5.3. Nested title pages. "The Owle," in *Poems: by Michael Drayton Esquire* (London: William Stansby for John Smethwick, 1619), 394–95, *STC* 7222 copy 1, reproduced by permission of the Folger Shakespeare Library.

the generic *mise-en-page* of a title page for a dramatic pamphlet, the date of imprint, and the printer's name. Pavier seems to have included these dates only after the initial plan was abandoned, modifying his product while it was still in press so that at whatever point the Quartos stopped being a preordered sequence of plays and started becoming a free-form structure of authorized units available for their readers' personal selection, they also acquired the title pages and the dates that construct them as printed objects of the past. Such tropes create the booklets as individually distinct units, each recovered from some lost storehouse, each possessing its own textual history. Thus, on a third level, each booklet's unique identity as a product is part and parcel of the overall design, printed into the almost-but-not-quite allegiance in the plays' interests that creates the tension between part and whole and that engages the individual purchaser in the process of representation. The Pavier Quartos are not simply material vehicles for otherwise-freestanding literary abstraction, but a material assembly program that the reader uses to represent literature, authorship, and the past.

This assembly program is tabled if we brand the Quartos illegitimate, Pavier a pirate.[12] In fact, there is little in Pavier's career to suggest illegality and much to suggest his tendency to plan and execute ambitious printing enterprises. Pavier was involved in the Stationers Company on an executive level and seems to have administered or designed a number of investment instruments: he was elected to the livery; he became an officer of the English Stock, first as keeper, then as committee member and auditor; and finally, in 1622, he rose to underwarden, which gave him executive powers over the company. In addition to approximately two hundred publications, over one hundred of which were religious material, Pavier produced sixteen plays above the nine Pavier Quartos, including two editions of Thomas Kyd's *Spanish Tragedy*. He worked with Jaggard and was continually alive to risk. His leading biographer, Gerald Johnson, writes that he was

> one of the most enterprising and successful publishers during the first decades of the seventeenth century. . . . Pavier's success as a

> publisher rested mainly upon his ability to negotiate deals with other stationers. Many of his publications, especially the popular books that went through multiple editions, were reprints whose copyrights he had taken over from other men, either by outright purchase or through an arrangement by which he paid the copyright-holder a certain amount for the copies published.[13]

Further, Massai argues that Pavier's preparation of the plays' copy suggests his care and planning of the Quartos overall. Both she and Andrew Murphy note that Pavier's ownership of rights to a number of the plays and his manifold connections with the Quarto printers, particularly with William Jaggard and Smethwick, suggest that he had strong connections to the Folio Syndicate overall.[14] Given this role, Pavier's dates seem less subterfuge than a functioning part of the way the individual quartos figure in a canonical Shakespearean miscellany.

The Pavier Quartos return to history not just as a thematic but as part of print poetics. From the start they invite the reader to construct a story of the past. Pavier's original plan launches this story with *The Whole Contention* and thus asks the reader to begin by imagining the Wars of the Roses and work through the literature of the past—*Pericles*—to some more personal selection, for regardless of how Pavier initially imagined the overall order, almost all the plays tell stories associated with English literary history: *King Lear* is a known part of the English chronicles, *Pericles* is told by the English poet Gower, *Midsommer Night's Dreame* has its origins in Chaucer's *Knight's Tale*, and *A Yorkshire Tragedie* is filled with local interest. Only *The Merchant of Venice* is a spectacular non-English addition. Within this imaginative field, this library of plots and characters, the plays are open to any number of connections.

For example, Pavier's title page to *The First Part of the True & Honorable History, of the Life of Sir Iohn Old-castle* announces Shakespeare as the play's author (Figure 5.4). The play is in fact simultaneously ancillary and central to the Shakespearean canon—ancillary because apocryphal (Philip Henslowe records that it was written by "mr monday mr drayton & mr wilsson & haythway" who are to be paid "for the first pte of the lyfe of Sr Jhon Ouldcasstell"); central

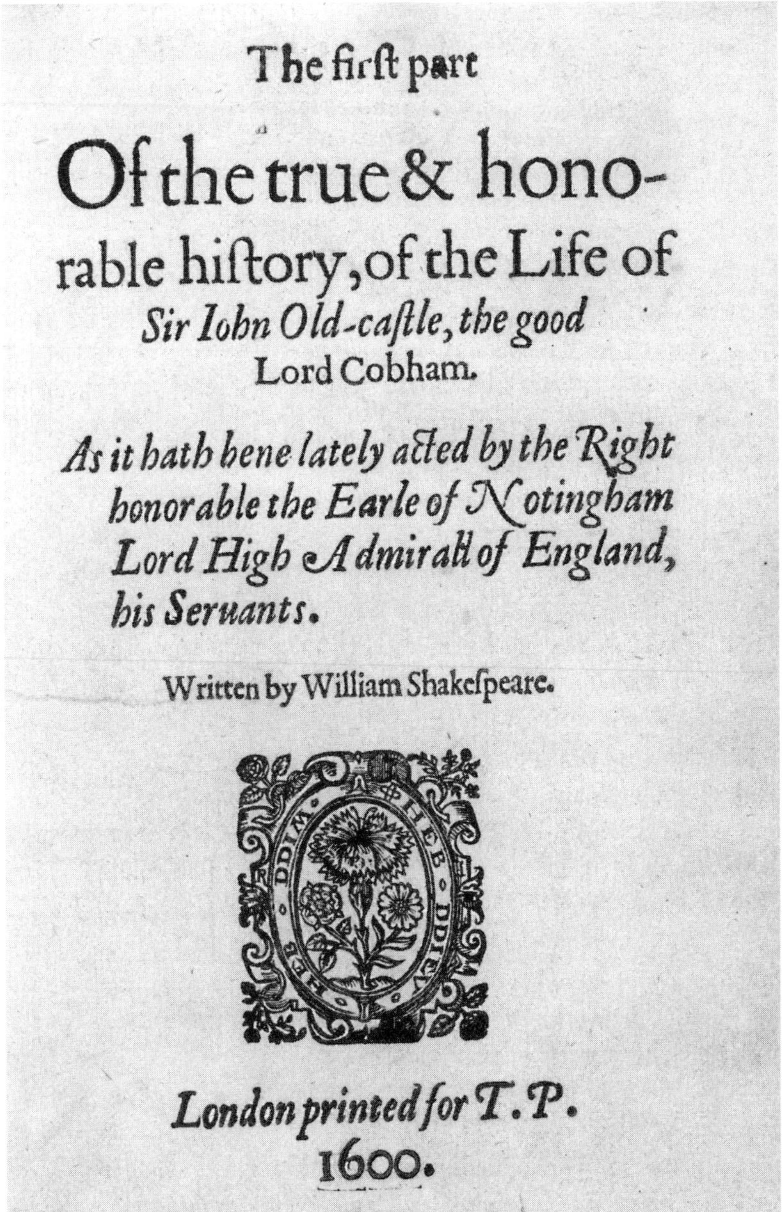

The firſt part

Of the true & hono-
rable hiſtory, of the Life of
Sir Iohn Old-caſtle, the good
Lord Cobham.

*As it hath bene lately acted by the Right
honorable the Earle of Notingham
Lord High Admirall of England,
his Seruants.*

Written by William Shakeſpeare.

London printed for T. P.
1600.

Figure 5.4. Recognition and misrecognition in the literary marketplace. *The First Part of the True & Honorable History, of the Life of Sir John Old-castle* (London: William Jaggard for Thomas Pavier, 1619), title page, *STC* 18796 copy 1, reproduced by permission of the Folger Shakespeare Library.

The Prologue.

THE doubtfull Title (Gentlemen) prefixt
Vpon the Argument we haue in hand,
May breed ſuſpence, and wrongfully diſturbe
The peacefull quiet of your ſetled thoughts:
To ſtop which ſcruple, let this breefe ſuffice.
It is no pamper'd Glutton we preſent,
Nor aged Councellour to youthfull ſinne;
But one, whoſe vertue ſhone aboue the reſt,
A valiant Martyr, and a vertuous Peere,
In whoſe true faith and loyalty expreſt
Vnto his Soueraigne, and his Countries weale:
We ſtriue to pay that tribute of our loue
Your fauours merit: Let faire Truth be grac'd,
Since forg'd inuention former time defac'd.

A 2

Figure 5.5. This is not Falstaff. "The Prologue," in *The First Part of the True & Honorable History, of the Life of Sir John Old-castle* (London: William Jaggard for Thomas Pavier, 1619), A2, *STC* 18796 copy 1, reproduced by permission of the Folger Shakespeare Library.

because reactionary, a response and attempt to clear up some lingering suspicion about the performance history of *1 Henry IV*. Both the 1600 and the misdated 1619 editions of the play contain a prologue that reflects on this tension, reacting apparently to theatre history by setting the record straight: "It is no pamper'd Glutton we present, / Nor aged Councellour to youthfull sinne," the Prologue insists, "But one, whose vertue shone aboue the rest, / A valiant Martyr, and a vertuous Peere" (Figure 5.5).[15] The lines seem to allude to a mid-1590s performance of *1 Henry IV* in which the character now known as Falstaff first appeared as Oldcastle. This identification of Oldcastle with Falstaff is corroborated by two external sources, a note by Nicholas Rowe in his 1709 edition of *The Works of Mr. William Shakespeare* and, closer to the First Folio, Dr. Richard James's dedicatory epistle appended to a poem by Thomas Hoccleve. James writes:

> That in Shakespeares first shewe of Harrie ye fift, ye person with which he vndertook to playe a buffone was not Falstaffe, but Sr Jhon Oldcastle, and that offence beinge worthily taken by personages decended from his [title,] as peradventure by manie others allso whoe ought to haue him in honourable memorie, the poet was putt to make an ignorant shifte of abusing Sr Jhon ~~Falstaffe or~~ Fastolphe, a man not inferior [of] Vertue though not so famous in pietie as the other, whoe gaue witnesse vnto the truth of our reformation with a constant and resolute martyrdom, vnto which he was pursued by the Priests, Bishops, Moncks, and Friers of those dayes.[16]

James copied Hoccleve's poem around 1625 as Bodleian Library, MS James 34, perhaps for a planned edition of Hoccleve's works.[17] The poem is now known as Hoccleve's "Remonstrance against Oldcastle," and, dated from 1415, shortly after Henry embarked for Harfluer, it heralds from exactly the period depicted by the plays *Henry the Fift* and *Sir Iohn Old-castle*. Whatever James's purpose in copying and annotating Hoccleve, it demonstrates a seventeenth-century reader engaged with Shakespeare's work as a way of returning to history. The issues of authority and history, of telling a historical story from the quartos of Shakespeare's legacy, is not simply the province of the modern critic but embedded in the Quartos themselves, and this is evident in the notes and prologues that accompany their passage through time.

Playing on the expectation and denial of Shakespeare's Falstaff, then, the prologue to *Sir Iohn Old-castle* participates in the tension of constructing a legitimate Shakespearean canon. Falstaff's popularity in the early seventeenth century is well established: Peter Blayney lists *1 Henry IV* as tied for the third best-selling play, and C. M. Ingleby, editor of the *Shakespeare Allusion-Book*, remarks that allusion to Falstaff "ranks second only to Hamlet."[18] The epilogue to the first quarto of *2 Henry IV*, printed in 1600 by Valentine Simmes for Andrew Wise as *The Second Part of Henrie the Fourth* and announcing "the humours of sir John Falstaffe, and swaggering Pistoll," also casts a distinction between Oldcastle and Falstaff. "For Olde-castle died Martyre," it states, "and this is not the man" (see Figure 5.6). Like the epistle to the *Troylus* and the prologue to *Old-castle*, this epilogue presents an elusive voice that chaperones the quarto. This voice presents itself as embodied ("my tongue is weary, when my legges are too, I wil bid you, good night"), speaking in the first person ("I was lately here in the end of a displeasing play"), and separate from the author of the play, whom it identifies on its title page ("written by William Shakespeare") and who it promises will provide a sequel ("our humble Author will continue the storie, with sir Iohn in it").

In further similarity to the *Troylus* epistle, it presents the play as a product ("I meant indeed to pay you with this, which if like an il venture it come vnluckily home, I breake, and you my gentle creditors loose") within a fluid system of exchange ("And yet that were but light payment, to daunce out of your debt, but a good conscience will make any possible satisfaction, and so woulde I"). The *Old-castle* prologue suggests its main concern is historical accuracy—"Let faire Truth be grac'd, / Since forg'd inuention former time defac'd"—but it too groups a number of similar issues—the forging and defacing of objects, the clouding of truth or brilliance by time—that cluster around the proper recognition of authority. In this, the prologue begs its own face: claiming to be "written by William Shakespeare" and printed in

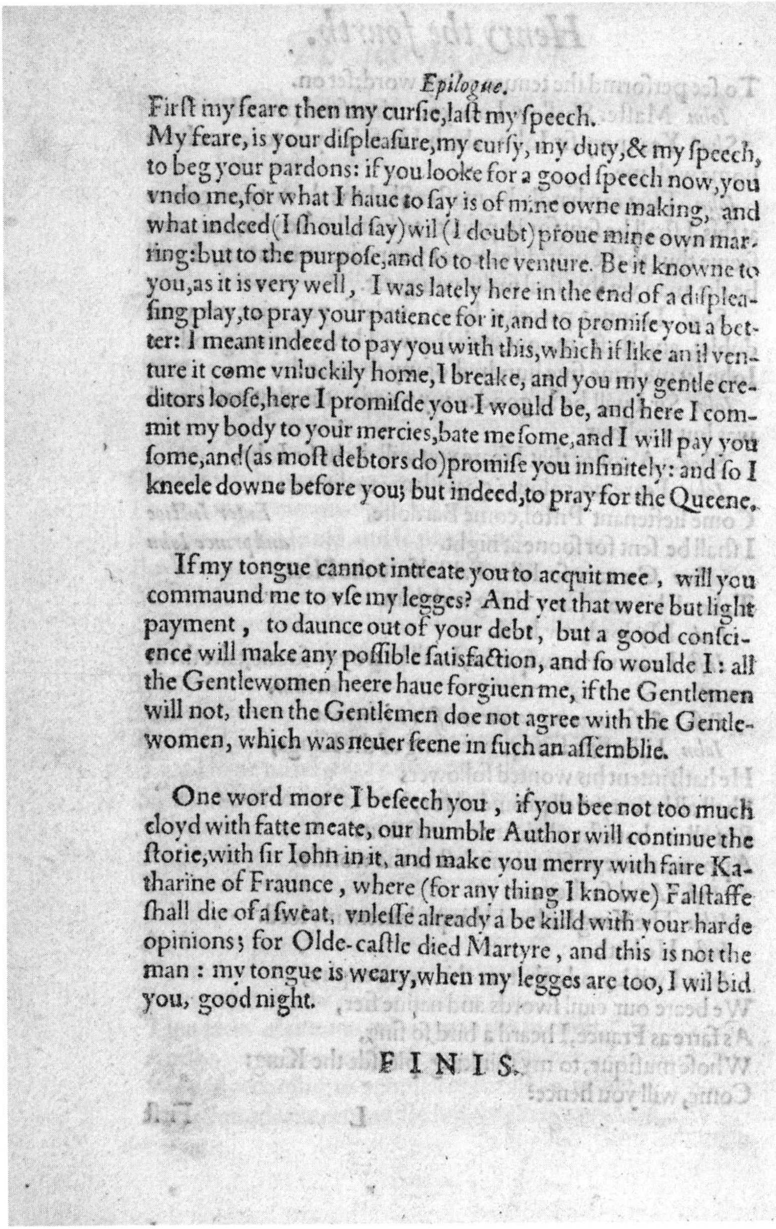

Epilogue.

Firſt my feare then my curſie,laſt my ſpeech.

My feare, is your diſpleaſure,my curſy, my duty,& my ſpeech, to beg your pardons: if you looke for a good ſpeech now,you vndo me,for what I haue to ſay is of mine owne making, and what indeed(I ſhould ſay)wil (I doubt)proue mine own marring:but to the purpoſe,and ſo to the venture. Be it knowne to you,as it is very well, I was lately here in the end of a diſpleaſing play,to pray your patience for it,and to promiſe you a better: I meant indeed to pay you with this,which if like an il venture it come vnluckily home,I breake, and you my gentle creditors looſe,here I promiſde you I would be, and here I commit my body to your mercies,bate me ſome,and I will pay you ſome,and(as moſt debtors do)promiſe you infinitely: and ſo I kneele downe before you; but indeed,to pray for the Queene.

If my tongue cannot intreate you to acquit mee , will you commaund me to vſe my legges? And yet that were but light payment , to daunce out of your debt, but a good conſcience will make any poſſible ſatisfaction, and ſo woulde I: all the Gentlewomen heere haue forgiuen me, if the Gentlemen will not, then the Gentlemen doe not agree with the Gentlewomen, which was neuer ſeene in ſuch an aſſemblie.

One word more I beſeech you , if you bee not too much cloyd with fatte meate, our humble Author will continue the ſtorie,with ſir Iohn in it, and make you merry with faire Katharine of Fraunce, where (for any thing I knowe) Falſtaffe ſhall die of a ſweat, vnleſſe already a be killd with your harde opinions; for Olde-caſtle died Martyre, and this is not the man : my tongue is weary,when my legges are too, I wil bid you, good night.

FINIS.

Figure 5.6. The Quarto's Body. "The Second Part of: Epilogue," in *The Second Part of Henrie the Fourth* (London: Valentine Simmes for Andrew Wise and William Aspley, 1600), L^{v}, *STC* 22288a copy 1, reproduced by permission of the Folger Shakespeare Library.

1600, the very title page of *Old-castle* is counterfeit, a forged coin in the circulation of playbooks. "The language of coinage," Jesse M. Lander writes, "attuned to the potential contradiction between the sovereign's stamp and the coin's alloy, conveys the complex intertwining of value and legitimacy."[19] In short, under cover of setting the record straight, the prologue to *Sir Iohn Old-castle* frames the central problem of the quarto format since A. W. Pollard took its measure: rather than clearly identifying themselves either as literature or as dramatic reconstruction, the early dramatic quartos come to us without portfolio and so leave us perplexed as to how to imagine their reception: as inconsequential accounts by nameless players and minor dramatists or as authorized copy, indeed, a corrective record to the stage. Without the prefaces and tables that contextualize the folio book, the quartos leave the reader alone, as the prologue says, in "the peacefull quiet of your setled thoughts," to ponder their legitimacy or, more bluntly, to recognize literary history from illegitimate fabrication, Falstaff from Oldcastle.

Within *Sir Iohn Old-castle* the task of recognition falls to Henry. Preparing for the Brewer's rebellion, for example, Henry circulates in disguise in a way purposefully reminiscent of the camp scene in *Henry the Fift* ("but you do know of old, / That I haue beene a perfect nightwalker," F3^{v}). Held up by Sir John Wrotham, a priest who is also "a singer, a drinker, a bencher, a wencher" (D), Henry recalls his own past: "Well, if thou wilt needs haue it, there it is: iust the Prouerbe, one theefe robs another. Where the diuel are all my old theeues? Falstaffe that villaine is so fat, hee cannot get on's horse, but me thinkes Poines and Peto should bee stirring hereabouts" (F2). Discovering that Henry is of the king's chamber, Sir John-the-Priest banks the promise of immediate ransom for that of a future pardon, to which Henry agrees, "so it be for no murther" (F2^{v}). They shake on the deal (F2^{v}):

Pri. Giue me thy hand of the same.
Kin. There tis.
Pri. Me thinkes the King should be good to theeues because
he has bin a theefe himselfe, though I thinke now
hee be turned true man.

Kin. Faith I haue heard indeede h'as had an ill name that way in's youth: but how canst thou tell he has beene a Theefe?

Priest. How? because he once robb'd me before I fell to the trade my selfe, when that foule villanous guts, that led him to all that Roguery, was in's company there, that Falstaffe.

King aside. Well, if he did rob thee then, thou art but euen with him now Ile be sworne: Thou knowest not the King now I thinke, if thou sawest him?

Pri. Not I yfaith.

K. aside. So it should seeme.

The connection between King Henry and Sir John-the-Priest is thick and personal: Henry's previous robbery of Sir John "before I fell to the trade my selfe" is shaded with the responsibility of creating him as a thief. John seems to sense Henry's former relationship to Falstaff—he remarks on it here, earlier (D), and later, too (G^v); it is a point with him. Neither recognizes the other; both recognize Falstaff as a fat villain. The issue of recognition is of particular concern to John now that he has promise of a pardon, and so he bites off a coin to mark their agreement: "Nay sirra, because I thinke indeede I shal haue some occasion to vse thee, and as thou comst oft this way, I may light on thee another time not knowing thee, here ile break this Angel, take thou halfe of it, this is a token betwixt thee and me" (F3). For John, the broken angel is a token of recognition that, like his memory, is only partial. For Henry, as for the reader, it is like Falstaff himself, a broken signifier, one that muddies the present, that threatens to confuse fiction with historical record, to mingle illegitimate play with canonical work, and to align the king with this unholy priest.

The recognition of authority is therefore a theme throughout *Sir Iohn Old-castle*, one the prologue's voice calls attention to and the characters discuss and think on privately. In many ways, *Henry the Fift* is also a play about recognition. For example, coming upon one of his "old theeues," Pistol, Henry distances himself from his past. Pistol, unable to recognize Henry in his nighttime disguise, nevertheless asserts their former intimacy (D3v):

> *Pist.* The Kings a bago, and a hart of gold,
> A lad of life, an impe of fame,
> Of parents good, of fist most valiant:
> I kis his durty shooe, and from my heart strings
> I loue the louely bully. What is thy name?

Like Sir John, Pistol's life has been shaped by his association with young Henry. For him, "the King's a bago"—he's complete; indeed, he's bursting full with "a hart of gold." Yet when Henry answers Pistol's question ("*King. Harry le Roy*"), Pistol is obtuse and misrecognizes the name entirely ("*Pist. Le Roy*, a Cornish man"). In any case, by this point Henry has already supported Flewellen's decision not to pardon Bardolfe, so when Pistol rants his objections to this anonymous soldier, Henry can only rebuff him. "Figa for thee then," Pistol spits back; "my name is *Pistoil*": figs for friendship, curses Pistol, and so he is left alone, repeating "*Pistoll* is my name," a statement of his angry, isolated retreat into self-sufficiency. He can no longer recognize his friends, but at least he can recognize himself. The scene runs a kind of parallel to that in *Sir Iohn Old-castle* between Sir John and Henry that is typical of the two plays overall—it is an encounter between the king and a lowly commoner that works through disguise and failed recognition—but its results are the opposite: rather than generating a token of memory, it is barren, and rather than affirming some lost connection, it denies everything but Pistol's name.

In fact, tokens *do* get exchanged in *Henry the Fift* but to no easy resolution. During his nocturnal rounds, Henry exchanges his glove with a less-than-admiring soldier. Their argument escalates until a third soldier defuses it (E):

> *3. Soul.* Be friends you fooles,
> We haue French quarrels enow in hand,
> We haue no need of English broyles.

> *King.* Tis no treason to cut French Crownes,
> For to morrow the King himselfe will be a clipper.

In *Sir Iohn Oldcastle* the clipping of crowns—the splitting of the broken angel—comes back when Sir John gambles with Henry in disguise (F4v):

> *Pri.* Sir, pay me Angel gold,
> Ile none of your crackt French Crownes nor Pistolets.
> Pay me faire Angel gold, as I pay you.
> *King.* No crackt French crownes? I hope to see more crackt
> French crownes ere long.
> *Pri.* Thou meanst of Frenchmens crowns, when the kings in
> France.

The scene doubles up on that of *Henrie the Fift* by continuing the pun on "French Crownes," even playing out a punning echo on Pistol's name, "pistolet." In this scene, Henry beats Sir John in gambling in due course, but John comes up with his last broken crown, which leads to their moment of recognition: "The King? Gods will, I am in a proper pickle" (G), declares Sir John upon realizing that he robbed the king. Henry's initial reaction is to have him hanged ("let him be hang'd vp for example sake," Gv). But John backpedals, banking the broken angel as far more than a literal marker: "your selfe (my Liege) haue bin a Theefe" (Gv), he asserts, recalling the entire history of allegiance and denial cloaked behind their earlier conversation.

So Sir John's broken angel evokes a threefold identification: once by recalling to Henry his own past as a thief; once again, in that by pardoning Sir John, Henry legitimates this past; and finally, in the very name of Sir John, which with its inexplicable and unexplained claim to title of the play itself, ties Sir John the priest to Sir John Oldcastle, the Lollard Knight. Indeed, this series of recognitions is essential to the play's plot, for it is because Sir John escapes execution here that he is able to stand as a witness later, exonerating the Lord and Lady Cobbham, Sir John Oldcastle and his wife (K3). Money itself is a persistent theme in the play. Henry is in need of it to pursue his war with France (B2), the Clergy are tight with it (B2), the populace cannot eat (B3v), a butler is robbed (C2), and even the rebels must take account of their war chest: "Fiue hundred man? fiue thousands not enough, / A hundred thousand will not pay our men" (D2). Money recalls too that the quarto itself is imagined as a coin in the prologue and that it is a commodity overall. The broken angel is an overdetermined representation that aligns the play's many themes in a process of recognition. That is, the Pavier Quartos present a similar set of questions of reading material and rhetorical forms, so that just as the reader is challenged to consider and weigh the quartos in the process of constructing them into a book, the plays ask him or her to consider and weigh Falstaff from Oldcastle, as well as from Henry. Within the prologues and plays, all of these modes of reading are tied up together in the coin, a symbol for recognizing quarto, character, and authority.

Recognition is not so easily celebrated in *Henry the Fift*. For example, where King Henry of *Old-castle* must come to terms with the broken angel for the plot to move ahead, the Henry of *Henry the Fift* never successfully resolves the exchanges he puts in place. He avoids the challenge implied by the exchange of gloves by using Flewellen as an intermediary, and though he takes back his glove (F2), he does so as king, divorced from his previous incarnation. Henry tries to be "a bago" about it all and fills the Second Soldier's gloves with crowns "till I do challenge it" (F3v), but the gesture fails, and the soldier refuses: "Ille none of your money sir, not I" (F3v). Relations remain clipped in *Henry the Fift* rather than matched, as in *Old-castle*. So, in *Henry the Fift*, Henry denies Falstaff, and this is stated explicitly when Flewellen compares Henry to "*Alexander* the big" (E4v). Here Captain Gower remarks, "I but our King is not like him in that, / For he neuer kild any of his friends" (F). Flewellen points out (F),

I speake in the comparisons, as *Alexander* is kill
His friend *Clitus:* so our King being in his ripe
Wits and iudgements, is turne away, the fat Knite
With the great belly doublet:
I am forget his name.
Gower. Sir Iohn Falstaffe.

The conversation between Flewellen and Gower underscores that the rigor of denial that defines Henry as a king is comparable to Alexander; it also forces the audience to remember Falstaff, to realize that in the context of the play this is no simple forgetting but an act of willful assertion. Premising its authority on the distinction of history, that Oldcastle is neither "pamper'd Glutton" nor "aged Councellour to youthfull sinne," *Sir Iohn Old-castle* proceeds to tell a story of recognition that *Henry the Fift* denies. Strangely, this is a distinction affirmed by a Captain named "Gower."

Like *Old-castle*, *Pericles* is also a Pavier Quarto play excised from the First Folio's canon. Further, like *Old-castle*, it too is fronted by a prologue, though unlike that play, *Pericles* is anchored by a historical speaker, Gower, who appears as a figure of sacrifice and of spectacle ("From ashes, auntient *Gower* is come"). He is anachronistic ("I life would wish") and retrograde ("If you, borne in those latter times, / When Witts more ripe, accept my rimes"), but neither obsolete nor inappropriate, for he comes to glad the ear, please the eye, and announce the value of antique letters. "I life would wish, and that I might / Waste it for you, like a Taper light": his is a literary precedence of sacrifice, of loss if not the martyrdom of the past as a performance. Nevertheless, Gower's emphasis on performance does not alleviate his textual identity, for in the quarto there are no scene divisions, and instead Gower's entrance and the dumb show he introduces is handled simply with a line (C, D4^{v}). Thus, a sense of the magisterial spectacle of the past defines Gower's role throughout the play, where he introduces and glosses no less than six dumb shows. Gower's function is both to introduce and to embody performance, as well as to mediate the reader's encounter with the text.

Again, this depiction seems to be created from the material presentation of Gower in the sixteenth century. Thomas Berthelette printed Gower's *Confessio amantis* in 1532 and again in 1554.[20] R. F Yeager reads the typographical representation in these editions as nuancing Gower's role towards that of a dramatic speaker:

> Berthelette, who imbeds the Latin prose in the poetry, apparently worked from a manuscript of the latter kind, replicating his me-

> dieval model as far as he could by changing his typefaces: larger black letter for the Middle English verse, smaller black letter for the interpretive Latin prose, and the roman for the Latin verses. The differing type maintains—even emphasizes—Gower's formalized "conversation," making especially the Latin prose seem to stand away from its placement in the column of English verse, as if (translating this into dramatic terms) speaking an aside. (Indeed, the overall effect has even led one critic to suggest Berthelette's "medieval" page layout as Shakespeare's inspiration for the role of Gower in the play.)[21]

This Gower is not the political author of *Vox clamantis* or even the lover of the *Confessio amantis*; rather, it is Gower as master of ceremonies, as loadstar for the ensuing performances, as didactic scholar, as Lydgate, author of mummings, who is to perform the effective glossing of the past. "Gower," then, whether of *Henry the Fift* or of *Pericles*, forces the recognition of the past. This recognition is psychological—the naming of Falstaff in Henry's biography—and historical, a coming to grips with the ways the past creates the present.

Sir Iohn Old-castle is about the recognition and misrecognition of the past from the start. Its prologue recognizes Falstaff and Oldcastle, which the central record of this controversy, Dr. Richard James's note appended to the Hoccleve manuscript, confirms. The play and this Hoccleve poem, "Remonstrance against Oldcastle," group a constellation of similar themes: heresy, treason, vulgar reading. In the play, Oldcastle is, as the prologue tells us, "a valiant Martyr." He is accused of "Wickliffes doctrine" ($A4^v$, C), and the play reports that his followers "giue themselues the name of Protestants" ($B1^v$). The play follows Foxe's *Book of Martyrs* by imagining the past as an allegorical precursor for contemporary reformation. The problem for the play is twofold: it has to nuance the allegory so that Oldcastle nevertheless remains loyal to King Henry the Fifth even in his disobedience to the church, and it has to recognize Henry's allegiance to the Catholic past even as it redeems him. Thus it follows Shakespeare in ultimately casting Henry as psychologically breaking from his childhood; it attempts to separate Oldcastle's Lollard sympathies from the charge of treason (E2), heresy, and the more general problem of vernacular reading. As a judge announces early in the play, "when the vulgar sort / Sit on their Ale-bench, with their cups and cans, / Matters of State be not their common talke, / Nor pure Religion by their lips prophan'd" (B).

Hoccleve grapples with the same problem: that Oldcastle's Lollard sympathies place him in opposition with his king.[22] So, Hoccleve berates Oldcastle for the Lollard "conceits" of opposing confession, sacrament, priestly exegesis of the Bible, transubstantiation, pilgrimage, idolatry, and clerical endowment. Hoccleve even presses the point to argue against the common reading of scripture in favor of tradition (153–60):

> Our*e* fadres olde & modres lyued wel,
> And taghte hir children / as he*m* self taght wer*e*
> Of holy chirche / & axid nat a del
> 'Why stant this worde heere?' / and 'why this word there?'
> 'Why spake god thus / and seith thus elles where?'
> 'Why dide he this wyse / and mighte han do thus?'
> Our fadres medled no thyng of swich gere:
> þat oghte been a good mirour to vs.

Hoccleve asserts a past of stability against the revolutionary present. With this, he condemns the close reading of texts, the questioning of why one word stands here, another there. Yet, follower of father Chaucer, he is one of the children he rebukes, and as a Chaucerian poet and a literary scribe of the major fourteenth-century poets, he cannot help but measure out each word, placing them here and there to develop his meter, rhyme, line breaks, and *mise-en-page*. By the writing of the poem, 1415, Arundel's Constitutions had specifically named Lollardy the English heresy, and so Hoccleve's stand against vernacular reading walks a fine line, for even as it espouses orthodoxy it furthers vernacular reading practices. The problem for the play and the poem alike is an apparent paradox: in Hoccleve's poem, the vernacular poet must denounce vernacular interpretation even as he develops it, and in Oldcastle's mythology, the Protestant martyr must stand with the Catholic king who legitimizes the Tudor line. Lancastrian and Elizabethan texts both grapple with the paradox of literary history—with progress and break—as they try to negotiate a place from a past that constitutes their possibilities for writing.

Although Hoccleve seems to censor literary engagement in the "Remonstrance against Oldcastle," his project is ultimately enabling. Hoccleve assembles a reading list for Oldcastle (193–200):

> Bewar Oldcastel / & for Crystes sake
> Clymbe no more / in holy writ so hie!
> Rede the storie of Lancelot de lake,
> Or Vegece of the aart of Chiualrie,
> The seege of Troie / or Thebes / thee applie
> To thynge þat may to thordre of knyght longe!
> To thy correcci*u*on / now haaste and hie,
> For thow haast been out of ioynt al to longe.

Hoccleve recommends the *Art of Chivalry*, romance, and the sieges of Troy and Thebes. These readings are intended to put Oldcastle back in joint—to align him, in a tangible way, with his role. And further, no sooner does Hoccleve warn Oldcastle from climbing so high in Holy Writ, he recommends a specific list of biblical reading (201–8):

> If thee list thyng rede of auctoritee,
> To thise stories sit it thee to goon:
> To Iudicum / Regum, and Iosue,
> To Iudith / & to Paralipomenon,
> And Machabe / & as siker as stoon,
> If þat thee list in hem bayte thyn ye,
> More autenike thing / thow fynde noon,
> Ne more pertinent to Chiualrie.

Judges, Kings, Joshua, Judith, Paralipomenon, and Maccabees—nothing is "more pertinent to Chiualrie" than the Bible, Hoccleve announces, pointing out that "Kynghtes so dide in tymes þ*a*t be past" (209). Overtly, Hoccleve's advice seems simply incoherent, prohibiting biblical reading in one stanza and then endorsing it in the next, and in this the poem expresses a tension he cannot escape, for his writing is premised on the authority of letters, and he is constituted through a tension of appropriation: push too hard, take too much, and Hoccleve will fall afoul of exactly the authority he wishes to use and be deemed a heretic. Push too lightly, take too little, and he cannot constitute himself in writing.

This same tension dominates Hoccleve's own reading practices as is clear in his major poem, the *Regement of Princes*, where he decries Lollard exegesis but then goes on to explicate Genesis himself. Written between 1410 and 1411, the *Regement* is a two-part poem dedicated to Henry V, when he was still Prince of Wales. In the first part of the *Regement*, Hoccleve, lamenting his desperate poverty in the fields outside London, meets an indigent old man who, after listening to his autobiography and his personal knowledge of Chaucer, encourages him to write a begging poem to the king. The second part of the *Regement* is just this poem, a *fürstenspiegl*. In the last section of *The Regement* Hoccleve presents Chaucer's image as a poet (see Figure 5.7). Hoccleve's particular lines, placed next to the portrait of Chaucer in the manuscript, suggest a relationship between the author and the book that goes beyond biography.

> Al þogh his lyfe be queynt þe resemblaunce
> Of him haþ in me so fressh lyflynesse
> Þat to putte othre men in remembraunce
> Of his p*er*sone I haue heere his lyknesse
> Do make to þis ende in sothfastnesse
> Þat þer þ[t] haue of him lest þought & mynde
> By þis þeynture may ageyn him fynde

The passage enacts a double appropriation: it first authorizes Chaucer by appropriating iconography toward a secular use—deifying Chaucer—and then selects that very image to define Hoccleve's own authority. For here Chaucer is the "more autentike thing" that underwrites Hoccleve's poetry, and Hoccleve's claim is that he, Hoccleve, knows this thing better than his reader does. He can put other men in remembrance because he has the authority to fashion the icon. Further, this icon embodies Chaucer's self in ways beyond the poetry, beyond any words that might put other men in remembrance of his person. Hoccleve fashions Chaucer as a recognizable self, a living Hector, and thus embeds Chaucer as a representation of poetic authority within his text, one that authorizes, not simply his own writing, but his entire autobiography. Hoccleve creates himself by first creating Chaucer as an author.

Immediately after setting the Chaucer portrait out, and constituting himself through the double appropriation of authorization and selection, however, Hoccleve decries the Lollard objection to iconography: "Yit so*m*me holden oppynyon and sey / Þat none ymages schuld I maked be / Þer erren foule & goon out of þe wey / Of trouth haue þer scant sensibilite."[23] In "Remonstrance against Oldcastle," too, Hoccleve continues this sense of visuality. "Right as a spectacle helpith feeble sighte, / Whan a man on the book redith or writ, / And causith him to see bet than he mighte" (417–19). The paradox for Hoccleve concerns the appropriation of this authority from previously authorized sources—the Bible, Chaucer. His way around this paradox is to mark it, to admonish Oldcastle and prohibit too much thinking on iconography, and thus position himself as congruent with the sources of authority, indeed, as entirely endorsing them, contributing to them, furthering their cause. In this allegiance, however, he also asserts his own authority and thus authorizes his own trespass into the authority he acknowledged as prohibited, which is accomplished within the book as a tangible object of that authority. Throughout all his major works, Hoccleve casts himself as the exception, the one who is able to counsel knights, princes, and kings. This exceptional status is constituted through a kind of double bind, the push and pull of acknowledgment and alienation, embedding and subordination, that we see throughout sixteenth-century literature, in which his prior familiarity with vernacular writing both authorizes his voice and allows him to use it to censor other writing as heresy.

Sir Iohn Old-castle deals with this same problem of vernacular reading. Ransacking Oldcastle's house for documents that will finally prove him heretical, the Bishop comes up with books (H2):

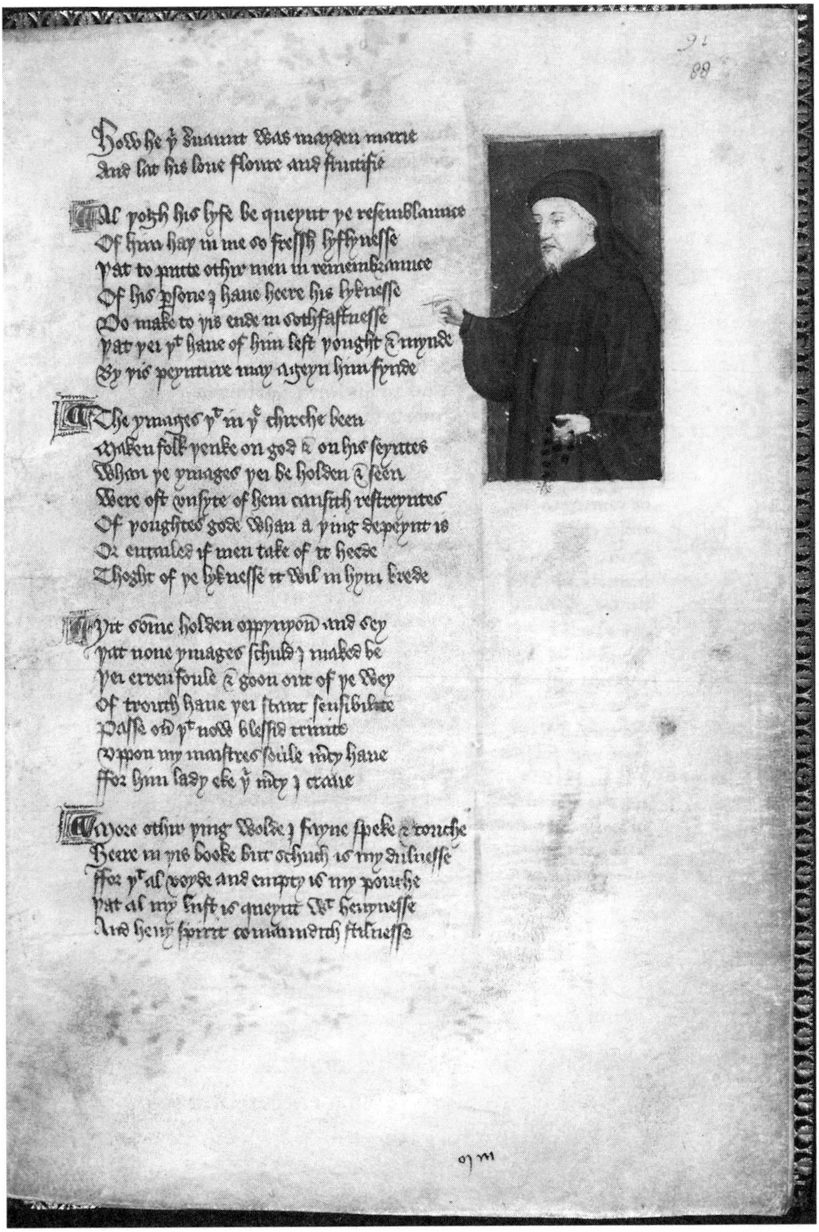

Hou he yt auctour was mayden marie
And lat his love floure and fructifie

Al yoȝh his lyfe be queynt ye resemblaunce
Of him hay in me so fressh lyflynesse
Yat to putte othir men in remembraunce
Of his persone I haue heere his lyknesse
Do make to yis ende in sothfastnesse
Yat yei yt haue of him lest yought & mynde
By yis peynture may aȝeyn him fynde

The ymages yt in ye chirche been
Maken folk yenke on god & on his seyntes
Whan ye ymages yei be holden & seen
Were oft vnsyte of hem causith restreyntes
Of youghtes gode Whan a ying depeynt is
Or entailed if men take of it heede
Thoght of ye lyknesse it wil in hym brede

Yit somme holden oppynyon and sey
Yat none ymages schuld I maked be
Yei erren foule & goon out of ye wey
Of trouth haue yei scant sensibilite
Passe ouer yt now blessid trinite
Vppon my maistres soule mercy haue
ffor him lady eke yi mercy I craue

More othir ying wolde I fayne speke & touche
Heere in yis booke but schuch is my dulnesse
ffor yt al voyde and empty is my pouche
Yat al my lust is queynt wt heuynesse
And heuy spirit commaundeth stilnesse

Figure 5.7. Knowing Chaucer. *The Regement of Princes*, British Library MS Harley 4866, fol.88,

Enter *Sumner with bookes.*

Bish. What bringst thou there? what, bookes of heresie?
Sum. yea my Lord, here's not a Latine booke,
No not so much as our Ladies Psalter:
Here's the Bible, the Testament, the Psalmes in meeter,
The sickmans salue, the Treasure of Gladnesse,
All English, no not so much but the Almanacke's English.
Bish. Away with them, to'th fire with them Clun,
Now fie vpon these vpstart heretikes,
All English, burne them, burne them quickly Clun.
Harpoo. But do not Sumner as you'l answer it, for I haue there English bookes my Lord, that Ile not part withal for your byshoppricke, Beuis of Hampton, Owleglasse, the frier and the boy, Ellen of Rumming, Robin-hood, and other such godly stories, which if ye burne, by this flesh ile make ye drink their ashes in S. Margets ale.
Exit

The Summoner discovers a welter of texts: religious (the Bible and psalms), commonplace (the almanac), and literary. Oldcastle's man, Harpoole, casts a distinction: "I haue there English bookes," he cautions, and these he means to protect. The books seem to constitute a small library of Middle English reading printed in the first quarter of the sixteenth century: *Bevis of Hampton* was printed at least once by de Worde in 1500, by Pynson in 1503, and by Julian Notary in 1510, and afterwards well into the seventeenth century.[24] *Howleglas* was printed in Antwerp by J. Van Doesborch in 1519 and then by William Copland in 1555 and 1560, and remains in a fragment dated at 1560.[25] John Skelton's *Eleanor Rumming* was printed by de Worde in 1521 and as part of a larger collection of Skelton's works by Richard Lant for Henry Tab in 1545, by John King for Thomas Marshe in 1554, and by John Day in 1563.[26] *The Frere and the Boye* was printed by de Worde around 1513 and reprinted by William Middleton in 1545, Edward Allde after 1584 and, beginning with Allde, numerous times in the seventeenth century.[27] Lastly, *Robin Hood* was printed quite often, beginning with Richard Pynson in 1500, de Worde in 1506, Hugo van der Goes in 1509, and Julian Notary in 1515.[28]

Absurdly anachronistic a library as this may be for Oldcastle's manor, it presents an argument in which English literature is inseparable from English heresy. The issue is not simply that the political instability of the period is contemporary with the interest in literary production, but that the one constitutes the other. To hunt out heresy is to discover medieval literature. Such is the representative force of the broken angel in *Sir Iohn Old-castle*. To recognize Falstaff from Oldcastle, then, is to recognize literary history. For Falstaff-Oldcastle constitutes the medieval as a locatable reality but also as an otherness, a heretical treason that is nevertheless true. Apocrypha and necessity, fiction and historical record, self and other, Falstaff is Jack Cade, the rebellious Brewer, the lord of misrule located in the past but always lurking in Henry's consciousness, usually denied but never eradicated.

In *Sir Iohn Old-castle*, Henry resolves this paradox when he is confronted with reports of Oldcastle's disloyalty by naming the past as the past (G3):

> *king*. I thinke the iron age begins but now,
> Which learned poets haue so often taught,
> Wherein there is no credit to he giuen
> To either words, or lookes, or solemne oaths:
> For if he were, how often hath he sworne,
> How gently tun'd the musicke of his tongue,
> And with what amiable face beheld he me,
> When all God knowes, was but hypocrisie.

Shocked at the possibility of Oldcastle's hypocrisy, Henry announces "the Iron Age," and in doing so, both names his own historical condition and provides the readers of the Pavier Quartos with an overarching conception, *a period*, for the collection's plays. Henry's name for the period, "the Iron Age"—damning as it is—acknowledges its literary capacity in its "learned poets" and the music of its courtiers' tongues. In this, he provides a vocabulary to both recognize and rationalize the past for the present, accomplishing a performance of periodization and sovereignty that breaks with the past, with his own past and the past of the nation, in a single gesture. "In this way," Kathleen Davis writes, "the paradox of a self-constituting modernity is folded into the cut of periodization itself, and the 'modern' can emerge as unproblematically sovereign."[29] Thus, if on one level the Pavier Quartos embrace the historical practices of manuscript book assembly, and if on a second level they couple these practices with the tropes of print, then on a third level they are explicitly recursive, their intellectual contents looping back on their physical manifestations to encounter the problem of history and construct authorship and canon through a synergy of forms dependent on, rather than oppositional to, the historical imagination. This process of recursion is multiply productive: it produces historical period by casting time as the Iron Age; it produces authorship by writing Gower-as-the-voice-of-the-past, Chaucer-as-absent, and Shakespeare-as-gentleman-writer; it produces the canon as a personal quarto collection; and, finally, it produces the reader as distancing the past but also participating in its construction.

In this, the Pavier Quartos contain the program necessary to assemble the fifteenth century and modernity alike. I mean this literally. We tend to think of books as static objects and of coded programs as interactive, so that the making of books is material and tangible, while programming is digital and abstract. When we refer to digital code we imagine a sequence of ones and zeroes that constitute a primary layer of instruction that build through various levels of machine language to abstract representation. Yet both printing and programming are digital in that each digit, each letter form, each one and each zero, must occupy a single space. There can be no blank space in the printer's form; each individual digit of type must be accounted for, each space assigned in order to hold the form together. The individual pieces of type may bear different letters or blanks, and the ink may cover those signs to varying degrees, but ultimately the pieces themselves are a mode of digital technology. In both cases the process of textual production uses discrete unities to signify presence and absence; in neither case does the composition process rely on variation in gradations of signal that would define it as analogue, and further, the ultimate representation is never defined exclusively by the primary layer of instruction but by the representation produced as the digital sequence is read back, processed, at higher and higher levels of abstraction.

In this sense, when Pavier's compositor set the title pages for the Quartos, one after the other, he composed a block of digital code. He used this block to create a representation and then modified it by pulling discrete elements of the code out—say the title "A / YORKSHIRE / TRAGEDIE. / *Not so New, as Lamentable* / and True"—and recoding in "THE LATE, / And much admired Play, / CALLED, / Pericles, Prince of / Tyre. / *With the true Relation of the whole Hi-*/story, aduentures, and fortunes of / the said Prince." What is significant, and often overlooked, is that the notion of digital textual production is not a twentieth-century concept but is in fact implicit in print, that slow-changing technology of the 1450s. The notion that printed books and electrical components are underwritten by a fundamental similarity may seem naïve, a confusion of pre- and postindustrial technological practices, but I submit that it is no more naïve than the notion that a single trope, recursion, can be operational across so many disciplines as music, the fine arts, mathematics, computer programming, artificial intelligence, linguistics, evolutionary biology, and, finally, literary history.

Thus, the Pavier Quartos present the reader with an assembly program. This assembly program is written as metonymy: a twofold tropic action that transforms parts into a whole and then changes the name of this whole from a collection of textual fragments to a witness of the Iron Age, from various quartos to authorial canon. Readers fluent in the tropes and schemes of what I am calling textual formalism, but what might simply be called the poetic language of books, must in some way use their imagination to activate the booklets' programming to construct author, canon, history, and literary authority from their physical structure. In this sense the reader of the Pavier Quartos must supply the matching half of Sir John's broken angel to animate the literary functions implicit in the text. Readers of screen-based poetry must do exactly the same thing by searching out the literary object and then participating with it, in whatever manner it insists, so as to construct its meaning. Both quarto and computer reader must develop a certain amount of skill and invest that skill into the reading process in order for the text to produce its meaning, which occurs at various levels of remove from the digital code work itself.

The First Folio operates according to a different register from that of the Pavier Quartos, and this colors its production of Shakespeare and the process of reading. The Folio's editors, John Heminge and Henry Condell, are explicit about this difference. In their opening, "Epistle Dedicatorie," to William, Earl of Pembroke, and Philip, Earl of Montgomery, they represent the book as a sum greater than its parts. "There is a great difference," they write, "whether any Booke choose his Patrones, or finde them" (A2^{v}):

> This hath done both. For, so much were your L L. likings of the seuerall parts, when they were acted as before they were published, the Volume ask'd to be yours. We haue but collected them, and done an office to the dead, to procure his Orphanes, Guardians; without ambition either of selfe-profit, or fame: onely to keepe the memory of so worthy a Friend, & Fellow aliue, as was our S H A K E S P E A R E, by humble offer of his playes, to your most noble patronage.

Heminge and Condell begin straightforwardly enough: the lords liked the plays as they were acted. Already, however, the plays are not simply separate events. They are "parts," "orphans" needing guardians, abandoned fragments looking to be made whole. "This hath done both": there appears something of a magnetic attraction in these parts to the patrons who would make them whole. As such a whole, the volume inhabits the "Go little book" trope we know from Chaucer and Spenser in which the book is capable of leaving its maker and adventuring on its own. In this case, the book does not go from Chaucer or Spenser to the steps of classical poetry or the fields of pastoral warbles but strangely stays within the real world to speak directly to the lords Pembroke and Montgomery. As a result, these scattered parts collected by Heminge and Condell become an office to the dead, an entity that changes its name from "volume" to "our S H A K E S P E A R E," asserting a unified self and book, the self and book of authorship, over the many selves and plays the man named Shakespeare produced.

The editors thus accomplish the two aspects of metonymy—part for whole and change of name—before the plays have even been presented. Where the Pavier Quartos demanded the readers' assembly of parts into a whole, the Folio is unified, reproduced at a rate of between 500 and 750 copies per print run. And although Heminge and Condell initially insist that they work "without ambition either of selfe-profit, or fame," they quickly reverse this in their next preface "To the great Variety of Readers" (A3):

> Well! It is now publique, & you wil stand for your priuiledges wee know: to read, and censure. Do so, but buy it first. That doth best commend a Booke, the Stationer saies. Then, how odde soeuer your braines be, or your wisedomes, make your licence the same, and spare not. Iudge your sixe-pen'orth, your shillings worth, your fiue shillings worth at a time, or higher, so you rise to the iust rates, and welcome. But, what euer you do, Buy.

Whatever you do, buy the book. Again, the reader is asked to weigh coins, to recognize the value of exchange and ratify the proper match. The First Folio is recorded as selling for 15s. unbound and £1 in calfskin.[30] At this price, the value of the Folio lies not in the experience of the plays so much as in the product. Gary Taylor explains, "for the price of the complete Shakespeare folio, you could stand in the yard of the Globe there 240 times." It lies not so much in the individual plays, either; Taylor continues, "at the standard price of sixpence each, you could buy 40 printed play quartos."[31] Given that the First Folio only delivers thirty-six plays, many already available in quarto, for the price of forty, its value lies elsewhere. Taylor reflects: "the 1623 object not only preserved texts of those 36 plays; it also bound them together. That act of binding structured subsequent acts of reading."[32] The act of reading is very much showcased in Heminge and Condell's lines, which accord the reader the role of judge and censor. Yet the judgment Heminge and Condell emphasize in the preface occurs at a much higher level of abstraction than we saw with the Pavier Quartos. Rather than thinking through the legitimacy of character or selecting certain quartos to be bound together as an edition, rather than supplying the matching half of the imaginary broken angel that will mark the text as part of a uniquely personal collection of plays, all the reader of the folio must do is weigh the price—six pennies, a shilling, five shillings!—not the texts, which will fall out as the readers' odd brains devise. In presenting the plays as a bound object, the First Folio accomplishes the poetic functions of the book—part for whole, change of name—in advance. What remains is for the individual reader to consecrate this function by paying for it. In short, the First Folio charges a supplementary price—two shillings to be exact—for performing the operations of metonymy.

For the reader of the First Folio, then, the experience of the past is replaced by the formal structures of authorship and genre, compilation and binding, through which Shakespeare's canon is routed. Examine its Catalogue (Figure 5.8), which eliminates *Pericles* and presents the plays according to fixed generic categories, of which history is only a subset. To this extent, the Catalogue is of a piece with Heminge and Condell's later announcement in their preface that "where (before) you were abus'd with diuerse stolne, and surreptitious copies, maimed, and deformed by the frauds and stealthes of iniurious impostors, that expos'd them: euen those, are now offer'd to your view cur'd, and perfect of their limbes."[33] The Pavier Quartos are no doubt part of this fraudulent textual past, one that falsified Shakespeare's texts and rendered his canon imperfect. So the Folio sheers it all away, dissolving the unity of *The Whole Contention*, removing any possible collaborators, eliminating Gower, banishing *Oldcastle* and the *Yorkshire Tragedie*, as well as Henry's pronouncement of the Iron Age, as the frauds and stealthes of injurious impostors; so it eliminates Shakespeare's nondramatic verse entirely; so it arrives at a moment of origins through the assertion of formal principles of literary organization—scene division, generic category, the complete folio book—as the dominant mode of conceptual organization. The first issue of the First Folio does not even contain the most recognizably Chaucerian title, *Troilus and Cressida*. In this, the First Folio banishes English literary history, particularly the Chaucerian literary history of production. In doing so, it also banishes the reader from the

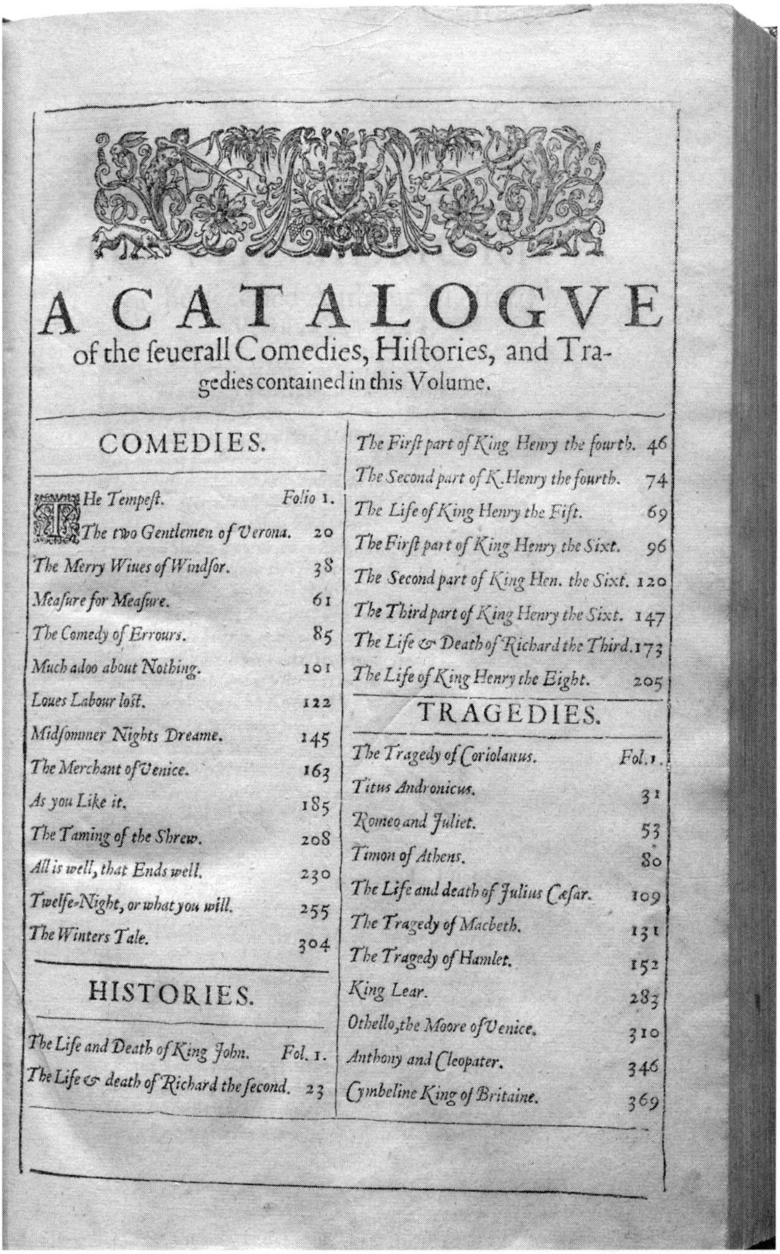

A CATALOGVE
of the ſeuerall Comedies, Hiſtories, and Tragedies contained in this Volume.

COMEDIES.

THe Tempeſt.	Folio 1.
The two Gentlemen of Verona.	20
The Merry Wiues of Windſor.	38
Meaſure for Meaſure.	61
The Comedy of Errours.	85
Much adoo about Nothing.	101
Loues Labour loſt.	122
Midſommer Nights Dreame.	145
The Merchant of Venice.	163
As you Like it.	185
The Taming of the Shrew.	208
All is well, that Ends well.	230
Twelfe-Night, or what you will.	255
The Winters Tale.	304

HISTORIES.

The Life and Death of King John.	Fol. 1.
The Life & death of Richard the ſecond.	23
The Firſt part of King Henry the fourth.	46
The Second part of K. Henry the fourth.	74
The Life of King Henry the Fift.	69
The Firſt part of King Henry the Sixt.	96
The Second part of King Hen. the Sixt.	120
The Third part of King Henry the Sixt.	147
The Life & Death of Richard the Third.	173
The Life of King Henry the Eight.	205

TRAGEDIES.

The Tragedy of Coriolanus.	Fol. 1.
Titus Andronicus.	31
Romeo and Juliet.	53
Timon of Athens.	80
The Life and death of Julius Cæſar.	109
The Tragedy of Macbeth.	131
The Tragedy of Hamlet.	152
King Lear.	283
Othello, the Moore of Venice.	310
Anthony and Cleopater.	346
Cymbeline King of Britaine.	369

Figure 5.8. Formalism and the protocols of auto-assembly. "A Catalogue," in *Mr. William Shakespeares Comedies, Histories, & Tragedies Published According to the True Originall Copies* (London: Isaac Jaggard and Edmund Blount for William Jaggard, Edmund Blount, John Smethwick, and William Aspley, 1623), A8, *STC* 22273 fol. 1 no .05, reproduced by permission of the Folger Shakespeare Library.

production process, effectively programming in an intellectual structure for Shakespeare that appears fixed.

If the Pavier Quartos are programmed according to the assembly codes of the Chaucerian past, the Folio is programmed for auto-assembly: its animating scripts enact the twofold metonymic process—parts into whole, change of name from book to "SHAKESPEARE"—regardless of the reader's engagement. George Donaldson argues that in contrast to Ben Jonson's *Workes*, "the First Folio's full audacity is to claim that it puts its readers directly in touch not only with his hand, but also with Shakespeare's mind."[34] The book's audacity is indeed impressive, but not original. Hoccleve asserts much the same in the *Regement* with regards to Chaucer, bringing to his readers Chaucer's very "p*er*sone," and we know that readers such as Thomas Speght and Richard James read Hoccleve and noted his text as they thought through the English canon. Thus I see the reading of the Middle Ages against modernity as a task less of reading a selection of texts by one author against the other—Chaucer's *Troilus and Criseyde* against Shakespeare's *Troilus and Cressida*, *Two Noble Kinsmen* against *The Knight's Tale*—than of tracing out the process of canon construction in the sixteenth century as it loops back on the Middle Ages, casting it as historically remote even as it makes use of its material and intellectual technologies.

What is created by the First Folio is the long shadow of modernity, a shade so complete it blocks out the past. In the First Folio the author is proclaimed dead, and his death seals the past away from the reader, closing it off as a period that cannot be accessed directly and, paradoxically, resurrecting him as immortal in its place. And so the First Folio imagines a break with the past into formalism, a break that casts any engagement with "the Iron Age" as excessive and that totalizes the most variegated of artistic endeavors—the theatre, the poet, the self, the book—under the rubric of all totalities: the Modern. For the Folio contrives literature as autonomous and formal, alienated from history, which—conceived of as existing externally to the book—must actively be brought to bear on the work of art if it is to influence what Greg so drolly referred to as "received opinion." As Jane Rickard writes, "Shakespeare's Folio, however, more fully achieves the separation of texts from the specific contexts in which they were produced, and the general contexts of authority and literary tradition."[35] Simultaneously closed and open, it presents the reader with a fait accompli that imagines a pure engagement with authorship, even as it presides over the author's death. The Pavier Quartos and the First Folio thus imagine history differently—the one names the past as the Iron Age, the other asserts a larger generic framework over this very construction—but both use the material form of the book to imagine the Shakespearean canon. The contrast between the two demonstrates the emergence not simply of Shakespeare as a dramatic author but of modernity as a formalist practice by which the past is bracketed off through a unified vision of the self as autonomous, existing forever in the present, living in death, speaking directly to the reader. In such a view, history must be brought to bear on the forms of literature—as anecdote, as additional information—if it is to make any difference. Thus, to read Shakespeare in the shadow of the First Folio is to subscribe to a notion of break—a break from the past, a break into literary forms—that isolates the text from history and, ultimately, from technology.

And so, over one hundred years later, Greg's argument continues to thrill. Not only does his conclusion of deception still broadly govern the critical assessment of the Pavier Quartos, but his brusque opposition between the New Bibliography and "received opinion" remains in play. As Stephen Cohen writes, "without overmuch simplification, the institutional history of literary studies, over the last hundred or so years can be characterized as a series of agonistic oscillations between the discipline's two mighty opposites, form and history."[36] Greg views the study of books as a science of forms, the demonstration of fact—as Nedig writes two years after Greg announced his analysis of the Quartos, "no argument of any kind is involved."[37] Of course, the opposition between form and history is elusive, and Greg and Nedig perhaps write tongue-in-cheek, for the end result of their analysis is both historical and polemical, a major revision of Shakespeare's bibliography. What nevertheless remains forceful about Greg's thesis is both the separation of the evidence under study, the physical book, from the field of study, literature, and the tacit assumption that the renovation of any methodological category for study—the New Bibliography, the New Historicism, the New Media—exists externally to the narrative of period, which is forever modern. For as Fredric Jameson reminds us, the narrative of modernity is attuned to the scandal of origins, the willingness to be shocked by yet another moment of novelty in the narrative's overall trajectory.

Jameson concludes that "we cannot not periodize" and accepts that modernity is an incomplete project. I suggest that we pursue this project at some risk. For when taken to the next step, a step Greg no doubt never imagined, the categorical science of textual forms as separate from "received opinion" has the power to eclipse the project of humanist study. Witness the development of New Media studies outside of literature departments, a discipline so secure in its claims to novelty, so confident in its break with the past, that it has no truck with history at all. Quite obviously, academic units devoted to commercially interested formalism are new players in the academic structure and stage a persuasive draw among students and administrations eager to finance education by engaging directly with the marketplace. In my view, each claim for the novelty of sixteenth-century print culture and authorship, each denial of the technologies of the past as somehow still in the cradle, obliquely confirms the validity of a contemporary rupture. We are in a time of transition if we allow ourselves to tell a narrative of births and rebirths. This depends chiefly on our narrative practice, and I suggest we experiment with narrative instead of merely subscribing to a story in which we are bit players, full of high sentence and glad to be of use.

The Renaissance may have invented the doctrine of artistic progress, but there is no reason that we must measure the literary arts accordingly. Reading in the shadow of the First Folio, in the sway of its tremendous gravitational pull, we often forget that it is a historical form. The one significant truth of the book, in all its forms, is that books are, as William Caxton terms them, "lyberal monumentis." They are simultaneously intimate and anonymous, deeply connected to the individual reader's experience and profligate, moving from reader to reader across centuries. They are also possessive of beautiful and sophisticated qualities, and this is true of the most elegant handmade medieval manuscripts and of the Kindle, both of which express the historical circumstances of their mode of production. In this, books present our twin charge—form and history—and reading them is an experience of participating in history and standing apart from it. Engaging with books returns us to both our contingency and our isolation. It sets us within time and within our imagination, and in doing so it allows us to cast multiple narratives simultaneously. Bridging the self and the other, the beauty of reading is that it demonstrates that we are all connected here.

I suggest that we recognize the agon of influence and creativity, as well as the enduring legacy of the past, as within the indomitable nature of literary reading. This process of realizing multiple narratives should remind us that we are well beyond the opposition between form and history at this point in literary studies. The literary imagination allows a powerful time travel, one that constructs the self from the forms of the past and, in so doing, breathes life into time. The great charge and command that Philosophy puts on all of us is to realize that this connection is not simply within a sequence of events we perceive as linear but across all time, which, amazingly, we can access through the technology of the book. Given this access, to imagine that our participation in the production of knowledge is entirely married to an incomplete modernity is ultimately to refuse to take up Philosophy's challenge in the hope of reaching some final point of immanence that could be called a true present. Thus I abandon the notion of periodicity in favor of a more fundamental subscription to literature, for literature is our choice and our charge, and in opening a book we ultimately find ourselves embedded within it.

NOTES

Introduction

1. Keith Richards, *Life* (New York: Little, Brown, 2010), 364.

2. Ibid., 365.

3. Gilles Deleuze and Félix Guattari, *A Thousand Plateaus: Capitalism and Schizophrenia*, trans. Brian Massumi (Minneapolis: University of Minnesota Press, 1987), 6.

4. Douglas R. Hofstadter, "Twentieth-Anniversary Preface," in *Gödel, Escher, Bach: An Eternal Golden Braid* (1979; rpt., New York: Vintage Books, 1999), P-2.

5. See, for example, John Guillory, *Cultural Capital: The Problem of Literary Canon Formation* (Chicago: University of Chicago Press, 1993).

6. See Curtis Perry and John Watkins's introduction to *Shakespeare and the Middle Ages* (Oxford: Oxford University Press, 2009), 1–18.

7. Lukas Erne, afterword to *Shakespeare's Book: Essays in Reading, Writing and Reception*, ed. Richard Meek, Jane Rickard, and Richard Wilson (Manchester, UK: Manchester University Press, 2008), 260.

8. I borrow the term "tangled loop" from Hofstadter's more technical reading of recursion in *Drawing Hands* in *Gödel, Escher, Bach*, 689–90.

9. Marshall McLuhan, *Understanding Media: The Extensions of Man* (1964; rpt., Cambridge, MA: MIT Press, 2001), 8. See the more recent elaboration of this view by Jay David Bolter and Richard Grusin, *Remediation: Understanding New Media* (Cambridge, MA: MIT Press, 1999).

10. Kathleen Davis, *Periodization & Sovereignty: How Ideas of Feudalism & Secularization Govern the Politics of Time* (Philadelphia: University of Pennsylvania Press, 2008), 5.

11. Jonathan Gil Harris, *Untimely Matter in the Time of Shakespeare* (Philadelphia: University of Pennsylvania Press, 2009), 16.

12. For Harris's discussion of metonymy, see ibid., 146.

13. Davis, *Periodization & Sovereignty*, 5.

14. Throughout *Recursive Origins* I make use of specific editions, modernizing long-s and w, expanding and italicizing abbreviations, and listing the edition by *Short-Title Catalogue* (*STC*) number in the notes. When I refer to a work in general, I use its modern title rather than the sprawling original titles.

15. Patrick Cheney, *Shakespeare's Literary Authorship* (Cambridge: Cambridge University Press, 2008), 22.

16. See William Kuskin, "Vernacular Humanism: Fifteenth-Century Self-Fashioning and the State-Crowned Laureates," chapter 6 of *Symbolic Caxton: Literary Culture and Print Capitalism* (Notre Dame, IN: University of Notre Dame Press, 2008).

Chapter One. Machine Language

1. David Wallace, *The Cambridge History of English Literature* (Cambridge: Cambridge University Press, 1999), 638.

2. *The Cambridge History of Early Modern English Literature,* ed. David Loewenstein and Janel Mueller (Cambridge: Cambridge University Press, 2002), 8, 88, and 108 respectively.

3. James Simpson, *1350–1547: Reform and Cultural Revolution*, vol. 2 of *The Oxford English Literary History* (Oxford: Oxford University Press, 2002), 1.

4. Paul Strohm, "Chaucer's Fifteenth-Century Audience and the Narrowing of the 'Chaucer Tradition,'" *Studies in the Age of Chaucer* 4 (1982): 3–32, and David Lawton, "Dullness and the Fifteenth Century," *English Literary History* 54 (1987): 761–99.

5. A. C. Spearing, *Medieval to Renaissance in English Poetry* (Cambridge: Cambridge University Press, 1985), 89.

6. Helen Cooper and Sally Mapstone, eds., *The Long Fifteenth Century: Essays for Douglas Gray* (Oxford: Clarendon Press, 1997).

7. Frederic Jameson, *A Singular Modernity: Essay on the Ontology of the Present* (New York: Verso, 2002), 34. See also the companion volume, *The Modernist Papers* (New York: Verso, 2009), as well as his similar argument in the foreword to *The Postmodern Condition: A Report on Knowledge* (1984; rpt., Minneapolis: University of Minnesota Press, 1989), vii–xxi.

8. Jameson, *Singular Modernity*, 29.

9. Ibid., 13.

10. See Robert J. Meyer-Lee, *Poets and Power from Chaucer to Wyatt* (Cambridge: Cambridge University Press, 2007), 27 and 40.

11. Jameson, *Singular Modernity*, 150.

12. Daniel Wakelin, *Humanism, Reading, and English Literature, 1430–1530* (Oxford: Oxford University Press, 2007), 86; Meyer-Lee, *Poets and Power*, 231.

13. Leah Marcus, "Reading Matter," *PMLA* 121 (2006): 11.

14. Jessica Brantley, "The Prehistory of the Book," *PMLA* 124 (2009): 632–39. Two recent monographs that follow out such a capacious history of books are Jennifer Summit, *Memory's Library: Medieval Books in Early Modern England* (Chicago: University of Chicago Press, 2008), and Siân Echard, *Printing the Middle Ages* (Philadelphia: University of Pennsylvania Press, 2008).

15. New Formalism has recently been discussed by Marjorie Levinson in "What is New Formalism?," *PMLA* 122 (2007): 558–68, and to some extent by Marjorie Perloff in her "Presidential Address 2006: It Must Change," *PMLA* 122 (2007): 652–62, and Stephen Cohen in his introduction to *Shakespeare and Historical Formalism* (Burlington, VT: Ashgate, 2007), 1–27, and "Between Form and Culture: New Historicism and the Promise of a Historical Formalism," in *Renaissance Literature and Its Formal Engagements*, ed. Mark David Rasmussen (New York: Palgrave, 2005), 17–42.

16. The masterwork on recursion is Douglas R. Hofstadter's *Gödel, Escher, Bach: An Eternal Golden Braid* (New York: Vintage Books, 1979), the claims of which are reiterated in *I Am a Strange Loop* (New York: Basic Books, 2007). Useful to understanding the basics of recursive programming are Robert T. Wainwright's *The Recursive Universe: Cosmic Complexity and the Limits of Scientific Knowledge* (New York: William Morrow 1985), and Joseph R. Shoenfield, *Recursion Theory* (Berlin: Springer-Verlag, 1993). See also N. Katherine Hayles's discussion of recursion in *How We Became Posthuman: Virtual Bodies in Cybernetics, Literature, and Informatics* (Chicago: University of Chicago Press, 1999).

17. Hofstadter, *Gödel, Escher, Bach*, 127.

18. W. Tecumseh Fitch, "Three Meanings of 'Recursion': Key Distinctions for Biolinguistics," in *The Evolution of Human Language*, ed. R. K. Larson, V. Déprez, and H. Yamakido (Cambridge: Cambridge University Press, 2010), 75.

19. *Fibonacci's Liber Abaci: A Translation into Modern English of Leonardo Pisan's Book of Calculation*, ed. L. E. Sigler (Springer: New York, 2002), 404–5. See also Joseph Gies and Frances Gies, *Leonard of Pisa and the New Mathematics of the Middle Ages* (New York: Thomas Y. Crowell, 1969).

20. K. K. Tung, *Topics in Mathematical Modeling* (Princeton, NJ: Princeton University Press, 2007), 5.

21. Ibid., 12.

22. Reviewed in the introduction to Larson, Déprez, and Yamakido, eds., *The Evolution of Human Language*, 1–13, and in Michael C. Corballis,

The Recursive Mind: The Origins of Human Language, Thought, and Civilization (Princeton, NJ: Princeton University Press, 2011), 5.

23. Marc D. Hauser, Noam Chomsky, and W. Tecumseh Fitch, "The Faculty of Language: What Is It, Who Has It, and How Did It Evolve?," *Science* 22 (2002): 1569; reprinted in Larson, Déprez, and Yamakido, eds., *The Evolution of Human Language*, 14–42.

24. Hayles, *How We Became Posthuman*, 225.

25. Fitch discusses this nicely in "Three Meanings of 'Recursion,'" 73–90; see especially his point that meta-mathematical recursion is not recursion at all (85).

26. Quoted and translated by William Fitzgerald in *Martial: The World of the Epigram* (Chicago: University of Chicago Press, 2007), 99.

27. Colin H. Roberts and T. C. Skeat, *The Birth of the Codex*, enl. and exp. ed. (London: Oxford University Press, 1987), 4.

28. Fitzgerald, *Martial*.

29. Harold Bloom, *A Map of Misreading* (Oxford: Oxford University Press, 1975), 102, and Gérard Genette, *Narrative Discourse: An Essay in Method* (Ithaca, NY: Cornell University Press, 1974).

30. Brian Cummings, "Metalepsis: The Boundaries of Metaphor," in *Renaissance Figures of Speech*, ed. Sylvia Adamson, Gavin Alexander, and Katrin Ettenhuber (Cambridge: Cambridge University Press, 2007), 221, contains an excellent review of the bibliography.

31. See M. B. Parkes, "The Influence of the Concepts of *Ordinatio* and *Compilatio* on the Development of the Book," *Medieval Learning and Literature: Essays Presented to Richard William Hunt*, ed. J. J. G. Alexander and M. T. Gibson (Oxford: Clarendon Press, 1976).

32. Ralph Hanna III and Traugott Lawler, "Textual Notes to *Boece*," in *The Riverside Chaucer*, ed. Larry D. Benson (Boston: Houghton Mifflin, 1987), 1151. See also *Chaucer According to William Caxton: Minor Poems and "Boece," 1478*, ed. Beverly Boyd (Lawrence, KS: Allen Press, 1978), 196.

33. Hofstadter, *Gödel, Escher, Bach*, 146.

34. Lotte Hellinga, *William Caxton and Early Printing in England* (London: The British Library, 2010), 45–51.

35. Paul de Man, *Blindness and Insight: Essays in the Rhetoric of Contemporary Criticism*, 2nd ed. rev. (Minneapolis: University of Minnesota Press, 1983), 148.

36. For the deployment of this title, as well as the more striking title "Arch-Poët," see *The Faerie Queen; The Shepheards Calendar: Together with the Other Works of England's Arch-Poët, Edm. Spencer; Collected into One Volume* (London: Humphrey Lownes, 1611), STC 23083.3.

37. Harold Bloom, *The Anxiety of Influence: A Theory of Poetry* (1973; rpt., Oxford: Oxford University Press, 1997), 11.

38. Ibid., xxviii.

39. See Bruce Holsinger, *The Premodern Condition: Medievalism and the Making of Theory* (Chicago: University of Chicago Press, 2005), and Summit, *Memory's Library.*

40. Bruno Latour, *We Have Never Been Modern*, trans. Catherine Porter (Cambridge, MA: Harvard University Press, 1993).

41. Bloom, *The Anxiety of Influence*, 141.

42. Jean-François Lyotard, "Answering the Question: What Is Postmodernism?," in *The Postmodern Condition: A Report on Knowledge*, trans. Geoff Bennington and Brian Massumi (1984; rpt., Minneapolis: University of Minnesota Press, 1989), 79.

Chapter Two. The Poet

1. Sir Philip Sidney, *An Apologie for Poetrie* (London: James Roberts for Henry Olney, 1595), I2v. Written between 1579 and 1583, Sidney's essay was printed twice in 1595, by Henry Olney as *An Apologie for Poetrie* (22534) and by William Ponsonby as *The Defence of Poesie* (22535/4.5). Michael Brennan writes, "It is relevant to note that Ponsonby's most textually unsatisfactory work was his edition of Sidney's *Defence* even though it was commissioned to supersede Olney's carefully edited but unauthorized version" ("William Ponsonby: Elizabethan Stationer," *Analytical and Enumerative Bibliography* 7 [1983]: 94). I cite from Olney's edition. The text is edited by Geoffrey Shepherd as *An Apology for Poetry, or, The Defense of Poesy*, 3rd ed., rev. and exp. by R. W. Maslen (Manchester, UK: Manchester University Press, 2002).

2. For specific arguments in terms of *The Shepheardes Calender*, with which this chapter is concerned, see Paul Alpers, "Pastoral and the Domain of Lyric in Spenser's *Shepheardes Calender*," *Representations* 12 (1985): 83–100; A. F. Marotti, *Manuscript, Print, and the English Renaissance Lyric* (Ithaca, NY: Cornell University Press, 1995); and David Lee Miller, *The Poem's Two Bodies: The Poetics of the 1590 "Faerie Queene"* (Princeton, NJ: Princeton University Press, 1988). The notion that fifteenth-century printing is fundamentally transitional is embedded in the very term by which it is recognized: the incunable. As a result, discussion of the way early printing engages with capitalism, canonicity, and nationalism is often deferred to the sixteenth century. I pursue this argument in more depth in my introduction to *Caxton's Trace: Studies in the History of English Printing*, ed. William Kuskin (Notre Dame, IN: University of Notre Dame Press, 2006).

3. Lynn Staley Johnson, *The Shepheardes Calender: An Introduction* (University Park: Pennsylvania State University Press, 1990), 12.

4. For the generic overlap between intellectual and material forms in *The Shepheardes Calender*, see Ruth Samson Luborsky, "The Allusive Presentation of *The Shepheardes Calender*," *Spenser Studies* 1 (1980): 29–67, and Bruce R. Smith, "On Reading *The Shepheardes Calender*," *Spenser Studies* 1 (1980): 69–93.

5. Listed in the *Short-Title Catalogue* as *STC* 5077, printed by Adam Islip for George Bishop; *STC* 5078, printed by Islip for Bonham Norton; and *STC* 5079, printed by Islip for Thomas Wight.

6. Listed as *STC* 5068, by Thomas Godfray, and then reprinted in 1542 by Richard Grafton for William Boham (*STC* 5069) and for John Reynes (*STC* 5070).

7. On Spenser's use of the "go little book" topos, see A. C. Spearing, *Medieval to Renaissance in English Poetry* (Cambridge: Cambridge University Press, 1985), 327–32, and Miller, *The Poem's Two Bodies*, 30–44. On the trope in general, see Anne Coldiron, *Canon, Period, and the Poetry of Charles of Orleans: Found in Translation* (Ann Arbor: University of Michigan Press, 2000); on Chaucer's use in *Troilus and Criseyde*, see Glending Olson's "Making and Poetry in the Age of Chaucer," *Comparative Literature* 31 (1979): 272–89.

8. My citations from *Troilus and Criseyde* and from Geoffrey Chaucer's poetry in general are taken from the 1561 edition, *The Woorkes of Geffrey Chaucer, Newly Printed, with Diuers Addicions, Whiche Were Neuer in Printe Before: with the Siege and Destruccion of the Worthy Citee of Thebes, Compiled by Ihon Lidgate, Monke of Berie* (London: John Kingston for John Wight, 1561), listed as *STC* 5076 and commonly referred to as Stow's edition. For Stow, see *John Stow (1525–1605) and the Making of the English Past*, ed. Ian Gadd and Alexandra Gillespie (London: British Library, 2004). The lines cited here appear on fol. cxliii.^{v} of the 1561 edition and correspond to lines V.1786–82 in *The Riverside Chaucer*, 3rd ed., ed. Larry D. Benson (Boston: Houghton Mifflin, 1987). For ease of reference, I note both the page numbers from the 1561 edition and the line numbers in the *Riverside*.

9. *The Shepheardes Calender* (London: Hugh Singleton, 1579), π¶.i.^{v} (*STC* 23089); see also the facsimile version, Edmund Spenser, *The Shepheardes Calender, 1579* (Menston, UK: Scolar Press, 1968), which reproduces Bodleian 40 F 2 (10) Art.BS.

10. For a review of the scholarship discussing E. K.'s identity, see chapter 1 of Patsy Scherer Cornelius, *E. K.'s Commentary on "The Shepheardes Calender"* (Salzburg: University of Salzburg, 1974), 1–13, as well as the more recent discussion of the issue in Frances M. Malpezzi, "E. K., A Spenserian Lesson in Reading," *Connotations* 4, no. 3 (1994/95): 181–91.

11. *The Woorkes of Geffrey Chaucer*, fol. clv.^{v}; *Riverside*, I.809.

12. *The Woorkes of Geffrey Chaucer*, fol. clxii.^{v}; *Riverside*, II.1026–29.

13. See also Seth Lerer, *Courtly Letters in the Age of Henry VIII: Literary Culture and the Arts of Deceit* (Cambridge: Cambridge University Press, 1997).

14. For recent scholarship on John Lydgate, see *Lydgate Matters: Poetry and Material Culture in the Fifteenth Century*, ed. Lisa H. Cooper and Andrea Denny-Brown (New York: Palgrave Macmillan, 2008); Robert J. Meyer-Lee, *Poets and Power from Chaucer to Wyatt* (Cambridge: Cambridge University Press, 2007); *John Lydgate: Poetry, Culture, and Lancastrian England*, ed. Larry Scanlon and James Simpson (Notre Dame, IN: University of Notre Dame Press, 2006); and Maura Nolan, *John Lydgate and the Making of Public Culture* (Cambridge: Cambridge University Press, 2005).

15. Henry Bergen, ed., *Lydgate's Fall of Princes*, Early English Text Society Early Series 121 (1924; rpt., London: Oxford University Press, 1967), I. 252.

16. James Simpson, *1350–1547: Reform and Cultural Revolution*, vol. 2 of *Oxford English Literary History*, ed. Jonathan Bate (Oxford: Oxford University Press, 2002), 42. See also John J. Thompson, "Reading Lydgate in Post-Reformation England," in *Middle English Poetry: Texts and Traditions: Essays in Honour of Derek Pearsall*, ed. A. J. Minnis (Woodbridge, UK: York Medieval Press, 2001), 181–209.

17. The *STC* records the *Fall of Princes* as printed by Richard Pynson in 1494 (*STC* 3175) and in 1527 (*STC* 3176), by John Wayland in 1554 (*STC* 3177.5/78), and by Richard Tottel (*STC* 3177).

18. The *STC* records the *Troy Book* as printed by Pynson in 1513 (*STC* 5579), by Thomas Marshe in 1555 (*STC* 5580), and by Thomas Purfoot in 1614 (*STC* 5581.5).

19. Wynkyn de Worde's 1497 *Storye of Thebes* is recorded as *STC* 17031.

20. Seth Lerer, *Chaucer and His Readers: Imagining the Author in Late-Medieval England* (Princeton, NJ: Princeton University Press, 1993), 7.

21. David Lawton, "Dullness and the Fifteenth Century," *English Literary History* 54 (1987): 771.

22. Marotti, *Manuscript, Print, and the English Renaissance Lyric*, 293. See also Wendy Wall, *The Imprint of Gender: Authorship and Publication in the English Renaissance* (Ithaca, NY: Cornell University Press, 1993), 12–13.

23. For example, John Skelton, *Here After Foloweth Certayne Bokes, Compyled by Mayster Skelton, Poet Laureat* (London: Richard Lant for Henry Tab, 1545), *STC* 22598; reprinted by John King and Thomas Marshe in 1554, *STC* 22599; and by John Day in 1563, *STC* 22600.

24. Jane Griffiths, *John Skelton and Poetic Authority: Defining the Liberty to Speak* (Oxford: Oxford University Press, 2007), 190.

25. Jane Griffiths, "What's in a Name? The Transmission of 'John Skelton, Laureate' in Manuscript and Print," *Huntington Library Quarterly*

67, no. 2 (2004): 217. For a strong argument regarding Skelton's conception of his name in print, see Lerer, *Chaucer and His Readers*. The *Eneydos* is *STC* 24796.

26. Miller, *The Poem's Two Bodies*, 48.

27. For example, in *The Chaucer Canon*, W. W. Skeat writes, "the most important book, with regard to the Chaucerian canon, is of course Thynne's first edition of Chaucer in 1532, as this was the first volume in which his Works were presented in a collected form" ([1900; rpt., New York: Hastell House, 1965], 94). This view has largely been picked up and repeated in comments such as Marotti's (note 22 above) and in A. S. G. Edwards's "Chaucer from Manuscript to Print: The Social Text and the Critical Text," *Mosaic* 28, no. 4 (1995): 1–12. As a literal observation of fact, the statement is quite true: Thynne's edition is the first single-volume printed edition of Chaucer's works.

28. See the oft-cited essay by Julia Boffey, "Richard Pynson's Book of Fame and the Letter of Dido," *Viator* 19 (1988): 339–53.

29. For the so-called Oxford Group of Chaucerian anthologies see E. P. Hammond's initial identification in "On the Editing of Chaucer's Minor Poems," *Modern Language Notes* 23 (1908): 20–21, and the more recent discussion by Julia Boffey and John J. Thompson in "Anthologies and Miscellanies: Production and Choice of Texts," in *Book Production and Publishing in Britain, 1375–1475*, ed. Jeremy Griffiths and Derek Pearsall (Cambridge: Cambridge University Press, 1989), 280–81.

30. For an updated list of Caxton's productions see Paul Needham, "Appendix D: Checklist of Caxton's Printing," in *The Printer and the Pardoner* (Washington, DC: Library of Congress, 1986), 83–91. The most recent complete biography of Caxton is N. F. Blake's *William Caxton*, vol. 3 of *English Writers of the Late Middle Ages*, ed. M. C. Seymour, Authors of the Middle Ages (Brookfield, VT: Ashgate, 1996), 1–67. For an excellent overview of Caxton's work, see Lotte Hellinga, *William Caxton and Early Printing in England* (London: British Library, 2010).

31. The *STC* records these texts as *Stans puer ad mensam* (*STC* 17030), *The Churl and the Bird* (*STC* 17008), *The Horse, the Sheep and the Goose* (*STC* 17018), the *Temple of Glass* (*STC* 17032), Chaucer's *Temple of Brass* (*STC* 5091) and *Queen Anelida and the False Arcite* (*STC* 5090), Caxton's 1483 *Canterbury Tales* (*STC* 5083), and *Troilus and Criseyde* (*STC* 5094).

On Caxton's composite volumes see Needham, *The Printer and the Pardoner*, 69–80. These have been discussed in terms of the Chaucerian tradition by Seth Lerer in "William Caxton," in *The Cambridge History of Medieval English Literature*, ed. David Wallace (Cambridge: Cambridge University Press, 1999), esp. 726. See also a number of articles by Alexandra Gillespie: "Caxton's Chaucer and Lydgate Quartos: Miscellanies from Manuscript to

Print," *Transactions of the Cambridge Bibliographical Society* 12 (2000): 1–26; "The Lydgate Canon in Print, 1476–1534," *Journal of the Early Book Society* (2000): 59–93; "Poets, Printers, and Early English *Sammelbände*," *Huntington Library Quarterly* 67, no. 2 (2004): 189–214; and her chapter "'Folowynge the Trace of Mayster Caxton': Some Histories of Fifteenth-Century Printed Books," in Kuskin, ed., *Caxton's Trace.*

32. For some account of these allusions, see two articles by N. F. Blake: "Caxton and Chaucer," *Leeds Studies in English* n.s., 1 (1967): 19–36, and "John Lydgate and William Caxton," *Leeds Studies in English* 16 (1985): 272–89.

33. For the first point see Blake's "Caxton and Chaucer," 36; for the second, Richard Firth Green, *Poets and Princepleasers: Literature and the English Court in the Late Middle Ages* (Toronto: University of Toronto Press, 1980), 159. See also Robert Costomiris, "Sharing Chaucer's Authority in Prefaces of Chaucer's Works from William Caxton to William Thynne," *Journal of the Early Book Society* 5 (2002): 1.

34. *Oxford English Dictionary*, s. v. Lodestar, definition 2.

35. For Dido see John Watkins, *The Specter of Dido: Spenser and the Virgilian Epic* (New Haven, CT: Yale University Press, 1995), as well as my discussion in *Symbolic Caxton: Literary Culture and Print Capitalism* (Notre Dame, IN: University of Notre Dame Press, 2008), 243–57.

36. Jonathan Goldberg, *Writing Matter: From the Hands of the English Renaissance* (Stanford, CA: Stanford University Press, 1990), 179.

37. *The Woorkes of Geffrey Chaucer*, fol. vi.[v]; *Riverside*, 1 [A].2059.

38. *The Woorkes of Geffrey Chaucer*, fol. clxxxv.[v]; *Riverside*, V.232.

39. *The Woorkes of Geffrey Chaucer*, fol. lxii.[v]; *Riverside*, V.1386–93.

40. Jennifer Summit, *Lost Property: The Woman Writer and English Literary History, 1380–1589* (Chicago: University of Chicago Press, 2000), 39. On this point, see also Lee Patterson's chapter "'Thirled with the Poynt of Remembraunce': The Theban Writing of *Anelida and* Arcite" in *Chaucer and the Subject of History* (Madison: University of Wisconsin Press, 1991), 68.

41. Watkins, *The Specter of Dido*, 64.

42. Listed in the *Short-Title Catalogue* as *STC* 12093 and 12097/.5. See Peter C. Herman, *Squitter-Wits and Muse-Haters: Sidney, Spenser, Milton and Renaissance Antipoetic Sentiment* (Detroit: Wayne State University Press, 1996).

43. For discussion of these two composite volumes, see Gillespie, "'Folowynge the Trace of Mayster Caxton.'"

44. See *The Siege of Thebes* in *The Woorkes of Geffrey Chaucer*, fol. ccclvi. See also *The Siege of Thebes*, ed. Robert R. Edwards (Kalamazoo, MI: Medieval Institute Publications, 2001), line 44.

45. See Germaine Warkentin, "Sidney's Authors," in *Sir Philip Sidney's Achievements*, ed. M. J. B. Allen, Dominic Baker-Smith, Arthur F. Kinney, and Margaret Sullivan (New York: AMS, 1990), 83. For a review of Sidney's library, see also Germaine Warkentin, "The World and the Book at Penshurst: The Second Earl of Leicester (1595–1677) and His Library," *Library*, 6th ser., 20, no. 4 (1998): 325–46. Also useful is *Sir Philip Sidney and the Interpretation of Renaissance Culture: The Poet in His Time and in Ours: A Collection of Critical and Scholarly Essays*, ed. Gary F. Waller and Michael D. Moore (London: Croom Helm, 1984).

46. *The Woorkes of Geffrey Chaucer*, fol. ccclvii; Edwards, *Siege of Thebes*, 200–210.

47. *The Woorkes of Geffrey Chaucer*, fol. ccclvi; Edwards, *Siege of Thebes*, Prologue, ln. 57.

48. *The Woorkes of Geffrey Chaucer*, fol. ccclvii and fol. ccclvi; Edwards, *Siege of Thebes*, ln. 1.190, and Prologue, ln. 1.48.

49. *The Woorkes of Geffrey Chaucer*, fol. ccclvii^{v}; Edwards, *Siege of Thebes*, ll. 331–33.

50. *The Woorkes of Geffrey Chaucer*, fol. ccclvii^{v}.

51. *The Woorkes of Geffrey Chaucer*, fol. ccclxi; Edwards, *Siege of Thebes*, ln. 1014.

52. Tim William Machan discusses this linguistic distance in his essay "Early Modern Middle English," in Kuskin, ed., *Caxton's Trace*, 299–322.

53. See, for example, George B. Harrison's generalization, "Roman type was reserved for books intended for a scholarly and cultured reader, black letter was the popular type. All ballads are in black letter, news pamphlets, novels and proclamations. Poetry, on the other hand, intended for gentlemen readers, was usually ornamentally printed in roman and italic, as were scholarly or technical works" ("Books and Readers, 1591–4," *Library* ser. 4, 8 [1927]: 283).

54. Zachary Lesser, "Typographic Nostalgia: Play-Reading, Popularity, and the Meanings of Black Letter," in *The Book of the Play: Playwrights, Stationers, and Readers in Early Modern England*, ed. Marta Straznicky (Amherst: University of Massachusetts Press, 2006), 99. Lesser provides an excellent review of the scholarship on black letter. For a more historical account see D. C. Greetham's *Textual Scholarship: An Introduction* (New York: Garland, 1994), 169–270.

55. Lesser, "Typographic Nostalgia," 106.

56. See Nicolas Barker, "Caxton's Typography," *Journal of the Printing Historical Society* 11 (1976/7): 131–32, and Hellinga, *William Caxton*, 102.

57. Stanley Morison, "Early Humanistic Script and the First Roman Type," *Library* 4th ser., 24, nos. 1–2 (1943): 6.

58. The *Sermo* is *STC* 21800, the *Oratio*, *STC* 12413. See Geoffrey Ashall Glaister, *Encyclopedia of the Book*, 2nd ed. (New Castle, DE: Oak Knoll Press, 1996).

59. *The Fall of Prynces; Gathered by John Bochas, From the Begynnyng of the World Vntyll His Time, Translated into English by John Lidgate Monke of Burye* (London: Printed by John Wayland, 1554), T.P.v *STC* 3177.5.

60. *The Woorkes of Geffrey Chaucer*, fol. ccxliiii.v; *Riverside*, 22–23.

61. Geoffrey Chaucer, *The Canterbury Tales* (Westminster: William Caxton, 1483), aii (*STC* 5083).

62. David R. Carlson, "Woodcut Illustrations of the *Canterbury Tales*, 1483–1602," *Library*, 6th ser., 19 (1997): 26.

63. See David R. Carlson, "A Theory of the Early English Printing Firm: Jobbing, Book-Publishing, and the Problem of Productive Capacity in Caxton's Work," in Kuskin, ed., *Caxton's Trace*.

64. Jonathan Gil Harris, *Untimely Matter in the Time of Shakespeare* (Philadelphia: University of Pennsylvania Press, 2009), 112.

65. For a useful discussion of the complex relationship in the manuscript editions of Chaucer, see Ralph Hanna III, *Pursuing History: Middle English Manuscript and Their Texts* (Stanford, CA: Stanford University Press, 1996). I follow out the complex transition from manuscript to print in *Symbolic Caxton*.

66. Edmund Spenser, *The Faerie Queen; The Shepheards Calendar: Together with the Other Works of England's Arch-Poët, Edm. Spencer; Collected into One Volume, and Carefully Corrected* (London: Humphrey Lownes for Matthew Lownes, 1611), *STC* 23083.3/.7.

67. For a suggestive discussion of the production and consumption of texts into these later periods, see Roger Chartier's *The Order of Books: Readers, Authors, and Libraries in Europe between the Fourteenth and Eighteenth Centuries* (Stanford, CA: Stanford University Press, 1994).

Chapter Three. The Dramatic Quarto

1. These are *An Apologie for Poetrie: Written by the Right Noble, Vertuous, and Learned, Sir Phillip Sidney, Knight* (London: James Roberts for Henry Olney, 1595), *STC* 22534, and *The Defence of Poesie by Phillip Sidney* (London: Printed for William Ponsonby, 1595), *STC* 22535 (with a variant issue, *STC* 22534.5, combining quires from the *Apologie* with the title page of the *Defence*); *The Countesse of Pembrokes Arcadia, Written by Sir Philippe Sidnei* (London: Printed by John Windet for William Ponsonby, 1590), *STC* 22539 and 22539a, *STC* 22540 (1593), *STC* 22541 (London: Printed by Richard Field for William Ponsonby, 1598), and *STC* 22542 (Edinburgh:

Robert Waldegraue, 1599); *Sir P. S. His Astrophel and Stella* (London: Printed by J. Danter for Thomas Newman, 1591), *STC* 22537, *STC* 22536 (Printed by John Charlewood for Thomas Newman, 1591), *STC* 22538 (London: Printed by Felix Kingston for Matthew Lownes, 1597), with an additional fragment.

2. *The Shepheardes Calender* (London: Printed by Hugh Singleton, 1579), *STC* 23089, *STC* 23090 (London: Thomas East for John Harrison, 1581), *STC* 23091 (London: John Wolfe for John Harrison, 1586), *STC* 23092 (London: Printed by John Windet for John Harrison, 1591), and *STC* 23093 (London: Printed by Thomas Creede for John Harrison, 1597); *Three Proper, and Wittie, Familiar Letters* (London: H. Bynneman, 1580), *STC* 23095; *De rebus gestis Britanniae commentarioli tres Ad ornatissimum virum M. Henricum Broncarem Armigerum. E. S.* (London: Henrici Binneman, 1582), *STC* 21488; *The Faerie Queene* (London: John Wolfe for William Ponsonby, 1590), *STC* 23081, 23080, 23081a, and *STC* 23082 (London: Printed by Richard Field for William Ponsonby, 1596); *Complaints* (London: William Ponsonby, 1591), *STC* 23078; *Daphnaïda* (London: Printed by T. Orwin for William Ponsonby, 1591), *STC* 23079; *Prosopopoia* (London: William Ponsonby, 1591), *STC* 23078; *Axiochus* (London: Cuthbert Burby, 1592), *STC* 19974.6; *Amoretti and Epithalamion* (London: Printed by P. Short for William Ponsonby, 1595), *STC* 23076; *Colin Clouts Come Home Againe* (London: Printed by Thomas Creede for William Ponsonby, 1595), *STC* 23077; *Fowre Hymnes* (London: Printed by Richard Field for William Ponsonby, 1596), *STC* 23086; *Prothalamion* (London: Printed by J. Orwin for William Ponsonby, 1596), *STC* 23088; and *The Second Part of The Faerie Queene* (London: Richard Field for William Ponsonby, 1596), *STC* 23082.

3. The major shift in the past decade of Shakespeare studies has been to view Shakespeare as concerned with his identity in print. This issue was powerfully broached by Lukas Erne's field-changing *Shakespeare as Literary Dramatist* (Cambridge: Cambridge University Press, 2003), and builds on the more general sense, as Marta Straznicky writes, "that the reading of drama (whether in the context of play production, censorship, pedagogy, or private leisure) was a recognized cultural practice in early modern England that only partially intersected with the culture of playgoing" ("Plays, Books, and the Public Sphere," in *The Book of the Play: Playwrights, Stationers, and Readers in Early Modern England*, ed. Marta Straznicky [Amherst: University of Massachusetts Press, 2006], 1). Erne's argument is more polemical, however, and suggests that Shakespeare consciously crafted himself as a literary maker in print. More recently, the thesis has been furthered by Patrick Cheney, in *Shakespeare's Literary Authorship* (Cambridge: Cambridge University Press, 2008).

The history of the earlier view is reviewed in Erne's introduction to his *Shakespeare as Literary Dramatist* and reiterated more recently in his "Reconsidering Shakespearean Authorship," *Shakespeare Studies* 36 (2008): 26–36. Note especially David Scott Kastan, *Shakespeare and the Book* (Cambridge: Cambridge University Press, 2001), and his rebuttal to Erne, "'To Think These Trifles Some-thing': Shakespearean Playbooks and the Claims of Authorship," *Shakespeare Studies* 33 (2005): 221–36; Andrew Murphy, *Shakespeare in Print: A History and Chronology of Shakespeare Publishing* (Cambridge: Cambridge University Press, 2003); and Douglas Brooks, *From Playhouse to Printing House: Drama and Authorship in Early Modern England* (Cambridge: Cambridge University Press, 2000).

4. Shakespeare, *Venus and Adonis* (London: Richard Field, 1593), *STC* 22354, discussed in Murphy, *Shakespeare in Print*, 287.

5. Peter W. M. Blayney, "The Publication of Playbooks," in *A New History of Early English Drama*, ed. John D. Cox and David Scott Kastan (New York: Columbia University Press, 1997), 385–86. Shakespeare's plays in print are usefully listed in Murphy's "Chronological Appendix," 287–386. The plays I mention above are *The First Part of the Contention* (London: Printed by Thomas Creede for Thomas Millington, 1594), *STC* 26099; *Lucrece* (London: Printed by Richard Field for John Harrison, 1594), *STC* 22345; *The Most Lamentable Romaine Tragedie of Titus Andronicus* (London: Printed by John Danter for Edward White and Thomas Millington, 1594), *STC* 22328; *Venus and Adonis* (*STC* 22355); *The True Tragedie of Richard Duke of Yorke and the Deth of Good King Henrie the Sixt* (London: Printed by Peter Short for Thomas Millington, 1595), *STC* 21006; and Harrison's third edition of *Venus and Adonis* (*STC* 22356).

6. Blayney, "Publication of Playbooks," 388.

7. Peter Stallybrass and Roger Chartier, "Reading and Authorship: The Circulation of Shakespeare 1590–1619," in *A Concise Companion to Shakespeare and the Text*, ed. Andrew Murphy (Malden, MA: Blackwell, 2007), 39.

8. Counting Shakespeare's editions is no straightforward task: Does one count poetry as well as drama? Apocrypha? Only first editions? What of variants and archival fragments? Murphy's "Chronological Appendix" in *Shakespeare in Print* (287–386) lists ninety-two items from 1593 through to the Pavier Quartos in 1619. Of these, sixty-four texts carry Shakespeare's name in some fashion.

9. Erne, *Literary Dramatist*, 63–64.

10. Ibid., 68.

11. Stallybrass and Chartier, "Reading and Authorship," 46.

12. See Peter Berek, "Genres, Early Modern Theatrical Title Pages, and the Authority of Print," in Straznicky, ed., *The Book of the Play*, 159–75.

13. Lukas Erne, "Print and Manuscript," in *The Cambridge Companion to Shakespeare's Poetry*, ed. Patrick Cheney (Cambridge: Cambridge University Press, 2007), 66. See also Patrick Cheney, *Shakespeare, National Poet-*

Playwright (Cambridge: Cambridge University Press, 2004), for discussion of the authorial overlap between poetry and drama.

14. "*Henry VI, Part 2*: Commodifying and Recommodifying the Past in Late-Medieval and Early-Modern England," in *Henry VI: Critical Essays,* ed. Thomas A. Pendleton (New York: Routledge, 2001), 187.

15. Erne, *Literary Dramatist*, 50.

16. Kastan, "'To Think These Trifles,'" 45.

17. David Lawton, "Dullness and the Fifteenth Century," *English Literary History* 54 (1987): 775.

18. *A Treatise Excellent and Compendious, Shewing and Declaring, in Maner of Tragedye, the Falles of Sondry Most Notable Princes and Princesses with Other Nobles, Through ye Mutabilitie and Change of Vnstedfast Fortune*... (London: Richard Tottel, 1554), fol. xxv (*STC* 3177).

19. Shakespeare, *Venus and Adonis*, H^{v}.

20. When I refer to Shakespeare's play in the abstract, I use the conventional title, *2 Henry VI*. Otherwise, I refer either to the 1594 *Contention* (*STC* 26099), which I note parenthetically as Q1 followed by the signature, or to the version in the 1623 Folio (*STC* 22273), *The Second Part of Henry the Sixt*. Ronald Knowles presents a convenient facsimile of *The Contention* in the Arden edition, *King Henry VI: Part 2* (1999; rpt., London: Thomson Learning, 2001). The *STC* lists the other editions I mention above as follows: 1595, *The True Tragedie*, *STC* 21006; 1600, *The First Part of the Contention*, *STC* 26100; 1600, *The True Tragedie*, *STC* 21006a; and 1619, *The Whole Contention*, *STC* 26101.

21. Murphy, *Shakespeare in Print*, 40.

22. This discussion is usefully reviewed by Thomas A. Pendleton in his introduction to *Henry VI: Critical Essays*, 1–25, and Knowles, *King Henry VI: Part 2*, "Appendix 2: Q1 and Q3 Variants," 408–33.

23. As Holinshed died in 1580, the final edition of the chronicles was assembled by a group of writers, known as the Syndicate, that included Richard Stanyhurst, Abraham Fleming, John Stow, Francis Thynne, John Hooker, and William Harrison. See Annabel Patterson, *Reading Holinshed's Chronicles* (Chicago: University of Chicago Press, 1994).

24. See Patrick Cheney, *Shakespeare's Literary Authorship*, chapter 5, "'Show of Love . . . Bookish Rule': Books, Theatre, and Literary History in *2 Henry VI*." More generally, see Charlotte Scott, *Shakespeare and the Idea of the Book* (Oxford: Oxford University Press, 2007).

25. Margaret Deanesly, "Vernacular Books in England in the Fourteenth and Fifteenth Centuries," *Modern Language Review* 15 (1920): 349.

26. Raphael Holinshed, et al., *The Firste Volume of the Chronicles of England, Scotlande, and Irelande* (London: Henry Denham for John Harrison,

George Bishop, Rafe Newberie, Henry Denham, and Thomas Woodcock, 1577), 430 (*STC* 13569.2pt 1).

27. Ibid., 432.

28. See Roger Chartier's analysis of Shakespeare's interest in merging these historical figures: "Jack Cade, the Skin of a Dead Lamb, and the Hatred for Writing," *Shakespeare Studies* 34 (2006): 77–89.

29. Holinshed, *The Firste Volume of the Chronicles of England*, 430.

30. Robert Adger Law, "The Chronicles and the Three Parts of *Henry VI*," *University of Texas Studies in English* 33 (1954): 13–32.

31. Holinshed, *The Firste Volume of the Chronicles of England*, 648–49.

32. I draw this distinction from Paul Needham's discussion in "Fragments in Books: Dutch Prototypography in the Van Ess Library," where he describes book history as closer to analytical bibliography in its evidentiary claims and the history of the book as larger in scope and more theoretical in practice (in *"So Precious a Foundation": The Library of Leander van Ess*, ed. Milton McCormick Gatch [New York: Union Theological Seminary & The Grolier Club, 1996]). See also my introduction to *Caxton's Trace: Studies in the History of English Printing*, ed. William Kuskin (Notre Dame, IN: University of Notre Dame Press, 2006), 25n3.

33. See Lister M. Matheson, *The Prose "Brut": The Development of a Middle English Chronicle* (Tempe: Arizona State University, 1998), 6.

34. Lister M. Matheson has stated the case for Caxton's authorship in "Printer and Scribe: Caxton, the *Polychronicon*, and the *Brut*," *Speculum* 60 (1985): 593–614.

35. Glossed by A. H. Thomas and I. D. Thornley, *The Great Chronicle of London* (1938; rpt. in microprint, Gloucester: Alan Sutton, 1983), 426.

36. Mary-Rose McLaren, *The London Chronicles of the Fifteenth Century: A Revolution in English Writing* (Cambridge: D. S. Brewer, 2002), 3.

37. C. L. Kingsford, *English Historical Literature* (Oxford: Clarendon Press, 1913), 99–100.

38. Thomas and Thornley, *The Great Chronicle of London*, 191.

39. Samuel K. Workman, "Versions by Skelton, Caxton and Berners of a Prologue by Diodorus Siculus," *Modern Language Notes* 56 (1941): 252–58.

40. Ranulf Higden and John of Trevisa, *Polychronicon* (Westminster: William Caxton, 1482), a^{v} (*STC* 13438).

41. Ibid., a3.

42. See Matheson, "Printer and Scribe," 595, 598, and 609, and *The Prose "Brut,"* 70–71, and 157–72.

43. Matheson, *The Prose "Brut,"* 6–8.

44. The 1482 *Chronicles* is *STC* 9992; the 1480 *Discripcion of Britayne* is *STC* 13440a.

45. Saint Albans, *Cronicles of Englonde with the Frute of Timis* (Saint Albans: Saint Albans Schoolmaster, 1485), *STC* 9995; William de Machlinia (*STC* 9993); Gerard de Leew, *Cronycles of the Londe of Englond* (*STC* 9994); Wynkyn de Worde (*STC* 9996).

46. De Worde 1502 (*STC* 9997), 1515 (*STC* 10000.5), 1520 (*STC* 10001), 1528 (*STC* 10002); Notary, 1504 (*STC* 9998), 1515 (*STC* 10000); and Pynson, 1510 (*STC* 9999). The 1520 edition appears not to have *The Descrypcyon of Englonde*.

47. I explore the question of production and consumption in my essay "'Onely Imagined': Vernacular Community and the English Press," in Kuskin, ed., *Caxton's Trace*, 199–240.

48. I discuss reproduction as an overall category in *Symbolic Caxton: Literary Culture and Print Capitalism* (Notre Dame, IN: University of Notre Dame Press, 2008).

49. The Saint Albans press is excellently reviewed by Lotte Hellinga in the *Catalogue of Books Printed in the XVth Century Now in the British Library: BMC Part XI, England* (Houten, The Netherlands: Hes & De Graaf Publishers, 2007), 10–11, 18–20, 301–6, 320–21, and 412–16 (hereafter referred to as *BMC XI*).

There are two bibliographical traditions stemming from E. Gordon Duff's early assessment of the text that continue to hold sway (see *Fifteenth Century English Books: A Bibliography of Books and Documents Printed in England and of Books for the English Market Printed Abroad*, Illustrated Monographs 18 [Oxford: Printed for the Bibliographical Society at Oxford University Press, 1917]): that the book was printed close to the 1486 *Boke of St Albans* to avoid an inexplicable delay, and that it is "not a reprint of Caxton's, but a separate compilation, comprising the same text, with a history of the Popes and other ecclesiastical matters interpolated throughout" (29). Still, the Schoolmaster twice dates the *Cronicles* at 1483 (aii and k viii^{v}), and the work matches Caxton's earlier text verbatim at many points. In the *Illustrium maioris Britanniae*, John Bale describes a compiler working with Caxton out of St Albans (*BMC XI*, 11). Hellinga adds: "The only fairly solid piece of evidence for a connection of Caxton with the Abbey of St Albans is a copy of an original note signed by Caxton. It is found in the contemporary binding of a manuscript of Mandeville's Travels in English, written by the printer Richard Tottel in 1579, and reads: 'This fair book I have from the Abbey at Saint Albans in this year of Our Lord 1490 the sixth day of April. William Caxton'" (*BMC XI*, 11).

50. *Cronycle of Englonde* (Westminster: Wynkyn de Worde, 1497), I.iii.

51. The Saint Albans press used four separate types: Types 2 and 3 are modeled on Caxton, and the final type, called Type 4, is a recasting of one of Caxton's; see Hellinga, *BMC XI*, 412–16.

52. Saint Albans, *Cronicles of Englonde,* aii. Citations hereafter noted parenthetically within the text.

53. See my discussion of printer's marks, "Affixing Value: The Bibliography of Material Culture," in *Symbolic Caxton*, 29–80.

54. Discussed in Nicolas Barker, "St Albans Press: The First Punch-Cutter in England and the First Native Typefounder?," *Transactions of the Cambridge Bibliographical Society* 7 (1979): 257–78.

55. The idea of the original copy is nicely articulated by William N. West in "Old News: Caxton, de Worde, and the Invention of the Edition," in Kuskin, ed., *Caxton's Trace*, 241–73.

56. Kuskin, *Symbolic Caxton*, 61.

57. Edward Hall and Richard Grafton, *The Union of the Two Noble and Illustre Famelies of Lancastre & Yorke* (London: Richard Grafton, 1548), [flueron] ii^{v} (*STC* 12721).

58. See the *Newe Cronycles of Englande and of Fraunce* (London: Richard Pynson, 1516), DD.iiii. (*STC* 10659), and the attributed and expanded version, *Fabyans Cronycle Newly Prynted* (London: William Rastell, 1533), kk.iii^{v} (*STC* 10660).

59. *The Union of the Two Noble and Illustre Famelies of Lancastre and Yorke* (*STC* 12722), fol. c.lxx^{v}.

60. The relationship between *The Great Chronicle of London* and Fabian's work remains unclear; see McLaren, *The London Chronicles,* 26–28.

61. D. R. Woolf, *Reading History in Early Modern England* (Cambridge: Cambridge University Press, 2000), 54.

62. Caxton, *Polychronicon*, a2^{v}.

63. Jonathan Gil Harris, *Untimely Matter in the Time of Shakespeare* (Philadelphia: University of Pennsylvania Press, 2009), 138.

64. Sarah Beckwith, "Medieval Penance, Reformation Repentance and *Measure for Measure*," in *Reading the Medieval in Early Modern England*, ed. Gordon McMullan and David Matthews (Cambridge: Cambridge University Press, 2007), 194.

Chapter Four. Form

1. See, for example, the essays collected in two recent editions, Martha W. Driver and Sid Ray, eds., *Shakespeare and the Middle Ages: Essays on the Performance and Adaptation of the Plays with Medieval Sources or Settings* (Jefferson, NC: McFarland, 2009), and Curtis Perry and John Watkins, eds., *Shakespeare and the Middle Ages* (Oxford: Oxford University Press, 2009).

2. See James Simpson's "Making History Whole: Diachronic History and the Shortcomings of Medieval Studies," in which he writes, "the break

in England was not restricted to a given discursive area, such as, say, ecclesiology or education. State-driven as the cultural revolution was in England, it affected the entire discursive landscape," in *Reading the Medieval in Early Modern England*, ed. Gordon McMullan and David Matthews (Cambridge: Cambridge University Press, 2007), 17.

3. Bruce Holsinger, "Lollard Ekphrasis: Situated Aesthetics and Literary History," *Journal of Medieval and Early Modern Studies* 35 (2005): 75.

4. For discussion of Chaucer and Shakespeare, see, for example, Ann Thompson, *Shakespeare's Chaucer: A Study in Literary Origins* (New York: Barnes & Noble, 1978); E. Talbot Donaldson, *The Swan at the Well: Shakespeare Reading Chaucer* (New Haven, CT: Yale University Press, 1985); and Jill Mann, "Shakespeare and Chaucer: 'What Is Criseyde Worth?'" in *The European Tragedy of Troilus*, ed. Piero Boitani (Oxford: Clarendon Press, 1989), 219–42. There is an older tradition of source study represented by Hyder E. Rollins, "The Troilus-Cressida Story from Chaucer to Shakespeare," *PMLA* 32 (1917): 383–429, and M. C. Bradbrook, "What Shakespeare Did to Chaucer's *Troilus and Criseyde*," *Shakespeare Quarterly* 9 (1958): 311–19, that sees Shakespeare as not fully understanding the dividing line between Chaucer and Henryson, effectively refuted by Donaldson, *The Swan at the Well*, 76–78.

5. Simpson emphasizes the importance of John Bale's literary history (*STC* 1295) and Gavin Douglas's *Eneados* (*STC* 24797) in chapter 1 of *1350–1547: Reform and Cultural Revolution*, vol. 2 of *The Oxford English Literary History*, ed. Jonathan Bate (Oxford: Oxford University Press, 2002), 7–33. Chapman's 1598 translations, *Achilles Shield* (*STC* 13635) and *Seauen Bookes of Iliades* (*STC* 13632), are widely cited in the literature on *Troilus and Cressida* and, with the *Eneados*, are discussed as significant markers of period by Julia Boffey and A. S. G. Edwards, "Literary Texts," in *The Cambridge History of the Book in Britain, Volume 3, 1400–1557*, ed. Lotte Hellinga and J. B. Trapp (Cambridge: Cambridge University Press, 1999), 575.

6. Caxton's *Recuyell of the Histories of Troye* has long been recognized as a major source for Shakespeare's play on grounds of plot similarity. See John S. P. Tatlock, "The Siege of Troy in Elizabethan Literature, Especially in Shakespeare and Heywood," *PMLA* 30 (1915): 673–770; Geoffrey Bullough, *Narrative and Dramatic Sources of Shakespeare* (New York: Columbia University Press, 1966), 6:83–111, with sample texts on 112–221; Kenneth Muir, *The Sources of Shakespeare's Plays* (New Haven, CT: Yale University Press, 1978), 141–57; and David M. Bevington, "'Instructed by the Antiquary Times': Shakespeare's Sources" in *Troilus and Cressida*, The Arden Shakespeare (1998; rpt., London: Thompson Learning, 2001), 375–97. Robert K. Presson provides a useful review of the early scholarship in *Shakespeare's "Troilus and Cressida" and the Legends of Troy* (Madison: University of

Wisconsin Press, 1953), though he weighs Chapman's Homer as the primary source. The consensus is that Shakespeare did not rely on Lydgate's *Troy Book*; see Elizabeth Stein, "Caxton's *Recuyell* and Shakespeare's *Troilus*," *Modern Language Notes* 45 (1930): 144–46.

7. There are seventeen English editions of *The Recuyell.* These are:

William Caxton, *The Recuyell of the Histories of Troye*, Folio, Bruges, 1473/74 (*STC* 15375). Caxton also produced a French edition of this text in 1474 with Colard Mansion, entitled *Recueil des histories de Troie*, which I do not number here.

Wynkyn de Worde, *The Recuyles or Gaderinge to Gyder of the Hystoryes of Troye*, Folio, London, 1502 (*STC* 15376), with a 1503 variant (*STC* 15377). A revised edition of *STC* 15375.

William Copland, *The Recuile of the Histories of Troie*, Folio, London, 1553 (*STC* 15378). A conflation of *STC* 15375 and 15376/7.

Thomas Creede and Valentine Simmes, *The Auncient Historie of the Destruction of Troy*, Quarto, London, 1596/97 (*STC* 15379). Revised by William Phiston. Books 1 and 2 are printed by Creede with title pages indicating 1596; book 3 by Simmes has a title page labeled 1597. This is the basis for all of the following editions to William Morris's version.

Thomas Creede, *The Ancient Historie, of the Destruction of Troy*, Quarto, London, 1607 (*STC* 15380).

Barnard Alsop, *The Ancient Historie of the Destruction of Troy*, Quarto, titled "Fifth Edition," London, 1617 (*STC* 15381).

Barnard Alsop and Thomas Fawcett, *The Ancient Historie of the Destruction of Troy*, Quarto, "Sixth Edition," London, 1636 (*STC* 15382).

Samuel Speed, *The Destruction of Troy*, Quarto, "Seventh Edition," London, 1663 (book 1, Wing L929; book 2, Wing L934; book 3, Wing L938). Here and following, Caxton's name is eliminated from the title page.

Thomas Passenger, *The Destruction of Troy*, Quarto, "Eight Edition," London, 1670 (book 1, Wing L930, printed by Tyler and Holt; book 2, Wing L935, printed with Speed; book 3, Wing L939, printed by Tyler & Holt).

Thomas Passenger, *The Destruction of Troy*, Quarto, "Ninth Edition," London, 1676 (Wing L931, L936, L940).

Thomas Passenger, *The Destruction of Troy*, Quarto, "Tenth Edition," London, 1680 (Wing L932, L937, L941).

Thomas Passenger, *The Destruction of Troy*, Quarto, "Eleventh Edition," London, 1684 (Wing L933, L937A, L941A).

Eben Tracey, *The Destruction of Troy*, Quarto, "Twelfth Edition," London, 1702.

Eben Tracy, *The Destruction of Troy*, Quarto, "Thirteenth Edition," London, 1708.

Thomas Browne, *The Destruction of Troy*, Quarto, "Eighteenth Edition," Dublin, 1738.

William Morris, *The Recuyell of the Historyes of Troye*, Hammersmith, 1892.

Ballantyne, Hanson & Co., *The Recuyell of the Historyes of Troye*, edited by H. Oskar Sommer for the Early English Text Society, London, 1894.

8. John Lydgate, *The Auncient Historie and Onely Trewe and Syncere Cronicle of the Warres Betwixte the Grecians and the Troyans . . . Translated in to Englyshe Verse by John Lydgate Moncke of Burye* (London: Thomas Marshe, 1555), *STC* 5580.

9. Following convention, I use the titles *Troilus and Cressida* to refer to Shakespeare's play and *Troilus and Criseyde* to refer to Chaucer's long poem in the abstract. When I discuss or cite the play, I refer to a specific printed title.

The criticism on *Troilus and Cressida* as a problem play is usefully summarized in Bevington's introduction to the Arden edition, 1–19. See also, W. R. Elton, *Shakespeare's Troilus and Cressida and the Inns of Court Revels* (Brookfield, VT: Ashgate, 2000), 1–17. *Troilus and Cressida* is often read as a local allegory, either for the political life of the Earl of Essex or for the Wars of the Theatres. See, for example, E. A. J. Honigmann's argument for the dating of the play at 1601 through the Essex rebellion in "The Date and Revision of Troilus and Cressida," in *Textual Criticism and Literary Interpretation*, ed. Jerome McGann (Chicago: University of Chicago Press, 1985), 38–54; and, more recently, Eric Mallin, "Emulous Factions and the Collapse of Chivalry: *Troilus and Cressida*," *Representations* 29 (1990): 145–79; and Heather James's *Shakespeare's Troy: Drama, Politics, and the Translation of Empire* (Cambridge: Cambridge University Press, 1997), chapter 3, "'Tricks We Play on the Dead': Making History in *Troilus and Cressida*," 85–118. See Robert Kimbrough's similar conclusion for the War of the Theatres, in "The Origins of *Troilus and Cressida*: Stage, Quarto, and Folio," *PMLA* 77 (1962): 195–96. Because Chapman's work can be connected to these twin themes through issues of patronage and allusion, it has been regarded as a source of overwhelming importance. Few critics have explored *The Recuyell* thematically, however, and I argue that if we open up *The Recuyell*, we find a much broader connection to *Troilus* around the issue of literary representation than has been recognized.

10. These are listed in the *STC* as *The Historie of Troylus and Cresseida* ("Qa," *STC* 22331) and *The Famous Historie of Troylus and Cresseid* ("Qb,"

STC 22332). They were entered into the Stationers' Register by Richard Bonian and Henry Walley on January 28, 1603. For publication details, see Philip Williams Jr., "The 'Second Issue' of Shakespeare's *Troilus and Cressida*, 1609," *Studies in Bibliography* 2 (1949–50): 26–35. The 1623 First Folio is *STC* 22273.

11. Leslie A. Fielder, "Shakespeare's Commodity-Comedy: A Meditation on the Preface to the 1609 Quarto of *Troilus and Cressida*," in *Shakespeare's "Rough Magic": Renaissance Essays in Honor of C. L. Barber*, ed. Peter Erickson and Coppélia Kahn (Newark: University of Delaware Press, 1985), 50.

12. For the Stationers' Register see Stanley Wells and Gary Taylor, *William Shakespeare: A Textual Companion* (Oxford: Clarendon Press, 1987), 424.

13. Gary Taylor suggests that the epistle was a late discovery in the printing process, some sort of remaindered essay from the play's early circulation at the Inns of Court only realized by the printer, George Eld, after production had begun; see Gary Taylor, "*Troilus and Cressida*: Bibliography, Performance, and Interpretation," *Shakespeare Studies* 15 (1982): 118–21, and Wells and Taylor, *A Textual Companion*, 424–26. Taylor dates the composition of the play at 1602 (*Textual Companion*, 123), though Honigmann and others date it at 1601 (see "The Date and Revision," 43, and Kimbrough, "The Origins," 196). Current views hold the quarto text as coming from an authorial manuscript. For the First Folio, Isaac Jaggard apparently possessed an unmarked version of this text, from which he set four pages of the play, placing it after *Romeo and Juliet*, but then stopped, moving the entire piece to come after *Henry the Eight* and switching to an annotated version. "It is generally assumed," Taylor writes, "that the initial setting of *Troilus* was abandoned because of difficulties over copyright" (*Textual Companion*, 425). In any case, the Folio's final version represents the quarto with annotations from a manuscript, perhaps a promptbook from a Globe production. The differences between the Quarto and Folio versions concern the prefatory material and a number of repeated lines, listed in Taylor and Wells, *Textual Companion*, 426–43. For a strong caution against Taylor's editorial conclusions, see Phebe Jensen, "The Textual Politics of *Troilus and Cressida*," *Shakespeare Quarterly* 46 (1995): 414–23.

14. See Elton, "Appendix II: Troilus and Legal Terms," in *Shakespeare's Troilus and Cressida*, 175.

15. *The Famous Historie of Troylus and Cresseid*, M^{v}. The First Folio presents this line as "hold-dore trade" (signed ¶¶¶); cf. Bevington, *Troilus and Cressida*, 5.11.51.

16. Wells and Taylor, *Textual Companion*, 425.

17. The first eleven chapters are reprinted in Copland's 1553 edition of *The Recuile*, Bk. III, fol. i–fol. xxiiii^{v}. These particular examples appear as

follows: the sixty and nine at the port of Athens (fol. xii), the Port of Thenedon (fol. xiiii), the Dardan plains (fol. xix^{v}), and the gates of Troy (fol. ii).

18. In Copland's 1553 edition of *The Recuile*, book 3, "orguyllous and proude" (fol. ii^{v}), "chauffyd" (fol. iii), "rauysshed" (fol. vii), "quarel" (fol. xii^{v}), and "pauyllon" (fol. xvii).

19. *Recuyles* (Wynkyn de Worde, 1503), Aa.vi.

20. In *The Destruction of Troy* (Thomas Creede and Valentine Simmes, 1596/97), "pride" (page 438), "insolent" (pages 439 and 480), "high minded" (page 466), and "hautinesse" (page 480).

21. Jacobus de Cessalis, *The Game and Play of Chess* (Bruges: William Caxton, 1474), chapter 5, pages unsigned and unnumbered (*STC* 4920); Raoul Lefèvre, *Historie of Iason* (Westminster: William Caxton, 1477), pages unsigned and unnumbered (*STC* 15383). Caxton uses the term in a number of editions, such the *Godefrey of Boloyne* (Westminster: William Caxton, 1481), i2^{v} and i3 (*STC* 13175), the 1483 *Curial*, i^{v} (*STC* 5057); Geoffroy de la Toure Landry, *Knyght of the Toure* (Westminster: William Caxton, 1484), aviii (*STC* 15296); and Christine de Pizan, *The Boke of the Fayt of Armes and of Chyualrye* (Westminster: William Caxton, 1484), Aiiii^{v} (*STC* 7269).

22. Thomas Malory, *Le Morte Darthur* (Westminster: William Caxton, 1485), zvi (*STC* 801).

23. Copland, *Recuile*, book 1, fol. iii. and fol. Ii^{v}, respectively.

24. *Oxford English Dictionary*, c.v., "Orgel." "Orgulous" appears across the sixteenth century in instances such as the triangular heading "Odyous / orgulyous / and flyblowen opinions" of John Skelton's *Replycacion* (London: Thomas Pynson, 1528), Aii^{v} (*STC* 22609), and William Wyrley's 1592 *The True Use of Armorie*: "I discontent for orgule that he did / Refuse: dischargd, and back to Poycters rid" (page 91), and "Which seen the English orgulous words did say / Gainst Lord *Cowcie*, which English houerd still, / Who was in Austrige warring at his will" (London: John Jackson for Gabriell Cawood, 1592), 150 (*STC* 26062).

25. Copland, *Recuile*, book 3, fol. xiiii^{v}.

26. Ibid., fol. xv.

27. Ibid., *Recuile*, fol. ii^{v}.

28. The pages of *Troylus and Cressida* in the First Folio are signed out of sequence with the volume overall. Ulysses's discussion with Nestor occurs on pages ¶2–¶2^{v}; cf. Bevington, 1.3.310–92.

29. First Folio, ¶^{v}; cf. Bevington, *Troilus and Cressida*, 1.3.125–26.

30. First Folio, ¶^{v}; cf. Bevington, *Troilus and Cressida*, 1.3.150–58.

31. Elton, *Shakespeare's Troilus and Cressida and the Inns of Court Revels*, 6.

32. Mallin, "Emulous Factions," 152.

33. First Folio, ¶^{v}; cf. Bevington, *Troilus and Cressida*, 1.3.103, and First Folio, ¶2^{v}; cf. Bevington, *Troilus and Cressida*, 2.1.6, respectively.

34. First Folio, ¶¶4; cf. Bevington, *Troilus and Cressida*, 4.5.239–40.

35. First Folio, ¶6^{v}; cf. Bevington, *Troilus and Cressida*, 3.2.197–99. On this point, see Linda Charnes, "'So Unsecret to Ourselves': Notorious Identity and the Material Subject in Shakespeare's *Troilus and Cressida*," *Shakespeare Quarterly* 40 (1989): 413–40.

36. First Folio, ¶¶6; cf. Bevington, *Troilus and Cressida*, 5.3.107.

37. Copland, *Recuile*, book 3, fol. i^{v}.

38. In Copland, *Recuile*, book 3, fol. xx^{v}, fol. iiii, and fol. x[i], respectively. For Ulysses's line, see Folio, ¶¶3^{v} ; cf. Bevington, *Troilus and Cressida*, 4.5.110.

39. Copland, *Recuile*, book 3, fol. xxiii^{v} and fol. xxvii.

40. In Copland, *Recuile*, book 3: the women's lament and Hector's response occurs from fol. xxiiii–fol. xxix; "Galathe" is mentioned five times, on fol. xx^{v}, xxi, xxii, and twice on fol. xxvi^{v}; Diomedes's taking of Troilus's horse is on fol. xx[vi]ii^{v} (signed "fol. xx ii^{v}"); Hector takes armor and captives on fol. xxi, fol. xxiii, and fol. xxx; Hector defeats Achilles on fol. xxiiii; and Achilles slays him on fol. xxx: "[Hector] had caste hys sheelde behinde him at his backe, & had lefte his breste discouerte and as he was in thys poynte & tooke none hede of Achilles that came pryueyly unto hym and put thys spere with in his body, and Hector fell downe dead, to the grounde."

41. See, for example, the discussion of "Helayne incontinent" in book 3 (*Recuile*, fol. viii), and of Breseyda (Cressida), fol. xx[vi]ii (signed "fol. xx ii").

42. See also Derek Pearsall's discussion of the *recueil* form in "The English Romance in the Fifteenth Century," *Essays and Studies* n.s., 29 (1976): 78.

43. Creede printed the first play attributed to Shakespeare for Millington, a 1594 variant of *Henry VI, Part 2*, known as *The First Part of the Contention* (*STC* 26099) and discussed in the previous chapter, and Simmes printed the first edition of *Hamlet* in 1603 (*STC* 22275) for Nicholas Ling and John Trundell. They continued to print quartos through the turn of the century, and though by 1610 they seem to have been superseded by Eld and Jaggard (Eld printing the quarto versions of *Troilus and Cressida* as well as *Shake-speares Sonnets* in 1609 for Thomas Thorpe, *STC* 22353a, and Jaggard printing the Pavier collection before going onto the Folio), discussed in the next chapter, both resurfaced in the beginning of the second decade with some final Shakespearean quartos. In 1611 Simmes printed an edition of *The Troublesome Raigne of Iohn King* for John Helme, flirtatiously attributed to "W. Sh." on its title page (*STC* 14646), and, more conjecturally, had some involvement in Eld's 1611 edition of *Hamlet* for John Smethwick (*STC* 22277), as noted by Andrew Murphy in *Shakespeare in Print: A History and*

Chronology of Shakespeare Publishing (Cambridge: Cambridge University Press, 2003), 298. Creede printed the 1612 editions of the *Merry Deuill of Edmonton* as it was acted by "his Majesties seruants, at the Globe" for Arthur Johnson (*STC* 7494) and *The Tragedie of King Richard the Third* (*STC* 22318).

44. *Pericles* (STC 22334) and *The Painful Aduentures of Pericles* (STC 25638.5) are discussed in Wells and Taylor, *A Textual Companion*, 557.

45. 1632 (by Cotes, *STC* 22274/with variants a–e), 1663 (by Roger Daniel, Alice Warren, and another, Wing S2913), and 1664 (Wing S2914). See note 7 for the editions of *The Recuyell.*

46. *The Auncient Historie of the Destruction of Troy*, (a).iv.

47. *The Vision of Pierce Plowman* (London: Richard Grafton for Robert Crowley, 1550), *.ii.[v], *STC* 19906.

48. *The True Copye of a Prolog* (London: Richard Grafton for Robert Crowley, 1550), π2, *STC* 25588.

49. *The Auncient Historie of the Destruction of Troy*, 427.

50. Ibid., 603.

51. Simpson, *Reform and Cultural Revolution*, 11.

52. See my discussion of these issues in *Symbolic Caxton: Literary Culture and Print Capitalism* (Notre Dame, IN: University of Notre Dame Press, 2008).

53. John Lydgate, *The Hystorye, Sege and Dystruccyon of Troye* (London: Richard Pynson, 1513), *STC* 5579.

54. John Lydgate, *The Auncient Historie and Onely Trewe and Syncere Cronicle of the Warres Betwixte the Grecians and the Troyans . . . Translated in to Englyshe Verse by Iohn Lydgate Moncke of Burye* (London: Thomas Marshe, 1555), π (*STC* 5580).

55. John Lydgate, *The Life and Death of Hector* (London: Thomas Purfoot, 1614), *STC* 5581.5.

56. Tatlock, "The Siege of Troy," 676–77. Robert Greene, *Euphues His Censure to Philautus* (London: John Wolfe for Edward White, 1587), *STC* 12239; George Peele, *A Tale of Troy* (London: John Charlewood for William White, 1589), *STC* 19537; Thomas Heywood, *Troia Britanica* (London: William Jaggard, 1609), *STC* 13366; Heywood, *The Golden Age* (London: Nicholas Okes for William Barrenger, 1611), *STC* 13325; Heywood, *The Brazen Age* (London: Okes for Samuel Rand, 1613), *STC* 13310; *The Siluer Age* (London: Okes for Benjamin Lightfoote, 1613), *STC* 13365; and Heywood, *The Iron Age* (London: Okes, 1632), *STC* 13340.5.

57. Copland, *Recuile*, book 3, fol. xxvii[v].

58. See Maura Nolan, "Social Forms, Literary Contents: Lydgate's Mummings," chapter 2 of *John Lydgate and the Making of Public Culture* (Cambridge: Cambridge University Press, 2005), 71–119.

59. See *The Riverside Chaucer*, ed. Larry Benson (Boston: Houghton Mifflin, 1987): Boethius's *Consolation of Philosophy*, book 2, prose 2, ln. 70, pp. 409–10, the *Prologue of the Monk's Tale*, ll. 1973–77, p. 241, and *Troilus and Criseyde*, ll. 1786–88, p. 584.

60. For example, Lydgate's modern editors are somewhat dismissive of his work here. Henry Bergen comments that "throughout almost this entire passage he has drawn on his own reading," *Lydgate's Troy Book*, Part IV, Early English Texts 126 (London: Oxford University Press, 1935), 121. Robert R. Edwards, Lydgate's most recent editor, writes that "the generic descriptions of comedy and tragedy are commonplaces"; see *John Lydgate: Troy Book Selections*, TEAMS Middle English Texts (Kalamazoo: Western Michigan University, 1998), 368.

61. M. H. Marshall points to Isidore of Seville's *Etymologies* as a likely source for Chaucer and Lydgate in "Theatre in the Middle Ages: Evidence from Dictionaries and Glosses," *Symposium* IV (1950): 9; Paul Strohm suggests that "a definition of tragedy of the sort Vincent [of Beauvais] and other medieval scholars would have known is that of the thirteenth century Catholicon of Johannes Januensis, in which he distinguishes between tragedy and comedy on the basis of the persons they treat, the levels of their styles, and the upward or downward movements of their plots," in "Storie, Spelle, Geste, Romaunce, Tragedie: Generic Distinctions in the Middle English Troy Narratives," *Speculum* 46 (1971): 356.

62. Lydgate, *Auncient Historie* (Marshe, 1555), F.vi; cf. Edwards, *Selections*, 2.842–914.

63. C. David Benson suggests that Lydgate's *Troy Book* reveals "a genuine sense of historical perspective that is not found in any of the other Middle English histories of Troy," in *The History of Troy in Middle English Literature: Gudio delle Colonne's Historia Destructionis Troiae in Medieval England* (Woodbridge: D. S. Brewer, 1980), 106–8.

64. M. H. Marshall identifies this as the "main error" of medieval understandings of classical drama ("Theatre in the Middle Ages," *Symposium* 4 [1950]: 375); nonetheless, this should not distract us from the fundamentally historical nature of Lydgate's attempt.

65. Lydgate, *Auncient Historie* (Marshe, 1555), S.iv; cf. Edwards, *Selections*, 3.5575–764.

66. Simpson, *Reform and Cultural Revolution*, 89.

67. Ibid., 103.

68. Compare Edwards, *Troy Book Selections*, book 4, ll. 603–7 and 649–52, with Benson, *Riverside Chaucer*, *Troilus and Criseyde*, book 1, ll. 266–73, 358–64, and 420.

69. Benson, *Riverside Chaucer*, *Troilus and Criseyde*, ln. 365.

70. Benson, *Riverside Chaucer*, "Explanatory Notes," 1026.

71. Patrick Cheney, *Shakespeare's Literary Authorship* (Cambridge: Cambridge University Press, 2008), 59.

Chapter Five. The Edition

1. For the First Folio see Peter W. M. Blayney, *The First Folio of Shakespeare* (Washington, DC: Folger Library Publications, 1991); Andrew Murphy, *Shakespeare in Print: A History and Chronology of Shakespeare Publishing* (Cambridge: Cambridge University Press, 2003), 41–56; and Gary Taylor, "Why Publish Shakespeare's Works?" Eleventh Annual D. F. McKenzie Lectures, unpublished manuscripts. January 20, 2006. See also Anthony James West, "The Life of the First Folio in the Seventeenth and Eighteenth Centuries," in *A Concise Companion to Shakespeare and the Text*, ed. Andrew Murphy (Malden, MA: Blackwell 2007), 71–90.

2. From Taylor, "Why Publish Shakespeare's Works?," I.8.

3. The analysis of the Pavier Quartos is one of the major feats of the New Bibliography. The main argument was articulated by W. W. Greg, but the initial similarity between a number of composite volumes collecting the same quartos was first noted by Alfred W. Pollard, who, in 1906, hypothesized a remainder market for Shakespeare's plays that Pavier bought out and combined with his own copies of unsold editions of *Henry V*, recorded in *Shakespeare Folios and Quartos* (London: Methuen, 1909). Two years later, Greg presented his "more revolutionary hypothesis" in his three-part essay, "On Certain False Dates in Shakespearian Quartos," *Library* n.s., 9, no. 34 (1908): 113–31, 381–409, which traced the paper stocks across the variously dated quartos to argue for their complete publication in 1619. In 1910 William Nedig followed out Greg's thesis by using high-resolution photography, "not unlike the modern Bertillon system of measuring criminals," to match the title pages and sequence the order of printing, in "The Shakespeare Quartos of 1619," *Modern Philology* 8 (1910): 145–63. Finally, in 1951 Allan Stevenson confirmed this finding by observing that the edition of *Henry the Fift* proclaiming 1608 on its title page had "PD1617" or "PD1619" inscribed in its watermark in tiny characters, and that the 1600 edition of *Sir Iohn Oldcastle* had a similar watermark announcing 1608; see Allan H. Stevenson, "Shakespearian Dated Watermarks," *Studies in Bibliography* 4 (1951–52): 159–64. Additionally, Edwin Eliott Willoughby, *A Printer of Shakespeare: The Books and Times of William Jaggard* (London: P. Allen, 1934), pointed out a May 1619 letter from the Lord Chamberlain blocking the publishing of plays, which is taken to be directed at Pavier. R. Carter Hailey has recently thoroughly revisited Greg's collation of the paper stocks in "The Shakespearian Pavier Quartos Revisited," *Studies in Bibliography* 57 (2005/06): 151–95.

The textual and historical evidence is reviewed by Stanley Wells and Gary Taylor, with John Jowett and William Montgomery, *William Shakespeare: A Textual Companion* (Oxford: Clarendon Press, 1987), 35ff., and Murphy, *Shakespeare in Print*, 36–56. References to the texts of the Pavier Quartos are hereafter cited parenthetically within the text.

4. Table adapted from Murphy, *Shakespeare in Print*, 40.

5. For this revision, see chiefly Lukas Erne's *Shakespeare as Literary Dramatist* (Cambridge: Cambridge University Press, 2003), a condensed version of which appears in "Shakespeare and the Publication of his Plays," *Shakespeare Quarterly* 53 (2002): 1–20; and Peter W. M. Blayney, "The Publication of Playbooks," in *A New History of Early English Drama*, ed. John D. Cox and David Scott Kastan (New York: Columbia University Press, 1997), 383–422. Blayney's argument is debated by Alan B. Famer and Zachary Lesser, "The Popularity of Playbooks Revisited," *Shakespeare Quarterly* 56 (2005): 1–32, and defended in Peter W. M. Blayney, "The Alleged Popularity of Playbooks," *Shakespeare Quarterly* 56 (2005): 33–50. See also Marta Straznicky's introduction to *The Book of the Play: Playwrights, Stationers, and Readers in Early Modern England*, ed. Marta Straznicky (Amherst: University of Massachusetts Press, 2006).

6. Greg, "On Certain False Dates, Pt. I," 128.

7. Sonia Massai, *Shakespeare and the Rise of the Editor in Print* (Cambridge: Cambridge University Press, 2007), 108.

8. The first such collection, the 1601 *Works of Samuel Daniel Newly Augmented* (*STC* 6236), lacks a table of contents and collects Daniel in discontinuous pagination and signatures, so that its initial title page announces the whole collection, but each work begins anew, with a new title page. The overall plan is fragmentary at best: witness the entire page given over to the signature Fiij. In a further similarity to the Pavier Quartos, Daniel's *Works* begins with his poem the "Civill Warres betweene the Two Houses of Lancaster and Yorke." The 1616 *Workes of Beniamin Ionson* (*STC* 14751) is more impressively unified than Daniel's *Works*, but not entirely different: the Catalogue stands alone, and the paratactic matter sets out Jonson's authority, but the plays are still arranged as separate units associated by continuous signatures and pagination, but each with its own title page announcing afresh the author, printer, and year.

9. *Poems: by Michael Drayton Esquire* (London: printed by W. Stansby for John Smethwick, 1619), STC 7222.

10. Michael Drayton, *The Barrons Wars in the Raigne of Edward the Second, with Englands Heroicall Epistles* (London: Printed by James Roberts for Nathan Ling, 1603), *STC* 7189; Michael Drayton, *The Tragicall Legend of Robert, Duke of Normandy* (London: Printed by James Roberts for Nathan Ling, 1596), *STC* 7232; and Michael Drayton, *Poems: Lyrick and Pastorall,*

Odes, Eglogs, the Man in the Moone (London: Printed by R. Bradock for Nathan Ling and J. Flasket, 1606), *STC* 7225.5.

11. Nedig, "The Shakespeare Quartos of 1619," 11–16.

12. Gerald D. Johnson, "Thomas Pavier, Publisher, 1600–25," *Library* ser. 6, 14 (1992): 12–50.

13. Ibid., 12–13.

14. Massai, *Shakespeare and the Rise of the Editor*; Murphy, *Shakespeare in Print*, 43.

15. On the Oldcastle controversy see Gary Taylor, "William Shakespeare, Richard James and the House of Cobham," *Review of English Studies* 38 (1987): 334–54; Jonathan Goldberg, *Shakespeare's Hand* (Minneapolis: University of Minnesota Press, 2003), 212–21; and Peter Corbin and Douglas Sedge, eds., *The Oldcastle Controversy: Sir John Oldcastle, Part I and The Famous Victories of Henry V* (Manchester, UK: Manchester University Press, 1991), who write, "there seems little doubt that Shakespeare first gained the idea of casting Oldcastle in the role of buffoon from the example of *Famous Victories*, though in the version known to Shakespeare the role may have been a more prominent one" (24).

16. Taylor, "William Shakespeare, Richard James and the House of Cobham," 335–36.

17. Israel Gollancz, *Hoccleve's Works* (Oxford: Oxford University Press, 1892), xliii. Further citations of Hoccleve's "Remonstrance against Oldcastle" are noted parenthetically within the text.

18. Cited in Peter Stallybrass and Roger Chartier, "Reading and Authorship: The Circulation of Shakespeare 1590–1619," in *A Concise Companion to Shakespeare and the Text*, ed. Andrew Murphy (Malden, MA: Blackwell, 2007), 54.

19. Jesse M. Lander, "'Crack'd Crowns' and Counterfeit Sovereigns: The Crisis of Value in *1 Henry IV*," *Shakespeare Studies* 30 (2002): 140.

20. John Gower, *Jo. Gower de confessione amantis* (London: Thomas Berthelette, 1532), *STC* 12143; reprinted in 1554, *STC* 12144.

21. R. F. Yeager, "Shakespeare as Medievalist: What It Means for Performing *Pericles*," in *Shakespeare and the Middle Ages: Essays on the Performance and Adaptation of the Plays with Medieval Sources or Settings*, ed. Martha W. Driver and Sid Ray (Jefferson, NC: McFarland, 2009), 217.

22. For Thomas Hoccleve, see Anthony J. Hasler, "Hoccleve's Unregimented Body," *Paragraph* 13 (1990): 164–83; Ethan Knapp, *The Bureaucratic Muse: Thomas Hoccleve and the Literature of Late Medieval England* (University Park: Pennsylvania State University Press, 2001); Derek Pearsall, "Hoccleve's *Regement of Princes*: The Poetics of Royal Self-Representation," *Speculum* 69 (1994): 386–410; Larry Scanlon, "The King's Two Voices: Narrative and Power in Hoccleve's *Regement of Princes*," in *Literary Practice and*

Social Change in Britain, ed. Lee Patterson (Berkeley: University of California Press, 1990), 216–47; James Simpson, "Nobody's Man: Thomas Hoccleve's *Regement of Princes*," in *London and Europe in the Later Middle Ages*, ed. Julia Boffey and Pamela King (London: Centre for Medieval and Renaissance Studies, Queen Mary and Westfield College, University of London, 1995), 149–80; and Paul Strohm, *England's Empty Throne: Usurpation and the Language of Legitimation, 1399–1422* (New Haven, CT: Yale University Press, 1998).

23. *Thomas Hoccleve: The Regiment of Princes*, ed. Charles R. Blyth (Kalamazoo: Medieval Institute of Western Michigan University, 1999), ll. 5006–9.

24. *Bevis of Hampton* (Westminster: Wynkyn de Worde, 1500), *STC* 1987/7.5; *Bevis of Hampton* (London: Richard Pynson 1503), *STC* 1988; and *Bevis of Hampton* (London: Julian Notary, 1510), *STC* 1988.2.

25. *Howe Howleglas Deseyued a Wynedrawer in Lubeke* (Antwerp: Jan Van Doesborch, 1519), *STC* 10563; *Here Beginneth a Merye Iest of a Man That Was Called Howleglas* (London: William Copland, 1555), *STC* 10563; *Here Beginneht a Merye Iest of a Man That Was Called Howleglas* (London: William Copland, 1560), *STC* 10564; and the fragment, *STC* 10563.5.

26. John Skelton, *The Tunning of Elinor Rumming* (London: Wynkyn de Worde, 1521), *STC* 22611.5, and the collections of his works: *Here After Foloweth Certayne Bokes, Compyled by Mayster Skelton, Poet Laureat* (London: Richard Lant for Henry Tab, 1545), *STC* 22598, reprinted by John King and Thomas Marshe in 1554 (*STC* 22599), and by John Day in 1563 (*STC* 22600).

27. *Here Begynneth a Mery Geste of the Frere and the Boye* (London: Wynkyn de Worde, 1513), *STC* 14522; *Here Begynneth a Mery Geste of the Frere and the Boye* (London: William Middleton, 1545), *STC* 14522.5; *Heer Beginneth a Mery Iest of the Frier and the Boy* (London: Edward Allde, 1589), *STC* 14522.7; *The Fryer, and the Boy* (London: Edward Allde, 1617), *STC* 14523; *Here Beginneth a Merry Iest, of the Fryer and the Boy* (London: Edward Allde, 1626), *STC* 14524.3; *The Frier and the Boy* (London, 1690), Wing F2205A; *The Frier and the Boy: Very Delectable Though Unpleasant to All Step-Mothers* (Glasgow, 1668), Wing F2205; and *The Frier and the Boy: Very Delectable Though Unpleasant to All Step-Mothers* (Glasgow, 1698), Wing F2206.

28. *A Little Gest of Robin Hood* (London: Richard Pynson, 1500), *STC* 13688; *Here Begynneth a Lytell Geste of Robyn Hood* (London: Wynkyn de Worde, 1506), *STC* 13689; *Here Begynneth a Lytell Geste of Robyn Hood* (York: Hugo van der Goes, 1509), *STC* 13689.3; and *Here Begynneth a Gest of Robyn Hode* (London: Julian Notary, 1515), *STC* 13690.

29. Kathleen Davis, "The Sense of an Epoch: Periodization, Sovereignty, and the Limits of Secularization," in *The Legitimacy of the Middle*

Ages: On the Unwritten History of Theory, ed. Andrew Cole and D. Vance Smith (Durham, NC: Duke University Press, 2010), 46.

30. West, "The Life of the First Folio," 71.

31. Taylor, "Why Publish Shakespeare's Works?," I.21.

32. Ibid., I.6.

33. *Mr. William Shakespeares Comedies, Histories, & Tragedies Published According to the True Originall Copies* (London: Isaac Jaggard and Edmund Blount for William Jaggard, Edmund Blount, John Smethwick, and William Aspley, 1623), A3 (*STC* 22273).

34. George Donaldson, "The First Folio: 'My Shakespeare'/'Our Shakespeare': Whose Shakespeare?," in *Shakespeare's Book: Essays in Reading, Writing and Reception*, ed. Richard Meek, Jane Rickard, and Richard Wilson (Manchester, UK: Manchester University Press, 2008), 204.

35. Jane Rickard, "The 'First' Folio in Context: The Folio Collections of Shakespeare, Jonson and King James," in *Shakespeare's Book*, 213.

36. Stephen Cohen, "Introduction" to *Shakespeare and Historical Formalism* (Burlington, VT: Ashgate, 2007), 1.

37. Nedig, "The Shakespeare Quartos of 1619," 10.

BIBLIOGRAPHY

Alpers, Paul. "Pastoral and the Domain of Lyric in Spenser's *Shepheardes Calender.*" *Representations* 12 (1985): 83–100.

Anon. *Bevis of Hampton.* Westminster: Wynkyn de Worde, 1500. *STC* 1987/7.5.

———. *Bevis of Hampton.* London: Richard Pynson, 1503. *STC* 1988.

———. *Bevis of Hampton.* London: Julian Notary, 1510. *STC* 1988.2.

———. *The Frier and the Boy.* London, 1690. Wing F2205A.

———. *The Frier and the Boy: Very Delectable Though Unpleasant to All Step-Mothers.* Glasgow, 1698. Wing F2206.

———. *The Fryer, and the Boy.* London: Edward Allde, 1617. *STC* 14523.

———. *Heer Beginneth a Mery Iest of the Frier and the Boy.* London: Edward Allde, 1589. *STC* 14522.7.

———. *Here Beginneth a Merry Iest, of the Fryer and the Boy.* London: Edward Allde, 1626. *STC* 14524.3.

———. *Here Beginneth a Merye Iest of a Man That Was Called Howleglas.* London: William Copland, 1555. *STC* 10563/.5.

———. *Here Beginneth a Merye Iest of a Man That Was Called Howleglas.* London: William Copland, 1560. *STC* 10564.

———. *Here Begynneth a Gest of Robyn Hode.* London: Julian Notary, 1515. *STC* 13690.

———. *Here Begynneth a Lytell Geste of Robyn Hood.* London: Wynkyn de Worde, 1506. *STC* 13689.

———. *Here Begynneth a Lytell Geste of Robyn Hood.* York: Hugo van der Goes, 1509. *STC* 13689.3.

———. *Here Begynneth a Mery Geste of the Frere and the Boye.* London: Wynkyn de Worde, 1513. *STC* 14522.

———. *Here Begynneth a Mery Geste of the Frere and the Boye.* London: William Middleton, 1545. *STC* 14522.5.

———. *Howe Howleglas Deseyued a Wynedrawer in Lubeke.* Antwerp: Jan Van Doesborch, 1519. *STC* 10563.

———. *A Little Gest of Robin Hood*. London: Richard Pynson, 1500. *STC* 13688.

Barker, Nicolas. "Caxton's Typography." *Journal of the Printing Historical Society* 11 (1976/77): 114–33.

———. "St Albans Press: The First Punch-Cutter in England and the First Native Typefounder?" *Transactions of the Cambridge Bibliographical Society* 7 (1979): 257–78.

Beckwith, Sarah. "Medieval Penance, Reformation Repentance and *Measure for Measure*." In *Reading the Medieval in Early Modern England*, edited by Gordon McMullan and David Matthews, 193–204. Cambridge: Cambridge University Press, 2007.

Benson, C. David. *The History of Troy in Middle English Literature: Guido delle Colonne's Historia Destructionis Troiae in Medieval England*. Woodbridge: D. S. Brewer, 1980.

Benson, Larry D., ed. *The Riverside Chaucer*. 3rd ed. Boston: Houghton Mifflin, 1987.

Berek, Peter. "Genres, Early Modern Theatrical Title Pages, and the Authority of Print." In *The Book of the Play: Playwrights, Stationers, and Readers in Early Modern England*, edited by Marta Straznicky, 159–75. Amherst: University of Massachusetts Press, 2006.

Bergen, Henry, ed. *Lydgate's Fall of Princes*. Early English Text Society Early Series 121. 1924. Reprint, London: Oxford University Press, 1967.

———. *Lydgate's Troy Book*. Part IV. Early English Text Society 126. London: Oxford University Press, 1935.

Bevington, David M. "'Instructed by the Antiquary Times': Shakespeare's Sources." In *Troilus and Cressida*, 375–97. The Arden Shakespeare, Third Series. 1998. Reprint, London: Thompson Learning, 2001.

Blake, N. F. "Caxton and Chaucer." *Leeds Studies in English* n.s., 1 (1967): 19–36.

———. "John Lydgate and William Caxton." *Leeds Studies in English* 16 (1985): 272–89.

———. *William Caxton*. Vol. 3 of *English Writers of the Late Middle Ages*, edited by M. C. Seymour, 1–67. Authors of the Middle Ages. Brookfield, VT: Ashgate, 1996.

Blayney, Peter W. M. "The Alleged Popularity of Playbooks." *Shakespeare Quarterly* 56 (2005): 33–50.

———. *The First Folio of Shakespeare*. Washington, DC: Folger Library Publications, 1991.

———. "The Publication of Playbooks." In *A New History of Early English Drama*, edited by John D. Cox and David Scott Kastan, 383–422. New York: Columbia University Press, 1997.

Bloom, Harold. *The Anxiety of Influence: A Theory of Poetry*. 1973. Reprint, Oxford: Oxford University Press, 1997.

———. *A Map of Misreading*. Oxford: Oxford University Press, 1975.

Blyth, Charles R., ed. *Thomas Hoccleve: The Regiment of Princes*. Kalamazoo: Medieval Institute of Western Michigan University, 1999.

Boffey, Julia. "Richard Pynson's Book of Fame and the Letter of Dido." *Viator* 19 (1988): 339–53.

Boffey, Julia, and A. S. G. Edwards. "Literary Texts." In *The Cambridge History of the Book in Britain: Volume 3, 1400–1557*, edited by Lotte Hellinga and J. B. Trapp, 555–75. Cambridge: Cambridge University Press, 1999.

Boffey, Julia, and John J. Thompson. "Anthologies and Miscellanies: Production and Choice of Texts." In *Book Production and Publishing in Britain, 1375–1475*, edited by Jeremy Griffiths and Derek Pearsall, 279–315. Cambridge: Cambridge University Press, 1989.

Bolter, Jay David, and Richard Grusin. *Remediation: Understanding New Media*. Cambridge, MA: MIT Press, 1999.

Boyd, Beverly, ed. *Chaucer According to William Caxton: Minor Poems and "Boece," 1478*. Lawrence, KS: Allen Press, 1978.

Bradbrook, M. C. "What Shakespeare Did to Chaucer's *Troilus and Criseyde*." *Shakespeare Quarterly* 9 (1958): 311–19.

Brantley, Jessica. "The Prehistory of the Book." *PMLA* 124 (2009): 632–39.

Brennan, Michael. "William Ponsonby: Elizabethan Stationer." *Analytical and Enumerative Bibliography* 7 (1983): 91–110.

Brooks, Douglas. *From Playhouse to Printing House: Drama and Authorship in Early Modern England*. Cambridge: Cambridge University Press, 2000.

Bullough, Geoffrey. *Narrative and Dramatic Sources of Shakespeare*. Vol. 6. New York: Columbia University Press, 1966.

Carlson, David R. "A Theory of the Early English Printing Firm: Jobbing, Book-Publishing, and the Problem of Productive Capacity in Caxton's Work." In *Caxton's Trace: Studies in the History of English Printing*, edited by William Kuskin, 35–68. Notre Dame, IN: University of Notre Dame Press, 2006.

———. "Woodcut Illustrations of the *Canterbury Tales*, 1483–1602." *Library*, 6th ser., 19 (1997): 25–67.

Caxton, William. *Boecius de consolacione philosophie*. Westminster: William Caxton, 1478. *STC* 3199.

———. *The Cronycles of Englond*. Westminster: William Caxton, 1482. *STC* 9992.

———. *The Cronycles of Englond*. London: William de Machlinia, 1486. *STC* 9993.

———. *Cronycles of the Londe of Englond*. Antwerp: Gerard de Leew, 1493. *STC* 9994.

———. *Eneydos*. Westminster: William Caxton, 1490. *STC* 24796.

———. *Godefrey of Boloyne*. Westminster: William Caxton, 1481. *STC* 13175.

Charnes, Linda. "'So Unsecret to Ourselves': Notorious Identity and the Material Subject in Shakespeare's *Troilus and Cressida*." *Shakespeare Quarterly* 40 (1989): 413–40.

Chartier, Alain. *Curial*. Westminster: William Caxton, 1483. *STC* 5057.

Chartier, Roger. "Jack Cade, the Skin of a Dead Lamb, and the Hatred for Writing." *Shakespeare Studies* 34 (2006): 77–89.

———. *The Order of Books: Readers, Authors, and Libraries in Europe between the Fourteenth and Eighteenth Centuries*. Stanford, CA: Stanford University Press, 1994.

Chaucer, Geoffrey. *Canterbury Tales*. Westminster: William Caxton, 1483. *STC* 5083.

———. *Queen Anelida and the False Arcite*. Westminster: William Caxton, 1477. *STC* 5090.

———. *Temple of Brass* [Parliament of Fowls]. Westminster: William Caxton, 1477. *STC* 5091.

———. *Troilus and Criseyde*. Westminster: William Caxton, 1483. *STC* 5094.

———. *The Workes of Geffray Chaucer Newly Printed, with Dyuers Workes Whiche Were Neuer in Print Before*. London: Printed by Thomas Godfray, 1532. *STC* 5068.

———. *The Workes of Geffray Chaucer Newly Printed, with Dyuers Workes Whiche Were Neuer in Print Before*. London: Printed by Richard Grafton for William Bonham, 1542. *STC* 5069.

———. *The Workes of Geffray Chaucer Newly Printed, with Dyuers Workes Whiche Were Neuer in Print Before*. London: Printed by Richard Grafton for John Reynes, 1542. *STC* 5070.

———. *The Woorkes of Geffrey Chaucer, Newly Printed, with Diuers Addicions, Whiche Were Neuer in Printe Before: With the Siege and Destruccion of the Worthy Citee of Thebes, Compiled by Ihon Lidgate, Monke of Berie*. London: Printed by John Kingston for John Wight, 1561. *STC* 5076.

———. *The Workes of Our Antient and Lerned English Poet, Geffrey Chaucer, Newly Printed*. London: Printed by Adam Islip for George Bishop, 1598. *STC* 5077.

———. *The Workes of Our Antient and Lerned English Poet, Geffrey Chaucer, Newly Printed*. London: Printed by Adam Islip for Bonham Norton, 1598. *STC* 5078.

———. *The Workes of Our Antient and Lerned English Poet, Geffrey Chaucer, Newly Printed*. London: Printed by Adam Islip for Thomas Wight, 1598. *STC* 5079.

Cheney, Patrick, ed. *The Cambridge Companion to Shakespeare's Poetry*. Cambridge: Cambridge University Press, 2007.

———. *Shakespeare, National Poet-Playwright*. Cambridge: Cambridge University Press, 2004.

———. *Shakespeare's Literary Authorship*. Cambridge: Cambridge University Press, 2008.

Cohen, Stephen. "Between Form and Culture: New Historicism and the Promise of a Historical Formalism," in *Renaissance Literature and Its Formal Engagements*, edited by Mark David Rasmussen, 17–42. New York: Palgrave, 2005.

———. *Shakespeare and Historical Formalism*. Burlington, VT: Ashgate, 2007.

Coldiron, Anne. *Canon, Period, and the Poetry of Charles of Orleans: Found in Translation*. Ann Arbor: University of Michigan Press, 2000.

Cole, Andrew, and D. Vance Smith, eds. *The Legitimacy of the Middle Ages: On the Unwritten History of Theory*. Durham, NC: Duke University Press, 2010.

Cooper, Helen, and Sally Mapstone, eds. *The Long Fifteenth Century: Essays for Douglas Gray*. Oxford: Clarendon Press, 1997.

Cooper, Lisa H., and Andrea Denny-Brown, eds. *Lydgate Matters: Poetry and Material Culture in the Fifteenth Century*. New York: Palgrave Macmillan, 2008.

Corballis, Michael C. *The Recursive Mind: The Origins of Human Language, Thought, and Civilization*. Princeton, NJ: Princeton University Press, 2011.

Corbin, Peter, and Douglas Sedge, eds. *The Oldcastle Controversy: Sir John Oldcastle, Part I and The Famous Victories of Henry V*. Manchester, UK: Manchester University Press, 1991.

Cornelius, Patsy Scherer. *E. K.'s Commentary on "The Shepheardes Calender."* Salzburg: University of Salzburg, 1974.

Costomiris, Robert. "Sharing Chaucer's Authority in Prefaces of Chaucer's Works from William Caxton to William Thynne." *Journal of the Early Book Society* 5 (2002): 1–13.

Cox, John D., and David Scott Kastan, eds. *A New History of Early English Drama*. New York: Columbia University Press, 1997.

Cummings, Brian. "Metalepsis: the Boundaries of Metaphor." In *Renaissance Figures of Speech*, edited by Sylvia Adamson, Gavin Alexander, and Katrin Ettenhuber, 217–36. Cambridge: Cambridge University Press, 2007.

Daniel, Samuel. *Works of Samuel Daniel Newly Augmented*. London, 1601. *STC* 6236.

Davis, Kathleen. *Periodization and Sovereignty: How Ideas of Feudalism and Secularization Govern the Politics of Time*. Philadelphia: University of Pennsylvania Press, 2008.

———. "The Sense of an Epoch: Periodization, Sovereignty, and the Limits of Secularization." In *The Legitimacy of the Middle Ages: On the*

Unwritten History of Theory, edited by Andrew Cole and D. Vance Smith, 39–69. Durham, NC: Duke University Press, 2010.

Deanesly, Margaret. "Vernacular Books in England in the Fourteenth and Fifteenth Centuries." *Modern Language Review* 15 (1920): 349–58.

De Cessalis, Jacobus. *The Game and Play of Chess.* Bruges: William Caxton, 1474. *STC* 4920.

De La Toure Landry, Geoffroy. *Knyght of the Toure.* Westminster: William Caxton, 1484. *STC* 15296.

Deleuze, Gilles, and Félix Guattari. *A Thousand Plateaus: Capitalism and Schizophrenia*. Translated by Brian Massumi. Minneapolis: University of Minnesota Press, 1987.

de Man, Paul. *Blindness and Insight: Essays in the Rhetoric of Contemporary Criticism*. 2nd ed., rev. Minneapolis: University of Minnesota Press, 1983.

De Pizan, Christine. *The Boke of the Fayt of Armes and of Chyualrye*. Westminster: William Caxton, 1484. *STC* 7269.

Donaldson, E. Talbot. *The Swan at the Well: Shakespeare Reading Chaucer*. New Haven, CT: Yale University Press, 1985.

Donaldson, George. "The First Folio: 'My Shakespeare'/'Our Shakespeare': Whose Shakespeare?" In *Shakespeare's Book: Essays in Reading, Writing and Reception*, edited by Richard Meek, Jane Rickard, and Richard Wilson, 187–206. Manchester, UK: Manchester University Press, 2008.

Drayton, Michael. *The Barrons Wars in the Raigne of Edward the Second, with Englands Heroicall Epistles*. London: Printed by James Roberts for Nathan Ling, 1603. *STC* 7189.

———. *Poems: by Michael Drayton Esquire*. London: Printed by William Stansby for John Swethwick, 1619. STC 7222.

———. *Poems: Lyrick and Pastorall, Odes, Eglogs, the Man in the Moone*. London: Printed by R. Bradock for Nathan Ling and J. Flasket, 1606. *STC* 7225.5.

———. *The Tragicall Legend of Robert, Duke of Normandy*. London: Printed by James Roberts for Nathan Ling, 1596. *STC* 7232.

Driver, Martha, and Sid Ray, eds. *Shakespeare and the Middle Ages: Essays on the Performance and Adaptation of the Plays with Medieval Sources or Settings*. Jefferson, NC: McFarland, 2009.

Duff, E. Gordon. *Fifteenth Century English Books: A Bibliography of Books and Documents Printed in England and of Books for the English Market Printed Abroad*. Illustrated Monographs 18. Oxford: Printed for the Bibliographical Society at Oxford University Press, 1917.

Early English Books Online. http://eebo.chadwyck.com.

Echard, Siân. *Printing the Middle Ages*. Philadelphia: University of Pennsylvania Press, 2008.

Edwards, A. S. G. "Chaucer from Manuscript to Print: The Social Text and the Critical Text." *Mosaic* 28, no. 4 (1995): 1–12.

Edwards, Robert R. *John Lydgate: Troy Book Selections*. TEAMS Middle English Texts. Kalamazoo: Western Michigan University, 1998.

———. ed. *The Siege of Thebes*. Kalamazoo, MI: Medieval Institute Publications, 2001.

Elton, W. R. *Shakespeare's Troilus and Cressida and the Inns of Court Revels*. Brookfield, VT: Ashgate, 2000.

English Short Title Catalogue. http://estc.bl.uk.

Erne, Lukas. Afterword to *Shakespeare's Book: Essays in Reading, Writing and Reception*, edited by Richard Meek, Jane Rickard, and Richard Wilson, 255–65. Manchester, UK: Manchester University Press, 2008.

———. "Print and Manuscript." In *The Cambridge Companion to Shakespeare's Poetry*, edited by Patrick Cheney, 54–71. Cambridge: Cambridge University Press, 2007.

———. "Reconsidering Shakespearean Authorship." *Shakespeare Studies* 36 (2008): 26–36.

———. "Shakespeare and the Publication of His Plays." *Shakespeare Quarterly* 53 (2002): 1–20.

———. *Shakespeare as Literary Dramatist*. Cambridge: Cambridge University Press, 2003.

Fabyan, Robert. *Fabyans Cronycle Newly Prynted*. London: William Rastell, 1533. *STC* 10660.

———. *Newe Cronycles of Englande and of Fraunce*. London: Richard Pynson, 1516. *STC* 10659.

Famer, Alan B., and Zachary Lesser. "The Popularity of Playbooks Revisited." *Shakespeare Quarterly* 56 (2005): 1–32.

Fibonnaci, Leonardo. *Fibonacci's Liber Abaci: A Translation into Modern English of Leonardo Pisano's Book of Calculation*. Translated by L. E. Sigler. New York: Springer, 2002.

Fiedler, Leslie A. "Shakespeare's Commodity-Comedy: A Meditation on the Preface to the 1609 Quarto of *Troilus and Cressida*." In *Shakespeare's "Rough Magic": Renaissance Essays in Honor of C. L. Barber*, edited by Peter Erickson and Coppélia Kahn, 50–60. Newark: University of Delaware Press, 1985.

Fitch, W. Tecumseh. "Three Meanings of 'Recursion': Key Distinctions for Biolinguistics." In *The Evolution of Human Language*, edited by R. K. Larson, V. Déprez, and H. Yamakido, 73–90. Cambridge: Cambridge University Press, 2010.

Fitzgerald, William. *Martial: The World of the Epigram*. Chicago: University of Chicago Press, 2007.

Gadd, Ian, and Alexandria Gillespie, eds. *John Stow (1525–1605) and the Making of the English Past*. London: British Library, 2004.

Genette, Gérard. *Narrative Discourse: An Essay in Method*. Ithaca, NY: Cornell University Press, 1974.

Gies, Joseph, and Frances Gies. *Leonard of Pisa and the New Mathematics of the Middle Ages*. New York: Thomas Y. Crowell, 1969.

Gillespie, Alexandra. "Caxton's Chaucer and Lydgate Quartos: Miscellanies from Manuscript to Print." *Transactions of the Cambridge Bibliographical Society* 12 (2000): 1–26.

———. "'Folowynge the Trace of Mayster Caxton': Some Histories of Fifteenth-Century Printed Books." In *Caxton's Trace: Studies in the History of English Printing*, edited by William Kuskin, 167–95. Notre Dame, IN: University of Notre Dame Press, 2006.

———. "The Lydgate Canon in Print, 1476–1534." *Journal of the Early Book Society* 4 (2000): 59–93.

———. "Poets, Printers, and Early English *Sammelbände*." *Huntington Library Quarterly* 67, no. 2 (2004): 189–214.

Glaister, Geoffrey Ashall. *Encyclopedia of the Book*. 2nd ed. New Castle, DE: Oak Knoll Press, 1996.

Goldberg, Jonathan. *Shakespeare's Hand*. Minneapolis: University of Minnesota Press, 2003.

———. *Writing Matter: From the Hands of the English Renaissance*. Stanford, CA: Stanford University Press, 1990.

Gollancz, Israel. *Hoccleve's Works*. Oxford: Oxford University Press, 1892.

Gosson, Stephen. *The Ephemerides of Phialo . . . And a Short Apologie of the Schoole of Abuse*. London: Thomas Woodcocke, 1579. *STC* 12093.

———. *The Schoole of Abuse*. London: Thomas Woodcocke, 1579. *STC* 12097/.5.

Gower, John. *Gower de confessione amantis*. London: Thomas Berthelette, 1554. *STC* 12144.

———. *Jo. Gower de confessione amantis*. London: Thomas Berthelette, 1532. *STC* 12143.

Green, Richard Firth. *Poets and Princepleasers: Literature and the English Court in the Late Middle Ages*. Toronto: University of Toronto Press, 1980.

Greene, Robert. *Euphues His Censure to Philautus*. London: John Wolfe for Edward White, 1587. *STC* 12239.

Greetham, D. C. *Textual Scholarship: An Introduction*. New York: Garland, 1994.

Greg, W. W. "On Certain False Dates in Shakespearian Quartos." *Library* n.s., 9, no. 34 (1908): 113–31, 381–409.

Griffiths, Jane. *John Skelton and Poetic Authority: Defining the Liberty to Speak*. Oxford: Oxford University Press, 2007.

———. "What's in a Name? The Transmission of 'John Skelton, Laureate' in Manuscript and Print." *Huntington Library Quarterly* 67, no. 2 (2004): 215–35.

Gryphus, Petrus. *Oratio*. London: Richard Pynson, 1509. *STC* 12413.

Guillory, John. *Cultural Capital: The Problem of Literary Canon Formation.* Chicago: University of Chicago Press, 1993.

Hailey, R. Carter. "The Shakespearian Pavier Quartos Revisited." *Studies in Bibliography* 57 (2005/06): 151–95.

Hall, Edward, and Richard Grafton. *The Union of the Two Noble and Illustre Famelies of Lancastre and Yorke*. London: Richard Grafton, 1548. *STC* 12721/2.

Hammond, E. P. "On the Editing of Chaucer's Minor Poems." *Modern Language Notes* 23 (1908): 20–21.

Hanna, Ralph, III. *Pursuing History: Middle English Manuscripts and Their Texts*. Stanford, CA: Stanford University Press, 1996.

Hanna, Ralph, III, and Traugott Lawler. "Textual Notes to *Boece*." In *The Riverside Chaucer*, edited by Larry D. Benson, 1151–52. Boston: Houghton Mifflin, 1987.

Harris, Jonathan Gil. *Untimely Matter in the Time of Shakespeare*. Philadelphia: University of Pennsylvania Press, 2009.

Harrison, George B. "Books and Readers, 1591–4." *Library* ser. 4, 8, no. 3 (1927): 273–302.

Hasler, Anthony J. "Hoccleve's Unregimented Body." *Paragraph* 13 (1990): 164–83.

Hauser, Marc D., Noam Chomsky, and W. Tecumseh Fitch. "The Faculty of Language: What Is It, Who Has It, and How Did It Evolve?" *Science* 298 (2002): 1569–79.

Hayles, N. Katherine. *How We Became Posthuman: Virtual Bodies in Cybernetics, Literature, and Informatics*. Chicago: University of Chicago Press, 1999.

Hellinga, Lotte. *Catalogue of Books Printed in the XVth Century Now in the British Library: BMC Part XI, England*. Houten, The Netherlands: Hes & De Graaf Publishers, 2007.

———. *William Caxton and Early Printing in England*. London: British Library, 2010.

Herman, Peter C. *Squitter-Wits and Muse-Haters: Sidney, Spenser, Milton and Renaissance Antipoetic Sentiment*. Detroit: Wayne State University Press, 1996.

Heywood, Thomas. *The Brazen Age*. London: Nicholas Okes for Samuel Rand, 1613. *STC* 13310.

———. *The Golden Age*. London: Printed by Nicholas Okes for William Barrenger, 1611. *STC* 13325.

———. *The Iron Age*. London: Nicholas Okes, 1632. *STC* 13340.5.

———. *The Siluer Age*. London: Nicholas Okes for Benjamin Lightfoote, 1613. *STC* 13365.

———. *Troia Britanica*. London: William Jaggard, 1609. *STC* 13366.

Higden, Ranulf. *Discripcion of Britayne*. Westminster: William Caxton, 1480. *STC* 13440a.

Higden, Ranulf, and John of Trevisa. *Polychronicon*. Westminster: William Caxton, 1482. *STC* 13438.

Hofstadter, Douglas R. *Gödel, Escher, Bach: An Eternal Golden Braid*. 1979. Reprinted with new introduction. New York: Vintage Books, 1999.

———. *I Am a Strange Loop*. New York: Basic Books, 2007.

Holinshed, Raphael, et al. *The Firste Volume of the Chronicles of England, Scotlande, and Irelande*. London: Henry Denham for John Harrison, George Bishop, Rafe Newberie, Henry Denham, and Thomas Woodcock, 1577. *STC* 13569.2pt 1.

Holsinger, Bruce. "Lollard Ekphrasis: Situated Aesthetics and Literary History." *Journal of Medieval and Early Modern Studies* 35, no. 1 (2005): 67–89.

———. *The Premodern Condition: Medievalism and the Making of Theory*. Chicago: University of Chicago Press, 2005.

Honigmann, E. A. J. "The Date and Revision of Troilus and Cressida." In *Textual Criticism and Literary Interpretation*, edited by Jerome McGann, 38–54. Chicago: University of Chicago Press, 1985.

James, Heather. *Shakespeare's Troy: Drama, Politics, and the Translation of Empire*. Cambridge and New York: Cambridge University Press, 1997.

Jameson, Frederic. "Forward." To *The Postmodern Condition: A Report on Knowledge*, vii–xxi. 1984. Reprint, Minneapolis: University of Minnesota Press, 1989.

———. *The Modernist Papers*. New York: Verso, 2009.

———. *A Singular Modernity: Essay on the Ontology of the Present*. New York: Verso, 2002.

Jensen, Phebe. "The Textual Politics of *Troilus and Cressida*." *Shakespeare Quarterly* 46 (1995): 414–23.

Johnson, Gerald D. "Thomas Pavier, Publisher, 1600–25." *Library* ser. 6, 14 (1992): 12–50.

Johnson, Lynn Staley. *The Shepheardes Calender: An Introduction*. University Park: Pennsylvania State University Press, 1990.

Jonson, Benjamin. *Workes of Beniamin Ionson*. London: 1616. *STC* 14751.

Kastan, David Scott. *Shakespeare and the Book*. Cambridge: Cambridge University Press, 2001.

———. "'To Think These Trifles Some-thing': Shakespearean Playbooks and the Claims of Authorship." *Shakespeare Studies* 33 (2005): 221–36.

Kimbrough, Robert. "The Origins of *Troilus and Cressida*: Stage, Quarto, and Folio." *PMLA* 77 (1962): 194–99.

Kingsford, C. L. *English Historical Literature*. Oxford: Clarendon Press, 1913.
Knapp, Ethan. *The Bureaucratic Muse: Thomas Hoccleve and the Literature of Late Medieval England*. University Park: Pennsylvania State University Press, 2001.
Kuskin, William, ed. *Caxton's Trace: Studies in the History of English Printing*. Notre Dame. IN: University of Notre Dame Press, 2006.
———. "'Onely Imagined': Vernacular Community and the English Press." In *Caxton's Trace: Studies in the History of English Printing*, edited by William Kuskin, 199–240. Notre Dame, IN: University of Notre Dame Press, 2006.
———. *Symbolic Caxton: Literary Culture and Print Capitalism*. Notre Dame, IN: University of Notre Dame Press, 2008.
Lander, Jesse M. "'Crack'd Crowns' and Counterfeit Sovereigns: The Crisis of Value in *1 Henry IV*." *Shakespeare Studies* 30 (2002): 137–61.
Langland, William. *The Vision of Pierce Plowman*. London: Richard Grafton for Robert Crowley, 1550. *STC* 19906.
Larson, R. K., V. Déprez, and H. Yamakido, eds. *The Evolution of Human Language*. Cambridge: Cambridge University Press, 2010.
Latour, Bruno. *We Have Never Been Modern*. Translated by Catherine Porter. Cambridge, MA: Harvard University Press, 1993.
Law, Robert Adger. "The Chronicles and the Three Parts of *Henry VI*." *University of Texas Studies in English* 33 (1954): 13–32.
Lawton, David. "Dullness and the Fifteenth Century." *English Literary History* 54 (1987): 761–99.
Lefèvre, Raoul. *The Ancient Historie, of the Destruction of Troy*. London: Thomas Creede, 1607. *STC* 15380.
———. *The Ancient Historie of the Destruction of Troy*. London: Barnard Alsop, 1617. *STC* 15381.
———. *The Ancient Historie of the Destruction of Troy*. London: Barnard Alsop and Thomas Fawcett, 1636. *STC* 15382.
———. *The Auncient Historie of the Destruction of Troy*. London: Thomas Creede and Valentine Simmes, 1596/97. *STC* 15379.
———. *The Destruction of Troy*. London: Samuel Speed, 1663. Book One, Wing L929; Book Two, Wing L934; Book Three, Wing L938.
———. *The Destruction of Troy*. London: Thomas Passenger, 1670. Wing L930, L935, L939.
———. *The Destruction of Troy*. London: Thomas Passenger. 1676. Wing L931, L936, L940.
———. *The Destruction of Troy*. London: Thomas Passenger. 1680. Wing L932, L937, L941.
———. *The Destruction of Troy*. London: Thomas Passenger. 1684. Wing L933, L937A, L941A.
———. *The Destruction of Troy*. London: Eben Tracey, 1702.

———. *The Destruction of Troy*. London: Eben Tracey, 1708.
———. *The Destruction of Troy*. Dublin: Thomas Browne, 1738.
———. *Historie of Iason*. Westminster: William Caxton, 1477. *STC* 15383.
———. *Recueil des histories de Troie*. Bruges: William Caxton, 1474.
———. *The Recuile of the Histories of Troie*. London: William Copland, 1553. *STC* 15378.
———. *The Recuyell of the Historyes of Troye*. Bruges: William Caxton, 1473/74. *STC* 15375.
———. *The Recuyell of the Historyes of Troye*. Hammersmith: William Morris, 1892.
———. *The Recuyell of the Historyes of Troye*. Edited by H. Oskar Sommer for the Early English Text Society. London: Ballantyne, Hanson, 1894.
———. *The Recuyles or Gaderinge to Gyder of the Hystoryes of Troye*. London: Wynkyn de Worde, 1502. *STC* 15376/a.
———. *The Recuyles or Gaderinge to Gyder of the Hystoryes of Troye*. London: Wynkyn de Worde, 1503. *STC* 15377.
Lerer, Seth. *Chaucer and His Readers: Imagining the Author in Late-Medieval England*. Princeton, NJ: Princeton University Press, 1993.
———. *Courtly Letters in the Age of Henry VIII: Literary Culture and the Arts of Deceit*. Cambridge: Cambridge University Press, 1997.
———. "William Caxton." In *The Cambridge History of Medieval English Literature*. Edited by David Wallace, 720–738. Cambridge: Cambridge University Press, 1999.
Lesser, Zachary. "Typographic Nostalgia: Play-Reading, Popularity, and the Meanings of Black Letter." In *The Book of the Play: Playwrights, Stationers, and Readers in Early Modern England*, edited by Marta Straznicky, 99–126. Amherst: University of Massachusetts Press, 2006.
Levinson, Marjorie. "What Is New Formalism?" *PMLA* 122 (2007): 558–68.
Lowenstein, David, and Janel Mueller, eds. *The Cambridge History of Early Modern English Literature*. Cambridge: Cambridge University Press, 2002.
Luborsky, Ruth Samson. "The Allusive Presentation of *The Shepheardes Calender*." *Spenser Studies* 1 (1980): 29–67.
Lydgate, John. *The Auncient Historie and Onely Trewe and Syncere Cronicle of the Warres Betwixte the Grecians and the Troyans . . . Translated in to Englyshe Verse by Iohn Lydgate Moncke of Burye*. Printed by Thomas Marshe, 1555. *STC* 5580.
———. *The Churl and the Bird*. Westminster: William Caxton, 1477. *STC* 17008.
———. *The Fall of Prynce; Gathered by Iohn Bochas, From the Begynnyng of the World Vntyll His Time, Translated into English by Iohn Lidgate Monke of Burye*. London: Printed by John Wayland, 1554. *STC* 3177.5/78.

———. *Here Begynnethe the Boke Calledde Iohn Bochas Descriuinge the Falle of Princis Princessis and Other Nobles Translated into Englissh by Iohn Ludgate Monke of the Monastery of Seint Edmundes Bury*. London: Printed by Richard Pynson, 1494. *STC* 3175.

———. *Here Begynneth the Boke of Iohan Bochas, Discryuing the Fall of Princes, Princesses, and Other Nobles: Translated into Englysshe by Iohn Lydgate Monke of Bury*. Printed by Richard Pynson, 1527. *STC* 3176.

———. *The Horse, the Sheep and the Goose*. Westminster: William Caxton, 1477. *STC* 17018.

———. *The Hystorye, Sege and Dystruccyon of Troye [The Troy Book]*. London: Richard Pynson, 1513. *STC* 5579.

———. *The Life and Death of Hector [The Troy Book]*. London: Thomas Purfoot, 1614. *STC* 5581.5.

———. *Stans puer ad mensam*. Westminster: William Caxton, 1476. *STC* 17030.

———. *The Storye of Thebes*. Westminster: Printed by Wynkyn de Worde, 1497. *STC* 17031.

———. *Temple of Glass*. Westminster: William Caxton, 1477. *STC* 17032.

———. *A Treatise Excellent and Compendious, Shewing and Declaring, in Maner of Tragedye, the Falles of Sondry Most Notable Princes and Princesses with Other Nobles, Through ye Mutabilitie and Change of Vnstedfast Fortune Together with Their Most Detestable and Wicked Vices; First Compyled in Latin by the Excellent Clerke Bocatius, an Italian Borne; And Sence That Tyme Translated into our English and Vulgare Tong, by Dan Iohn Lidgate Monke of Burye*. London: Printed by Richard Tottel, 1554. *STC* 3177.

Lyotard, Jean-François. *The Postmodern Condition: A Report on Knowledge*. Translated by Geoff Bennington and Brian Massumi. 1984. Reprint, Minneapolis: University of Minnesota Press, 1989.

Machan, Tim William. "Early Modern Middle English." In *Caxton's Trace: Studies in the History of English Printing*, edited by William Kuskin, 299–322. Notre Dame, IN: University of Notre Dame Press, 2006.

Mallin, Eric. "Emulous Factions and the Collapse of Chivalry: *Troilus and Cressida*." *Representations* 29 (1990): 145–79.

Malory, Thomas. *Le Morte Darthur*. Westminster: William Caxton, 1485. *STC* 801.

Malpezzi, Frances M. "E. K., A Spenserian Lesson in Reading." *Connotations* 4, no. 3 (1994/95): 181–91.

Mann, Jill. "Shakespeare and Chaucer: 'What Is Criseyde Worth?'" In *The European Tragedy of Troilus*, edited by Piero Boitani, 219–42. Oxford: Clarendon Press, 1989.

Marcus, Leah. "Reading Matter." *PMLA* 121 (2006): 9–16.

Marotti, A. F. *Manuscript, Print, and the English Renaissance Lyric*. Ithaca, NY: Cornell University Press, 1995.

Marshall, M. H. "Theatre in the Middle Ages: Evidence from Dictionaries and Glosses." *Symposium* 4, no. 1 (1950): 1–39, 366–89.

Matheson, Lister M. "Printer and Scribe: Caxton, the *Polychronicon*, and the *Brut*." *Speculum* 60 (1985): 593–614.

———. *The Prose "Brut": The Development of a Middle English Chronicle*. Tempe: Arizona State University Press, 1998.

Massai, Sonia. *Shakespeare and the Rise of the Editor in Print*. Cambridge: Cambridge University Press, 2007.

McLaren, Mary-Rose. *The London Chronicles of the Fifteenth-Century: A Revolution in English Writing*. Cambridge: D. S. Brewer, 2002.

McLuhan, Marshall. *Understanding Media: The Extensions of Man*. 1964. Reprint, Cambridge, MA: MIT Press, 2001.

Meyer-Lee, Robert J. *Poets and Power from Chaucer to Wyatt*. Cambridge: Cambridge University Press, 2007.

Miller, David Lee. *The Poem's Two Bodies: The Poetics of the 1590 "Faerie Queene."* Princeton, NJ: Princeton University Press, 1988.

Morison, Stanley. "Early Humanistic Script and the First Roman Type." *Library* 4th ser., 24, nos. 1–2 (1943): 1–29.

Muir, Kenneth. *The Sources of Shakespeare's Plays*. New Haven, CT: Yale University Press, 1978.

Murphy, Andrew, ed. *A Concise Companion to Shakespeare and the Text*. Malden, MA: Blackwell, 2007.

———. *Shakespeare in Print: A History and Chronology of Shakespeare Publishing*. Cambridge: Cambridge University Press, 2003.

Nedig, William. "The Shakespeare Quartos of 1619." *Modern Philology* 8 (1910): 145–63.

Needham, Paul. "Fragments in Books: Dutch Prototypography in the Van Ess Library." In *"So Precious a Foundation": The Library of Leander van Ess*, edited by Milton McCormick Gatch, 85–110. New York: Union Theological Seminary & The Grolier Club, 1996.

———. *The Printer and the Pardoner*. Washington, DC: Library of Congress, 1986.

Nolan, Maura. *John Lydgate and the Making of Public Culture*. Cambridge: Cambridge University Press, 2005.

Olson, Glending. "Making and Poetry in the Age of Chaucer." *Comparative Literature* 31 (1979): 272–89.

Parkes, M. B. "The Influence of the Concepts of *Ordinatio* and *Compilatio* on the Development of the Book." In *Medieval Learning and Literature: Essays Presented to Richard William Hunt*, edited by J. J. G. Alexander and M. T. Gibson, 115–41. Oxford: Clarendon Press, 1976.

Patterson, Annabel. *Reading Holinshed's Chronicles*. Chicago: University of Chicago Press, 1994.

Patterson, Lee. *Chaucer and the Subject of History*. Madison: University of Wisconsin Press, 1991.
Pearsall, Derek. "The English Romance in the Fifteenth Century." *Essays and Studies* n.s., 29 (1976): 56–83.
———. "Hoccleve's *Regement of Princes*: The Poetics of Royal Self-Representation." *Speculum* 69 (1994): 386–410.
Peele, George. *A Tale of Troy*. London: Printed by John Charlewood for William White, 1589. *STC* 19537.
Pendleton, Thomas A., ed. *Henry VI: Critical Essays*. New York: Routledge, 2001.
Perloff, Marjorie. "Presidential Address 2006: It Must Change." *PMLA* 122 (2007): 652–62.
Perry, Curtis, and John Watkins, eds. *Shakespeare and the Middle Ages*. Oxford: Oxford University Press, 2009.
Pollard, Alfred W. *Shakespeare Folios and Quartos*. London: Methuen, 1909.
Presson, Robert K. *Shakespeare's "Troilus and Cressida" and the Legends of Troy*. Madison: University of Wisconsin Press, 1953.
Purvey, John. *The True Copye of a Prolog*. London: Richard Grafton for Robert Crowley, 1550. *STC* 25588.
Richards, Keith. *Life*. New York: Little, Brown, 2010.
Rickard, Jane. "The 'First' Folio in Context: The Folio Collections of Shakespeare, Jonson and King James." In *Shakespeare's Book: Essays in Reading, Writing and Reception*, edited by Richard Meek, Jane Rickard, and Richard Wilson, 207–32. Manchester, UK: Manchester University Press, 2008.
Roberts, Colin H., and T. C. Skeat. *The Birth of the Codex*. Enlarged and expanded ed. London: Oxford University Press, 1987.
Rollins, Hyder E. "The Troilus-Cressida Story from Chaucer to Shakespeare." *PMLA* 32 (1917): 383–429.
Saint Albans Schoolmaster. *Cronicles of Englonde with the Frute of Timis*. Saint Albans: Saint Albans Schoolmaster, 1485. *STC* 9995.
———. *The Cronycles of Englond.* London: Wynkyn de Worde, 1520. *STC* 10001.
———. *The Cronycles of Englond* (with "*The Descrypcyon of Englonde*"). Westminster: Wynkyn de Worde, 1497. *STC* 9996.
———. *The Cronycles of Englond* (with "*The Descrypcyon of Englonde*"). London: Wynkyn De Worde, 1502. *STC* 9997.
———. *The Cronycles of Englond* (with "*The Descrypcyon of Englonde*"). London: Julian Notary, 1504. *STC* 9998.
———. *The Cronycles of Englond* (with "*The Descrypcyon of Englonde*"). London: Richard Pynson, 1510. *STC* 9999.
———. *The Cronycles of Englond* (with "*The Descrypcyon of Englonde*"). London: Julian Notary, 1515. *STC* 10000.

———. *The Cronycles of Englond* (with "*The Descrypcyon of Englonde*"). London: Wynkyn de Worde, 1515. *STC* 10000.5.

———. *The Cronycles of Englond* (with "*The Descrypcyon of Englonde*"). London: Wynkyn de Worde, 1528. *STC* 10002.

Savonarola, Girolamo. *Sermo Fratris Hieronymi de Ferraria in vigilia Natiuitatis domini coram fratribus suis recitatus*. London: Richard Pynson, 1509. *STC* 21800.

Scanlon, Larry. "The King's Two Voices: Narrative and Power in Hoccleve's *Regement of Princes*." In *Literary Practice and Social Change in Britain*, edited by Lee Patterson, 216–47. Berkeley: University of California Press, 1990.

———. *Narrative, Authority, and Power: The Medieval Exemplum and the Chaucerian Tradition*. Cambridge: Cambridge University Press, 1994.

Scanlon, Larry, and James Simpson, eds. *John Lydgate: Poetry, Culture, and Lancastrian England*. Notre Dame, IN: University of Notre Dame Press, 2006.

Scott, Charlotte. *Shakespeare and the Idea of the Book*. Oxford: Oxford University Press, 2007.

Shakespeare, William. *The Famous Historie of Troylus and Cresseid* London : Imprinted by G. Eld for R. Bonian and Henry Walley, 1609. *STC* 22332.

———. *The First Part of the Contention*. London: Printed by Thomas Creede for Thomas Millington, 1594. *STC* 26099.

———. *The First Part of the Contention*. London: Printed by Valentine Simmes for Thomas Millington, 1600. *STC* 26100.

———. *The Historie of Troylus and Cresseida*. London: Printed by George Eld for Richard Bonian and Henry Walley, 1609. *STC* 22331.

———. *The History of Henrie the Fourth*. London: Printed by Simon Stafford for Andrew Wise, 1599. *STC* 22281.

———. *King Henry VI: Part 2*. The Arden Shakespeare. Edited by Ronald Knowles. 1999. Reprint, London: Thomson Learning, 2001.

———. *Loves Labour's Lost*. London: Printed by William White for Cuthbert Burby, 1598. *STC* 22294.

———. *Lucrece*. London: Printed by Richard Field for John Harrison, 1594. *STC* 22345.

———. *The Merry Wives of Windsor*. London: Printed by Thomas Creede for Arthur Johnson, 1602. *STC* 22299.

———. *The Most Lamentable Romaine Tragedie of Titus Andronicus*. London: Printed by John Danter for Edward White and Thomas Millington, 1594. *STC* 22328.

———. *Mr. William Shakespeares Comedies, Histories, & Tragedies Published According to the True Originall Copies*. London: Isaac Jaggard and Edmund Blount for William Jaggard, Edmund Blount, John Smethwick, and William Aspley, 1623. *STC* 22273.

———. *Pericles*. London: Printed by William White and Thomas Creede for Henry Gosson, 1609. STC 22334.

———. *Shake-speares Sonnets Neuer Before Imprinted.* London: By George Eld for Thomas Thorpe, 1609. *STC* 22353a.

———. *The Tragedie of King Richard the Second*. London: Printed by Valentine Simmes for Andrew Wise, 1598. *STC* 22308/9.

———. *The Tragedie of King Richard the Third*. London: Printed by Thomas Creede, for Andrew Wise, 1602. *STC* 22316.

———. *The Tragedie of King Richard the Third*. London: Printed by Thomas Creede for Matthew Lane, 1612. *STC* 22318.

———. *The Tragedy of Hamlet Prince of Denmarke*. London: Printed [by George Eld] for Iohn Smethwicke, 1611. *STC* 22277.

———. *The Tragicall Historie of Hamlet Prince of Denmarke*. London: Printed by Valentine Simmes for Nicholas Ling and Iohn Trundell, 1603. *STC* 22275.

———. *The Troublesome Raigne of Iohn King*. London: Printed by Valentine Simmes for John Helme, 1611. *STC* 14646.

———. *The True Tragedie of Richarde Duke of Yorke and the Death of Good King Henrie the Sixt*. London: Printed by William White for Thomas Millington, 1600. *STC* 21006a.

———. *The True Tragedie of Richard Duke of Yorke and the Deth of Good King Henrie the Sixt*. London: Printed by Peter Short for Thomas Millington, 1595. *STC* 21006.

———. *Venus and Adonis*. London: Richard Field, 1593. *STC* 22354.

———. *Venus and Adonis*. London: Printed by Richard Field for John Harrison, 1594. *STC* 22355.

———. *Venus and Adonis*. London: Printed by Richard Field for John Harrison, 1595. *STC* 22356.

———. *The Whole Contention*. London: Printed by William Jaggard for Thomas Pavier, 1619. *STC* 26101.

Shakespeare, William, Thomas Dekker, and Thomas Heywood. *Merry Deuill of Edmonton*. London: Printed by Thomas Creede for Arthur Johnson, 1612. *STC* 7494.

Shepherd, Geoffrey, ed. *An Apology for Poetry, or, The Defense of Poesy*. 3rd ed. Revised and expanded by R. W. Maslen. Manchester, UK: Manchester University Press, 2002.

Shoenfield, Joseph R. *Recursion Theory*. Berlin: Springer-Verlag, 1993.

Sidney, Sir Philip. *An Apologie for Poetrie: Written by the Right Noble, Vertuous, and Learned, Sir Phillip Sidney, Knight*. London: James Roberts for Henry Olney, 1595. *STC* 22534.

———. *The Countesse of Pembrokes Arcadia, Written by Sir Philippe Sidnei*. London: Printed by John Windet for William Ponsonby, 1590. *STC* 22539/a.

———. *The Countesse of Pembrokes Arcadia, Written by Sir Philippe Sidnei.* London: Printed by John Windet for William Ponsonby, 1593. *STC* 22540.

———. *The Countesse of Pembrokes Arcadia, Written by Sir Philippe Sidnei.* London: Printed by Richard Field for William Ponsonby, 1598. *STC* 22541.

———. *The Countesse of Pembrokes Arcadia, Written by Sir Philippe Sidnei.* Edinburgh: Robert Waldegraue, 1599. *STC* 22542.

———. *The Defence of Poesie.* London: William Ponsonby, 1595. *STC* 22535/4.5.

———. *Sir P. S. His Astrophel and Stella.* Printed by John Charlewood for Thomas Newman, 1591. *STC* 22536.

———. *Sir P. S. His Astrophel and Stella.* London: Printed by J. Danter for Thomas Newman, 1591. *STC* 22537.

———. *Sir P. S. His Astrophel and Stella.* London: Printed by Felix Kingston for Matthew Lownes, 1597. *STC* 22538.

Simpson, James. "Making History Whole: Diachronic History and the Shortcomings of Medieval Studies." In *Reading the Medieval in Early Modern England*, edited by Gordon McMullan and David Matthews, 17–30. Cambridge: Cambridge University Press, 2007.

———. "Nobody's Man: Thomas Hoccleve's *Regement of Princes*." In *London and Europe in the Later Middle Ages*, edited by Julia Boffey and Pamela King, 149–80. London: Centre for Medieval and Renaissance Studies, Queen Mary and Westfield College, University of London, 1995.

———. *1350–1547: Reform and Cultural Revolution.* Volume 2 of *The Oxford English Literary History*. Edited by Jonathan Bate. Oxford: Oxford University Press, 2002.

Skeat, W. W. *The Chaucer Canon.* 1900. Reprint, New York: Hastell House, 1965.

Skelton, John. *Here After Foloweth Certayne Bokes, Compyled by Mayster Skelton, Poet Laureat.* London: Richard Lant for Henry Tab, 1545. *STC* 22598.

———. *Here After Foloweth Certayne Bokes, Compyled by Mayster Skelton, Poet Laureat.* London: John King and Thomas Marshe, 1554. *STC* 22599.

———. *Here After Foloweth Certayne Bokes, Compyled by Mayster Skelton, Poet Laureat.* London: John Day, 1563. *STC* 22600.

———. *Replycacion.* London: Thomas Pynson, 1528. *STC* 22609.

———. *The Tunning of Elinor Rumming.* London: Wynkyn de Worde, 1521. *STC* 22611.5

Smith, Bruce R. "On Reading *The Shepheardes Calender*." *Spenser Studies* 1 (1980): 69–93.

Smith, M. Rick. "*Henry VI, Part 2*: Commodifying and Recommodifying the Past in Late-Medieval and Early-Modern England." In *Henry VI:*

Critical Essays, edited by Thomas A. Pendleton, 177–204. New York: Routledge, 2001.
Spearing, A. C. *Medieval to Renaissance in English Poetry*. Cambridge: Cambridge University Press, 1985.
Spenser, Edmund. *Amoretti and Epithalamion*. London: Printed by P. Short for William Ponsonby, 1595. *STC* 23076.
———. *Axiochus*. London: Cuthbert Burby, 1592. *STC* 19974.6.
———. *Colin Clouts Come Home Againe*. London: Printed by Thomas Creede for William Ponsonby, 1595. *STC* 23077.
———. *Complaints*. London: William Ponsonby, 1591. *STC* 23078.
———. *Daphnaïda*. London: Printed by T. Orwin for William Ponsonby, 1591. *STC* 23079.
———. *De rebus gestis Britanniae commentarioli tres Ad ornatissimum virum M. Henricum Broncarem Armigerum. E.S.* London: Henrici Binneman, 1582. *STC* 21488.
———. *The Faerie Queene*. London: John Wolfe for William Ponsonby, 1590. *STC* 23080/a/1a.
———. *The Faerie Queene*. London: Printed by Richard Field for William Ponsonby, 1596. *STC* 23082.
———. *The Faerie Queen; The Shepheards Calendar: Together with the Other Works of England's Arch-Poët, Edm. Spencer; Collected into One Volume, and Carefully Corrected.* London: Humphrey Lownes for Matthew Lownes, 1611. *STC* 23083.3/.7.
———. *Fowre hymnes*. London: Printed by Richard Field for William Ponsonby, 1596. *STC* 23086.
———. *Prosopopoia*. London: William Ponsonby, 1591. *STC* 23078.
———. *Prothalamion*. London: Printed by J. Orwin for William Ponsonby, 1596. *STC* 23088.
———. *The Second Part of The Faerie Queene*. London by Richard Field for William Ponsonby, 1596. *STC* 23082.
———. *The Shepheardes Calender*. London: Hugh Singleton, 1579. *STC* 23089.
———. *The Shepheardes Calender*. London: Thomas East for John Harrison, 1581. *STC* 23090.
———. *The Shepheardes Calender*. London: John Wolfe for John Harrison, 1586. *STC* 23091.
———. *The Shepheardes Calender*. London: Printed by John Windet for John Harrison, 1591. *STC* 23092.
———. *The Shepheardes Calender*. London: Printed by Thomas Creede for John Harrison, 1597. *STC* 23093.
———. *The Shepheardes Calender, 1579*. Menston, UK: Scolar Press, 1968.
———. *Three Proper, and Wittie, Familiar Letters*. London: H. Bynneman, 1580. *STC* 23095.

Stallybrass, Peter, and Roger Chartier. "Reading and Authorship: The Circulation of Shakespeare 1590–1619." In *A Concise Companion to Shakespeare and the Text*, edited by Andrew Murphy, 35–56. Malden, MA: Blackwell, 2007.

Stein, Elizabeth. "Caxton's *Recuyell* and Shakespeare's *Troilus*." *Modern Language Notes* 45 (1930): 144–46.

Stevenson, Allan H. "Shakespearian Dated Watermarks," *Studies in Bibliography* 4 (1951–52): 159–64.

Straznicky, Marta, ed. *The Book of the Play: Playwrights, Stationers, and Readers in Early Modern England*. Amherst: University of Massachusetts Press, 2006.

———. "Plays, Books, and the Public Sphere." In *The Book of the Play: Playwrights, Stationers, and Readers in Early Modern England*, edited by Marta Straznicky, 1–19. Amherst: University of Massachusetts Press, 2006.

Strohm, Paul. "Chaucer's Fifteenth-Century Audience and the Narrowing of the 'Chaucer Tradition.'" *Studies in the Age of Chaucer* 4 (1982): 3–32.

———. *England's Empty Throne: Usurpation and the Language of Legitimation, 1399–1422*. New Haven, CT: Yale University Press, 1998.

———. "Storie, Spelle, Geste, Romaunce, Tragedie: Generic Distinctions in the Middle English Troy Narratives." *Speculum* 46 (1971): 348–59.

Summit, Jennifer. *Lost Property: The Woman Writer and English Literary History, 1380–1589*. Chicago: University of Chicago Press, 2000.

———. *Memory's Library: Medieval Books in Early Modern England*. Chicago: University of Chicago Press, 2008.

Tatlock, John S. P. "The Siege of Troy in Elizabethan Literature, Especially in Shakespeare and Heywood." *PMLA* 30 (1915): 673–770.

Taylor, Gary. "*Troilus and Cressida*: Bibliography, Performance, and Interpretation." *Shakespeare Studies* 15 (1982): 99–136.

———. "Why Publish Shakespeare's Works?" Eleventh Annual D. F. McKenzie Lectures. Unpublished Manuscripts. January 20, 2006.

———. "William Shakespeare, Richard James and the House of Cobham." *Review of English Studies* 38 (1987): 334–54.

Thomas, A. H., and I. D. Thornley. *The Great Chronicle of London*. 1938. Reprint in microprint, Gloucester: Alan Sutton, 1983.

Thompson, Ann. *Shakespeare's Chaucer: A Study in Literary Origins*. New York: Barnes and Noble, 1978.

Thompson, John J. "Reading Lydgate in Post-Reformation England." In *Middle English Poetry: Texts and Traditions: Essays in Honour of Derek Pearsall*, edited by A. J. Minnis, 181–209. Woodbridge, UK: York Medieval Press, 2001.

Tung, K. K. *Topics in Mathematical Modeling*. Princeton, NJ: Princeton University Press, 2007.

Wainwright, Robert T. *The Recursive Universe: Cosmic Complexity and the Limits of Scientific Knowledge*. New York: William Morrow, 1985.

Wakelin, Daniel. *Humanism, Reading, and English Literature, 1430–1530*. Oxford: Oxford University Press, 2007.

Wall, Wendy. *The Imprint of Gender: Authorship and Publication in the English Renaissance*. Ithaca, NY: Cornell University Press, 1993.

Wallace, David. *The Cambridge History of English Literature*. Cambridge: Cambridge University Press, 1999.

Waller, Gary F., and Michael D. Moore, eds. *Sir Philip Sidney and the Interpretation of Renaissance Culture: The Poet in His Time and in Ours: A Collection of Critical and Scholarly Essays*. London: Croom Helm, 1984.

Warkentin, Germaine. "Sidney's Authors." In *Sir Philip Sidney's Achievements*, edited by M. J. B. Allen, Dominic Baker-Smith, Arthur F. Kinney, and Margaret Sullivan, 69–89. New York: AMS, 1990.

———. "The World and the Book at Penshurst: The Second Earl of Leicester (1595–1677) and His Library." *Library*, 6th ser., 20, no. 4 (1998): 325–46.

Watkins, John. *The Specter of Dido: Spenser and the Virgilian Epic*. New Haven, CT: Yale University Press, 1995.

Wells, Stanley, and Gary Taylor. *William Shakespeare: A Textual Companion*. Oxford: Clarendon Press, 1987.

West, Anthony James. "The Life of the First Folio in the Seventeenth and Eighteenth Centuries." In *A Concise Companion to Shakespeare and the Text*, edited by Andrew Murphy, 71–90. Malden, MA: Blackwell, 2007.

West, William N. "Old News: Caxton, de Worde, and the Invention of the Edition." In *Caxton's Trace: Studies in the History of English Printing*, edited by William Kuskin, 241–73. Notre Dame, IN: University of Notre Dame Press, 2006.

Wilkins, George, *The Painful Aduentures of Pericles*. London: Printed by Thomas Purfoot for Nathaniel Butter, 1608. *STC* 25638.5.

Williams, Philip, Jr. "The 'Second Issue' of Shakespeare's *Troilus and Cressida*, 1609." *Studies in Bibliography* 2 (1949–50): 26–35.

Willoughby, Edwin Eliott. *A Printer of Shakespeare: The Books and Times of William Jaggard*. London: P. Allen, 1934.

Woolf, D. R. *Reading History in Early Modern England*. Cambridge: Cambridge University Press, 2000.

Workman, Samuel K. "Versions by Skelton, Caxton and Berners of a Prologue by Diodorus Siculus." *Modern Language Notes* 56 (1941): 252–58.

Wyrley, William. *The True Use of Armorie*. London: John Jackson for Gabriell Cawood, 1592. *STC* 26062.

Yeager, R. F. "Shakespeare as Medievalist: What It Means for Performing *Pericles*." In *Shakespeare and the Middle Ages: Essays on the Performance and Adaptation of the Plays with Medieval Sources or Settings*, edited by Martha W. Driver and Sid Ray, 215–31. Jefferson, NC: McFarland, 2009.

INDEX

Page numbers in *italics* indicate illustrative material.

WILLIAM KUSKIN

is professor of English at the University of Colorado at Boulder. He is the editor of *Caxton's Trace: Studies in the History of English Printing* and author of *Symbolic Caxton: Literary Culture and Print Capitalism,* both published by the University of Notre Dame Press.